KALLIS' REDESIGNE

MW00873912

SAT®
WRITING &
LANGUAGE
PATTERN

KALLIS' Redesigned SAT Writing & Language Pattern

KALLIS EDU, INC.
7490 Opportunity Road, Suite 203
San Diego, CA 92111
info@kallisedu.com
www.kallisedu.com

ISBN: 978-1535296120

Our **Redesigned SAT Writing & Language Pattern** provides thorough overviews for all SAT Writing and Language topics, helping students review familiar concepts and master unfamiliar ones.

A wide variety of assignments, ranging from single-sentence questions to full-length practice tests, challenge students while building fundamental skills. Finally, our detailed Answers and Explanations sections help students clear up any lingering confusion.

KALLIS

KALLIS'

SAT®

WRITING & LANGUAGE PATTERN

LEARNING THE WAY YOU WANT IT

Table of **Contents**

Getting Started

About SAT Writing & Language

The Redesigned SAT Writing and Language section is meant to assess your ability to improve written information. The test consists of four passages accompanied by 11 questions each, for a total of 44 questions. You will have 35 minutes to complete the section.

The four passages fit loosely into the categories of careers, science, history/social science, and humanities. In addition, a visual display of data accompanies one or two of the passages.

Writing and Language Questions

In the passages, the number "1" followed by underlined words or phrases in the text correlates with Question 1, and so on. Some questions are expressed as sentences, while other questions are implied by the answer choices.

Each multiple-choice question has four answer choices, and only one is correct. As with other sections of the SAT, you will not be penalized for incorrect answers.

For some questions, more than one answer may be technically correct, but just one is the "most effective" at conveying the information.

Certain types of questions will appear in nearly every question set. A set will often include questions related to precise vocabulary. Also, passages that are accompanied by graphs, charts, or tables, will contain questions about how effectively and accurately the passage makes use of the data.

Expression of Ideas

A little more than half of the questions for each passage require you to make judgments about the content of a passage. You must evaluate whether the writer should support, lengthen, shorten, delete, reorganize, or change information. Sometimes you are asked why a writer has included or should include particular information.

Standard English Conventions

Nearly half of the questions in the Redesigned SAT Writing and Language section require you to identify language errors and choose the best option for improvement. You will not be tested on the names of grammatical structures. We have used grammar terms in these pages only for reference.

Answer Strategy

- Read the whole passage quickly and carefully. That prepares you to answer questions about content.
- Read the first question and locate the underlined section in the passage.
- Look carefully at the four answer choices. Try to determine what is being tested in the question. What parts of the answers change from choice to choice?
- Select an answer and, before marking it on the answer sheet, check to make sure it would fit into the surrounding sentence or paragraph.

GRAMMAR TERMS

Noun	a person (or people), place(s), thing(s), or idea(s).
Pronoun	a word that replaces and refers to a noun, noun phrase, or another pronoun.
Subject	the term or phrase that performs an action or is being described in a sentence.
Object	the term or phrase that is affected by the verb, or that completes the preposition.
Article	a word that indicates whether the noun it precedes is specific or general. The three articles in English are "the," "a," and "an." • "The" indicates a specific noun or nouns. *The family next door met* **the** *other families that live on this street.* • "A" and "an" refer to a single, general noun. **A** *new family is always interesting to neighbors.*
Adjective	a word that describes or limits a noun. • An adjective is often placed in front of the noun(s) it describes. *A* **cheerful** *melody came from the* **outdoor** *cafe.* • An adjective can also appear after a linking verb. *The cafe is* **charming**.
Gerund	an action that acts as a noun. Gerunds are formed by adding "ing" to the end of a verb's base form. **Singing** *releases stress.*
Infinitive verb	the most basic form of a verb (i.e. *to see, to do, to play*). • Infinitive verb forms often act as nouns. **To befriend** *a dog, throw a toy for it. Most dogs love* **to play**.
Participle	a modifier (a word that describes or limits) that looks like a verb ending in "ing," "en," or "ed," as in "**living** *organism*," or "**decorated** *cake*." • A **participial phrase** is a group of words that begins with a participle and works together to modify a noun, noun phrase, or pronoun. *The children walked by,* **laughing among themselves**.
Main Verb	a verb from that supplies a subject's action or describes its state-of-being. • An **action verb** describes a subject's activity. *I* **went** *to Hawaii. Please* **call** *me later.* • A **linking verb** connects a noun, noun phrase, or pronoun to a "state of being" description. Common linking verbs include forms of *be, become, appear, stay, grow, seem, feel, look, taste,* and *smell.* *I* **am** *busy. The room* **grew** *quiet.*
Auxiliary verb	also called a "helping verb." It precedes a main verb in order to help express a wide array of tense and meaning, or to form questions and negative statements. • Common auxiliary verbs include forms of *be, do, have, can, must, might, should,* and *may.* *I* **am working**. **Can** *you* **text** *me? We* **did not tell** *him the code.*
Tense	a quality of verbs that expresses the time in which an action or state occurred. The three main tenses are past, present, and future.
Adverb	a modifier that describes or limits a verb, adjective, or another adverb. An adverb tells a reader *where, when, how,* or *how often* something occurs, and usually end in "-ly." • An adverb describing a verb: *The cat ate* **delicately**. • An adverb describing an adjective: *The sandwich was* **immensely** *filling.* • An adverb describing another adverb: *Simone felt as though she did* **very** *well on her geography midterm.*

Preposition	a word that shows direction, location, or time. Prepositions include "to," "from," "on," "under," "over," "about," "in," "out," and "from."
Conjunction	a word that joins ideas and expresses relationships between them. The most common conjunctions are "and" and "but." • "And" expresses agreement and addition. *We shopped **and** cooked.* • "But" expresses contrast or opposition. *We shopped, **but** we were too tired to cook.*
Sentence	a group of words that forms a complete thought. A sentence begins with a capital letter, contains at minimum a subject and a verb, and ends with a period, a question mark, or an exclamation point.
Clause	a group of words containing a subject and a verb.
Apostrophe (')	a punctuation mark which indicates that a noun shows possession, or which identifies that one or more letters have been omitted from a word or a contraction. • Showing possession: *Adam has become good friends with **Sarah's** brother.* • Showing omission: *"I **don't** think **I'll** ever pass calculus!" the discouraged student moaned.*
Colon (:)	a punctuation mark that separates a term/phrase from a definition or description of, or an elaboration on that term/phrase. • In formal written English, an independent clause must always precede a colon, but the information that follows a colon can be a single word, a phrase, or an entire clause. *Richard had set three goals for the day**:** avoid hitting the "snooze" button on his alarm clock, pack a lunch, and arrive to work on time.*
Comma (,)	a punctuation mark that, generally speaking, denotes a brief pause in a sentence. A comma can be used to separate a term, phrase, or an entire clause from the rest of a sentence. Common uses for commas include: • separating the items of a list. *Jolene purchased sugar, flour, and milk from the grocery store.* • separating grammatically non-essential phrases from the rest of a sentence. *Banksy, an enigmatic and reclusive street artist, directed the 2010 film Exit Through the Gift Shop.* • separating clauses from one another. *Asia is the world's largest continent, and it has the highest population.*
Semicolon (;)	a punctuation mark that can effectively replace a period whenever a period separates sentences containing closely related information. Note that the first letter in the word following a semicolon should not be capitalized.
Period (.)	a punctuation mark most commonly used to denote the end of a sentence.
Parentheses ( )	punctuation marks that are always used in pairs. They enclose additional, grammatically non-essential information that is added to a sentence.
Em Dash (—)	a versatile punctuation mark that can effectively replace commas, parentheses, or colons. • Generally, em dashes are considered less formal, but more dramatic, than commas, parentheses, or colons.

Mastering
Writing & Language

Successful people **keep moving**. They make mistakes, but they **don't quit**.

— Conrad Hilton

001 *Question Topic*

→ **SUBJECT-VERB AGREEMENT**

Terms and Structures

Verbs in sentences change to reflect the subject, noticeable mainly when an "s" is added to the end of third-person singular verbs in the present tense, or when conjugating the verb "to be":

> *I laugh whenever* **he laughs***; I can't help it.*
> **Honesty is** *of vital importance in any close relationship.*
> *Math teacher* **Ms. Abbott tries** *to encourage school spirit among students.*

The Arctic tern <u>migrate</u> up to 44,000 miles each year.

(A) NO CHANGE
(B) The Arctic tern to migrate
(C) The Arctic tern migrates
(D) The Arctic tern migrating

The subject, "The Arctic tern," is a third-person singular noun, so the main verb of the sentence must also reflect this person and number. The only choice that does so is (C). The verb used in choice (A)—"migrate"—is the wrong person and number, while choices (B) and (D) are incorrect because infinitives and participles cannot act as main verbs.

002 *Question Topic*

→ **SINGULAR SUBJECTS THAT LOOK PLURAL**

Terms and Structures

Some nouns that end in "-s" act as singular nouns even though they may look plural. Common examples include books and films with plural titles (*Minions*, *Star Wars*); country names (the Philippines, the United States); academic subjects (mathematics, physics); diseases (measles, mumps); and organizations or businesses (Friends of the Earth, Sylvia's Carpets). These names agree with third-person *singular* verbs.

> *Stay tuned,* **the news is** *next.*
> **Shingles** *often* **manifests** *in older adults.*
> **Marvel Comics introduces** *several new X-Men in its latest comic book.*

The United States <u>celebrate</u> its independence from Britain each year on the fourth day of July.

(A) NO CHANGE
(B) are celebrating
(C) celebrating
(D) celebrates

The subject of the sentence is the third-person singular noun "The United States," which agrees with the third-person singular verb, "celebrates," making (D) the correct choice.

1. During the "Raksha Bandhan" festival in parts of India, friends and family members <u>exchanges gifts</u> and sweets.

   (A) NO CHANGE
   (B) is an exchange of gifts
   (C) exchange gifts
   (D) traditionally gives gifts

2. On the morning of the festival, <u>a sister give</u> a braided bracelet with protective symbolism to each of her brothers, and they vow to protect her as well.

   (A) NO CHANGE
   (B) sisters give
   (C) sisters gives
   (D) a sister gives

3. Another interesting festival occurs when the <u>Netherlands celebrate</u> "King's Day" in April.

   (A) NO CHANGE
   (B) the Netherlands celebration of
   (C) the Netherlands' celebrate
   (D) the Netherlands celebrates

4. Music and <u>street festivals abounds,</u> and many people wear orange to honor the royal family.

   (A) NO CHANGE
   (B) street festivals abound,
   (C) street festival abounds,
   (D) street festivals abounding,

5. "Junkanoo" street festivals also take place several times a year in the Bahamas, <u>which have cultural traditions</u> held over from days when the majority of the population was slaves.

   (A) NO CHANGE
   (B) which has cultural traditions
   (C) which have a cultural tradition
   (D) which revive cultural traditions

6. Junkanoo parades start around 2 a.m. on December 26 and <u>create a joyous uproar</u> of color, noise, music, and dancing.

   (A) NO CHANGE
   (B) creating a joyous uproar
   (C) to create joyous uproars
   (D) creates a joyous uproar

7. <u>There is a number of</u> encyclopedic resources for travelers interested in cultural celebrations.

   (A) NO CHANGE
   (B) A number of
   (C) There are a number of
   (D) There is a few

8. David Brown and Arthur Findlay's *501 Must-Be-There Events* <u>provide descriptions</u> and background of many celebrations and festivals around the globe.

   (A) NO CHANGE
   (B) have provided descriptions
   (C) provides descriptions
   (D) providing descriptions

☑	1		3		5		7	
	2		4		6		8	

8 ~ 7	6 ~ 5	4 ~ 3	2 ~ 1
EXCELLENT	VERY GOOD	GOOD	NEEDS WORK

003 Question Topic

→ **SUBJECTS THAT ARE SEPARATED FROM THEIR ACTIONS**

Terms and Structures

To check for subject-verb agreement, you must always be able to locate the subject, even if a number of words separate the subject and verb. When checking for subject-verb agreement in longer sentences, try eliminating all information that is "extra," such as parenthetical phrases.

The Tyrannosaurus, *a large, carnivorous dinosaur that lived 68 million years ago,* **shows up** *in many fictional books and films.*

The Czech city of **Prague**, *which is often referred to as one of Europe's "crown jewels,"* **ha**s *some of central Europe's most stunning architecture.*

"Few who choose to sail through the Bermuda Triangle <u>is</u> ever seen again," the old sea captain intoned solemnly.

(A) NO CHANGE
(B) was
(C) be
(D) are

The correct choice is (D) because the subject of the sentence, "Few," agrees with a third-person plural form of the verb "to be," making "are" the only appropriate choice.

004 Question Topic

→ **INDEFINITE PRONOUN SUBJECTS**

Terms and Structures

Words such as "anyone" and "somebody" are called *indefinite* pronouns because they do not refer to a *definite* person or thing. Words ending in singular nouns "one," "body," and "thing" always take singular verbs:

Someone *in the room* **is** *humming.*   **Everything is** *turning out well.*

Within certain phrases, "what" and "whatever" also form singular pronouns:

I see **what is** *happening.*   *Do* **whatever needs** *doing.*

The term "each" always takes a singular verb:

Each *animal* **has** *its own trainer.*

"Either of…." And "neither of…" sentences refer to one of two things, and thus take singular verbs:

Neither of my parents is *here right now.*

The main verb in an "either...or" or a "neither...nor" sentence always agrees with the second listed term:

Either *scissors* **or a knife is** *suitable for the task at hand.*
Neither *the shirt* **nor the socks** *that Timothy received for his birthday* **fit** *him.*

Neither of the two television reporters <u>is willing</u> to set foot on the creaky porch of the dilapidated old house.

(A) NO CHANGE
(B) are willing
(C) be willing
(D) were willing

The correct choice is (A) because the subject of the sentence, "neither," refers to two individuals and thus takes takes the third-person singular form of a verb — in this case, "is."

1. People in Japan's Ryukyu islands, of which Okinawa is the largest, <u>tends to have</u> longer, healthier lives than people elsewhere.

   (A) NO CHANGE
   (B) tend to have
   (C) is tending to have
   (D) DELETE underlined portion

2. As a result, everything about the Okinawan lifestyle—diet, exercise, social life—<u>are</u> of interest to researchers.

   (A) NO CHANGE
   (B) were
   (C) being
   (D) is

3. Genetic researchers say that anyone who lives for a century or more <u>is</u> 20 times more likely to have a long-lived relative than the average person, indicating a genetic component to longevity.

   (A) NO CHANGE
   (B) to be
   (C) will be
   (D) are

4. Yet most researchers have concluded that it is neither lifestyle nor genes that <u>make</u> Okinawans so healthy, but a combination of the two.

   (A) NO CHANGE
   (B) makes
   (C) is making
   (D) are making

5. People on some Italian and Greek islands, in some Nordic regions, and on the Nicoya peninsula in Costa Rica also <u>are enjoyable</u> unusually long, healthy lives.

   (A) NO CHANGE
   (B) is enjoying
   (C) enjoy
   (D) enjoys

6. Something that these long-lived populations share <u>are diets</u> high in vegetables and low in sugar.

   (A) NO CHANGE
   (B) is a diet
   (C) being diets
   (D) are a diet

7. For protein, each of the populations <u>rely on their own</u> culturally specific combination of fish, dairy, legumes, nuts, and seeds, rather than red meat.

   (A) NO CHANGE
   (B) rely on
   (C) relies on its own
   (D) are relying on

8. Thus, it is not necessary to choose between the Mediterranean diet and the Okinawan diet; either <u>serve healthful models.</u>

   (A) NO CHANGE
   (B) one.
   (C) serve as a healthful model.
   (D) serves as a healthful model.

☑	1		3		5		7	
	2		4		6		8	

8 ~ 7	6 ~ 5	4 ~ 3	2 ~ 1
EXCELLENT	VERY GOOD	GOOD	NEEDS WORK

005 Question Topic

→ **ACTIONS AS SUBJECTS**

Terms and Structures

Infinitives (to + verb base form) and gerunds (verb base form with "-ing" ending) allow for an action to serve as the subject of a sentence. They are considered singular nouns that take third-person singular verbs.

> *Even* **sleeping requires** *energy.*
> **To arrive** *early on your first day at a new job* **is** *wise.*

Remembering passwords <u>are</u> no longer crucial with new technology.

(A) NO CHANGE
(B) is
(C) were
(D) have

The correct choice is (B) because "remembering" acts as a noun in the sentence. Action nouns are considered to be singular, thus "remembering" must take the singular verb form "is."

006 Question Topic

→ **SUBJECTS AND PREPOSITIONAL PHRASES**

Terms and Structures

When a subject includes a prepositional phrase, make sure you know which term is the actual subject that the verb must agree with. One way to locate the subject of a sentence or clause is to remember that the subject will never come immediately after a preposition. The most common preposition is "of":

> **The queen** *of hearts* **is** *indispensable.*
> **The towers** *of the castle* **look** *out over the surrounding countryside.*

The most common <u>symptoms of a pollen allergy is</u> red eyes, itchy skin, and runny nose.

(A) NO CHANGE
(B) symptoms of a pollen allergy are
(C) symptom of an allergy to pollen are
(D) symptom of allergies to pollen are

The subject of the sentence is the plural noun "symptoms," which agrees with the plural verb "are," making (B) correct. Choice (A) is incorrect because the plural subject "symptoms" does not agree with "is." Choice (C) and (D) are incorrect because the singular noun "symptom" does not agree with "are," and does not make sense because more than one symptom is listed.

1. The stories told by militant extremists <u>are</u> similar, regardless of culture or cause, according to experts.

   (A) NO CHANGE
   (B) is
   (C) being
   (D) would be

2. Describing how the past was glorious for the group, but that now others are denying the group its rightful place, <u>are hallmarks</u> of such organizations.

   (A) NO CHANGE
   (B) are a hallmark
   (C) being a hallmark
   (D) is a hallmark

3. To create a perfect, utopian world (as defined by the extremist group) <u>being possible,</u> according to its narrative.

   (A) NO CHANGE
   (B) are possibilities,
   (C) is possible,
   (D) is to be,

4. Militant extremist groups tend to believe that their norms are absolute truths, and that tolerating differences from the norms <u>is unacceptable.</u>

   (A) NO CHANGE
   (B) are unacceptable.
   (C) will be unacceptable.
   (D) unaccepting.

5. The recruitment of idealistic youth for extremist groups is not uncommon; for these young people, stopping at nothing to further the group's goals <u>is a compelling idea.</u>

   (A) NO CHANGE
   (B) were compelling ideas.
   (C) are compelling ideas.
   (D) compel them.

6. Members of the mainstream community <u>has a role to play</u> in countering extremist groups' versions of reality.

   (A) NO CHANGE
   (B) have a role to play
   (C) playing roles
   (D) has roles

7. Demonstrating that change for the better can occur by working peacefully on issues <u>are among</u> the many effective strategies.

   (A) NO CHANGE
   (B) is among
   (C) among
   (D) being among

8. Young people can learn to recognize and question systems of thought <u>that categorizes everyone and everything</u> as either "perfect" or "vile."

   (A) NO CHANGE
   (B) to be categorizing everyone and everything
   (C) that has categorized everyone and everything
   (D) that categorize everyone and everything

☑	1		3		5		7	
	2		4		6		8	

8 ~ 7	6 ~ 5	4 ~ 3	2 ~ 1
EXCELLENT	VERY GOOD	GOOD	NEEDS WORK

007 *Question Topic*

SHOWING POSSESSION

Terms and Structures

Possessive nouns act like adjectives: after all, possession means *describing* who or what is showing ownership. Because they act like adjectives, possessive nouns cannot serve as the subject of a sentence, although whatever it is that they possess can.

>*Alejandro's* **friend is** *interested in physics.*   *Alejandro's* **friends are** *interested in physics.*

When a possessive pronoun immediately precedes the noun it shows possession over, the pronoun is considered a possessive adjective. The possessive adjectives are "my," "your," "his," "her," "its," "our," and "their." As with possessive nouns, possessive adjectives cannot be the subject of a sentence.

>*Your* **social media profile is** *great.*   *Your* **photos are** *funny.*

Her necklace shone in the light, and <u>hers</u> earrings twinkled.

(A) NO CHANGE
(B) she's
(C) her
(D) her's

The possessive adjective "her" indicates that a female possesses the earrings; adjectives do not change when they describe plural nouns, making (C) the correct answer.

008 *Question Topic*

COMMON ERRORS WITH POSSESSIVE ADJECTIVES

Terms and Structures

When combining another person with the adjective "my," the other person is listed first and has an apostrophe. It is never correct to use "I's" in place of "my."

>**My friend's and my** *plan was to meet in front of the school.*

When two nouns (not pronouns) possess one thing, one apostrophe appears after the second noun.

>**Violeta and Anthony's** *project got an "A."*

Completely different meanings are expressed by words that sound the same as "its" and "their."

The contraction of "it is" contains an apostrophe ("it's") while the possessive adjective "its" never needs one, as it already indicates possession:

>*Before serving the soup,* **it's** *important to check* **its** *flavor.*

Both the word "there" and the contraction of "they are," "they're," sound the same as the possessive adjective "their":

>**They're** *on* **their** *way over* **there**.

It's time to feed the goldfish; <u>it's</u> stomach is probably growling.

(A) NO CHANGE

(B) the

(C) hers

(D) its

The word "its" describes the stomach as belonging to the goldfish. No apostrophe is needed to show possession, making (D) the correct answer.

1. My college dormitory was nice, but unfortunately, <u>my roommate and my</u> windows faced the dumpsters behind it.

   (A) NO CHANGE
   (B) my roommate's and mine
   (C) my roommate's and my
   (D) my roommate and I's

2. My dorm also seemed to have skunks burrowed beneath it, <u>based on its</u> pervasive odor.

   (A) NO CHANGE
   (B) based on their
   (C) based on our
   (D) based on it's

3. I was impressed at <u>my roommates</u> resourceful use of incense to improve the room's atmosphere.

   (A) NO CHANGE
   (B) my roommate's
   (C) the roommate of
   (D) our roommates'

4. The dining hall's food was not bad; <u>their</u> menu always included at least three entree choices.

   (A) NO CHANGE
   (B) there
   (C) it's
   (D) its

5. My roommate and I, along with some of the other <u>freshmen whose rooms</u> were on our floor, went to the dining hall together for meals.

   (A) NO CHANGE
   (B) freshmens' rooms who
   (C) freshmen who's rooms
   (D) freshmen whose rooms'

6. One day, a group of us accompanied a friend who was getting <u>her's hair</u> cut downtown.

   (A) NO CHANGE
   (B) her hair
   (C) she's hair
   (D) herself's hair

7. We had sushi; it felt good to eat food that was not <u>the dining halls.</u>

   (A) NO CHANGE
   (B) the dining halls'.
   (C) of the dining hall's.
   (D) the dining hall's.

8. We went to a theater that specialized in classic films; <u>their feature that night was Orson Welles'</u> *Citizen Kane.*

   (A) NO CHANGE
   (B) their feature that night was Orson Welles
   (C) its feature that night was Orson Welles'
   (D) it's feature that night was Orson Welles's

   it is

☑	1		3		5		7	
	2		4		6		8	

8 ~ 7	6 ~ 5	4 ~ 3	2 ~ 1
EXCELLENT	VERY GOOD	GOOD	NEEDS WORK

009 Question Topic

→ **COUNTABLE/UNCOUNTABLE SUBJECT NOUNS**

Terms and Structures

Many nouns are always singular because they are "uncountable" on their own. This category includes undivided or unmeasured quantities, as well as abstract nouns. Some uncountable nouns are "air," "water," "sand," "time," and "snow."

Some nouns can be both countable or uncountable, depending on how they are used. When referring to multiple cakes, "cake" is countable. But when a cake is to be divided into pieces, it is treated as uncountable, as in, "How much cake is left?"

Uncountable nouns can be described by **much, little,** and **less**:
> **Little money** *is left, but we expect* **much improvement** *in the situation soon.*

Countable nouns can be plural, and can be described by **many** and **few**:
> **Many** *of us are finished with the test.* **A few** *of the students are still working.*

The most common student error regarding countable and uncountable nouns is misusing the adjectives "**less**" and "**fewer**." Never use "less" to describe something you can count:
> *Because I only had a few items, I went to the "15 items or* **fewer**" *register at the grocery store.*

Only a little papers go to waste in this office.

(A) NO CHANGE
(B) Only a few papers go
(C) Not very many paper goes
(D) Very little paper goes

Unless the "papers" in the sentence are newspapers or school essays, the noun should be uncountable and thus singular. We do not usually speak of papers, but rather of "pieces of paper." The word "little" correctly indicates a small part of an uncountable thing, making (D) the correct choice.

010 Question Topic

→ **NOUN AGREEMENT**

Terms and Structures

Checking for noun agreement means making sure that number (singular or plural) stays consistent when a noun or group of nouns is referenced two or more times. Thus, singular nouns must remain singular, and plural nouns must remain plural. Some tricky cases of noun agreement include:

- Singular noun and singular noun are...**plural noun**
  Sneezing and *itchiness* are two common **symptoms** *of a dust allergy.*

- Either singular noun or singular noun...**singular noun**
  You may choose either soup *or* salad *as* **a side dish** *for your meal.*

- Neither singular noun nor singular noun...**singular noun**
  "Neither choice A *nor* choice B *is* **the correct answer**," *said the teacher.*

"We will watch either *Annie Hall* or *Manhattan* as the movies of the week," Brian announced.

(A) NO CHANGE
(B) motion pictures
(C) film
(D) viewing

The two singular nouns in an "either...or" phrase must always be referenced in the singular. Thus, the correct choice is (C) because the underlined noun refers to one of the two films.

1. "Traditional" American <u>cuisine combines</u> indigenous ingredients and recipes with Old World immigrants' customs.

   (A) NO CHANGE
   (B) cuisines combines
   (C) cuisine combine
   (D) cuisine is combining

2. Maize (corn) cultivation originated in Mexico 9,000 years ago, and in <u>a little millennia</u> spread to the tribes of the American northeast.

   1,000 period

   (A) NO CHANGE
   (B) millennia
   (C) a small millennium
   (D) a few millennia

3. European colonial cooks learned from Native Americans how to grow, dry, and pound maize, and then to <u>boil it in water as porridges</u>—similar to today's "grits."

   (A) NO CHANGE
   (B) boil it in water as porridge
   (C) boil them in water as porridges
   (D) boil them in water as porridge

4. Although European settlers came from a wheat-baking culture, they had to make bread and cake with cornmeal or other grains, since there was <u>not a lot of</u> wheat flour available until the 1860s.

   (A) NO CHANGE
   (B) not much   non-count
   (C) a little
   (D) few   countable

5. Eighteenth-century and early nineteenth-century American bakers may have used different types of flour for <u>a lot of versions</u> of "Election Cake."

   (A) NO CHANGE
   (B) much of the versions
   (C) many versions
   (D) a version

6. Election Cake was a huge pan of pull-apart bread, requiring quantities of flour, sugar, butter, yeast, nutmeg, and raisins; bakers probably struggled to <u>get them</u> to rise and bake evenly.

   (A) NO CHANGE
   (B) manage them
   (C) get ready
   (D) get it

7. In the early years of the United States, Election Cake was created because traveling and transporting one's own food <u>was a necessary part</u> of voting.

   (A) NO CHANGE
   (B) been a necessary part
   (C) were necessary parts
   (D) are necessary parts

8. Today in the American South, cornbread remains especially popular, along with hushpuppies— <u>balls of corn doughs fried in oils and served with fishes.</u>

   (A) NO CHANGE
   (B) balls of corn dough fried in oil and served with fish.
   (C) corn doughs fried in oil and served with fish.
   (D) balls of corn dough that is fried in oil and served with fish.

☑	1		3		5		7	
	2		4		6		8	

8 ~ 7	6 ~ 5	4 ~ 3	2 ~ 1
EXCELLENT	VERY GOOD	GOOD	NEEDS WORK

011 *Question Topic*

→ **PRONOUNS AS SUBJECTS**

Terms and Structures

Pronouns that replace *subject* nouns are *subjective* pronouns. Subjective pronouns include "I," "you," "he," "she," "it," "we," and "they." For questions, the subjective person pronoun is "who."

> **I** *always wear white, and* **she** *always wears green.* **Who** *always wears red?*

Because pronouns function as stand-ins, they must always represent the noun correctly. This can be a challenge with third-person singular subjects whose gender is not specified. Although attitudes are changing on the acceptability of using gender-neutral "they" to replace a singular third-person noun, conventional written English still requires pronouns to agree in number with the nouns.

> **A person** *must work hard if* **he or she** *is to succeed.*

Every actor must take parts that are not completely satisfying if <u>they want</u> to maintain a productive career.

(A) NO CHANGE
(B) they wants
(C) he or she wants
(D) it wants

The subject, "Every actor," is singular, so the pronoun used to refer to the subject must also be singular. Thus, choices (A) and (B) are incorrect because "they" refers to a plural subject. (C) is correct because the two pronouns each refer to a singular human subject. (D) is incorrect because "it" is used to refer to objects, and frequently to animals.

012 *Question Topic*

→ **PRONOUNS AS OBJECTS**

Terms and Structures

A pronoun that replaces the *object* of a clause or prepositional phrase is an *objective* pronoun. Objective pronouns include "me," "you," "him," "her," "it," "us," or "them." For questions, the objective person pronoun is "whom."

When a pronoun follows a preposition, such as "of," "to," "at," or "for," it is the *object* of the preposition. After a preposition, use objective pronouns even when mentioning another person first:

> *The teacher looked* **at** *Zachary and* **me**.

> *The quarrels* **between** *my brother and* **me** *began when I was just twelve," wrote Benjamin Franklin in his* Autobiography.

To <u>who</u> did you send the text message?

(A) NO CHANGE
(B) whom
(C) which
(D) whose

Because the pronoun at the underlined portion is the object of the sentence and the preposition "to," choice (B) correct. (A) is incorrect because it is a subjective pronoun. (C) and (D) are incorrect because they do not make sense in the sentence; (C) refers to a thing or category rather than a particular person, and (D) indicates possession.

1. Insurance is a pool of money that people contribute to in case they experience misfortune.

   (A) NO CHANGE
   (B) one experiences
   (C) he or she experiences
   (D) we experience

2. All the contributors agree that if any of them suffers a big, unexpected financial loss, some of the pooled money will go to them.

   (A) NO CHANGE
   (B) us.
   (C) him or her.
   (D) they.

3. Insurance is a mechanism for community stability; they benefit you and me.

   (A) NO CHANGE
   (B) they benefit all of us.
   (C) they benefit you and I.
   (D) it benefits all of us.

4. An insurance company manages the pool of money, deciding how much a given client contribute to them each month.

   (A) NO CHANGE
   (B) contributes to them
   (C) contributes to us
   (D) contributes to it

5. For my spouse and me, auto insurance is expensive because the company considers us to be "high risk."
   (A) NO CHANGE
   (B) For me and my spouse,
   (C) For my spouse and I,
   (D) For I and my spouse,

6. Auto insurers may charge a client a higher monthly fee if they have been at fault in several accidents, commutes long distances, or gets speeding tickets.

   (A) NO CHANGE
   (B) he or she has
   (C) one has
   (D) we have

7. My cousin works as an insurance company claims adjuster; she evaluates how much money should be paid and to who.

   (A) NO CHANGE
   (B) to whose.
   (C) to whom.
   (D) to them.

8. If you or I crash our cars, us can claim reimbursement from our auto insurance companies.

   (A) NO CHANGE
   (B) you and me crash our cars, we
   (C) you or I crash our cars, each of us
   (D) you and I crash, you and I

☑	1		3		5		7	
	2		4		6		8	

8 ~ 7	6 ~ 5	4 ~ 3	2 ~ 1
EXCELLENT	VERY GOOD	GOOD	NEEDS WORK

013 Question Topic

→ **PRONOUN CLARITY**

Terms and Structures

It should always be clear which noun or noun phrase a pronoun refers to. A pronoun is *ambiguous* when it does not clearly refer to a particular noun. Usually this happens when there are multiple nouns with the same person and number in a sentence. If a pronoun is ambiguous, replace it to ensure sentence clarity.

   Ambiguous: *The doctor talked softly to the patient.* **She** *seemed tired.*

The sentence above is unclear because we cannot determine whether the doctor or the patient seemed tired. Rewritten for clarity, the sentence reads:

   Clear: *The doctor talked softly to the patient.* **The doctor** *seemed tired.*

Both Austin and Cole have a passion for swimming, but <u>he</u> is slightly faster.

(A) NO CHANGE
(B) Cole
(C) that one
(D) him

Because the sentence references "Austin" and "Cole," both of which are singular third-person masculine nouns, the use of the pronoun "he" is ambiguous — the reader does not know which of the two is faster. Thus, the correct choice, (B), replaces the ambiguous pronoun with a particular noun.

014 Question Topic

→ **POSSESSIVE PRONOUNS**

Terms and Structures

Stand-alone pronouns that indicate possession are "mine," "yours," "his," "hers," "its," "ours," and "theirs." Note that except for "mine," they end with "s."

   Whose phone is this? It is **yours***, isn't it?*

   No, it's not **mine***. I think it's* **his***.*

The bear clearly indicated that the cave was <u>hers,</u> and that she did not want to share

(A) NO CHANGE
(B) she's,
(C) the bear's,
(D) her's,

(A) is correct because the correct possessive pronoun stands in for the female bear. (B) is incorrect because it is a contraction of "she is." (C) is incorrect because it is redundant to use "the bear" twice so closely together; and (D) is incorrect because the word "hers" already indicates possession, so that an apostrophe is never necessary.

Quiz

5 min.

1. My friend Nikki works at Fashion Fiend; her job is more glamorous than <u>yours and mines.</u>

   (A) NO CHANGE
   (B) yours or mine.
   (C) your or my job.
   (D) you and I have.

2. Hunter worked summers as a lifeguard, a camp counselor, and a catering assistant, and found that <u>he liked it better.</u>

   (A) NO CHANGE
   (B) he liked them better.
   (C) it was best overall.
   (D) he liked catering best.

3. It should be easy to find your tutoring clients today; <u>theres is</u> the last house on the left.

   (A) NO CHANGE
   (B) there's
   (C) theirs is
   (D) their is

4. <u>Chloe and Ben led the horses, prancing in excitement, their manner gentle but insistent.</u>

   (A) NO CHANGE
   (B) The prancing horses were led by Chloe and Ben, their manner gentle but insistent.
   (C) Prancing in excitement, Chloe and Ben led the horses, their manner gentle but insistent.
   (D) In a gentle but insistent manner, Chloe and Ben led the prancing horses.

5. We hired our neighbors' son to walk our dogs each morning at the same time he walked theirs, but <u>they</u> did not get along.

   (A) NO CHANGE
   (B) the son and the dogs
   (C) our dogs and his
   (D) our neighbors and their son

6. During the morning shift, collecting the guests' room keys and payment <u>is theirs,</u> while keeping the coffee and pastries replenished is ours.

   (A) NO CHANGE
   (B) is yours,
   (C) is our job,
   (D) is their job,

7. My sister and I work part-time painting houses, but no one would know that by looking <u>at ours.</u>

   (A) NO CHANGE
   (B) at the house.
   (C) at the house of my sister and I.
   (D) DELETE the underlined portion.

8. Every afternoon, the two place the same orders: <u>his café au lait, and hers,</u> tea and three cake pops.

   (A) NO CHANGE
   (B) his, café au lait, and hers,
   (C) café au lait, and
   (D) theirs is café au lait, and

☑	1		3		5		7	
	2		4		6		8	

8 ~ 7	6 ~ 5	4 ~ 3	2 ~ 1
EXCELLENT	VERY GOOD	GOOD	NEEDS WORK

015 Question Topic

TITLES AND APPOSITIVE PHRASES FOR IDENTIFICATION

Terms and Structures

A noun or noun phrase that comes immediately before the noun or noun phrase it identifies is usually a **title**. A title is never preceded by an article, and it does not need to be separated from the term it identifies with any punctuation.

Paleontologist *Jim Jensen discovered the first Utahraptor specimen in 1975.*

When the additional identifying noun or noun phrase begins with an article ("a/an" or "the"), it is considered an **appositive phrase** that must be set off with punctuation (usually commas):

A fearsome predator, *the Utahraptor measured over 20 feet long.*

Or: *The Utahraptor,* **a fearsome predator,** *measured over 20 feet long.*

Remember that an appositive phrase does not include the noun that it describes.

Redwood <u>trees are the tallest organisms on Earth,</u> can be found in the Pacific Northwest.

(A) NO CHANGE
(B) trees, tallest organisms on Earth,
(C) trees, the tallest organisms on Earth,
(D) trees, and the tallest organisms on Earth,

The underlined portion should describe redwood trees, making (C) correct. (A) is incorrect because it is a complete idea, not a description of what "can be found in the Pacific Northwest." (B) and (D) are incorrect because they blur the description, making it unclear whether the "tallest organisms on Earth" are the redwood trees or something else.

016 Question Topic

CONCISION: ADJECTIVES AND PARTICIPLES

Terms and Structures

A void redundant and overgeneralized descriptive words. Saying "the big crowd" is not as descriptive as saying "the immense crowd." At the same time, the description does not become more precise with redundant words. There is no need to say "the big, immense crowd."

Redundant: *The auditorium filled up* **quickly and suddenly** *just minutes after the doors opened.*

Concise: *The auditorium filled up* **quickly** *just minutes after the doors opened.*

Participles can also help maintain concision. Instead of saying "the cookies *that were baked,*" you can say "the **baked** cookies."

The skiing expert ignored <u>the ski runs that had been prepared</u> and found other slopes to ski.

(A) NO CHANGE
(B) the runs that had been prepared for skiing
(C) the ski runs
(D) the prepared ski runs

Choice (A) is not incorrect, but (D) is the best answer because it is specific yet concise. (B) is incorrect because it adds unnecessary wording, and (C) fails to indicate which ski runs were ignored.

1. Atoms and molecules must be measured in nanometers, <u>a length which has been defined as</u> one billionth of a meter.

    (A) NO CHANGE
    (B) a length that is
    (C) a length that is defined as
    (D) defined as

2. Such particles are not visible; a single nanometer is <u>so tiny that it is smaller and shorter in length</u> than a wavelength of light.

    (A) NO CHANGE
    (B) tiny, small, and shorter
    (C) shorter
    (D) shorter in length   *redundant*

3. <u>Nanotechnology, the science of manipulating matter at the molecular level,</u> makes use of chemical, biological, and physical properties.

    (A) NO CHANGE
    (B) Nanotechnology, manipulated molecules,
    (C) Nanotechnology the science of manipulating matter at the molecular level,
    (D) Nanotechnology the science, manipulates matter at the molecular level,

4. <u>University and industry, nanotechnologists,</u> work in labs to create "recipes" for specialized nano materials.

    (A) NO CHANGE
    (B) University, industry nanotechnologists
    (C) University and industry nanotechnologists
    (D) University and industry nanotechnologists,

5. An example of a nanotechnology product is <u>dissolved metallic particles that have been designed to attach and connect to cancer cells.</u>

    (A) NO CHANGE
    (B) dissolved metallic particles designed to attach to cancer cells.
    (C) metallic particles, dissolved, which are designed to attach to cancer cells.
    (D) metallic particles designed to dissolve and also to attach to cancer cells.

6. <u>A doctor injects the dissolved metallic particles solution into a cancer patient, whereupon the</u> dissolved metallic nanoparticles bind to the cancer cells.

    (A) NO CHANGE
    (B) Injected into a cancer patient,
    (C) Dissolved and injected,
    (D) Injected,

7. Once the nanoparticles and <u>the human cells that are cancerous</u> have bonded, medical technicians can then apply a special light that super-heats the metallic particles.

    (A) NO CHANGE
    (B) cancer cells
    (C) cells, the cancerous ones,
    (D) certain cells

8. <u>Super-heated nanoparticles, destroy the cancer cells that they attached to</u> without damaging any surrounding healthy cells.

    (A) NO CHANGE
    (B) Super-heated nanoparticles destroy
    (C) Super-heated nanoparticles, destroy attached cancer cells
    (D) The super-heated nanoparticles destroy the attached cancer cells

☑	1		3		5		7	
	2		4		6		8	

8 ~ 7	6 ~ 5	4 ~ 3	2 ~ 1
EXCELLENT	VERY GOOD	GOOD	NEEDS WORK

017 Question Topic

→ **ADJECTIVES THAT COMPARE ONE NOUN TO ONE NOUN**

Terms and Structures

Use the **comparative degree** to compare ONE term to ONE other term. Comparative statements follow the word pattern "*x is ____ than y,*" where the blank contains one of the following adjective structures:

1. Adjectives with one or two syllables add "-er" to the end:

   Honey is **sweeter** *than sugar.*

2. Many adjectives with two syllables and all those with three or more are preceded by **more** or **less**:

   Molly is **more advanced** *in hip-hop dance than I am.*

"Good" and "bad" are expressed with **better** and **worse**, respectively:

   The limes look **better** *than the lemons today.*   *Usually the flu is* **worse** *than the common cold.*

The pattern "*x is as (adjective) as y*" describes an equal quality:

   Nathan is **as old as** *Michael is.*

Italian greyhounds are <u>worse at being trainable</u> than poodles.

(A) NO CHANGE
(B) less easier to train
(C) less good at training
(D) less trainable

(D) correctly pairs a three-syllable adjective with "less." The other answers are wordy and confusing.

018 Question Topic

→ **ADJECTIVES THAT COMPARE ONE NOUN TO TWO OR MORE NOUNS**

Terms and Structures

Use the **superlative degree** to compare ONE term to every member of its same group (TWO OR MORE other terms). In other words, the superlative degree describes how one noun stands out of a group. Superlative adjective are formed using one of the following two methods:

1. Most one-syllable adjectives and some two-syllable ones add "-est" to the end:

   Honey is the **sweetest** *ingredient in the cupboard.*

2. Some adjectives with two syllables and all those with three or more add **most** or **least**:

   Molly is the **most advanced** *student in the dance school.*

"Good" and "bad" become **best** and **worst**:

   Limes are the **best** *flavoring for avocado.*   *This is the* **worst** *cold I have ever had.*

My dog is the <u>most pretty</u> dog in town.

(A) NO CHANGE
(B) most prettiest
(C) prettiest
(D) best prettiest

Only (C) correctly adds an -est ending to the word "pretty" to compare the dog to others in town. All of the other choices add unnecessary and incorrect terms.

1. The two <u>most large</u> nations in the world abut the Arctic Circle: Russia and Canada.

   (A) NO CHANGE
   (B) larger
   (C) largest
   (D) most largest

2. In addition to being the second-smallest nation in the world, Monaco is also the <u>richest and crowded.</u>

   (A) NO CHANGE
   (B) richer and more crowded.
   (C) richer and crowded more than others.
   (D) richest and most crowded.

3. China is the nation with the highest population; at this point China is <u>more populous</u> than second-place India, but many predict that will change by 2050.

   (A) NO CHANGE
   (B) most populated
   (C) best in population
   (D) higher population

4. The continent with the youngest population is Africa, where the median age was 19.7 in 2012, much <u>most lower</u> than the worldwide median age of 30.4.

   (A) NO CHANGE
   (B) more lower
   (C) more low
   (D) lower

5. The smallest African nation is the Seychelles, a country of 115 islands that has been called "<u>the idyllic</u> place on Earth."

   (A) NO CHANGE
   (B) more idyllic
   (C) the most idyllic
   (D) better idyllic

6. Tourists to the Seychelles have different opinions about which beach has <u>the softest, whitest sand, and the clearest blue water.</u>

   (A) NO CHANGE
   (B) softer, whiter sand, and clearer blue water.
   (C) soft, white sand, and more clear blue water.
   (D) most soft, most white sand, and the most clear blue water.

7. Quite possibly <u>the rainiest spot</u> on Earth is the Indian state of Meghalaya, home of the famous "living bridges" woven from the aerial roots of banyan trees.

   (A) NO CHANGE
   (B) spot that is rainier
   (C) more rainy of spots
   (D) best rainier spot

8. Antarctica gets less precipitation than any desert, and the spot with <u>the lesser amount</u> of precipitation in the world is Antarctica's Dry Valleys region.

   (A) NO CHANGE
   (B) the least amount
   (C) less amount of
   (D) the most little

☑	1		3		5		7	
	2		4		6		8	

8 ~ 7	6 ~ 5	4 ~ 3	2 ~ 1
EXCELLENT	VERY GOOD	GOOD	NEEDS WORK

019 *Question Topic*

ACTIVE PHRASES THAT DESCRIBE NOUNS (PARTICIPIAL)

Terms and Structures

Participial phrases begin with a past or present participle, such as "rested" or "resting," and they describe a noun. They are usually separated from the rest of a sentence using commas.

Setting a quick pace, *Andrew started running.*   *Isaac,* **determined to win**, *ran faster.*

A common error is separating participial phrases from the nouns they describe, or failing to add the intended noun at all. This results in a **dangling modifier**.

Confusing: **Resting later**, *one could mistake them for twins, but they were not even brothers.*
(Who is resting?)

Clear: **Resting later**, **they** *could be mistaken for twins, although they were not even brothers.*

Confusing: **Leaving**, *shadows were long in the evening light.* (Who is leaving?)

Clear: **Leaving, they** *cast long shadows in the evening light.*

Taught to play the guitar almost before she could walk or talk, <u>I think she mostly communicated through music.</u>

(A) NO CHANGE
(B) I think music was her way of communicating.
(C) it is thought that she mostly communicated through music.
(D) she mostly communicated through music, I think.

Only (D) clearly indicates the subject of the sentence, "she." Choices (A) and (B) incorrectly indicate that it was the speaker who was "taught to play guitar..." Choice (C) muddles the meaning by not clarifying who was "taught to play the guitar..."

020 *Question Topic*

WH- CLAUSES THAT DESCRIBE NOUNS (RELATIVE CLAUSES)

Terms and Structures

A relative clause comes after a noun. It describes the noun using the words "which," "who/whom/whose," "that," "where," or "when":

The town **where I grew up** *is friendly.*

Some relative clauses should not be separated from the rest of a sentence using punctuation because they provide a description that provides context essential to the sentence's meaning:

The television **that I wanted** *would have covered a whole wall.*
(Without "that I wanted," the sentence would not make sense.)

If the relative clause provides information that is extra, and the sentence would make sense without it, separate the clause from the rest of the sentence with commas.

My grandma, **who was buying the television**, *had different ideas.*

The city of <u>Saskatoon, which sits at a bend of Canada's Saskatchewan River, is</u> known for its many bridges.

(A) NO CHANGE
(B) Saskatoon which sits at a bend of of Canada's Saskatchewan River, is
(C) Saskatoon, which sits at a bend of Canada's Saskatchewan River is
(D) Saskatoon which sits at a bend of Canada's Saskatchewan River is

Only (A) correctly separates the non-essential relative clause from the rest of the sentence with commas.

1. The music label <u>Motown founded in 1960,</u> had an enormous impact on American popular music.

   (A) NO CHANGE
   (B) Motown founded in 1960
   (C) Motown, founded in 1960,
   (D) Motown that was founded in 1960,

2. Working at the time on one of the many automobile assembly lines in the city of Detroit, <u>but wishing to be a songwriter, was Berry Gordy.</u>

   (A) NO CHANGE
   (B) Berry Gordy dreamed of being a songwriter.
   (C) was would-be songwriter Berry Gordy.
   (D) but with hopes of being a songwriter, was Berry Gordy.

3. Gordy wondered if he could create an <u>"assembly line" record label that could take young African Americans like himself</u> and turn them into sophisticated pop stars.

   (A) NO CHANGE
   (B) "assembly line" record label, that could take young African Americans like himself,
   (C) "assembly line" record label, that could take young African Americans, like himself,
   (D) "assembly line" record label and taking young African Americans like himself,

4. Borrowing $800 from family members, <u>a rhythm and blues (R&B) record company was started,</u> with one of its labels a shortened version of "Motor Town."

   (A) NO CHANGE
   (B) Gordy started a rhythm and blues (R&B) record company,
   (C) and starting a rhythm and blues (R&B) record company,
   (D) a rhythm and blues (R&B) record company started,

5. Motown formed vocal <u>groups, that recording</u> songs penned by staff songwriters and who were backed by in-house musicians.

   (A) NO CHANGE
   (B) groups, which recording
   (C) groups, who recorded
   (D) groups that recorded

6. Motown <u>groups, that studied poise and charm, wore</u> suits or gowns and executed subtle dance moves in unison.

   (A) NO CHANGE
   (B) groups who studied poise and charm wore
   (C) groups, poised and charmed, wore
   (D) groups, schooled in poise and charm, wore

7. Diana Ross and the Supremes, the Jackson 5 (including the youngest, Michael Jackson), and Stevie Wonder were just a few of the Motown <u>artists who</u> were tremendously successful.

   (A) NO CHANGE
   (B) artists, who
   (C) artists, that
   (D) artists and

8. <u>Becoming "crossover hits,"</u> popular with white audiences, which helped break down prejudice against African Americans.

   (A) NO CHANGE
   (B) "Crossover hits" were
   (C) Many Motown songs became "crossover hits"
   (D) Becoming "crossover hits" and

☑	1		3		5		7	
	2		4		6		8	

8 ~ 7	6 ~ 5	4 ~ 3	2 ~ 1
EXCELLENT	VERY GOOD	GOOD	NEEDS WORK

021 *Question Topic*

→ SIMPLE VERB TENSES

Terms and Structures

The simple present tense describes conditions ("*I* **am** *fine, thank you*"), routine actions, general facts, and universal truths. In addition, it is used to talk about characters in stories, films, and art.

> *A new nursing shift at the hospital* **starts** *daily at 7 a.m.*
>
> *The Sun* **converts** *millions of tons of hydrogen into energy every second.*
>
> *In the movie, the aliens* **transform** *into cars and radios.*

The phrase "used to" plus a base verb describes habitual actions or conditions in the past.

> *We* **used to see** *each other on the bus every morning.*

The simple past tense describes an action or condition in the past; the simple future tense does the same for the future.

> *Arianna* **ate** *lunch at noon.*   *She* **will eat** *dinner at 5 p.m.*

It was a good movie; I <u>liked the part where the</u> <u>mother saw</u> her son again

(A) NO CHANGE
(B) like the part when the mother saw
(C) liked the part where the mother <u>sees</u>
(D) like the part where the mother has seen

The speaker saw the movie in the past, thus the description of what the speaker liked can be in the past. The actions of characters in fictional movies and books, however, are usually described in the present tense, making (C) the best answer.

---

022 *Question Topic*

→ PROGRESSIVE TENSES

Terms and Structures

The present progressive tense uses forms of "to be" and verb bases ending in "ing" to describe what a subject is in the process of doing at the present moment.

> *I* **am taking** *a test right now.*   *The hamster* **is sleeping** *again.*   *What* **are** *you* **talking** *about?*

The present progressive tense with the word "going" plus an infinitive indicates plans and definite expectations.

> *She* **is going to arrive** *soon.*
>
> *We* **are going to have** *a party; would you like to come?*

Past continuous tense describes an action that was ongoing in the past when something else happened.

> *He* **was playing** *the piano when he got an idea.*   *What* **were** *you* **doing** *when I called?*

Many economists say that wage growth <u>does</u> <u>not keep up</u> with inflation (at the current time)

(A) NO CHANGE
(B) will not keep up
(C) did not keep up
(D) is not keeping up

"Keeping up" is a process, and the sentence describes it as (not) happening "at the current time." Therefore, (D) is the correct choice because the present progressive is appropriate.

---

1. <u>It would be</u> common to affix the title "the Great" to the ends of a few historical leaders' names.

   (A) NO CHANGE
   (B) It was
   (C) It is
   (D) It will be

2. The term does not necessarily mean that the leaders were good and kind, but rather that they <u>were building empires; some were even giving</u> themselves the title.

   (A) NO CHANGE
   (B) built empires; some even gave
   (C) built empires; some even give
   (D) will build empires; some are even giving

3. Russian Tsar Peter the Great (1672-1725) came to power in 1696 when the rest of Europe <u>embraced</u> new ways of thinking.

   (A) NO CHANGE
   (B) was going to embrace
   (C) was embracing
   (D) is embracing

4. While European scholars, inventors, entrepreneurs and explorers transformed European society, <u>Russia remained</u> isolated and feudal.

   (A) NO CHANGE
   (B) Russia remains
   (C) Russia was remaining
   (D) Russia was going to remain

5. Peter went undercover in Europe, pretending to be an ordinary Russian traveler so that <u>he can study</u> technologies and political structures.

   (A) NO CHANGE
   (B) he could be studying
   (C) he can be studying
   (D) he could study

6. Peter founded schools of math and science in Russia and started industries; today many historians <u>will applaud</u> his reforms.

   (A) NO CHANGE
   (B) would applaud
   (C) are applauding
   (D) applaud

7. However, critics say that all of his actions <u>were designed</u> to improve his military might and suppress his people.

   (A) NO CHANGE
   (B) were designing
   (C) are designed
   (D) being a design

8. Most likely, historians <u>would never completely agree</u> on the legacy of Peter the Great.

   (A) NO CHANGE
   (B) will never completely agree
   (C) are never completely agreeing
   (D) were never completely agreed

☑	1		3		5		7	
	2		4		6		8	

8 ~ 7	6 ~ 5	4 ~ 3	2 ~ 1
EXCELLENT	VERY GOOD	GOOD	NEEDS WORK

023 Question Topic

→ PERFECT TENSES

Terms and Structures

Present perfect tense uses forms of "to have" and past participles to indicate that an action or condition occurred before the time under consideration; the time it took place is irrelevant.

> Thank you for the offer, but I **have eaten** lunch already.
>
> We **have talked** about going skydiving, but we **haven't decided** yet.
>
> That swimming team **has swum** the English Channel.

Past perfect tense describes actions and conditions that occurred before some past point in time:

> My parents **had heard** the news even before I called them.

When perfect tense verbs are incorporated into a conditional statement, it indicates something that might have happened, but did not:

> If I **had gotten** that job, I **would have skipped** college.

Future perfect tense predicts that something will be true by some point in the future:

> Within five years, this technology **will have become** obsolete.

In 1910, few Americans <u>had ever seen</u> a movie.

(A) NO CHANGE
(B) have ever seen
(C) have never seen
(D) would have not seen

Of course, 1910 is a specific point in the past, and the sentence is about actions that occurred (or in this case, did not occur) at some unspecified point before that. Thus, the past perfect tense is the correct tense, making (A) the correct choice.

---

024 Question Topic

→ ACTIVE VOICE, PASSIVE VOICE

Terms and Structures

The active voice is a way of structuring sentences so that the subject appears before the verb, as in "**Ericka threw** the ball." The active voice is simpler and more direct than the passive voice, and is usually preferable.

The passive voice places the direct object first, adding a form of "to be" and a past participle, as in "**The ball was thrown** by Ericka." Thus, it can be used to emphasize either the object or the subject of the sentence:

> **The ball was** definitely **thrown** by Ericka, not by me.
>
> **A ball was thrown** by Ericka, not a rock.

The passive voice does not always name a subject, as in "**The ball was thrown**." Thus, it is useful when the subject is unimportant or unknown, as in "*Recently*, **the window was replaced**."

<u>Humor can be used as</u> a powerful tool for social commentary

(A) NO CHANGE
(B) Humor can be
(C) People can use humor as
(D) Humor can be used by everyone as

Choice (B) is active, simple, and concise, making it a better choice than the passive voice in (A). Choices (C) and (D) add obvious information to the sentence.

---

1. This semester, I took Psychology 1; I <u>have not taken</u> Abnormal Psychology yet.

   (A) NO CHANGE
   (B) had not taken
   (C) will not have taken
   (D) did not take

2. At my university, a cross-discipline major called "Computational Biology" <u>is recently added.</u>

   (A) NO CHANGE
   (B) has recently added.
   (C) has recently been added.
   (D) had recently been added.

3. If we hadn't gone to community college before transferring to the university, we <u>would having been had</u> more debt when we graduated.

   (A) NO CHANGE
   (B) would have had
   (C) would had
   (D) had had

4. Incoming freshmen should know that by the time they finish college, they <u>probably changed</u> majors at least once.

   (A) NO CHANGE
   (B) will probably change
   (C) probably have changed
   (D) will probably have changed

5. The Introduction to Sociology class is a prerequisite to all other sociology classes, but it <u>offers</u> only in the fall semester.

   (A) NO CHANGE
   (B) becomes offered
   (C) is offered
   (D) will have been offered

6. Earlier today, William told me that he <u>has to decide to pursue</u> a double major in Film Studies and Political Science.

   (A) NO CHANGE
   (B) will have decided and pursued
   (C) has decided to pursue
   (D) has had to decide, pursuing

7. By the time she finished kindergarten, Neftali <u>had already decided</u> that she wanted to become a teacher.

   (A) NO CHANGE
   (B) has already decided
   (C) will have decided
   (D) already decides

8. Philosophy <u>has never considered</u> a lucrative major, but sometimes philosophy majors land excellent jobs.

   (A) NO CHANGE
   (B) was never considered
   (C) has not considered
   (D) has never been considered

☑	1		3		5		7	
	2		4		6		8	

8 ~ 7	6 ~ 5	4 ~ 3	2 ~ 1
EXCELLENT	VERY GOOD	GOOD	NEEDS WORK

025 Question Topic → CONDITIONAL STATEMENTS

Terms and Structures

Conditional sentences express possible/probable outcomes given a set of circumstances (conditions):

If it snows (condition), *school will be canceled* (outcome).

Note that the phrases can be in either order, but if the outcome is mentioned first, no comma is used:

School will be canceled (outcome) *if it snows* (condition).

Present-tense "if" sentences pair with "can," "will," "might," or "may" and a verb base; they sound more definite than past-tense conditionals.

If the team **continues** *to play this well, it* **can win**.

We **will come** *over if you* **need** *us.*

Use of the past tense with "could" or "would" and a verb base expresses less certainty.

If the team **improved** *its offense, it* **could** *win.*

I **would be** *worried if you* **went** *on that ride.*

Use of the past-perfect tense with "could," "would," "will," "might," or "may" and a perfect-tense verb speculates on the outcome of an altered history.

You **might have gotten** *the job if you* **had gone** *to the job interview.*

If I **had not changed** *schools, I* **would not have met** *my best friend.*

If I go sailing on a stormy day, <u>I'd be getting</u> seasick.

(A) NO CHANGE
(B) I will get
(C) I will have gotten
(D) I would get

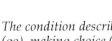

The condition described is in the present tense (go), making choice (B) correct. In the present, the possibility of going sailing still exists. Choices (A),(C), and (D) shift to past tenses, which does not make sense.

026 Question Topic → EXPRESSING THE UNLIKELY (SUBJUNCTIVE)

Terms and Structures

The subjunctive verb form expresses wishes or situations that are impossible or untrue. It is most noticeable with the use of "were" instead of "was" to describe that which is not the case.

I wish that she **were** *here right now.*

If Earth's gravity **were** *weaker, sofas would have seat belts.*

Unfortunately, I am in a rush at the moment; if I **were not**, *I would love to chat.*

That film star probably wishes that she <u>was not</u> hounded by paparazzi.

(A) NO CHANGE
(B) is not
(C) won't be
(D) were not

Because the sentence above implies that the wish is currently impossible, the underlined portion must contain "were," making (D) the correct choice.

1. If Mongolians <u>were not skilled horse riders, they would not be being</u> able to conquer lands from China to the Black Sea in the 1200s.

    (A) NO CHANGE
    (B) have not been skilled horse riders, they could not be
    (C) were not skilled horse riders, it could not be that they were
    (D) had not been skilled horse riders, they would not have been

2. In the Mediterranean region of the 1330s, shipbuilding and navigation had improved so much that if merchants <u>wanted to trade, they could move</u> cargo easily by sea.

    (A) NO CHANGE
    (B) want to trade, they will move
    (C) had wanted to trade, they could have moved
    (D) were wanting to trade, they would have moved

3. Seafaring ships and overland trade routes within the Mongolian Empire opened up a golden era for Eurasian trade in the 1300s; if they <u>did not, the bubonic plague pandemic may have been</u> more contained.

    (A) NO CHANGE
    (B) had not, the bubonic plague pandemic was
    (C) would not have, the bubonic plague pandemic would be
    (D) had not, the bubonic plague pandemic may have been

4. If a bubonic plague-carrying flea <u>bites a mammal, the flea will regurgitate</u> into the mammal's blood, infecting it with the disease.

    (A) NO CHANGE
    (B) has bitten a mammal, the flea would regurgitate
    (C) bit a mammal, the flea regurgitates
    (D) would bite a mammal, the flea would

5. Naturally, if people, rats, and farm animals <u>occupying the same farms, they will all be bitten</u> by the same fleas, and the disease can spread.

    (A) NO CHANGE
    (B) were occupying the same farms, they had been all bitten
    (C) occupy the same farms, they will all be bitten
    (D) have occupied the same farms, they will all be bitten

6. If the population count of the Eurasian continent and North Africa in the mid-1300s <u>is known, it would be</u> easier to estimate how many millions of people died from the plague.

    (A) NO CHANGE
    (B) was known, it were
    (C) were known, it would be
    (D) were known, it was

7. Although Europe <u>were</u> devastated by the plague, parts of Russia, China, northern Africa, and the Middle East fared even worse and were essentially depopulated.

    (A) NO CHANGE
    (B) is
    (C) was
    (D) had been

8. History <u>would have been very different if people had realized</u> that fleas carried the disease.

    (A) NO CHANGE
    (B) would be very different if people were realizing
    (C) had been very different if people realized
    (D) would have been very different if people would realize

✓	1		3		5		7	
	2		4		6		8	

8 ~ 7	6 ~ 5	4 ~ 3	2 ~ 1
EXCELLENT	VERY GOOD	GOOD	NEEDS WORK

027 Question Topic

→ **AUXILIARY VERBS**

Terms and Structures

When used as auxiliary verbs, forms of the verbs *be*, *have*, and *do* help other verbs form various tenses. They also help construct negatives, questions, and the passive voice. These verb phrases can be contracted, (I am = I'm, did not = didn't), **but contractions do not appear in formal writing**.

> The archaeologist **was digging** *for pottery when he found the bone fragment.*
>
> He **had not expected** *to find human or animal remains at this dig site.*
>
> "**Have** *you* **seen** *any more fossilized remains here?" he asked his coworker, Savannah.*

"Modal" auxiliary verbs include *can, could, may, might, must, should, ought to, will, would,* and *shall.* They do not change forms for tense.

> *"You* **should check** *with the interns," Savannah replied. "They* **might have seen** *something."*

Many species of rabbit <u>don't leave</u> their burrows in daylight in order to avoid airborne predators.
(A) NO CHANGE
(B) can't leave
(C) should not leave
(D) do not leave

Choice (D) is correct because the sentence provides a general fact about rabbit species, so a negative statement in the simple present tense ("do not leave") is appropriate. Choices (A) and (B) are incorrect because they use contractions, and (C) is incorrect because it creates a suggestion ("should").

---

028 Question Topic

→ **ADVERBS**

Terms and Structures

Adverbs describe verbs, adjectives, or other adverbs, explaining where, when, how, or how often something occurs. They often end in -ly, but not always. Common adverbs include *very, much, many,* and *too.* (Note that in the following examples, the adverbs are in **bold** text and the phrases they modify are <u>underlined</u>.)

Adverbs can appear before or after a verb phrase:

> *Jeremy* **usually** <u>*goes to bed*</u> **early**.

When an adverb describes an clause, the adverb should go at the beginning or the end of the clause:

> **Lately**, <u>*Jeremy has had trouble sleeping.*</u> <u>*He took a nap*</u> **yesterday**.

When there is an auxiliary verb, adverbs usually appear after it:

> *I* <u>*will*</u> **never** <u>*understand*</u> *that. It* <u>*has*</u> **only** <u>*happened*</u> *once.*

Adverbs can form two-part descriptions of nouns with past participles:

> *It was a* **frequently** *(adverb)* **traveled** *(past participle) road.*
> *I stopped for* **freshly squeezed** *lemonade.*

<u>Slowed by her recent injured knee,</u> Christine took a long time to walk back down the mountain.
(A) NO CHANGE
(B) Slowly by her recently injured knee,
(C) Slowed by her recently injured knee,
(D) Slowed by her injured knee recently,

Choice (C) is correct; "recently" should come immediately before the phrase it describes, "injured knee." Choice (A) is incorrect because "recent" is an adverb, and cannot modify "injured." Choice (B) is incorrect because "slowed" introduces a participial phrase, and must therefore be a participle, not an adverb. Choice (D) is incorrect because it misplaces the adverb "recently."

1. The artist <u>isn't not primarily attempting</u> to create images, but rather to carve out mental space for community building.

   (A) NO CHANGE
   (B) really don't attempt
   (C) is not primarily attempting
   (D) primarily is not attempting

2. The <u>contrived cleverly film</u> sequences lead viewers through a virtual maze.

   (A) NO CHANGE
   (B) cleverly contrived film
   (C) cleverly contriving film
   (D) contrived film cleverly

3. The photographs in the exhibit <u>ought to fit</u> together, but instead the effect is jarring.

   (A) NO CHANGE
   (B) must fit
   (C) do fit
   (D) will fit

4. With each consecutive panel, the artist <u>holds viewers' attention good.</u>

   (A) NO CHANGE
   (B) holds good viewers' attention.
   (C) holds viewers' attention well.
   (D) holds well viewers' attention.

5. In the corner of the painting, a lone figure seems to be on the verge of action; it is as though she <u>sudden might sing—or scream.</u>

   (A) NO CHANGE
   (B) might sing sudden—or scream.
   (C) might sing—or scream—suddenly.
   (D) might suddenly sing—or scream.

6. The garden will be formal; a sundial <u>wouldn't not be</u> out of place in it.

   (A) NO CHANGE
   (B) won't being
   (C) would not
   (D) would not be

7. <u>Surprisingly, splatters of color suggest precision</u> in the painting.

   (A) NO CHANGE
   (B) Splatters of color suggest precision surprisingly
   (C) Splatters of color suggest surprisingly precision
   (D) Splatters, surprising, of color suggest precision

8. Viewers <u>must discard all of their nearly previous</u> assumptions about gravity.

   (A) NO CHANGE
   (B) nearly must discard all of their previous
   (C) must discard nearly all of their previous
   (D) must discard all nearly of their previous

☑	1		3		5		7	
	2		4		6		8	

8 ~ 7	6 ~ 5	4 ~ 3	2 ~ 1
EXCELLENT	VERY GOOD	GOOD	NEEDS WORK

029 Question Topic

→ **DEPENDENT CLAUSES**

Terms and Structures

A clause is a group of words that contains a subject and verb. Two types of clauses are **independent** and **dependent clauses**. An independent clause can stand on its own as a sentence, but a dependent clause cannot; it *depends* on additional information to make sense.

Dependent clauses begin with subordinate conjunctions. Some of the most common subordinate conjunctions express relationships of:

Time: **as, before, since, until, once, while**

Cause and Effect: **because, since**

Conditional: **as, if, provided, that, unless, whereas**

Difference: **although, though, whereas**

(In the following examples, subordinate conjunctions are in **bold** and dependent clauses are underlined.)

I'll take the last piece of pie **unless** <u>you want it.</u>

Though <u>cherry pie is not my favorite</u>, I will have a bite or two.

Since <u>it is sunny</u>, let's go for a walk.

<u>Although the company experienced</u> a massive turnaround in sales.

(A) NO CHANGE
(B) Since the company, experienced
(C) The company, experiencing
(D) The company experienced

Choice (D) is correct because it is the only choice that forms a complete sentence. Choices (A) and (B) begin with dependent conjunctions, making them dependent clauses, which cannot stand alone as sentences. (C) is incorrect because it uses a participle—"experiencing"—where there should be a main verb.

---

030 Question Topic

→ **DEPENDENT CLAUSES AND COMMAS**

Terms and Structures

Dependent clauses can appear before or after independent clauses:

Because <u>it was hot</u>, we went swimming.   We went swimming **because** <u>it was hot</u>.

Note that when a dependent clause appears first, it must be followed by a comma. If a dependent clause appears after an independent clause, placing a comma between the two clauses is optional.

While Kelsey stopped every few minutes to take <u>photos Max</u> went ahead on the well-marked the trail.

(A) NO CHANGE
(B) photos. Max
(C) photos, Max
(D) photos: Max

(C) is correct because "While Kelsey stopped every few minutes to take photos" is a dependent clause; since it appears before the main clause, it must be followed by a comma. (A) is a run-on sentence, and (B) creates an incomplete sentence out of the clause. (D) creates a sentence that does not make sense.

Quiz

5 min.

1. <u>Resulting of several factors,</u> sales of athletic shoes are booming worldwide.

   (A) NO CHANGE
   (B) With several factors,
   (C) As several factors,
   (D) As a result of several factors,

2. Sales of comfortable shoes may be rising in <u>the U.S. Because</u> more people are working from home.

   (A) NO CHANGE
   (B) the U.S.: because
   (C) the U.S. because
   (D) the U.S.;

3. "Casual" and "retro" athletic shoes had the strongest sales growth in the previous <u>quarter. Although,</u> sales of basketball and running shoes are also rising.

   (A) NO CHANGE
   (B) quarter although
   (C) quarter although,
   (D) quarter, yet although,

4. Since more people are exercising <u>outdoors, the</u> "rugged" shoe category is expected to perform well in the near future.

   (A) NO CHANGE
   (B) outdoors the
   (C) outdoors. The
   (D) outdoors: the

5. Increasing public awareness of what it means to lead a healthy lifestyle may fuel the athletic shoe <u>market. Though</u> it does not guarantee that people will actually wear the shoes to exercise.

   (A) NO CHANGE
   (B) market, though
   (C) market; though
   (D) market, though,

6. The eco-friendly shoe category has strong growth <u>potential if analysts are right consumers want</u> to demonstrate eco-consciousness.

   (A) NO CHANGE
   (B) potential if analysts are right; consumers want
   (C) potential; if analysts are right, consumers want
   (D) potential, if analysts are right, consumers want

7. <u>That</u> previous decades saw little overlap in leisure wear and athletic gear, the 2010s saw the rise of athletic/leisure ("athleisure") clothing.

   (A) NO CHANGE
   (B) Because
   (C) Whereas
   (D) If

8. Because of the growth of "athleisure" <u>fashion even top</u> fashion designers introduced comfortable women's shoes such as chic "pajama sandals" and "pool slides."

   (A) NO CHANGE
   (B) fashion. Even top
   (C) fashion: even top
   (D) fashion, even top

☑	1		3		5		7	
	2		4		6		8	

8 ~ 7	6 ~ 5	4 ~ 3	2 ~ 1
EXCELLENT	VERY GOOD	GOOD	NEEDS WORK

031 Question Topic

JOINING INDEPENDENT CLAUSES IN A SENTENCE

Terms and Structures

Longer sentences often contain two or more independent clauses. Each independent clause could make sense as a complete sentence, since it contains a subject and a verb and comprises a complete thought. However, joining multiple independent clauses in the same sentence sometimes sounds smoother:

> *We argued. We both apologized. We made up.*

> *We argued,* **but** *we both apologized,* **and** *we made up.*

Independent clauses can be joined with a comma and a coordinating conjunction (*for, and, nor, but, or, yet, so*). The acronym "FANBOYS" can help you remember the seven coordinating conjunctions.

> *The snake was not dangerous to humans,* **so** *the ranger just watched it slither by.*

> *I like vanilla,* **and** *I like chocolate, too.*   *I like dessert,* **but** *I will eat vegetables.*

If the relationship between the two clauses needs no explanation, a semicolon can be used to join the two sentences:

> *My mom saw my haircut**;** she looked shocked.*

Nocturnal animals tend to have large <u>eyes, they</u> need to take in every bit of light there is.

(A) NO CHANGE
(B) eyes, for they
(C) eyes so they
(D) eyes; then they

Choice (B) is correct because it combines the two independent clauses with a comma and a coordinating conjunction ("for"). Choice (A) lacks a conjunction, and choice (C) lacks a comma. Choices (C) and (D) use connecting words that do not make sense.

032 Question Topic

ADDITIONAL CONNECTING WORDS

Terms and Structures

Topics 028 and 030 discuss the functions of the most common connecting words: subordinate and coordinate conjunctions. However, these are not the only words that are used to show relationships within sentences.

Relative pronouns include the words *who, whom, whose, when, which, that, where,* and *wherever*. Although relative pronouns are not conjunctions, they still act as "connecting" words that introduce a relative clause, which modifies the noun or noun phrase that comes immediately before it.

Correlative conjunctions are used to describe how two or more ideas relate to each other. They consist of pairs of words in a specific pattern:

both *A* **and** *B*	**whether** *A* **or** *B*	**not** *A* **but** *B*	**either** *A* **or** *B*
A **as well as** *B*	**between** *A* **and** *B*	**not only** *A* **but also** *B*	**neither** *A* **nor** *B*

> *I can meet him on* **either** *Monday* **or** *Tuesday.*   **Not only** *is the lake long,* **but** *it is* **also** *deep.*

City mayors must become familiar with plans for proposed <u>developments</u>, quite detailed.

(A) NO CHANGE
(B) developments, which can be
(C) developments, they may be
(D) developments, who are

Choice (B) is correct because it uses the appropriate relative pronoun, "which," to refer precisely to the preceding "plans for proposed developments." Choices (A) and (D) fail to clarify what is "detailed," while choice (C) begins another independent clause without a proper conjunction.

For questions 1 - 4, select the choice that most effectively combines the sentences at the underlined portion.

1. The Goosefish can hide its six-foot-long body in the sea <u>bed. It</u> lures prey with a protruding frond that looks like a fishing rod.

   (A) bed, because it
   (B) bed, for it
   (C) bed, it
   (D) bed, and it

2. The Portuguese man-of-war looks somewhat like a <u>jellyfish. It</u> is a colony several types of organisms called "polyps" and "medusoids."

   (A) jellyfish; it
   (B) jellyfish, and it
   (C) jellyfish, but it
   (D) jellyfish, since

3. A squid moves by means of jet <u>propulsion. It</u> shoots water out of its body to rocket backward.

   (A) propulsion: it
   (B) propulsion, it
   (C) propulsion, yet it
   (D) propulsion, though it

4. The icefish of the Antarctic coastal waters has no red blood <u>cells. Its</u> blood is clear-colored.

   (A) cells, but its
   (B) cells, nor its
   (C) cells, yet its
   (D) cells; its

5. Queen triggerfish live in <u>coral reefs. Where</u> they can back into a crevice and use upright spines on their backs to "lock" themselves in place.

   (A) NO CHANGE
   (B) coral reefs—where
   (C) coral reefs, where
   (D) coral reefs; where

6. Living in the world's southern oceans, the male sea spider has 20 or more walking <u>legs, as well,</u> two more for carrying fertilized eggs until they hatch.

   (A) NO CHANGE
   (B) legs, as well as
   (C) legs, as well as,
   (D) legs: well,

7. Sea otters <u>rest both day, night,</u> by floating on their backs and wrapping themselves in kelp seaweed.

   (A) NO CHANGE
   (B) rest day, and night,
   (C) rest not only day and night
   (D) rest both day and night

8. Humpback whales communicate by singing complicated <u>songs, whatever they</u> may repeat for hours at a time.

   (A) NO CHANGE
   (B) songs, so they
   (C) songs, which they
   (D) songs—that

☑	1		3		5		7	
	2		4		6		8	

8 ~ 7	6 ~ 5	4 ~ 3	2 ~ 1
EXCELLENT	VERY GOOD	GOOD	NEEDS WORK

033 Question Topic

→ **PARALLEL STRUCTURE**

Terms and Structures

Lists of words or phrases within sentences should parallel each other. Single terms should be the same part of speech, and phrases and clauses should maintain the same word pattern. Listed verbs should express the same tense, number, and person, and nouns should usually be all singular or all plural.

> The doctor **asked** about his symptoms and **checked** his health history.
>
> My mom looked for her keys **on the table**, **under the bed**, *and* **out on the patio**.
>
> Usually the **bigger**, **stronger**, **faster** team wins.

The boy was from a ranch in Mexico, and he already knew all about <u>grazing, how to herd, and he could care for cattle.</u>

(A) NO CHANGE
(B) graze and herding, he could care for cattle.
(C) how to graze, how to herd, and how to care for cattle.
(D) grazing, herding, and caring for cattle.

Choice (D) is the best answer because it is parallel and concise. Choices (A) and (B) use three different verb structures; choice (C) is unnecessarily wordy.

034 Question Topic

→ **LOGICAL COMPARISONS**

Terms and Structures

When comparing nouns, check that the nouns are truly comparable; for instance, it is logical to compare *Mozart* to *Beethoven* because both are composers, but it is illogical to compare *Mozart* to *Beethoven's Ninth Symphony* because a person cannot logically be compared to a composition. Comparing two different parts of speech results in an **illogical comparison**. It only takes a forgotten word or two to render comparisons illogical.

> Illogical: *More tornadoes occur in Kansas than in any state.*
> Logical: *More tornadoes occur in Kansas than in any **other** state.*

When the terms of a comparison include prepositional phrases or possession, the noun of the second term can often be replaced by either "that" or "those."

Use the pronoun "that" to replace or refer to a singular noun in a comparison.

> **The bird's song** *was more beautiful than* **that** *of any singer.*

Use the pronoun "those" to replace or refer to a plural noun.

> **The temple's imposing columns** *were even larger than* **those** *of the Parthenon in Athens.*

The birds near your house are <u>louder than mine.</u>

(A) NO CHANGE
(B) louder than my house.
(C) louder than the ones near mine.
(D) louder than at mine.

Choice (C) is correct because it clearly compares birds to other birds. Choices (A) and (B) seem to compare the birds to the speaker's house, which is illogical, of course. Choice (D) could be understood to mean that the same birds are louder at "your house" than when they are at "mine."

1. Great Britain established a universal emergency telephone number in 1937, decades before <u>the United States in 1968.</u>

   (A) NO CHANGE
   (B) the United States did in 1968.
   (C) 1968 in the United States.
   (D) the United States.

2. Proper first aid can sometimes save a person's life, especially if the person is bleeding heavily, has <u>stopped breathing, or something poisoned him or her.</u>

   (A) NO CHANGE
   (B) been stopping breathing, or was poisoned.
   (C) is stopped breathing, or poison got into him or her.
   (D) stopped breathing, or has been poisoned.

3. When a person is unconscious and not breathing, quick, regular compression of the chest may be <u>more effective for untrained people</u> than mouth-to-mouth resuscitation would be.

   (A) NO CHANGE
   (B) more effectively provided for untrained people
   (C) more effectively provided by untrained people
   (D) provided more effectively to untrained people

4. In the event of a life-threatening injury, people on the scene should first take a moment to look around and <u>have to assess</u> safety risks to themselves.

   (A) NO CHANGE
   (B) be assessing
   (C) assessed
   (D) assess

5. It is important that people call 9-1-1 and describe the situation clearly, <u>and should avoid</u> moving fallen victims unless it is clearly necessary.

   (A) NO CHANGE
   (B) and they should be avoiding
   (C) that they avoid
   (D) and that they avoid

6. Loss of blood, <u>heat stroke, and heart attack</u> are some of the conditions that can cause shock, according to medical experts.

   (A) NO CHANGE
   (B) heat strokes, or heart attacks
   (C) loss of coolness, or loss of heart function
   (D) and heat stroke or heart attack

7. Going into shock means <u>no ability to pump</u> enough oxygenated blood to the brain and other organs.

   (A) NO CHANGE
   (B) not being able to pump
   (C) not able to pump
   (D) no pumping of

8. While waiting for an ambulance, victims of shock should be kept lying down and warm, with their legs raised slightly <u>higher than them</u> so that blood can flow to the heart.

   (A) NO CHANGE
   (B) higher
   (C) higher than the rest of their body
   (D) higher than the victims

☑	1		3		5		7	
	2		4		6		8	

8 ~ 7	6 ~ 5	4 ~ 3	2 ~ 1
EXCELLENT	VERY GOOD	GOOD	NEEDS WORK

035 *Question Topic*

SEMICOLONS: TWO USES

Terms and Structures

The most common use for a semicolon is to join two independent clauses when the relationship between the clauses is self-evident:

> *The downpour lasted three days; houses flooded and streets became fast-moving streams.*

> *White sage is an aromatic shrub native to the southwestern United States and northwestern Mexico; its leaves can be dried and used for tea or incense.*

Semicolons also punctuate lists when one or more of the list items on the list already involve commas:

> *At the resort you can join a guided hike; swim, snorkel, and sunbathe at the beach; or just relax in a hammock.*

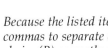

The novel is set in <u>Chicago, Illinois, Brooklyn, New York, and San Diego, California.</u>

(A) NO CHANGE
(B) Chicago, Illinois; Brooklyn, New York; and San Diego, California.
(C) Chicago, Illinois and Brooklyn, New York and San Diego, California.
(D) Chicago, Illinois; Brooklyn, New York and San Diego, California.

Because the listed items must use commas to separate city and state names, choice (B) correctly uses semicolons to separate the items of the complex list.

036 *Question Topic*

COLONS AND DASHES

Terms and Structures

A **colon** connects an idea to an elaboration on a definition of that idea. A colon can only appear after a complete thought.

> *It seemed that the kitten had only two desires: to understand everything, and to attack it.*

An **em dash** can be used in place of a comma, though it is less formal. Dashes can take the place of commas for a more dramatic effect.

> *Shoelaces, plastic bottle caps, hair ties—our brave kitten vanquished them all.*

Bella knew that setting the world record for most consecutive jumping jacks <u>she would need: a witness</u> and video evidence.

(A) NO CHANGE
(B) had two crucial requirements: a witness
(C) she: needed a witness
(D) she needs—a witness

Choice (B) is correct because it is the only choice that includes a complete thought before the colon.

1. Many species of Felinae evolved to hunt prey that is too small to <u>share, rodents, birds, lizards, and insects.</u>

   (A) NO CHANGE
   (B) share: rodents, birds, lizards, and insects.
   (C) share; birds; lizards; and insects.
   (D) share rodents, birds, lizards, and insects.

2. People often describe pet cats as being unsocial <u>or aloof they</u> sleep for 16 to 20 hours a day and seem to spend their waking hours grooming themselves.

   (A) NO CHANGE
   (B) or aloof; they
   (C) or aloof, they
   (D) or aloof when they

3. Pet cats are descended from the Near Eastern wildcat, which is relatively small and is preyed upon by <u>wolves; the wildcat's</u> cautious, "aloof" behavior is an adaptation to its habitat.

   (A) NO CHANGE
   (B) wolves: the wildcat's
   (C) wolves, but the wildcat's
   (D) wolves; and the wildcat's

4. Cats stay attuned to their environment using their rotating, sensitive <u>ears, their large, light-capturing eyes...and</u> the extraordinarily informative whiskers on their noses, ears, jaws, and forelegs.

   (A) NO CHANGE
   (B) ears, their large, light-capturing, eyes, and
   (C) ears; their large, light-capturing eyes; and
   (D) ears and their large, light-capturing eyes, and

5. Cats also exercise caution by scent-marking their individual hunting <u>territories: thus</u> avoiding lethal conflicts with other cats.

   (A) NO CHANGE
   (B) territories. Thus
   (C) territories, thus
   (D) territories and

6. When there is abundant food, feral cats, especially females, have been known to <u>form: loosely</u> structured colonies.

   (A) NO CHANGE
   (B) form loosely
   (C) form, loosely
   (D) form—loosely—

7. Many pet cats love the company of a particular <u>person, a person</u> whose legs they have almost certainly rubbed against, scent-marking and thereby claiming as territory.

   (A) NO CHANGE
   (B) person, and a person
   (C) person;
   (D) person—a person

8. Cats show affection very differently than do <u>dogs; cats</u> may simply sit near a person, purring.

   (A) NO CHANGE
   (B) dogs, cats
   (C) dogs while cats
   (D) dogs cats

☑	1		3		5		7	
	2		4		6		8	

8 ~ 7	6 ~ 5	4 ~ 3	2 ~ 1
EXCELLENT	VERY GOOD	GOOD	NEEDS WORK

IDENTIFYING COMMONLY CONFUSED WORDS

Terms and Structures

In the English language, it is not uncommon for words with very different meanings to sound similar or the same. When speaking, the differences rarely matter. But in writing, using the correct word is crucial for expressing thoughts accurately. The chart below includes some of the most commonly confused words:

NOTE: The following definitions/synonyms only summarize the most common uses for each word.

Commonly Confused Words	Part of Speech	Definition/Synonyms
accept	verb	receive, gain; accept something as true, believe
except	preposition	not including, besides
affect	verb	influence, have an impact on
effect	noun	a change resulting from a cause, result, consequence
adverse	adjective	harmful, unlucky, unfavorable
averse	adjective	having a strong feeling of opposition
bare	verb, adjective	(verb) uncover, expose; (adjective) simple, unclothed
bear	verb, noun	(verb) transport, support; tolerate; (noun) a type of large mammal
capital	noun	money; a city or town with political and economic importance;
capitol	noun	a building that houses the legislative branch of a government
complement	verb, noun	(verb) improve something by adding a part or component; (noun) an addition that completes something
compliment	verb, noun	(verb) mildly praise someone or something; (noun) an expression of mild praise
its	pronoun	gender-neutral third-person singular possessive pronoun
it's	contraction	the shortened form of the words "it is"
lose	verb	have something taken away, misplace
loose	adjective	unsecured, detached
passed	verb (past tense)	leave behind, progress, travel
past	adjective, noun	(adjective) no longer existing; (noun) the time before the present moment, former times
principal	adjective, noun	(adjective) main, primary; (noun) a person of authority, director
principle	noun	a concept that serves as the foundation of a behavior or system
their	pronoun	third-person plural possessive pronoun
there	demonstrative/ existential pronoun	(demonstrative) a pronoun that answers the question "where?"; (existential) a pronoun that indicates that something exists
they're	contraction	the shortened form of the words "they are"
to	preposition	indicating a particular direction, identifying something that is affected
too	adverb	extremely, excessively; additionally, also
two	number	2
whose	determiner/ pronoun	showing that something belongs to or is associated with a person
who's	contraction	the shortened form of the words "who is"

1. The plot of the 2004 film *I, Robot*, starring Will Smith, rests on the <u>principle</u> that robots can be programmed to apply logic to new situations.

   (A) NO CHANGE
   (B) printable
   (C) principal
   (D) rule

2. *I, Robot* is based on the ideas of science fiction writer Isaac Asimov, <u>who's</u> book of the same name was published in 1950.

   (A) NO CHANGE
   (B) who is
   (C) his
   (D) whose

3. Asimov's 1942 story "Runaround" was his first to imagine a society where human-like robots are programmed to obey humans, <u>accept</u> when doing so may harm other humans.

   (A) NO CHANGE
   (B) except
   (C) exempt
   (D) accessible

4. Many of Asimov's stories explore various unintended <u>affects</u> of programming robots in such a manner.

   (A) NO CHANGE
   (B) episodes
   (C) upsets
   (D) effects

5. The 1999 film *The Matrix* envisions a dystopian future where most humans are unaware that <u>they're</u> day-to-day life experiences are artificially supplied by machines.

   (A) NO CHANGE
   (B) there
   (C) their
   (D) they

6. The plots of *The Matrix* and *I, Robot* echo a "Frankenstein" theme: humans <u>lose</u> control over their own creations, and become controlled by them.

   (A) NO CHANGE
   (B) in lieu of
   (C) loose
   (D) loosely

7. In contrast, the 2007 film *Transformers* introduced "robotic organisms" from another planet— individuals who feel either friendly or <u>avatar</u> to humans.

   (A) NO CHANGE
   (B) adverse
   (C) averse
   (D) advantageous

8. In the film, transformers act on strong feelings about <u>passed</u> events that did not necessarily involve humans.

   (A) NO CHANGE
   (B) past
   (C) pasted
   (D) passable

☑	1		3		5		7	
	2		4		6		8	

8 ~ 7	6 ~ 5	4 ~ 3	2 ~ 1
EXCELLENT	VERY GOOD	GOOD	NEEDS WORK

038 *Question Topic*

→ **EDITING FOR DEVELOPMENT OF TOPIC**

CHAPTER 1

Terms and Structures

Consider the way a child may often draw a person. First, the child draws the outlines of a head and a body, then adds details such as hair, eyes, mouth, and fingers, and finally colors in the figure's clothing.

Similarly, writers introduce topics, convey their basic ideas, and then elaborate. "Developing" a topic means to fully explain and support main points. At the same time, writers should leave out distracting, irrelevant information.

Read the passage and analyze the sentences for the questions that follow.

Adults often grouse over the amount of time that teenagers spend playing video games. **1** In the United States, according to a 2008 study by the Pew Internet & American Life Project, 97 percent of teens play video games of some sort. **2** Some adults worry that the habit is creating a solitary, anti-social generation with severe mental deficits; however, the concerns do not hold up to scrutiny.

3 First, video games can inspire more, not less, social learning. The Pew study found that typically, teens play video games with other people either online or offline much of the time. Moreover, many respondents reported becoming more civic-minded through narrative games. **4** Seventy-six percent of respondents in the study said that they helped others while gaming, and 44 percent said that they have learned about a problem in society. **5** More than half of the teens in the study said that they played games that made them think about moral and ethical issues.

6 Some adults also assume that video games involve nothing but repetitive gun violence. But the Pew study found that the average young person plays at least five different types of video games. The most popular categories include racing, puzzles, sports, and action/adventure. **7** Many gamers say that the games greatly enhance their imaginations and thinking skills. The games allow players to solve problems, explore fantastical settings, and interact with high-quality art and music. Games also frequently allow playing the role of a hero, which is the timeless secret behind many good stories. **8** Humans find it compelling to identify with characters who overcome great obstacles.

---

1. What is the function of the sentence that follows?

   In the United States, according to a 2008 study by the Pew Internet & American Life Project, 97 percent of teens play video games of some sort.

   (A) To provide context for the passage's main claim
   (B) To state the passage's main claim

2. What is the function of the sentence that follows?

   Some adults worry that the habit is creating a solitary, anti-social generation with severe mental deficits; however, the concerns do not hold up to scrutiny.

   (A) To support a claim with facts and details
   (B) To state the passage's main claim

3. What is the function of the sentence that follows?

   First, video games can inspire more, not less, social learning.

   (A) To introduce the paragraph's main argument
   (B) To transition logically to a new paragraph

4. What is the function of the sentence that follows?

   Seventy-six percent of respondents in the study said that they helped others while gaming, and 44 percent said that they have learned about a problem in society.

   (A) To support a claim with facts and details
   (B) To state the passage's main claim

5. Why has the writer included the following?

   More than half of the teens in the study said that they played games that made them think about moral and ethical issues.

   (A) To explain the paragraph's argument
   (B) To elaborate on the paragraph's argument

6. What is one purpose of the sentence that follows?

   Some adults also assume that video games involve nothing but repetitive gun violence.

   (A) To illustrate a general principle
   (B) To acknowledge a counter-argument

7. What is one purpose of the sentence that follows?

   Many gamers say that the games greatly enhance their imaginations and thinking skills.

   (A) To set up the examples that follow
   (B) To reinforce the information in the previous sentence

8. What is one purpose of the sentence that follows?

   Humans find it compelling to identify with characters who overcome great obstacles.

   (A) To reformulate the passage's main claim
   (B) To explain the previous sentence

☑	1		3		5		7	
	2		4		6		8	

8 ~ 7	6 ~ 5	4 ~ 3	2 ~ 1
EXCELLENT	VERY GOOD	GOOD	NEEDS WORK

039 *Question Topic*

EDITING FOR ORGANIZATION

Terms and Structures

If you wanted to tell your teacher that the dog ate your homework, you would present the facts in logical order, from your dog acquiring your homework to her finishing it off. You would be certain to mention that the dog left a small piece of the homework uneaten, because that explains logically how you knew it was the dog.

In essays as well as in life, sequence and cohesion matter a great deal. Writers must make their case in a way that readers can follow easily.

Read the passage and analyze its organization for the questions that follow.

1.

1 <u>It is probable that</u> the "flight" of flying squirrels could more accurately be called a specialized leap. They jump from high up in a tree and sail downward to a lower spot on another tree. They are able to do so **2** <u>nevertheless from</u> loose, furry membranes attached between wrist and ankle on each side. [1] When they leap into the air, they stretch the membranes tight, so that their bodies look like square handkerchiefs. [2] The extra surface area provides extra "lift" by pushing down a bit on the air. **3**

2.

[1] Flying squirrels, quiet and nocturnal, migrated to other continents during periods when forested land bridges existed, eventually becoming 43 separate species. [2] Flying squirrels appear to have descended from North American tree squirrels, adapting to a distinct ecological niche. [3] In many forests, flying squirrels disperse plant seeds and fungal spores as a result of their diet. [4] They are also an important prey animal. **4**

3.

5 <u>Gliding through the air toward a tree trunk</u> would be quite dangerous without having a way to brake. Flying squirrels stop in time by pulling their long tails down. The motion swings them up to face the tree, **6** <u>and the tail creates a dragging force</u>. They pull their four limbs forward, so that their sail becomes a parachute, slowing them more. **7** Thus they are able to land smoothly with all four feet grasping the vertical tree trunk, ready to scramble around to the other side in case an owl is chasing them. **8**

1. Which choice would serve as the most effective introduction to the paragraph?

   (A) NO CHANGE
   (B) Despite the name,

2. (A) NO CHANGE
   (B) because of

3. The writer wants to add the following sentence to the paragraph.

   It is similar to the physics of a paper airplane.

   The best placement is

   (A) before sentence [1].
   (B) after sentence [2].

4. To make the paragraph more logical, sentence [2] should be placed

   (A) before sentence [1].
   (B) before sentence [4].

5. Which choice most effectively links the paragraph to the rest of the passage?

   (A) NO CHANGE
   (B) Gliding using aerodynamics and gravity

6. The writer is considering deleting the underlined portion. Should the writer make this change?

   (A) Yes, because it provides irrelevant details.
   (B) No, because it explains the previous statement.

7. Which choice most logically completes the paragraph?

   (A) NO CHANGE
   (B) They move their limbs in such a way as to make sharp turns, helping them to steer through smaller branches and evade flying predators.

8. Considering the passage as a whole, paragraph 2 should be placed

   (A) where it is now.
   (B) before paragraph 1.

☑	1		3		5		7	
	2		4		6		8	

8 ~ 7	6 ~ 5	4 ~ 3	2 ~ 1
EXCELLENT	VERY GOOD	GOOD	NEEDS WORK

Mastering
Writing & Language

It's hard to beat a person who
never gives up.
— Babe Ruth

1) Tobacco farming is <u>a leading</u> agricultural activity in Virginia.

(A) NO CHANGE
(B) a lead
(C) a leaded
(D) their leading

2) Pine trees are <u>the source of</u> an oily substance called "turpentine," which has various medicinal and industrial uses.

(A) NO CHANGE
(B) the source of creation for
(C) the source if you want
(D) sourced as

3) Only a few species of plants and animals <u>are surviving</u> in an environment that lacks oxygen.

(A) NO CHANGE
(B) survives
(C) be surviving
(D) can survive

4) The genus *Panthera* includes the only species of cats that can <u>roar; tigers,</u> lions, leopards, and jaguars.

(A) NO CHANGE
(B) roar: tigers,
(C) roar. Tigers,
(D) roar, tigers,

5) <u>Despite their</u> towering skyscrapers, bustling port, and iconic Manhattan Bridge, New York City's downtown is one of the world's most recognizable cityscapes.

(A) NO CHANGE
(B) Despite its
(C) Because of their
(D) Because of its

6) As early as 1670, some American colonies observed fast <u>day. This was a time of</u> prayer and penitence that preceded the planting of crops in spring.

Which choice most effectively combines the sentences at the underlined portion?

(A) day; being a time of
(B) day, which had been a time of
(C) day, a time of
(D) day, where

7) <u>Beginning in the Middle Ages,</u> politicians in Western Europe started keeping records of their actions <u>will</u> be stored in libraries for posterity.

(A) NO CHANGE
(B) so they could
(C) and when to
(D) that

8) Located near Naworth Castle in Northern England, <u>the 12th century saw the construction of Lanercost Priory out of stones taken from Hadrian's Wall.</u>

(A) NO CHANGE
(B) stones taken from Hadrain's wall were used to construct Lanercost Priory in the 12th century.
(C) Lanercost Priory was constructed in the 12th century using stones taken from Hadrian's Wall.
(D) the construction of Lanercost Priory was undertaken in the 12th century using stones taken from Hadrian's Wall.

9) The *Stegosaurus* is an armored herbivorous dinosaur from the Jurassic Period who's fossilized remains have been found in Portugal and the western United States.

(A) NO CHANGE
(B) whose
(C) for who
(D) with whom

10) Although tablet computers have existed in some form for over half a century, <u>those</u> did not achieve widespread popularity until the introduction of the iPad in 2010.

(A) NO CHANGE
(B) they
(C) this
(D) it

11) The goal of many forms of psychotherapy <u>were</u> to help patients understand what they need to do to live a more functional, productive life.

(A) NO CHANGE
(B) being
(C) are
(D) is

12) Locust trees, <u>whose</u> long, compound leaves and fragrant white flowers, can reach heights of up to 80 feet.

(A) NO CHANGE
(B) which have
(C) which have and include
(D) DELETE underlined portion.

13) Director Spike Lee's attempt to adapt the <u>2003 Korean cult classic</u> *Old Boy* for the American market proved both critically and financially unsuccessful.

(A) NO CHANGE
(B) 2003, Korean, cult, classic
(C) 2003 Korean, cult classic
(D) 2003 Korean cult classic,

14) Most cultures consider the color yellow to be bright, happy, warm, and in some cases even holy. Consequently, it is associated with illness or used to warn against danger.

(A) NO CHANGE *So*
(B) Furthermore, *and*
(C) Nonetheless, *but*
(D) Likewise, *and*

but

15) Males born with Klinefelter's syndrome possess two or more X chromosomes. Klinefelter's syndrome is a chromosomal disorder that encompasses a wide variety of symptoms, the most prominent of which is sterility.

Which choice most effectively combines the sentences above?

(A) Klinefelter's syndrome, a disorder in which males are born with two or more X chromosomes, encompasses a wide variety of symptoms, the most prominent of which is sterility.
(B) A chromosomal disorder encompassing a wide variety of symptoms—with the most prominent being sterility—males born with Klinefelter's syndrome possess two or more X chromosomes.
(C) Sterility is the most prominent of the wide variety of symptoms experienced by those with Klinefelter's syndrome; this is a chromosomal disorder in which males possess two or more X chromosomes.
(D) Two or more X chromosomes in males are a chromosomal disorder called Klinefelter's syndrome, which encompasses a wide variety of symptoms, the most prominent of which being sterility.

☑	1		4		7		10		13	
	2		5		8		11		14	
	3		6		9		12		15	

15 ~ 13	12 ~ 10	9 ~ 7	6 ~ 0
EXCELLENT	VERY GOOD	GOOD	NEEDS WORK

CHAPTER 2

1) The state of Washington is famous for its apples, the production of which <u>contributes</u> greatly to its economy.

(A) NO CHANGE
(B) contribute
(C) does contribute
(D) contributing

2) <u>Of all the factors affecting human psychological development, family dynamic is the one it influences children</u> the most.

(A) NO CHANGE
(B) that influences children
(C) children are influenced
(D) which influences

3) William Kirby, now considered the Father of Entomology—the scientific study of insects—first <u>met</u> attention in the scientific community for his comprehensive study of English bees.

(A) NO CHANGE
(B) honored
(C) increased
(D) garnered

4) The Amazon is home to a species of ant that has been observed creating life rafts out of their own <u>bodies. By doing so, they are able to safely transport their queen across water.</u>

Which choice most effectively combines the sentences at the underlined portion?

(A) bodies: thus enabling the safe transport of their queen across a body of water.
(B) bodies to safely transport their queen across a body of water.
(C) bodies, so that they are then able to transport their queen across a body of water.
(D) bodies; safely transporting their queen across water.

5) The reality television show *Candid Camera,* which captures <u>unsuspecting participants' reactions</u> on film, was actually derived from a radio show called *Candid Microphone.*

(A) NO CHANGE
(B) reactions of participants who are unsuspecting
(C) participants' unsuspected reactions
(D) unsuspected participants' reactions

6) <u>The microscope, though now inextricably linked to science and medicine,</u> was initially just a very expensive toy.

(A) NO CHANGE
(B) The microscope now inextricably linked to science and medicine,
(C) The microscope is now inextricably linked to science and medicine,
(D) The microscope: now inextricably linked to science and medicine,

7) Social psychologists apply the term "negativity bonding" to the ancient precept that even bitter enemies can bond <u>at</u> danger from a common enemy.

(A) NO CHANGE
(B) toward
(C) in the face of
(D) in front of

8) Russian researchers trying to domesticate the fox were surprised that the study subjects' evolution of domestic characteristics <u>was as fast.</u>

(A) NO CHANGE
(B) was faster.
(C) was as fast as that.
(D) was as fast as it was.

9) The Spanish government originally perceived the Lewis and Clark Expedition to be a threat to <u>their</u> territory, and sent a retinue of mercenaries, Native Americans, and Spanish soldiers to attempt to capture the entire American expedition.

(A) NO CHANGE
(B) there
(C) its
(D) it's

10) Although Ernest Hemingway's *A Farewell to Arms* is set in Italy, <u>its publication was forbidden there</u> until about twenty years after its American release.

(A) NO CHANGE
(B) its banned publication was forbidden there in Italy
(C) its publication was forbidden and banned there
(D) its publication was forbidden in Italy there

11) Hannibal <u>Barca a Carthaginian general, famous for leading war elephants over the Alps, actually</u> spent much of his later life in flight and voluntary exile, culminating in tragedy when he was betrayed to the Romans.

(A) NO CHANGE
(B) Barca, a Carthaginian general famous for leading war elephants over the Alps, actually
(C) Barca, a Carthaginian general famous for leading war elephants over the Alps actually
(D) Barca: a Carthaginian, general famous for leading war elephants over the Alps, actually

12) <u>While</u> the Ptolemy world map was advanced for its time in the 15th century, it was actually based on 2nd-century knowledge of the continents.

(A) NO CHANGE
(B) Because
(C) In fact
(D) DELETE the underlined portion.

13) One could travel across many of the world's smaller countries in the time it takes to drive from San Diego <u>and</u> San Francisco.

(A) NO CHANGE
(B) at
(C) or
(D) to

14) When soccer was first developing in the Middle Ages, players were allowed to use significantly more force than is permitted <u>today. The results could be fatal.</u>

Which choice most effectively combines the sentences at the underlined portion?

(A) today; the results could be fatal.
(B) today, and the results being possibly fatal to players on both teams.
(C) today, which did cause the potential for fatal results.
(D) today; having fatal results.

15) An extension of the esophagus, called a "crop," is present in most birds and allows them to store food prior to digestion <u>by the body's digestive system.</u>

(A) NO CHANGE
(B) by the rest of the system.
(C) systematically by the digestive system.
(D) DELETE the underlined portion.

✓	1		4		7		10		13	
	2		5		8		11		14	
	3		6		9		12		15	

15 ~ 13	12 ~ 10	9 ~ 7	6 ~ 0
EXCELLENT	VERY GOOD	GOOD	NEEDS WORK

1) Salmon live most of their lives in the ocean, but <u>give</u> birth to their young in freshwater streams.

(A) NO CHANGE
(B) gives
(C) giving
(D) to have given

2) The outer layer of the eye, <u>includes</u> the cornea, conjunctiva, and sclera, protects the organ from becoming dry and allows light to enter.

(A) NO CHANGE
(B) which includes
(C) include
(D) which include

3) Fishing may be among the world's oldest <u>hobby,</u> although its importance and popularity have varied from time to time.

(A) NO CHANGE
(B) leisure activity,
(C) diversion,
(D) pastimes,

4) The best known books of Earl Biggers, <u>is the</u> early 20th century detective novelist, feature the fictional private detective Charlie Chan.

(A) NO CHANGE
(B) is an
(C) they are by
(D) an

5) Well over three decades after its 1982 release, Michael Jackson's *Thriller* <u>sustains</u> the best-selling album of all time.

(A) NO CHANGE
(B) maintains
(C) remains
(D) triumphs

6) The Barbary macaque is one of only a few mammal species to rear its young through *alloparenting*, wherein members other than the biological parents participate in <u>nurturing and caring for</u> offspring.

(A) NO CHANGE
(B) raising and nurturing
(C) raising
(D) DELETE underlined portion.

7) The ancient Mesopotamian *Epic of Gilgamesh* was recorded as early as <u>2100 BCE in Akkadian, one of the oldest-known written languages.</u>

Which choice completes the sentence with relevant information?

(A) NO CHANGE
(B) 2100 BCE, so it predates the invention of the printing press by over 3,000 years.
(C) 2100 BCE, which is the same millennium as the construction of the Great Pyramid of Giza.
(D) 2100 BCE, and Gilgamesh and Enkidu fight before becoming best friends.

8) Of the approximately 3,400 known snake species worldwide, 725 species are <u>venomous, so</u> 250 species can kill a human with a single bite.

(A) NO CHANGE
(B) venomous, and
(C) venomous so
(D) venomous and

9) The United States landed on the Moon for the fifth time in 1972; <u>after</u> the U.S. has not been back, favoring other missions instead.

(A) NO CHANGE
(B) because
(C) since then
(D) that is

10) The United States did not participate in World War
II combat until 1941. The United States supplied
arms to European democracies from 1939 onward.

Which choice most effectively combines the
sentences at the underlined portion?

(A) The United states did not participate in World
War II combat until 1941, the country that
(B) When the United states did not participate in
World War II combat until 1941, it
(C) Although the United States did not participate
in World War II combat until 1941, the country
(D) The United States did not participate in World
War II combat until 1941, with it having

11) I cowered in a corner while my roommate killed the
spider lurking in the bathroom. Afterward, I said to
her, "You must be unafraid of spiders because that
one was quite large."

The author wants to use hyperbole (exaggeration)
as a rhetorical style. Which choice best accomplishes
this goal?

(A) NO CHANGE
(B) "You are my hero! That spider was bigger than
my head!"
(C) "Thank you so much! That spider was
terrifying."
(D) "Thanks, but I could have taken care of that
myself."

12) In mammals, a *gestation period* is the amount of
time it takes a fetus to develop, measured from
fertilization until birth.

(A) NO CHANGE
(B) develop; measured
(C) develop: measured
(D) develop, and measured

13) Above the mesosphere, so much thicker layer
of atmosphere called the thermosphere extends
upward.

(A) NO CHANGE
(B) a
(C) since
(D) still

14) Over his four-decade career, Prince (born Prince
Rogers Nelson) released dozens of albums,
experimented with many styles of music, and even
been a director and starred in several films.

(A) NO CHANGE
(B) and even directing and starring in several films.
(C) and even having directed and starred in several
films.
(D) and even directed and starred in several films.

15) The 1990s CBS television series *Northern Exposure*
attempted to portray its Native American characters
as modern individuals rather than stereotype
"Eskimos."

(A) NO CHANGE
(B) a type of Eskimos.
(C) outdated "Eskimos."
(D) stereotypical "Eskimos."

☑	1		4		7		10		13	
	2		5		8		11		14	
	3		6		9		12		15	

15 ~ 13	12 ~ 10	9 ~ 7	6 ~ 0
EXCELLENT	VERY GOOD	GOOD	NEEDS WORK

1) In 1835, American Richard Lawrence carried <u>out</u> a failed assassination attempt on President Andrew Jackson, who proceeded to beat his assailant with a cane.

(A) NO CHANGE
(B) on
(C) through
(D) with

2) <u>The</u> still large portions of the thickly forested Amazon that remain unexplored.

(A) NO CHANGE
(B) It is
(C) These
(D) There are

3) Caravaggio's 1593 painting *Boy with a Basket of Fruit* highlights many of the artist's <u>strengths. Dramatic</u> lighting, startling realism, and vibrant textures.

(A) NO CHANGE
(B) strengths; dramatic
(C) strengths: dramatic
(D) strengths, dramatic

4) As a crop, watermelons <u>exhibit</u> <u>remarkable and resistance</u> to both extreme heat and disease.

(A) NO CHANGE
(B) remarkable, resistant
(C) remarkably resistant
(D) remarkable resistance

5) In the 980s, Norwegian Erik the Red became the first European to establish a settlement on the island of <u>Greenland. While in Greenland, it is likely that he encountered</u> native Inuit people during summer expeditions.

Which choice most effectively combines the sentences at the underlined portion?

(A) Greenland, being likely to encounter
(B) Greenland, where he likely encountered
(C) Greenland, having there been likely to encounter
(D) Greenland; in Greenland, he likely encountered

6) Since his breakthrough performance in the <u>1994 film *Pulp Fiction*, Samuel</u> L. Jackson has appeared in over 70 films.

(A) NO CHANGE
(B) 1994 film, *Pulp Fiction*, Samuel
(C) 1994 film *Pulp Fiction* Samuel
(D) 1994 film *Pulp Fiction*: Samuel

7) Reginald Fessenden <u>transferred</u> the first entertainment radio broadcast to the people of Brant Rock, Massachusetts in 1906.

(A) NO CHANGE
(B) transported
(C) transmitted
(D) recounted

8) Feeling woefully unprepared for the upcoming marathon, I stood at the starting line. <u>"I wish I had trained more,"</u> I muttered to myself.

The author wants to use sarcasm as a rhetorical style. Which choice best accomplishes this goal?

(A) NO CHANGE
(B) "Well, this should be easy,"
(C) "I do not think that I can do this,"
(D) "A marathon involves over 26 miles of running,"

9) Some of the last wooly mammoths roamed present-day Siberia <u>during</u> the Great Pyramid of Giza was being constructed in Egypt.

(A) NO CHANGE
(B) since
(C) for
(D) when

10) *Titus Andronicus*, the bloodiest and most brutal of Shakespeare's plays, <u>tell</u> the story of a denounced Roman general's quest for revenge.

(A) NO CHANGE
(B) tells
(C) told
(D) telling

11) Fresh olives are very bitter and <u>must be treated with</u> a special brine solution <u>if they are to be</u> consumed as food.

(A) NO CHANGE
(B) when to be
(C) that they are
(D) as they are

12) In 1803, President Thomas Jefferson commissioned the Corps of Discovery Expedition, led by Meriwether Lewis and William Clark; <u>he</u> hoped that the expedition would help establish an overland route in the newly acquired American territory.

(A) NO CHANGE
(B) it
(C) who
(D) Jefferson

13) Professor Hiddleston argued that Ernest Hemingway's writing style was more influential than <u>any other 20th century author.</u>

(A) NO CHANGE
(B) those of 20th century authors.
(C) that of any other 20th century author.
(D) any other author alive during the 20th century.

14) Russian-American author Vladimir Nabokov famously lectured that a good reader must <u>be able to imagine, have a memory,</u> a dictionary, and some artistic sense.

(A) NO CHANGE
(B) possess imagination, memory,
(C) be imagining, memorizing, having
(D) be able to imagine, memorize,

15) <u>Ansel Adams took photographs in black and white. They provide stunning glimpses into the heart of the American west. The photographs often focus on nature.</u>

Which choice most effectively combines the sentences above?

(A) Ansel Adams's black-and-white photographs, which often focus on nature, provide stunning glimpses into the heart of the American west.
(B) Providing stunning glimpses into the heart of the American west and focusing on nature, Ansel Adams taking photographs in black and white.
(C) Ansel Adams's black-and-white photographs, providing stunning glimpses into the heart of the American west, often focusing on nature.
(D) Providing stunning glimpses into the heart of the American west, a focus on nature is what the black-and-white photographs of Ansel Adams have.

✓	1		4		7		10		13	
	2		5		8		11		14	
	3		6		9		12		15	

15 ~ 13	12 ~ 10	9 ~ 7	6 ~ 0
EXCELLENT	VERY GOOD	GOOD	NEEDS WORK

1) <u>Because</u> light from the sun takes approximately eight minutes to reach Earth, it takes an average of five-and-a-half hours to reach the dwarf planet Pluto.

(A) NO CHANGE
(B) Although
(C) Whereas
(D) Before

2) Among some species of termites, queens—the termites that lay a <u>colonies eggs</u>—can live for up to 50 years.

(A) NO CHANGE
(B) colony's eggs
(C) colonies egg's
(D) colonies' eggs

3) The term "ecology," which describes an interdisciplinary field that incorporates biology, Earth science, and geology, was <u>discovered</u> by 19th century scientist Ernst Haeckel.

(A) NO CHANGE
(B) founded
(C) coined
(D) uncovered

4) <u>The planet Venus is relatively close to Earth and reflects nearly 70 percent of sunlight. Venus</u> is one of the brightest objects in Earth's night sky.

Which choice most effectively combines the sentences at the underlined portion?

(A) Because Venus is relatively close to Earth and reflects nearly 70 percent of sunlight, the planet
(B) The planet Venus is relatively close to Earth and reflects nearly 70 percent of sunlight; it
(C) While being relatively close to Earth and reflecting nearly 70 percent of sunlight, the planet Venus
(D) In order to be relatively close to Earth and reflect nearly 70 percent of sunlight, the planet Venus

5) Opened in 1825, <u>western New York and the Great Lakes were able to be settled because of the Erie Canal.</u>

(A) NO CHANGE
(B) the Great Lakes and western New York were able to be settled because of the Erie Canal.
(C) American settlements in western New York as well as in the Great Lakes were facilitated by the Erie Canal.
(D) the Erie Canal facilitated American settlements in western New York as well as the in Great Lakes.

6) The Grand Canyon, one of the Seven Natural Wonders of the World, <u>first sighting</u> Francisco Coronado in 1540.

(A) NO CHANGE
(B) first sighted
(C) was first sighted by
(D) when first sighted by

7) Although the on-court chemistry <u>between Shaquille O'Neal and Kobe Bryant</u> led the Los Angeles Lakers to three straight NBA Championships, their off-court relationship was fraught with conflict.

(A) NO CHANGE
(B) between Shaquille O'Neal or Kobe Bryant
(C) within Shaquille O'Neal and Kobe Bryant
(D) within Shaquille O'Neal or Kobe Bryant

8) As of 2015, each U.S. penny costs 1.7 cents to produce while <u>U.S. nickels costs</u> 8 cents.

(A) NO CHANGE
(B) U.S. nickels cost
(C) the U.S. nickels cost
(D) each U.S. nickel costs

9) In the United States, the average annual salary of a physician is higher than <u>being a registered nurse.</u>

(A) NO CHANGE
(B) that of a registered nurse.
(C) those of registered nurses.
(D) getting to be a registered nurse.

10) The Public Library of Science (PLOS) publishes a variety of scientific <u>literature. The content published through PLOS is</u> free to access, reproduce, and distribute provided that it is properly cited and referenced.

Which choice most effectively combines the sentences at the underlined portion?

(A) literature; being
(B) literature, all of which is
(C) literature, of which all of it is
(D) literature; you will find that it is

11) Whereas popular animated films such as *Tangled, The Little Mermaid,* and *Mulan* end happily, the folk stories <u>on which they are</u> based often end in tragedy.

(A) NO CHANGE
(B) on which it is
(C) where they are
(D) where it is

12) The challenges of running a good business are compounded by the difficulty <u>stemming from finding reliable</u> employees.

(A) NO CHANGE
(B) that originates in finding reliable
(C) that is finding reliable
(D) of finding reliable

13) When fighting a forest fire, it is usually <u>most effective</u> to move fuel such as trees out of the fire's path than to try to douse it all with water.

(A) NO CHANGE
(B) better effectively
(C) more effective
(D) DELETE underlined portion.

14) The ash and debris ejected by Mount Krakatoa during <u>it's</u> cataclysmic eruption in 1883 darkened the sky worldwide for years afterward.

(A) NO CHANGE
(B) its
(C) they're
(D) their

15) American artist and writer Harvey Darger, Jr. is known today for <u>his fantasy manuscript titled *The Story of the Vivian Girls*. The expansive work</u> includes 15,000 single-spaced pages and hundreds of illustrations.

Which choice most effectively combines the sentences at the underlined potion?

(A) his expansive fantasy manuscript titled *The Story of the Vivian Girls,* which
(B) his fantasy manuscript, which is expansive and titled *The Story of the Vivian Girls*; it
(C) his fantasy manuscript titled *The Story of the Vivian Girls,* which, in addition to being expansive,
(D) his expansive fantasy manuscript titled *The Story of the Vivian Girls*; being expansive, it

☑	1		4		7		10		13	
	2		5		8		11		14	
	3		6		9		12		15	

15 ~ 13	12 ~ 10	9 ~ 7	6 ~ 0
EXCELLENT	VERY GOOD	GOOD	NEEDS WORK

CHAPTER 2

1) Hydrogen is the lightest and <u>most abundant</u> in the universe.

(A) NO CHANGE
(B) most abundant element
(C) most in abundance of elements
(D) most abundant of all the elements

2) Although many people associate sushi with raw fish, the word *sushi* actually means "sour-tasting" and <u>refer</u> to any dish that includes vinegared rice.

(A) NO CHANGE
(B) referring
(C) referred
(D) refers

3) In 1932, a small military <u>force armed with two machine guns and 10,000 rounds of ammunition was</u> sent to Western Australia to curb the region's emu bird population but met with little success.

(A) NO CHANGE
(B) force armed with two machine guns and 10,000 rounds of ammunition—was
(C) force armed with two machine guns and 10,000 rounds of ammunition, was
(D) force armed with two machine guns, and 10,000 rounds of ammunition was

4) <u>He is an outstanding American painter,</u> Winslow Homer is best known for his watercolors and oil paintings of the sea.

(A) NO CHANGE
(B) Outstanding American painter,
(C) An outstanding American painter,
(D) Being an outstanding American painter,

5) The North American passenger pigeon, whose population once numbered in the billions, <u>are extinct</u> because of overhunting and deforestation in the 19th and 20th centuries.

(A) NO CHANGE
(B) extinct
(C) was driven to extinction
(D) were driven to extinction

6) Often used to explain the origins of life on Earth, *abiogenesis* is a theoretical process through which organisms capable of reproduction <u>arise from</u> non-living organic compounds.

(A) NO CHANGE
(B) arose from
(C) ascend out of
(D) ascended out of

7) The first transcontinental airplane flight across the United States <u>that occur</u> in 1911.

(A) NO CHANGE
(B) it occurred
(C) and it occurred
(D) occurred

8) Archaeologists and anthropologists have learned much from studying <u>painting, imprints, and fossilized remains</u> present in the caves inhabited by prehistoric humans.

(A) NO CHANGE
(B) the paintings, imprints, and additionally the fossilized remains
(C) the paintings, imprints, and fossilized remains
(D) paintings, imprint, and fossilized remains

9) <u>A plant's</u> roots are removed or destroyed, the entire plant will eventually die.

   (A) NO CHANGE
   (B) If a plant's
   (C) That a plant's
   (D) When it is plant's

10) In the United Sates, fortune cookies are generally <u>confused</u> with Chinese cuisine, but they were actually invented and introduced to America by the Japanese.

   (A) NO CHANGE
   (B) associated
   (C) allied
   (D) conflated

11) In 1613, Dutch immigrants to America established a settlement called New <u>Amsterdam. The British later renamed the colony New York.</u>

   Which choice most effectively combines the sentences at the underlined portion?

   (A) Amsterdam, which the British later renamed New York.
   (B) Amsterdam, being renamed New York by the British later.
   (C) Amsterdam, a name that was changed by the British to New York later.
   (D) Amsterdam; this name was changed by the British later to New York.

12) In response to the Great Depression of the 1920s and 1930s, the United States government enacted <u>many numerous social and economic programs</u> jointly referred to as "the New Deal."

   (A) NO CHANGE
   (B) many social and numerous economic programs
   (C) a number of social programs and many economic ones
   (D) a number of social and economic programs

13) Joyce C. Hall was still a student in high school <u>when she</u> established Hallmark Cards, Inc. with her brother Rollie.

   (A) NO CHANGE
   (B) which she
   (C) that
   (D) who

14) The massive sequoia trees of Northern California can live to be over 3,000 <u>years old. They are among</u> the longest-lived organisms on Earth.

   Which choice most effectively combines the sentences at the underlined portion?

   (A) years old; because they live so long, they are among
   (B) years old, an age that makes them among
   (C) years old; for this reason, they are placed among
   (D) years old, making them among

15) <u>Contrary against popular belief,</u> learned Europeans in the Middle Ages understood that the Earth was spherical, not flat.

   (A) NO CHANGE
   (B) Contradicting against popular belief,
   (C) Contrary to popular belief,
   (D) Contradictory,

☑	1		4		7		10		13	
	2		5		8		11		14	
	3		6		9		12		15	

15 ~ 13	12 ~ 10	9 ~ 7	6 ~ 0
EXCELLENT	VERY GOOD	GOOD	NEEDS WORK

1) Many automobile manufacturers have developed <u>electric automobiles,</u> which require no fossil fuels and release no environmentally harmful emissions.

(A) NO CHANGE
(B) an electric car,
(C) an electric vehicle,
(D) an electric means of transportation,

2) The claim that lightning never strikes the same place twice is a myth. <u>Moreover, some very unlucky individuals have been struck by lightning more than once.</u>

Which choice provides evidence that best supports the claim made in the previous sentence?

(A) NO CHANGE
(B) In fact, lightning strikes the Empire States Building approximately 100 times each year.
(C) Often, the brighter a lightning strike appears, the louder its corresponding thunder.
(D) Nevertheless, the saying remains popular to this day.

3) <u>Since</u> the United States' Declaration of Independence was finalized on July 4, 1776, the signing of the document did not occur until August 2 of the same year.

(A) NO CHANGE
(B) While
(C) As
(D) When

4) Legal disputes <u>involve</u> two or more parties are often settled in a court of law.

(A) NO CHANGE
(B) involved
(C) involving
(D) are involved

5) It takes significantly longer to travel from Glasgow to London by bus than <u>trains do.</u>

(A) NO CHANGE
(B) a train does.
(C) a train will go.
(D) it does by train.

6) For tens of thousands of years, humans have depended on fire not only for warmth <u>and also</u> for cooking food.

(A) NO CHANGE
(B) as well
(C) but also
(D) yet

7) <u>The vast majority—of diamonds found on Earth—were formed under conditions</u> of extreme heat and pressure nearly 100 miles beneath the planet's surface.

(A) NO CHANGE
(B) The vast majority of diamonds, found on Earth, were formed under conditions
(C) The vast majority of diamonds found on Earth, were formed (under conditions)
(D) The vast majority of diamonds found on Earth were formed under conditions

8) Since the dawn of life on Earth, it is estimated that over five billion species of plants and animals have existed. <u>However,</u> less than one percent of these species are alive today.

(A) NO CHANGE
(B) Therefore,
(C) Regardless,
(D) For this reason,

9) Jack and Kyle took the stage, and the crowd went wild as <u>he</u> picked up the guitar and immediately launched into an extended solo.

(A) NO CHANGE
(B) Jack
(C) they
(D) it

10) Over 10,000 years ago in present-day <u>Iraq, wheat and barley</u> were farmed and harvested to make beer and soup.

(A) NO CHANGE
(B) Iraq, it was here that wheat and barley
(C) Iraq, where wheat and barley
(D) Iraq, when wheat and barley

11) My colleague, a native of Hawaii. jumped into the frigid Arctic waters, letting out a shocked yell as his tan skin turned milk pale. <u>"That's a bit colder than I'm used to,"</u> he said to no one in particular.

The author wants to use understatement as a rhetorical style. Which choice best accomplishes this goal?

(A) NO CHANGE
(B) "I feel like I'm going to freeze,"
(C) "How do people swim in water this cold?"
(D) "Why did I decide to come here, anyway?"

12) The only man-made objects visible to astronauts from outer space <u>is</u> the glowing city lights on the night side of Earth.

(A) NO CHANGE
(B) was
(C) being
(D) are

13) <u>The oldest confirmed and established star</u> in the Milky Way Galaxy formed approximately 13.2 billion years ago.

(A) NO CHANGE
(B) The oldest and confirmed
(C) The oldest confirmed star
(D) The oldest and most ancient confirmed star

14) "Becoming the best in any field requires discipline, hard work, and <u>persevering,</u>" lectured the motivational speaker.

(A) NO CHANGE
(B) to persevere,
(C) perseverance,
(D) being able to persevere,

15) The fall of the Berlin Wall in 1989 is often regarded as the symbolic end of the Soviet <u>Union. The official</u> dissolution of the Soviet Union occurred in 1991.

Which choice most effectively combines the sentences at the underlined portion?

(A) Union, so the official
(B) Union, but the official
(C) Union, in which the official
(D) Union, making it so that the official

✓	1		4		7		10		13	
	2		5		8		11		14	
	3		6		9		12		15	

15 ~ 13	12 ~ 10	9 ~ 7	6 ~ 0
EXCELLENT	VERY GOOD	GOOD	NEEDS WORK

CHAPTER 2

1) Most works of literature created during Europe's Middle Ages <u>was</u> religious in nature.

(A) NO CHANGE
(B) which were
(C) being
(D) were

2) Completed in the early 7th century CE, <u>the primary function of the Grand Canal of China was to transport grain to the nation's capital.</u>

(A) NO CHANGE
(B) transporting grain to the nation's capital was the primary function of the Grand Canal of China.
(C) grain transportation to the nation's capital being the primary function of the Grand Canal of China.
(D) the Grand Canal of China's primary function was to transport grain to the nation's capital.

3) Sharks have existed for over 350 million years. All the while, they have ruled Earth's oceans as apex predators.

Which choice most effectively combines the information in the sentences above?

(A) Sharks have ruled Earth's oceans as apex predators for over 350 million years.
(B) Existing for over 350 million years, and ruling Earth's oceans all the while, are sharks.
(C) Ruling Earth's oceans during their 350-million-year existence, sharks are apex predators.
(D) Sharks rule Earth's oceans as apex predators, and they have ruled for over 350 million years.

4) Orchids are the most <u>diverse</u> family of flowering plant, with over 27,000 known species.

(A) NO CHANGE
(B) divisive
(C) miscellaneous
(D) dissimilar

5) The massive sperm whale is still a poorly understood animal because <u>it spends much of it's</u> time hunting hundreds of meters underwater.

(A) NO CHANGE
(B) it spends much of its
(C) they spend much of they're
(D) they spend much of their

6) Before achieving <u>international stardom,</u> American actress Marilyn Monroe spent her youth in foster homes and orphanages.

(A) NO CHANGE
(B) internationally,
(C) international stardom everywhere,
(D) worldwide stardom internationally,

7) Post-Impressionist Dutch painter Vincent van Gogh <u>created over</u> 2,100 works of art, yet he sold only one in his lifetime.

(A) NO CHANGE
(B) formed above
(C) painted beyond
(D) made upon

8) Marsupials, which include kangaroos, opossums, and <u>the koala</u>, share many physiological characteristics with mammals, but unlike mammals, most marsupials carry their young in pouches.

(A) NO CHANGE
(B) koalas
(C) a koala
(D) the koala does

9) The paintings of 19th century artist Joseph Pickett are often categorized as *naïve art. Pickett's paintings ignore* formal conventions of perspective and proportionality.

Which choice most effectively combines the sentences at the underlined portion?

(A) *naïve art*, they ignore
(B) *naïve art*, these are ignoring
(C) *naïve art* because they ignore
(D) *naïve art*; for the reason that they ignore

10) Few events have proven <u>as environmentally devastating over</u> the *Deepwater Horizon* oil spill of 2010, in which over 200 million gallons of oil spilled into the Gulf of Mexico.

(A) NO CHANGE
(B) more environmentally devastating as
(C) as environmentally devastating more than
(D) as environmentally devastating as

11) Michigan's natural resources include vast forests, rich yields of iron ore, and <u>abundant water supplies.</u>

(A) NO CHANGE
(B) water supplies are abundant.
(C) supplying abundant water.
(D) supplies abundant water.

12) In ancient Egypt, scribes were among the most valued and respected <u>tasks.</u>

(A) NO CHANGE
(B) members of society.
(C) assignments.
(D) ideas.

13) All citizens of the United States are required <u>law</u> to pay income taxes on their income and property.

(A) NO CHANGE
(B) by law
(C) on law
(D) for law

14) <u>Backgammon—one of the oldest known board games, combines</u> strategy with an element of luck.

(A) NO CHANGE
(B) Backgammon, one of the oldest known board games—combines
(C) Backgammon, one of the oldest known board games, combines
(D) Backgammon, one of the oldest known board game, combines

15) <u>Although</u> all of Shakespeare's plays are well-regarded by critics and audiences alike, *Hamlet* and *King Lear* are often regarded as the bard's greatest works.

(A) NO CHANGE
(B) Due to the fact that
(C) Because
(D) Wherever

☑	1		4		7		10		13	
	2		5		8		11		14	
	3		6		9		12		15	

15 ~ 13	12 ~ 10	9 ~ 7	6 ~ 0
EXCELLENT	VERY GOOD	GOOD	NEEDS WORK

1) The gravitational forces of the sun and the moon are two of the main <u>factor of</u> Earth's tides.

(A) NO CHANGE
(B) reason for
(C) influence on
(D) causes of

2) The Cyclades are a chain of over 200 islands located in the Aegean Sea, the <u>larger of</u> them being the island of Naxos.

(A) NO CHANGE
(B) largest of
(C) large one of
(D) large among

3) The population of the state of California <u>expects</u> 38 million people, which is more than 12 percent of the total population of the United States.

(A) NO CHANGE
(B) outdoes
(C) exceeds
(D) beats

4) <u>The Copts are a Christian denomination that began in Alexandria in the first century CE. They remain</u> the largest sect of Christianity in modern-day Egypt, with over 10 million followers.

Which choice most effectively combines the sentences at the underlined portion?

(A) The Copts, a Christian denomination that began in Alexandria in the first century CE, remain
(B) The Copts are a Christian denomination that began in Alexandria in the first century CE despite remaining
(C) The Copts are a Christian denomination that began in Alexandria in the first century CE, yet they remain
(D) A Christian denomination that began in Alexandria in the first century CE are the Copts, remaining

5) <u>Because</u> we now regard Abraham Lincoln as one of America's greatest presidents, he was an incredibly divisive figure when he took office in 1861.

(A) NO CHANGE
(B) Where
(C) Although
(D) If

6) Oftentimes, talking about a troublesome issue with friends or family members can help put the problem <u>on perspective.</u>

(A) NO CHANGE
(B) in perspective
(C) over perspectives
(D) from a perspective

7) In 1977, the National Highway Traffic Safety Administration noted dangerous defects in Ford Pinto fuel systems. <u>Interestingly, the Pinto out-produced its domestic competitors during its 10-year run.</u>

Which choice contains information that logically follows the contents of the first sentence?

(A) NO CHANGE
(B) The Pinto was designed by Robert Eidschun, and the first model was released in 1971.
(C) The Pinto was released as a two-door sedan, a hatchback, and a wagon.
(D) Subsequently, Ford recalled 1.5 million Pintos so they could undergo safety modifications.

8) Many scientists speculate that humans have eyebrows to keep sweat and rain out of their <u>eyes. Eyebrows'</u> arched shape channels moisture away from the eyes.

Which choice most effectively combines the sentences at the underlined portion?

(A) eyes, and as a result their
(B) eyes, yet their
(C) eyes, as eyebrows'
(D) eyes with eyebrows'

9) Astronauts may become up to <u>3 percent taller</u> <u>during long stays in zero gravity, but they</u> shrink to their original height when they return to Earth.

(A) NO CHANGE
(B) 3 percent taller, during long stays in zero gravity, but they
(C) 3 percent taller during long stays, in zero gravity, but they
(D) 3 percent taller, during long stays in zero gravity but they

10) Norman Rockwell, an American illustrator, <u>who is</u> best known for his paintings of small-town people that were featured in *The Saturday Evening* Post.

(A) NO CHANGE
(B) he is
(C) is
(D) and is

11) It took Apollo 11, which bore astronauts Neil Armstrong, Buzz Aldrin, and Michael Collins where no men had gone before, approximately 4 days and 7 hours <u>and reached</u> the moon.

(A) NO CHANGE
(B) for reaching
(C) reaching
(D) to reach

12) The now-internationally popular Teenage Mutant Ninja Turtles franchise <u>were created</u> in 1984 in order to parody some of the most popular comics of the time.

(A) NO CHANGE
(B) was created
(C) being created
(D) a creation

13) The commonest color combination on national flags <u>being</u> red, white, and blue.

(A) NO CHANGE
(B) were
(C) are
(D) is

14) In 17th century English taverns, <u>some patrons who</u> <u>were customers</u> would give extra money to waiters "to insure promptitude," giving rise to the acronym *tip*.

(A) NO CHANGE
(B) they
(C) some patrons
(D) some of the customer clientele

15) Although Joseph began his climb of the 551 stairs to the top of St. Peter's Basilica with zeal, he quickly realized that he <u>will rather have taken</u> the elevator.

(A) NO CHANGE
(B) would rather have taken
(C) will rather be taking
(D) would rather took

☑	1		4		7		10		13	
	2		5		8		11		14	
	3		6		9		12		15	

15 ~ 13	12 ~ 10	9 ~ 7	6 ~ 0
EXCELLENT	VERY GOOD	GOOD	NEEDS WORK

1) From a young age, Jody showed an interest in journalism. Her passions were writing and photography.

Which choice most effectively combines the sentences at the underlined portion?

(A) journalism, yet her passions were writing
(B) journalism: writing
(C) journalism of writing
(D) journalism; her passions were writing

2) Ronald Reagan became the oldest United States president ever elected when he entered office in 1981 aged for sixty-nine.

(A) NO CHANGE
(B) the age
(C) at the age
(D) he was the age

3) Most students earn his or her undergraduate degrees in four to five years.

(A) NO CHANGE
(B) their undergraduate degrees
(C) their undergraduate degree's
(D) his or her undergraduate degree

4) Although its comfortable climate, excellent beaches, and luxury hotels, Acapulco is one of Mexico's most popular resort cities.

(A) NO CHANGE
(B) Among
(C) Because of
(D) Where there is

5) In the 19th century, Georges Polti created *The Thirty-Six Dramatic Situations*, an attempt to group and categorize every dramatic literary situation.

(A) NO CHANGE
(B) group and classify every dramatic literary situation into categories.
(C) classify every dramatic literary situation into categories by grouping.
(D) categorize every dramatic literary situation.

6) Up to 5.7 billion people, which amounts to about 80 percent of the world's population, regularly consume at least one of over 1,700 edible insect species.

Which choice best clarifies that the majority of the world's population consumes insects?

(A) NO CHANGE
(B) is about what the total world population was in 1995,
(C) is nearly 18 times greater than the population of the United States,
(D) is quite surprising because this practice is not popular in the United States,

7) The *carambola*, also called "starfruit" for its resemblance to a star when viewed from the top or bottom, grows in hot, tropical regions and have a distinct sweet-citrusy flavor.

(A) NO CHANGE
(B) bottom, grows
(C) bottom, and grows
(D) bottom, growing

8) The *Rococo* style of art and architecture, characterized by delicate and asymmetrical ornamentation, was popular in 18th-century France and is strongly associated with the rule of King Louis XV.

(A) NO CHANGE
(B) in strength and association
(C) a strong association
(D) a strong associated

9) Approximately one percent of people are ambidextrous, meaning that they are equally adept at using <u>both their right or left hands.</u>

(A) NO CHANGE
(B) both their right also left hands.
(C) both their right, left hands.
(D) both their right and left hands.

10) Released in 1927, *The Jazz Singer* was the first film to include sound, causing a sensation in the United States and <u>heralded</u> the decline of the silent film era.

(A) NO CHANGE
(B) heralding
(C) heralds
(D) herald

11) The outdoor game horseshoes, in which two players throw horseshoes at stakes planted in the ground, likely developed from *quoits*, a game <u>who's</u> origins extend back to ancient Greece.

(A) NO CHANGE
(B) which
(C) whose
(D) whom

12) Early 20th century actor, director, and screenwriter Lon Chaney used elaborate makeup to portray deformed <u>characters, it earned</u> him the nickname "Man of a Thousand Faces."

(A) NO CHANGE
(B) characters, earning
(C) characters, this earned
(D) characters, and earning

13) Used to treat the bites and stings of venomous animals, antivenom is created by harvesting and diluting an animal's venom, injecting it into a mammal species, and <u>the antibodies created by that mammal's immune response to the venom are harvested.</u>

(A) NO CHANGE
(B) then we harvest the antibodies created by that mammal's immune response to the venom.
(C) harvesting the antibodies created by that mammal's immune response to the venom.
(D) the mammal's immune response to the venom creates antibodies that are harvested.

14) The U.S. state name "Arizona" comes from the Pima Indian word *Arizuma,* <u>to mean</u> "little spring."

(A) NO CHANGE
(B) meaning
(C) it means
(D) the word means

15) Actor and martial artist Bruce Lee was born in San Francisco <u>in 1940. He grew up</u> in Hong Kong, where he began his prolific film career.

Which choice most effectively combines the sentences at the underlined portion?

(A) in 1940, but he grew up
(B) in 1940, where he grew up
(C) in 1940, to grow up
(D) in 1940, having grown up

☑	1		4		7		10		13	
	2		5		8		11		14	
	3		6		9		12		15	

15 ~ 13	12 ~ 10	9 ~ 7	6 ~ 0
EXCELLENT	VERY GOOD	GOOD	NEEDS WORK

1) Tweed is a durable fabric made of wool woven into <u>many of</u> different patterns.

(A) NO CHANGE
(B) many
(C) much
(D) much of

2) All radioactive elements decay over time. Hassium is a radioactive element.

Which choice most effectively combines the sentences above?

(A) Decaying over time, Hassium is like all radioactive elements.
(B) Like all other radioactive elements, Hassium decays over time.
(C) All radioactive elements, of which Hassium is, decay over time.
(D) Being a radioactive element, Hassium decays like all other radioactive elements do.

3) Some species of ant form *supercolonies*, wherein multiple ant colonies of the same species join together <u>eliminating</u> other nearby ant species.

(A) NO CHANGE
(B) and had eliminated
(C) to eliminate
(D) eliminated

4) Today's computers differ greatly from <u>the past.</u>

(A) NO CHANGE
(B) those passing.
(C) that in the past.
(D) those of the past.

5) Shortly after Charles Darwin introduced his theory of evolution in *On the Origin of Species,* biologist Thomas Huxley <u>recommended</u> an evolutionary link between birds and dinosaurs.

(A) NO CHANGE
(B) scheduled
(C) planned
(D) proposed

6) The aurora borealis, or "northern lights," occurs when charged particles from the sun transfer energy to electrons in Earth's <u>atmosphere; the energy</u> is then released by the electrons as photons of light that illuminate the night sky.

(A) NO CHANGE
(B) atmosphere; which
(C) atmosphere, the energy
(D) atmosphere, in which the energy

7) Feathery cirrus clouds often <u>precede a thunderstorm, which they come before.</u>

(A) NO CHANGE
(B) come before a thunderstorm that they precede.
(C) precede and herald a thunderstorm.
(D) precede a thunderstorm.

8) While most of Earth's landmasses have been explored, <u>remaining uncharted are the vast majority of Earth's oceans.</u>

(A) NO CHANGE
(B) people are not yet charting the vast majority of Earth's oceans.
(C) the vast majority of Earth's oceans remain uncharted.
(D) uncharted remain the vast majority of the oceans of Earth.

9) The four gas giants in our solar system (Jupiter, Saturn, Uranus, and Neptune) have rings, although Saturn's are the largest and most well-known.

(A) NO CHANGE
(B) system (being Jupiter, Saturn, Uranus, and Neptune) have
(C) system (Jupiter) (Saturn) (Uranus) and (Neptune) have
(D) system—Jupiter, Saturn, Uranus, and Neptune have

10) The ancient Greeks developed a limited knowledge of human anatomy although the body was considered sacred, so dissection of human corpses was not commonly practiced.

(A) NO CHANGE
(B) because
(C) when
(D) if

11) The diet of the Greenland shark, one of the only shark species found in Arctic waters, consisting at least in part of the carcasses of large mammals that sink to the ocean's floor.

(A) NO CHANGE
(B) consisted
(C) consists
(D) consist

12) Located on the Canada-United States border, the end of the Ice Age was when the Great Lakes formed, when shrinking ice sheets carved the lakes' basins and filled them with glacial waters.

(A) NO CHANGE
(B) the Great Lakes formed at the end of the Ice Age,
(C) the Ice Age's ending formed the Great Lakes,
(D) when the Ice Age ended the Great Lakes formed,

13) Chimpanzees in the wild spend over half of it's waking hours foraging for food.

(A) NO CHANGE
(B) its
(C) they're
(D) their

14) In response to the increasing rates of literacy in the Victorian-era United Kingdom, cheap works of serialized fiction called "penny dreadfuls" were produced for mass consumption.

(A) NO CHANGE
(B) massive consuming.
(C) the consumption of mass.
(D) a massive consumption.

15) The World Health Organization ranked Delhi, India as the regions with the highest levels of air pollution in 2015.

(A) NO CHANGE
(B) locations
(C) lands
(D) metropolitan area

☑	1		4		7		10		13	
	2		5		8		11		14	
	3		6		9		12		15	

15 ~ 13	12 ~ 10	9 ~ 7	6 ~ 0
EXCELLENT	VERY GOOD	GOOD	NEEDS WORK

CHAPTER 2

1) <u>While American's refer</u> to the flat, burrowing sea urchins found on many beaches as "sand dollars," New Zealanders call them "sea cookies" or "snapper biscuits," and South Africans refer to them as "pansy shells."

(A) NO CHANGE ·
(B) While Americans refer
(C) When American's refer
(D) When Americans refer

2) The Museum of Modern Art in New York houses an outstanding collection of 20th century <u>paintings, including</u> Salvador Dali's *The Persistence of Memory* and Roy Lichtenstein's *Drowning Girl*.

(A) NO CHANGE
(B) paintings include
(C) paintings, includes
(D) paintings, these include

3) Whereas crocodiles have pointed, v-shaped snouts, alligators have more <u>rounder,</u> u-shaped snouts.

(A) NO CHANGE
(B) rounding,
(C) rounded,
(D) the rounder,

4) The British rock group the Beatles famously held their <u>last final public performance</u> on the roof of a building in London on January 30, 1969.

(A) NO CHANGE
(B) final performance for the public in concert
(C) last concert performed in public
(D) final public performance

5) The social reformer known as "Mother Jones" <u>playing</u> an important role in the creation of the Industrial Workers of the World Union in 1905.

(A) NO CHANGE
(B) who played
(C) played
(D) plays

6) After spending 20 years playing in the NBA for the Los Angeles Lakers, Kobe Bryant <u>retired</u> professional basketball on April 13, 2016.

(A) NO CHANGE
(B) retired from
(C) retired on
(D) retiring

7) One of the first computer programming languages, <u>IBM Corporation published FORTRAN (an acronym for FORMula TRANslating system) in 1957.</u>

(A) NO CHANGE
(B) 1957 saw the publication of FORTRAN (an acronym for FORMula TRANslating system) by IBM Corporation.
(C) FORTRAN (an acronym for FORMula TRANslating system) was published by IBM Corporation in 1957.
(D) in 1957 IBM Corporation published FORTRAN (an acronym for FORMula TRANslating system).

8) In 1971, <u>Nike co-founder Philip Knight paid</u> graphic designer Carolyn Davidson just 35 dollars to design the now-famous Nike "swoosh" logo, although he later rewarded her handsomely for her contribution.

(A) NO CHANGE
(B) Nike, co-founder Philip Knight paid
(C) Nike co-founder, Philip Knight, paid
(D) Nike co-founder Philip Knight, paid

9) Human rights activist Malcolm X began his political activism and <u>involving himself</u> in the Nation of Islam religious movement after being incarcerated for larceny in 1948.

(A) NO CHANGE
(B) involve
(C) involved
(D) involvement

10) Orcas, also called killer whales, are the largest members of the dolphin family and among the ocean's most fearsome <u>animal.</u>

(A) NO CHANGE
(B) predators.
(C) creature.
(D) hunter.

11) Although inventors Nikola Tesla and Thomas Edison were colleagues, the scientific accomplishments of Edison receive wider recognition today than <u>Tesla does.</u>

(A) NO CHANGE
(B) does that of Tesla.
(C) do those of Tesla.
(D) does Tesla.

12) Claudius, Roman Emperor from 41 to 54 CE, was regarded as a fool and a cripple by his <u>contemporaries. Modern</u> historians recognize that he helped restore financial and social stability to the Roman Empire.

Which choice most effectively combines the sentences at the underlined portion?

(A) contemporaries, yet modern
(B) contemporaries, so modern
(C) contemporaries, if modern
(D) contemporaries, and these modern

13) The earliest sea crafts were likely <u>congregated</u> by *Homo erectus*, the ancestor of modern humans, up to 900,000 years ago in order to travel to the South East Asian island of Flores.

(A) NO CHANGE
(B) mustered
(C) assembled
(D) rallied

14) Black holes cannot be "seen" using telescopes because even light itself cannot escape their gravitational pull, but <u>it</u> can be detected by the intense radiation they emit.

(A) NO CHANGE
(B) theirs
(C) those who
(D) they

15) <u>Stephen Crane was the author of such works as *The Red Badge of Courage* and "The Open Boat." He died at the young age of 29. His works</u> have had a lasting influence on American literature.

Which choice most effective combines the sentences at the underlined portion?

(A) Although Stephen Crane, author of such works as *The Red Badge of Courage* and "The Open Boat," died at the young age of 29, his works
(B) Author of such works as *The Red Badge of Courage* and "The Open Boat" was Stephen Crane, who died at the young age of 29, but his works
(C) *The Red Badge of Courage* and "The Open Boat" were written by author Stephen Crane, whose works, although he died at the young age of 29,
(D) At the young age of 29, died did the author of such works as *The Red Badge of Courage* and "The Open Boat," Stephen Crane, but his works

☑	1		4		7		10		13	
	2		5		8		11		14	
	3		6		9		12		15	

15 ~ 13	12 ~ 10	9 ~ 7	6 ~ 0
EXCELLENT	VERY GOOD	GOOD	NEEDS WORK

1) Bats are not blind. <u>Nevertheless,</u> some species of bats have exceptionally good vision.

   (A) NO CHANGE
   (B) Thus,
   (C) In fact,
   (D) Despite this,

2) Lake Louise, a tourist resort in southwest Alberta, Canada, was named <u>for honoring</u> Queen Victoria's daughter, Princess Louise.

   (A) NO CHANGE
   (B) the honor for
   (C) to honored
   (D) in honor of

3) The 206 bones in an adult human's body are composed of two types of <u>tissue: compact</u> and spongy.

   (A) NO CHANGE
   (B) tissue: being compact
   (C) tissue; compact
   (D) tissue: these are compact

4) <u>Academy Awards for Best Actor have been received by Tom Hanks</u> for his roles in *Philadelphia* and *Forrest Gump.*

   (A) NO CHANGE
   (B) By Tom Hanks, Best Actor Academy Awards have been received
   (C) Receiving Best Actor Academy Awards has been Tom Hanks
   (D) Tom Hanks has received Best Actor Academy Awards

5) The Fahrenheit and Celsius scales <u>have read</u> the same temperature at –40 degrees.

   (A) NO CHANGE
   (B) read
   (C) are read
   (D) were reading

6) Orangutans are the heaviest arboreal (tree-dwelling) animals in the world, with males weighing <u>up to as much as</u> 250 pounds.

   (A) NO CHANGE
   (B) up to
   (C) a total of up to
   (D) as much as, in total,

7) Although red hair is most commonly associated with Northern Europeans, especially the Scottish and Irish, the trait likely <u>roused</u> in Iran about 20,000 years ago.

   (A) NO CHANGE
   (B) formulated
   (C) originated
   (D) hatched

8) Unlike fish, <u>sharks cannot bend their pectoral fins upwards,</u> which prevents them from stopping or swimming backwards.

   (A) NO CHANGE
   (B) the pectoral fins of sharks cannot bend upwards,
   (C) bending upwards is not something the pectoral fins of sharks can do,
   (D) upwards is a direction that the pectoral fins of sharks cannot bend,

9) Thai food uses a variety of spices and seasoning, including three types of <u>basil. They are called holy basil,</u> Thai basil, and lemon basil.

Which choice most effectively combines the sentences at the underlined portion?

(A) basil: holy basil,
(B) basil, and they are holy basil,
(C) basil; you call them holy basil,
(D) basil; their names are holy basil,

10) Popular until the 19th century, *Ohaguro* is <u>Japanese practices</u> that involves dying one's teeth black, a color associated with beauty.

(A) NO CHANGE
(B) the Japanese observances
(C) Japanese traditions
(D) a Japanese custom

11) The first female writer to be published in North America, poet Anne Bradstreet <u>immigrated</u> to Massachusetts Bay Colony in 1630.

(A) NO CHANGE
(B) emigrated
(C) intimidated
(D) initiated

12) When harvesting flax, farmers must pull the plants up with the roots because cutting <u>damage</u> the fibers.

(A) NO CHANGE
(B) damages
(C) damaged
(D) is damaging

13) <u>Free verse, which is</u> poetry without a regular meter or rhyme scheme.

(A) NO CHANGE
(B) Free verse is
(C) Free verse—
(D) Free verse, this is

14) Few countries are <u>more linguistically diverse as</u> China, which has nearly 300 living languages.

(A) NO CHANGE
(B) as linguistically diverse more than
(C) as linguistically diverse is
(D) as linguistically diverse as

15) Unable to compose a couplet to complete his sonnet, the poet threw down his pen in frustration. <u>"I have the worst case of writer's block,"</u> he lamented.

The author wants to use metaphor as a rhetorical style. Which choice best accomplishes this goal?

(A) NO CHANGE
(B) "Curse this confounding couplet,"
(C) "My genius is a well run dry,"
(D) "I have the worst luck in the world,"

☑	1		4		7		10		13	
	2		5		8		11		14	
	3		6		9		12		15	

15 ~ 13	12 ~ 10	9 ~ 7	6 ~ 0
EXCELLENT	VERY GOOD	GOOD	NEEDS WORK

1) While excessive sun exposure presents health risks, sun exposure in small doses it ensures a person is not deficient <u>of</u> vitamin D.

(A) NO CHANGE
(B) for
(C) from
(D) in

2) Uric acid is produced when a person's metabolism breaks down certain <u>substances. The amount of uric acid</u> in the bloodstream is regulated by the kidneys.

Which choice most effectively combines the sentences at the underlined portion?

(A) substances, and in turn the amount of uric acid
(B) substances, the uric acid
(C) substances; consequently, the amount of uric acid
(D) substances; the amount of uric acid

3) <u>Retired professional tennis player, Jennifer</u> Capriati had an early start in her career, notably ranking in the French Open at only fourteen years old.

(A) NO CHANGE
(B) Retired professional tennis player Jennifer
(C) Retired, professional tennis player, Jennifer
(D) Retired, professional tennis player Jennifer

4) Fossil evidence indicates that crabs <u>have remained</u> largely unchanged in appearance for millions of years.

(A) NO CHANGE
(B) remain
(C) remained
(D) had remained

5) Indian mathematician Brahmagupta is responsible for the concept of zero as a numeral, <u>who</u> has affected mathematics since its conception in 628 CE.

(A) NO CHANGE
(B) which
(C) and
(D) so

6) The life of a Roman gladiator was full of not only physical preparation,<u> and</u> psychological preparation to face death without protest upon defeat.

(A) NO CHANGE
(B) and also
(C) but also
(D) as well as

7) During the 19th century, a personal and ideological rivalry <u>has taken place</u> between the Romantic painter Eugene Delacroix and staunch Neoclassicist Jean-Auguste-Dominique Ingres.

(A) NO CHANGE
(B) flared up
(C) underwent
(D) interacted

8) Today, Edgar Allan Poe is chiefly known for his poems and short stories, yet in his day he was also famous <u>as being particularly harsh as a literary critic.</u>

(A) NO CHANGE
(B) for he was a particularly harsh literary critic.
(C) as literary criticism.
(D) for his particularly harsh literary criticisms.

9) Doctors have reported that placebos—inert substances that patients think are medicines—<u>can drastically reduce</u> symptoms in some situations.

(A) NO CHANGE
(B) drastically can reduce
(C) reducing drastic
(D) can reduce drastically

10) Author F. Scott Fitzgerald died at the age of 44, having suffered a variety of physical <u>ailments</u> from a young age.

(A) NO CHANGE
(B) anomalies
(C) abnormalities
(D) eccentricities

11) According to creator Stan Lee, the concept of the Hulk was partly <u>derived by</u> Mary Shelley's *Frankenstein*.

(A) NO CHANGE
(B) derived of
(C) derived from
(D) depreciated in

12) A Hoover wagon refers to <u>a Depression-era automobile altered to be drawn by horses.</u>

(A) NO CHANGE
(B) the Depression era, when automobiles were altered to be drawn by horses.
(C) the time during the Depression era when automobiles were altered to be drawn by horses.
(D) the altering of a Depression-era vehicle that can be drawn by horses.

13) The octane rating of gasoline is directly related to the fuel's ability to <u>prevent from</u> igniting too soon.

(A) NO CHANGE
(B) cease
(C) undermine
(D) avoid

14) Although he published many of his stories in cheap pulp magazines, Edgar Rice Burroughs is responsible for one of the most enduring characters of the 20th <u>century. Tarzan.</u>

(A) NO CHANGE
(B) century; Tarzan.
(C) century: Tarzan.
(D) century; it was Tarzan.

15) When British millionaire Ben Rea died in 1988, his will provided his children with <u>less monies</u> than his cat, Blackie, who received 7 million pounds.

(A) NO CHANGE
(B) fewer monies
(C) less money
(D) fewer money

✓	1		4		7		10		13	
	2		5		8		11		14	
	3		6		9		12		15	

15 ~ 13	12 ~ 10	9 ~ 7	6 ~ 0
EXCELLENT	VERY GOOD	GOOD	NEEDS WORK

1) Unlike other <u>alloys, stainless steel that is</u> highly resistant to corrosion and rust.

   (A) NO CHANGE
   (B) alloys, stainless steel is
   (C) alloys, it is stainless steel that
   (D) alloys; the alloy stainless steel is

2) <u>Because he invented the cotton gin,</u> Eli Whitney was still a young man.

   (A) NO CHANGE
   (B) Whereas he invented the cotton gin,
   (C) Having invented the cotton gin,
   (D) When he invented the cotton gin,

3) Vegetables are among the best <u>sourced for</u> essential vitamins.

   (A) NO CHANGE
   (B) sources that
   (C) for sourcing
   (D) sources of

4) The phrase "survival of the fittest" is often attributed to naturalist Charles <u>Darwin. The phrase was actually coined by</u> English academic Herbert Spencer, who was influenced by Darwin's work.

   Which choice most effectively combines the sentences at the underlined portion?

   (A) Darwin, being actually coined by
   (B) Darwin, so actually, the coining was done by
   (C) Darwin, but it was actually coined by
   (D) Darwin; coining it in actuality was

5) The Tarahumara, Native American inhabitants of northwestern Mexico, are well-known for their endurance <u>running, participating</u> in footraces that span up to 200 miles.

   (A) NO CHANGE
   (B) running, to participate
   (C) running that participates
   (D) running and to participate

6) Ginger is widely recognized as one of the best <u>cure</u> for an upset stomach.

   (A) NO CHANGE
   (B) remedies
   (C) treatment's
   (D) medicine

7) To determine whether or not an egg is rotten, simply place it in a pot of water. If the egg sinks, it is good to <u>eat. If it floats,</u> it is likely rotten.

   Which choice most effectively combines the sentences at the underlined portion?

   (A) NO CHANGE
   (B) eat; floating
   (C) eat, and to float
   (D) eat; if it floats,
   (E) eat, so a floating egg

8) Excluding Earth itself, every planet in the solar system (Mercury, Venus, Mars, Jupiter, Saturn, Uranus, and Neptune) could fit in the gap <u>between the Earth, and also the Moon.</u>

   (A) NO CHANGE
   (B) between the Earth and the Moon.
   (C) between the Earth or the Moon.
   (D) between: the Earth and the Moon.

9) To compete in the ten events that comprise a decathlon, an athlete must be a proficient sprinter, hurdler, jumper, thrower, and <u>be able to pole vault.</u>

(A) NO CHANGE
(B) have tried the pole vault.
(C) pole vaulting.
(D) pole vaulter.

10) New Jersey and Oregon are the only states that <u>have banned</u> self-service gasoline in order to reduce the risk of accidents.

(A) NO CHANGE
(B) is banning
(C) has banned
(D) are banned

11) The pupil of the human eye will <u>interact</u> quickly to fluctuations in brightness.

(A) NO CHANGE
(B) reply
(C) react
(D) affect

12) The Sentinelese, a tribe native to the Andaman Islands in the Indian Ocean, are hunter-gatherers not known to use fire or <u>practicing</u> agriculture.

(A) NO CHANGE
(B) for the practice of
(C) have practiced
(D) practice

13) The <u>world's oldest and most ancient written recipe</u> is a 4,000 year-old Mesopotamian recipe for beer, supposedly passed down to humans by the Sumerian god Enki.

(A) NO CHANGE
(B) world's oldest written recipe
(C) world's oldest recorded recipe that has been written
(D) world's most ancient (and oldest) recorded recipe

14) On land, a league is equal to three miles; at sea, a league is three nautical miles, <u>which are</u> slightly longer than miles measured on land.

(A) NO CHANGE
(B) they are
(C) who is
(D) that is

15) Completed in 1653, <u>20,000 workers spent 22 years completing the Taj Mahal complex of Agra, India.</u>

(A) NO CHANGE
(B) in Agra, India it took 22 years and 20,000 workers to complete the Taj Mahal complex.
(C) 22 years and 20,000 workers were required to construct the Taj Mahal complex of Agra, India.
(D) the Taj Mahal complex of Agra, India took 22 years and 20,000 workers to construct.

☑	1		4		7		10		13	
	2		5		8		11		14	
	3		6		9		12		15	

15 ~ 13	12 ~ 10	9 ~ 7	6 ~ 0
EXCELLENT	VERY GOOD	GOOD	NEEDS WORK

CHAPTER 2

1) Helium is said to be an inert <u>gas. It</u> does not burn or react with other materials.

(A) NO CHANGE
(B) gas because it
(C) gas, and it
(D) gas; for this reason, it

2) Agatha Christie was the world's <u>foremost leading</u> author of detective fiction during the 20th century.

(A) NO CHANGE
(B) premier foremost
(C) foremost
(D) most

3) While kiwifruit is commonly associated with New Zealand, it is also the national fruit of China, <u>where it is called</u> *yang tao*, meaning "strawberry peach."

(A) NO CHANGE
(B) who call it
(C) whom call it
(D) when it was called

4) Established in 1929, <u>over 2,000 sandstone arches are contained in the nearly 77,000 acres that comprise Arches National Park in Utah.</u>

(A) NO CHANGE
(B) the 77,000 acres that comprise Arches National Park in Utah contain over 2,000 sandstone arches.
(C) in Utah over 2,000 sandstone arches are contained in the nearly 77,000 acres that comprise Arches National Park.
(D) Arches National Park in Utah covers an area of nearly 77,000 acres and contains over 2,000 sandstone arches.

5) Since the early 2000s, the revenue Las Vegas generates from non-gambling activities, such as dining and shopping, has exceeded <u>gambling.</u>

(A) NO CHANGE
(B) people's gambling.
(C) gambling in Las Vegas.
(D) the revenue it generates from gambling.

6) The U.S. Route 66 <u>extends</u> nearly 2,500 miles from Chicago, Illinois to Santa Monica, California.

(A) NO CHANGE
(B) expands
(C) enlarges
(D) envelops

7) While Martin Luther King, Jr. and Malcolm X <u>is the man</u> most closely associated with the Civil Rights Movement, its success required the participation of thousands, if not millions, of activists.

(A) NO CHANGE
(B) was the individuals
(C) are the figures
(D) be the people

8) *Teacher Strategies* <u>build</u> the case for differentiated instruction in order to meet each student's unique learning needs, and offers several chapters on how to go about it.

(A) NO CHANGE
(B) build up
(C) are building
(D) builds

9) Common cuckoos engage in *brood parasitism,* wherein they trick another species of bird to raise their <u>young. The cuckoos do so by laying their eggs</u> in another bird's nest.

Which choice most effectively combines the sentences at the underlined portion?

(A) young, they do so by laying their eggs
(B) young by laying their eggs
(C) young; lay their eggs
(D) young with eggs

10) <u>Information</u> is fed into a computer, the computer's processor must decide what to do with it.

(A) NO CHANGE
(B) When information
(C) Because of information
(D) Information that

11) In 2005, the collapse of New Orleans' levies during Hurricane Katrina submerged much of the city, <u>affecting</u> millions of people.

(A) NO CHANGE
(B) effecting
(C) infecting
(D) perfecting

12) William Shakespeare's best plays are known for their witty dialogue and <u>constructed tight plots.</u>

(A) NO CHANGE
(B) plots are tightly constructed.
(C) tightly constructed plots.
(D) constructing of tight plots.

13) The gingko tree has small, fan-shaped leaves <u>are serving</u> as the symbol of Japan's Tokyo prefecture.

(A) NO CHANGE
(B) that serves
(C) that serve
(D) to serve

14) The *escape velocity* of Earth—that is, the speed an object must travel <u>to freely break Earth's</u> gravitational pull—is approximately 25,000 miles per hour.

(A) NO CHANGE
(B) breaking freely Earth's
(C) to break the freedom of Earth's
(D) to break free of Earth's

15) When they set off in 1804, <u>neither Merriweather Lewis or William Clark</u> could have imagined that their names would become synonymous with exploration and adventure.

(A) NO CHANGE
(B) neither Merriweather Lewis nor William Clark
(C) either Merriweather Lewis nor William Clark
(D) both Merriweather Lewis nor William Clark

☑	1		4		7		10		13	
	2		5		8		11		14	
	3		6		9		12		15	

15 ~ 13	12 ~ 10	9 ~ 7	6 ~ 0
EXCELLENT	VERY GOOD	GOOD	NEEDS WORK

CHAPTER 2

1) Because the Pythagorean Theorem is often attributed to Greek philosopher and mathematician Pythagoras, it is more likely that the theorem was developed by one of his successors.

(A) NO CHANGE
(B) Since
(C) Although
(D) If

2) Some species of pig has tusks while other species do not.

(A) NO CHANGE
(B) has been having
(C) is having
(D) have

3) Jeans are named after Genoa, Italy. It is here that the now-ubiquitous denim trousers were first produced.

Which choice most effectively combines the sentences at the underlined portion?

(A) Italy, the city in which
(B) Italy; it was in Genoa, Italy that
(C) Italy because Genoa, Italy is where
(D) Italy, here

4) Pressing a piano key triggers a small hammer that strikes a string within the instrument, causing the string to vibrate and fabricate a tone.

(A) NO CHANGE
(B) concoct
(C) produce
(D) manufacture

5) While fewer than one percent of bacteria are known to cause disease: most viruses are disease-causing.

(A) NO CHANGE
(B) disease, most viruses
(C) disease; it is most viruses
(D) disease, and most viruses

6) Wind results when air moves from an area of higher atmospheric pressure to this of lower pressure.

(A) NO CHANGE
(B) one
(C) ones
(D) those

7) "I think the most important task is determining how to consolidate general relativity with quantum field theory?" the professor concluded.

(A) NO CHANGE
(B) theory." the
(C) theory," the
(D) theory;" the

8) During Rome's long-lived conflict with the Carthaginian Empire, Roman statesman Cato the Elder would end virtually all of his speeches with some variation of the phrase, "Carthage must be destroyed."

(A) NO CHANGE
(B) Roman, statesman, Cato the Elder
(C) Roman statesman, Cato the Elder,
(D) Roman statesman (Cato the Elder)

9) Launched in 1977, the Voyager 1 space probe reached interstellar space in 2014. The probe will not be operational long enough to encounter any other star systems.

Which choice most effectively combines the sentences at the underlined portion?

(A) 2014, being unable to be
(B) 2014, thus not being
(C) 2014, or it will not be
(D) 2014, but it will not be

10) The Tardigrade, a micro-animal more commonly called a "water bear," is perhaps the most durable organism on Earth. <u>As the name implies, water bears thrive in aquatic environments, but they are capable of surviving outside of water, too.</u>

Which choice provides the best support for the information in the previous sentence?

(A) NO CHANGE
(B) While it thrives in water, it can survive crushing pressures, extreme temperatures, ionizing radiation, and even the vacuum of outer space.
(C) Despite their durability, these tiny organisms reach a maximum size of only 0.5 micrometers.
(D) Most species are herbivorous, but some will feed on smaller species of water bear.

11) Until its unification in the 1870s, the Hungarian capital of Budapest was actually two cities: Buda and Pest, occupying the west and east banks of the Danube River <u>respectfully.</u>

(A) NO CHANGE
(B) prospectively.
(C) respectively.
(D) reasonably.

12) The legend of the Pied Piper of Hamlin tells of a rat-catcher who plays music on his pipe to lure all the rats from an infested German town; when he is refused payment for his services, he <u>exacts revenge</u> by luring the town's children to their doom.

(A) NO CHANGE
(B) enacts revenge
(C) extracts revenge
(D) exacts the revenges

13) The present-day territory of Texas declared independence from Mexico in 1836, becoming a country called the Republic of Texas until <u>they</u> joined the United States in 1845.

(A) NO CHANGE
(B) this
(C) that
(D) it

14) Joseph Campbell's 1949 book *The Hero With a Thousand Faces* demonstrated the <u>widespread pervasiveness of the "hero's journey"</u> in myth and religion.

(A) NO CHANGE
(B) universally pervasive nature of the "hero's journey"
(C) pervasiveness of the widespread "hero's journey"
(D) universality of the "hero's journey"

15) A <u>countries</u> Gross Domestic Product (GDP) is the dollar value of the services and goods that it has produced in a given period.

(A) NO CHANGE
(B) countries'
(C) country's
(D) country is

☑	1		4		7		10		13	
	2		5		8		11		14	
	3		6		9		12		15	

15 ~ 13	12 ~ 10	9 ~ 7	6 ~ 0
EXCELLENT	VERY GOOD	GOOD	NEEDS WORK

1) <u>As well as</u> growing underground, potatoes are not roots—they are a type of stem called a "tuber."

(A) NO CHANGE
(B) Despite
(C) Since
(D) Even where

2) The human body is about 60 percent water, making it the body's most <u>abundant</u> substance.

(A) NO CHANGE
(B) excessive
(C) disproportionate
(D) lavish

3) Some American colleges and universities have unusual mascots: to name but a few, Scottsdale Community College has Artie the Fighting Artichoke, <u>Sammy the Banana Slug is UC Santa Cruz's mascot,</u> and Stanford has the Tree.

(A) NO CHANGE
(B) UC Santa Cruz's mascot is Sammy the Banana Slug,
(C) Sammy the Banana Slug at UC Santa Cruz,
(D) UC Santa Cruz has Sammy the Banana Slug,

4) Applying alcohol to a wound is still among the most effective <u>way of</u> cleaning it.

(A) NO CHANGE
(B) technique for
(C) methods of
(D) system of

5) <u>The Italian ghost town of Craco has been uninhabited since the 1970s. It</u> has become a popular filming location and tourist destination in recent decades.

Which choice most effectively combines the sentences at the underlined portion?

(A) If the Italian ghost town of Craco has been uninhabited since the 1970s, it
(B) Uninhabited since the 1970s, the Italian ghost town of Craco
(C) Since the 1970s being uninhabited, the Italian ghost town of Craco
(D) Craco, an Italian ghost town, uninhabited since the 1970s,

6) Some <u>plants, such as flax and cotton, are</u> grown specifically for the production of clothing fiber.

(A) NO CHANGE
(B) plants such as: flax and cotton, are
(C) plants such as flax, and cotton are
(D) plants, such as flax and cotton; are

7) The marathon, a 26.2-mile footrace, is derived from the legend of Pheidippides, a Greek soldier <u>whom ran</u> from the battlefield at Marathon to the city of Athens to report the Greek victory over the Persians.

(A) NO CHANGE
(B) who ran
(C) who's run
(D) whose running

8) Although Mercury is the closest planet to the sun, the average temperatures on the surface of Venus are higher than <u>Mercury.</u>

(A) NO CHANGE
(B) Mercury's surface.
(C) found on the planet Mercury.
(D) those on the surface of Mercury.

9) The lyrics to United States national anthem "The Star-Spangled Banner" come from a poem written by American lawyer Francis Scott Key. He wrote the poem after witnessing the bombardment of Fort McHenry by British troops during the War of 1812.

Which choice most effectively combines the sentences at the underlined portion?

(A) Key, witnessing
(B) Key; after witnessing
(C) Key after he witnessed
(D) Key, which he did after witnessing

10) Dogs were almost certainly the first animals domesticated by humans, although when dogs were first domesticated being still debated.

(A) NO CHANGE
(B) this is
(C) are
(D) is

11) London, England is the only city to have hosted the modern Olympic Games three times—in 1908, 1948, and 2012.

(A) NO CHANGE
(B) times; the times being in
(C) times those are in
(D) times. In

12) The great Mississippi River flood of 1927 destroys 300 million dollars in property and left 700,000 people homeless.

(A) NO CHANGE
(B) destroyed
(C) was destroying
(D) having destroyed

13) Russia embraces nine contiguous time zones and is the largest country on Earth.

(A) NO CHANGE
(B) envelops
(C) encompasses
(D) surrounds

14) In 1937 Disney released its first feature-length animated film, *Snow* White and the Seven Dwarfs.

(A) NO CHANGE
(B) first, feature-length, animated, film *Snow*
(C) first, feature-length animated film *Snow*
(D) first feature-length animated film; *Snow*

15) To the casual listener, Irish and Scottish folk music may sound almost identical. However, Scotland is part of Great Britain whereas Ireland is an island to the west of Great Britain.

Which choice provides the best support for the information in the previous sentence?

(A) NO CHANGE
(B) Having listened to some Irish and Scottish music, I can confirm that this is true.
(C) Traditionally, folk music has no known composer and is passed on orally.
(D) Indeed, both are heavily influenced by Celtic musical traditions.

☑	1		4		7		10		13	
	2		5		8		11		14	
	3		6		9		12		15	

15 ~ 13	12 ~ 10	9 ~ 7	6 ~ 0
EXCELLENT	VERY GOOD	GOOD	NEEDS WORK

CHAPTER 2

1) While George Washington Carver is most famous for finding more than 100 uses for peanuts, he also experimented with numerous other crops and <u>advocating</u> sustainable agricultural practices.

(A) NO CHANGE
(B) advocated
(C) could advocate
(D) being an advocate

2) Each year the Girl Scouts of the USA sells more than 200 million boxes of Thin Mints, <u>who make</u> up approximately 25 percent of all Girl Scout cookie sales.

(A) NO CHANGE
(B) these make
(C) this makes
(D) which make

3) Strong hind legs and a flexible spine <u>allowing</u> the average house cat to jump six times its own height.

(A) NO CHANGE
(B) allow
(C) allows
(D) to allow

4) <u>For</u> those looking to surf at a beach with no waves, kitesurfing and windsurfing are both valid options.

(A) NO CHANGE
(B) If
(C) With
(D) Although

5) In Thailand stray dogs are referred to as <u>*soi dogs.* In Bangkok</u> alone there are over 300,000 *soi dogs.*

Which choice most effectively combines the sentences at the underlined portion?

(A) *soi dogs*; consequently, in Bangkok
(B) *soi dogs*, meaning that in Bangkok
(C) *soi dogs*, and in Bangkok
(D) *soi dogs*, so in Bangkok

6) Polish scientist Marie Curie is the only woman to have won Nobel Prizes in two <u>fields, the fields are physics and chemistry.</u>

(A) NO CHANGE
(B) fields being physics and chemistry.
(C) fields are physics, chemistry.
(D) fields, physics and chemistry.

7) There is an ongoing scientific debate over whether dinosaurs <u>being warm- or cold-blooded,</u> though recent findings weigh in favor of warm-blooded dinosaurs.

(A) NO CHANGE
(B) were warm- or cold-blooded,
(C) being warm- and cold-blooded,
(D) were warm- and cold-blooded,

8) Recent estimates claim that Earth is home to over three trillion <u>trees. There are</u> approximately 400 trees for every human.

Which choice most effectively combines the sentences at the underlined portion?

(A) trees, which means that there are
(B) trees because there are
(C) trees, yet there are
(D) trees, if there are

9) Much of humanity's knowledge of the size and structure of the universe comes from observational <u>tool</u> that do not rely on visible light, such as radio, infrared, and gamma-ray telescopes.

(A) NO CHANGE
(B) device
(C) instruments
(D) machine

10) Competing in the earliest televised golf tournaments, <u>superstardom was what American Arnold Palmer achieved because of his skill, charisma, and modest upbringing.</u>

(A) NO CHANGE
(B) skill, charisma, and a modest upbringing helped American Arnold Palmer rise to superstardom.
(C) achieved by American Arnold Palmer was superstardom because of this skill, charisma, and modest upbringing.
(D) American Arnold Palmer rose to superstardom because of his skill, charisma, and modest upbringing.

11) A predominantly French style, Gothic architecture <u>generated</u> in the 12th century from Romanesque traditions.

(A) NO CHANGE
(B) reinforced
(C) developed
(D) broadened

12) <u>Prolific writer,</u> Joyce Carol Oates has won many honors for her works, including the National Book Award.

(A) NO CHANGE
(B) A prolific writer,
(C) A prolific writer who
(D) She is a prolific writer,

13) <u>Few blues artists</u> have had a more auspicious career than guitarist BB King, who helped define the Chicago sound and whose work is still popular today.

(A) NO CHANGE
(B) The few blues artists
(C) The blues artists are few
(D) Few are the blues artists

14) According to the Schmidt Sting Pain Index, the sting of a bullet ant is much more painful than <u>those of a honeybee.</u>

(A) NO CHANGE
(B) a honeybee.
(C) from a honeybee.
(D) that of a honeybee.

15) Scientific progress is cumulative, and even the greatest minds must understand the developments of the past to create the future. <u>For instance, Arthur C. Clarke once wrote, "Any sufficiently advanced technology is indistinguishable from magic."</u>

Which quote provides the best support for the information in the previous sentence?

(A) NO CHANGE
(B) Indeed, even the great Isaac Newton claimed, "If I have seen further it is by standing on the shoulders of giants."
(C) In fact, Einstein once asked, "If we knew what we were doing, it would not be called research, would it?"
(D) As author Terry Pratchett quipped, "Time is a drug. Too much of it kills you."

☑	1		4		7		10		13	
	2		5		8		11		14	
	3		6		9		12		15	

15 ~ 13	12 ~ 10	9 ~ 7	6 ~ 0
EXCELLENT	VERY GOOD	GOOD	NEEDS WORK

1) Everett, Washington is the home of aerospace manufacturer Boeing's final assembly plant— being the largest building in the world.

   (A) NO change
   (B) the largest
   (C) as the largest
   (D) this is the largest

2) In 1869 the first college football game took place against Princeton and Rutgers, but it was not until the 1880s that Walter Camp formalized the rules that standardized the sport.

   (A) NO CHANGE
   (B) against Princeton or Rutgers,
   (C) between Princeton or Rutgers,
   (D) between Princeton and Rutgers,

3) From 2008 to 2015, the films in Marvel's Cinematic Universe franchise, which include the *Iron Man, Captain America,* and *Avengers* series, grossed over 3.5-billion dollars worldwide.

   (A) NO CHANGE
   (B) includes
   (C) is including
   (D) has included

4) Feelings of embarrassment may cause the body to release adrenalin, which increases heart rate and causing blood vessels to dilate, causing a person to blush.

   (A) NO CHANGE
   (B) dilates blood vessels,
   (C) dilating blood vessels,
   (D) causes the dilation of blood vessels,

5) Insects do not breathe using lungs. Nevertheless, they breathe through a series of small holes along their abdomen called "spiracles," which feed oxygen to an insect's body through tubes called "trachea."

   (A) NO CHANGE
   (B) Consequently,
   (C) Moreover,
   (D) Instead,

6) Even though its highly porous structure, the igneous rock pumice will float in water.

   (A) NO CHANGE
   (B) Since
   (C) Because of
   (D) For

7) It takes most people about five to ten minutes to fall asleep.

   (A) NO CHANGE
   (B) for sleep.
   (C) to fall into a sleeping state.
   (D) for sleep to overcome them.

8) Although New York City is much larger than Albany, it is the capital of the state of New York.

   (A) NO CHANGE
   (B) its
   (C) the latter
   (D) which

9) Miguel Cervantes's *Don Quixote* is often rated as the first modern novel at least in part because it was among the first long fictional works to be written in prose.

   (A) NO CHANGE
   (B) considered
   (C) contemplated
   (D) evaluated as

10) With well over two billion adherents, Christianity is the world's largest religion. Islam is the world's fastest growing religion.

Which choice most effectively combines the sentences at the underlined portion?

(A) religion, it is Islam that is
(B) religion, and Islam being
(C) religion, so is Islam
(D) religion, but Islam is

11) A turtle's shell is part of its skeletal system, and consists largely of ribs and vertebrae that fuse during development.

Which choice provides the best support for the information in the previous sentence?

(A) NO CHANGE
(B) turtles evolved over 150 million years ago, making them among the oldest groups of reptile.
(C) although many species of turtle are aquatic, they all breathe air and lay their eggs on dry land.
(D) the shell of the largest turtle can grow over 6 feet long, with the turtle itself weighing over 2,000 pounds.

12) The sugar alcohol sorbitol is a popular sugar substitute in diet foods. It contains fewer calories per gram than regular sugar does.

Which choice most effectively combines the sentences at the underlined portion?

(A) foods with its
(B) foods, it containing
(C) foods and containing
(D) foods because it contains

13) Whereas most mammals rely on eye movement to take in their surroundings, many bird species rely on head movement. Paradoxically, many birds bob their heads when they walk to compensate for the movement of the rest of their bodies and stabilize their visual surroundings.

(A) NO CHANGE
(B) However,
(C) Thus,
(D) Nevertheless,

14) With morale and food supplies running low, the three climbers decided to risk the vertical ascent to the mountain's summit.

(A) NO CHANGE
(B) assent
(C) asset
(D) incense

15) The solo career of Paul McCartney has been more financially successful than his former bandmate, Ringo Starr.

(A) NO CHANGE
(B) that of his former bandmate, Ringo Starr.
(C) those of his former bandmate, Ringo Starr.
(D) the success of his former bandmate, Ringo Starr.

☑	1		4		7		10		13	
	2		5		8		11		14	
	3		6		9		12		15	

15 ~ 13	12 ~ 10	9 ~ 7	6 ~ 0
EXCELLENT	VERY GOOD	GOOD	NEEDS WORK

1) Throughout the 20th century, the New York Zoological Society (later renamed the Wildlife Conservation Society) offered a large financial reward for a live, healthy snake measuring over 30 feet in length.

(A) NO CHANGE
(B) Society, later renamed (the Wildlife Conservation Society), offered
(C) Society (It was later renamed the Wildlife Conservation Society.) offered
(D) Society—being renamed later the Wildlife Conservation Society—offered

2) According to the International Energy Agency, the United States is set to overwhelm Saudi Arabia as the world's largest oil producer by 2020.

(A) NO CHANGE
(B) outdistance
(C) upstage
(D) overtake

3) It is estimated that 70 to 80 percent of the atmosphere's oxygen is provided by marine plant life, which are mainly consisting of algae.

(A) NO CHANGE
(B) is mainly consisted
(C) mainly consists
(D) have mainly consisted

4) As the most massive object in the solar system, the sun dwarfs even the gas giants Jupiter and Saturn. Indeed, it takes sunlight approximately 43 minutes to travel to Jupiter and 79 minutes to travel to Saturn.

Which choice provides the best support for the information in the previous sentence?

(A) NO CHANGE
(B) the sun accounts for over 99 percent of all the mass in the solar system.
(C) the sun is only a medium-sized star when compared to other stars in the Milky Way.
(D) the sun is about 4.5 billion years old, and it is estimated to last another 5 billion years.

5) Japan comprises over 6,800 islands, but the vast majority of its population resides on Honshu, the country's largest island.

(A) NO CHANGE
(B) Honshu being the country's largest island.
(C) Honshu as the largest island in the country.
(D) the largest island, which is Honshu, in the country.

6) While about six percent of the salt manufactured in the world having use for human consumption, eight percent is used to de-ice highways and roads.

(A) NO CHANGE
(B) is used
(C) has use
(D) uses

7) In the United States, a politician who lacks policy-making authority because they are about to leave office is known as a "lame duck."

(A) NO CHANGE
(B) one is
(C) being
(D) he or she is

8) Wherever no sound can travel in the vacuum of outer space, many television shows and films insist on including rumbling engines and raucous explosions during space flight.

(A) NO CHANGE
(B) If
(C) Although
(D) When

9) The works of American composer Philip Glass are often categorized as classical music, but he has <u>both an influence on and worked with</u> many rock and electronic artists.

(A) NO CHANGE
(B) both influenced or worked with
(C) both influenced and worked with
(D) both influenced while working with

10) The President of the United States has the power to veto, or reject, decisions made by <u>Congress. There are ways that Congress can in turn override a presidential veto.</u>

Which choice most effectively combines the sentences at the underlined portion?

(A) Congress, which can in turn override a presidential veto.
(B) Congress; Congress has ways of overriding a presidential veto in turn.
(C) Congress, has ways in turn of overriding a presidential veto.
(D) Congress, it in turn has ways that it can override a presidential veto.

11) All of Earth's weather occurs in the troposphere, which is the lowest <u>levels</u> of Earth's atmosphere.

(A) NO CHANGE
(B) portion
(C) layered
(D) sections

12) In 1893 New Zealand became the first autonomous nation to grant all women <u>over the age above</u> 21 the right to vote.

(A) NO CHANGE
(B) beyond ages
(C) more than the age
(D) over the age of

13) Venus takes less time to orbit the Sun than it does to complete one <u>rotation. A day</u> on the planet takes longer than an entire year.

Which choice most effectively combines the sentences at the underlined portion?

(A) rotation because a day
(B) rotation if a day
(C) rotation, so a day
(D) rotation, yet a day

14) While some Americans still get a portion of their news from print and television sources, social media sites such as Facebook and Twitter <u>has</u> become increasingly important news resources for many.

(A) NO CHANGE
(B) having
(C) have
(D) DELETE underlined portion.

15) Consisting of over 40 books, <u>Terry Pratchett wrote Discworld, which ranks among the most critically and financially successful fantasy series.</u>

(A) NO CHANGE
(B) Terry Pratchett's *Discworld* ranks among the most critically and financially successful fantasy series.
(C) and ranking among the most critically and financially successful fantasy series is Terry Pratchett's *Discworld.*
(D) of all fantasy series, Terry Pratchett's *Discworld* ranks among the most critically and financially successful.

☑	1		4		7		10		13	
	2		5		8		11		14	
	3		6		9		12		15	

15 ~ 13	12 ~ 10	9 ~ 7	6 ~ 0
EXCELLENT	VERY GOOD	GOOD	NEEDS WORK

1) Although American performer Beyoncé is <u>the best</u> known for her musical career, she has also worked extensively in film, television, retail, and as a journalist.

(A) NO CHANGE
(B) a best
(C) best
(D) as the best

2) The five interlocking rings that serve as the most recognizable symbol of the Olympic Games were designed in 1912 by Pierre de <u>Coubertin the founder</u> of the International Olympic Committee.

(A) NO CHANGE
(B) Coubertin, being the founder
(C) Coubertin, he is the founder
(D) Coubertin, founder

3) The university's research results raise new ethical dilemmas that policymakers <u>would have to</u> address immediately.

(A) NO CHANGE
(B) were having to
(C) will be having to
(D) will have to

4) The blue whale is the largest animal to ever have lived, <u>measuring up to 98 feet in length and weighing more upwards</u> of 170 tons.

(A) NO CHANGE
(B) measuring up to a length of 98 feet long and weighing more than upwards
(C) measuring up to 98 feet long in length and weighing upwards
(D) measuring up to 98 feet long and weighing upwards

5) <u>Fighting</u> between the United Kingdom and the Zanzibar Sultanate, the Anglo-Zanzibar War is the shortest war in recorded history, ending in British victory after only 38 minutes.

(A) NO CHANGE
(B) Fought
(C) Fight
(D) To fight

6) <u>While the board game is referred to as "checkers" in America, people from the United Kingdom call it "draughts."</u> Ancient game boards have been discovered in Mesopotamia and Egypt, and references to the game are made in several ancient Greek texts.

Which choice most effectively introduces the information that follows it?

(A) NO CHANGE
(B) The board game that Americans refer to as "checkers" has existed in some form for at least 5,000 years.
(C) Variations on the game Americans call "checkers" are played around the world.
(D) Referred to as "checkers" in America, the game involves players moving pieces diagonally across a checkered board.

7) Wisconsin is the American leader of cheese production largely due to the efforts of Stephen Babcock and Harry <u>Russell, both of whom helped develop the</u> cold-curing process of ripening cheese in 1897 through the University of Wisconsin at Madison.

(A) NO CHANGE
(B) Russell, they are known for the
(C) Russell, both whose help developing
(D) Russell, both of who helped develop the

8) The Great Plains tornado <u>belt is a tornado-rich area of the Central United States. This area forms</u> at least in part because warm, moist air from the Gulf of Mexico meets cold, dry air from Canada.

Which choice most effectively combines the sentences at the underlined portion?

(A) belt is tornado rich, and it is located in the Central United States; the tornado-rich area forms
(B) belt, an area of the Central United States, being tornado-rich, and it forms
(C) belt, a tornado-rich area of the Central United States, forms
(D) belt being a tornado rich area of the Central United States, is forming

9) Some people claim that American astronauts have never set foot on the moon, and that renowned film director Stanley Kubrick directed a fake moon landing that was <u>passed away</u> as genuine.

(A) NO CHANGE
(B) passed on
(C) passed through
(D) passed off

10) At half-time, the coach gathered his team and said to them, "This is it, the last game of the season, so now more than ever there's no quitting. <u>Either we go down fighting and also</u> we go home winners."

(A) NO CHANGE
(B) Either we go down fighting nor
(C) Either we go down fighting and
(D) Either we go down fighting or

11) The planet Venus is covered in thick clouds that reflect the majority of sunlight back into <u>space. Venus is the</u> brightest object in Earth's night sky.

Which choice most effectively combines the sentences at the underlined portion?

(A) space, making Venus the
(B) space, Venus being the
(C) space, yet Venus is the
(D) space, being the

12) The average National Football League (NFL) game <u>last</u> a little over 3 hours, but the ball is in play for only about 11 minutes of that time.

(A) NO CHANGE
(B) lasts
(C) lasting
(D) lasted

13) A pipeline network <u>total</u> 800 miles connects oil fields in northern Alaska to refineries on Prince William Sound.

(A) NO CHANGE
(B) totals
(C) totaling
(D) it totals

14) French authors Ausguste Maquet and Alexander Dumas collaborated to produce some of fiction's most enduring <u>works. Their collaborations are</u> *The Three Musketeers* and *The Count of Monte Cristo.*

Which choice most effectively combines the sentences at the underlined portion?

(A) works, and these are
(B) works being
(C) works, with
(D) works:

15) At the 1968 Democratic Convention, the anarchist Youth International Party sowed <u>discord</u> by nominating a pig for President of the United States.

(A) NO CHANGE
(B) argument
(C) discredit
(D) renunciation

☑	1		4		7		10		13	
	2		5		8		11		14	
	3		6		9		12		15	

15 ~ 13	12 ~ 10	9 ~ 7	6 ~ 0
EXCELLENT	VERY GOOD	GOOD	NEEDS WORK

CHAPTER 2

1) The sentence "The quick brown fox jumps over the lazy dog" has been used to test typing equipment since the 19th century because <u>of its using</u> every letter in the alphabet at least once.

(A) NO CHANGE
(B) of their use of
(C) they use
(D) it uses

2) In the 2015 fiscal year, the U.S. federal budget totaled 3.8 trillion <u>dollars. That year, the federal budget was</u> just over 20 percent of the U.S. economy as measured by the nation's GDP.

Which choice most effectively combines the sentences at the underlined portion?

(A) dollars was
(B) dollars, which was
(C) dollars; this amount totaled
(D) dollars being in amount

3) Several ancient Greek scholars, including philosopher Xenophanes and historian Herodotus, correctly theorized that <u>much of Earth's surface</u> was once underwater based on discoveries of marine animal fossils well above sea level.

(A) NO CHANGE
(B) much of Earths surface
(C) much of Earths' surface
(D) many of Earth's surfaces

4) Romani people, often referred to as "Gypsies" by English-speakers, originated in Northern India and probably <u>have begun immigrating</u> to Europe in the 12th century.

(A) NO CHANGE
(B) begin to immigrate
(C) beginning an immigration
(D) began immigrating

5) During the 19th and 20th centuries, the U.S. government hired Indian agency <u>police. Each officer was</u> assigned a Native American tribe and tasked with enforcing federal and state laws on that tribe's reservation.

Which choice most effectively combines the sentences at the underlined portion?

(A) police, being
(B) police, and were
(C) police; each officer was
(D) police, yet each of the officers was

6) During the formation of the solar system, all the planets formed from a disk-like plane of space dust. <u>However,</u> the solar system's eight planets are coplanar—that is, their orbits around the sun occur on a shared plane.

(A) NO CHANGE
(B) For this reason,
(C) Despite this,
(D) In reality,

7) <u>That</u> humans have been producing music for tens of thousands of years, detailed musical notation has only existed since the European Middle Ages.

(A) NO CHANGE
(B) Although
(C) Provided that
(D) Whether

8) Diamond is the hardest naturally occurring <u>material</u> found on Earth.

(A) NO CHANGE
(B) matters
(C) of substances
(D) things

9) By definition herbivores are plant-eaters, yet a few herbivore species—notably cows and some species of deer—<u>are being observed</u> eating live birds, presumably to nutritionally supplement their otherwise plant-based diets.

(A) NO CHANGE
(B) is being observed
(C) have been observed
(D) has been observed

10) Over 200 million years ago the Central Pangean Mountain Range spanned much of the supercontinent <u>Pangea; North</u> America's Appalachian Mountains and Scotland's Highlands are remnants of this once-massive mountain range.

(A) NO CHANGE
(B) Pangea and North
(C) Pangea, with North
(D) Pangea, North

11) In 1931 General Ho Chein banned Lewis Carroll's *Alice's Adventures in Wonderland* in the Hunan Province of China because the book includes <u>anthropomorphic, human-like animals that use human language,</u> which General Ho Chein deemed demeaning to humans.

(A) NO CHANGE
(B) human-like animals that use human language and speech,
(C) anthropomorphic, human-like animals with human speech,
(D) anthropomorphic animals that use human language,

12) As the hurricane raged through the small town, Daniel burst through the front door with emergency supplies in hand. He announced to his wife and son, "Sorry that took so <u>long, but the stormy conditions make traveling incredibly dangerous."</u>

The author wants to use understatement as a rhetorical style. Which choice best accomplishes this goal?

(A) NO CHANGE
(B) long; walking into the wind was as hard as trudging through wet concrete."
(C) long, but it's a little bit windy out there."
(D) long; I got lost because the heavy rains affect visibility."

13) "Kickback" refers to a scheme in which an insider—an employee or elected official—helps someone cheat an organization or government agency, and in return, <u>they "kick back"</u> some of the profit to the insider.

(A) NO CHANGE
(B) he "kicks back"
(C) the someone "kicks back"
(D) that person "kicks back"

14) Wolves were once the <u>commanding</u> predators in Great Britain, but overhunting and deforestation led to their extermination from the island centuries ago.

(A) NO CHANGE
(B) dominant
(C) assertive
(D) governing

15) Even though the brain detects pain in other parts of the <u>body. The</u> brain itself has no pain receptors.

(A) NO CHANGE
(B) body the
(C) body, the
(D) body: the

☑	1		4		7		10		13	
	2		5		8		11		14	
	3		6		9		12		15	

15 ~ 13	12 ~ 10	9 ~ 7	6 ~ 0
EXCELLENT	VERY GOOD	GOOD	NEEDS WORK

CHAPTER 2

1) In most countries, one drives on the right side of the road, but in the United Kingdom and in most former British colonies, <u>you drive</u> on the left side of the road.

(A) NO CHANGE
(B) driving is
(C) one drives
(D) drive

2) In 1948 Margaret Chase Smith <u>becomes</u> the first woman to be elected to both the U.S. Senate and the House of Representatives.

(A) NO CHANGE
(B) was becoming
(C) has become
(D) became

3) The underside of a starfish contains hundreds of small, tubular <u>legs. Starfish use their legs</u> to move, grip rocks, and hold prey.

Which choice most effectively combines the sentences at the underlined portion?

(A) legs that the starfish uses
(B) legs, and these legs allow the starfish
(C) legs because the starfish uses them
(D) legs; the legs of a starfish are used

4) Found on every continent except Antarctica, huntsman spiders do not build webs to catch prey. <u>These spiders are known for their speed and size, with leg spans measuring up to 12 inches.</u>

Which choice provides evidence that best supports the claim made in the previous sentence?

(A) NO CHANGE
(B) Rather, they forage and hunt for food, which consists of insects and small invertebrates.
(C) They are called "rain spiders" in southern Africa because they often enter people's houses to seek shelter from rainstorms.
(D) Their bites are venomous but nonlethal.

5) In 1854 English physician John Snow <u>decided</u> that a London cholera outbreak was caused by contaminated drinking water, a discovery that had a lasting impact on public health.

(A) NO CHANGE
(B) diagnosed
(C) tallied
(D) determined

6) Rocks are often categorized based on how they form: sedimentary rocks form when sediment gradually layers on top of itself, igneous rocks form when magma crystallizes, and <u>metamorphic rocks form</u> when the structures of sedimentary or igneous rocks are altered by pressure and heat.

(A) NO CHANGE
(B) a metamorphic rock forms
(C) metamorphic rocks will form
(D) the metamorphic rock will form

7) Many students are taught that the three states of matter are solid, liquid, and gas, yet 99.9 percent of the matter in the universe is actually <u>a fourth state of matter plasma.</u>

(A) NO CHANGE
(B) plasma that is a fourth state of matter.
(C) plasma, a fourth state of matter.
(D) a fourth state—plasma—of matter.

8) The United States' military spending exceeds <u>any other country.</u>

(A) NO CHANGE
(B) that of any other country.
(C) those of any other country.
(D) any other country's does.

9) The common cold is usually associated with the <u>rhinovirus. There are</u> over 200 viruses known to cause cold-like symptoms.

Which choice most effectively combines the sentences at the underlined portion?

(A) rhinovirus, so there are
(B) rhinovirus, there being
(C) rhinovirus, yet there are
(D) rhinovirus is one of

10) Educators have long debated whether or not a student's standardized test scores <u>repeat honestly</u> his or her academic abilities.

(A) NO CHANGE
(B) correctly echo
(C) acceptably mirror
(D) accurately reflect

11) Visitors to Ethiopia's National Museum can see a replica of the fossilized bones of "Lucy," a female hominid who lived 3.2 million years ago; <u>the actual fossils are housed in the museum but cannot be displayed.</u>

(A) NO CHANGE
(B) the museum is housing the actual fossils but it cannot display them.
(C) museum staff members are housing the actual fossils, but they cannot display them.
(D) museum directors house the actual fossils but they cannot display them.

12) American gymnast Kerri Strug is best remembered <u>for vaulting</u> on a seriously injured leg in order to secure a U.S. gold medal win in the women's gymnastics team competition during the 1996 Olympic Games.

(A) NO CHANGE
(B) vaulting
(C) to vault
(D) for vault

13) Pearl S. Buck was awarded the Pulitzer Prize in 1932 for her novel *The Good Earth,* <u>while exploring</u> the lives of a rural Chinese family in the early 20th century.

(A) NO CHANGE
(B) which explores
(C) who explores
(D) where it explores

14) Oil prices are listed per barrel of crude oil, which is equal to 42 gallons. <u>Rather,</u> each barrel only produces about 19 gallons of usable gasoline.

(A) NO CHANGE
(B) For instance,
(C) Consequently,
(D) However,

15) The 2010 *Deepwater Horizon* oil spill is estimated to have <u>infused</u> over 8,000 animal species.

(A) NO CHANGE
(B) effected
(C) affected
(D) influenced

☑	1		4		7		10		13	
	2		5		8		11		14	
	3		6		9		12		15	

15 ~ 13	12 ~ 10	9 ~ 7	6 ~ 0
EXCELLENT	VERY GOOD	GOOD	NEEDS WORK

1) In 2010, a herd of goats <u>was hired</u> to consume weeds and invasive plant species on the property surrounding the Vanderbilt Mansion.

(A) NO CHANGE
(B) were hired
(C) is hired
(D) hired

2) Water lilies are believed to be <u>toward</u> the earliest groups of angiosperms (flowering plants).

(A) NO CHANGE
(B) at
(C) around
(D) among

3) Thailand's Mae Klong River is home to a species of freshwater stingray <u>who measures</u> over four meters long and weigh up to 800 pounds.

(A) NO CHANGE
(B) that can measure
(C) where it measures
(D) when measured

4) James <u>Buchanan was the 15th President of the United States. He served</u> just before the start of the Civil War, and many historians criticize his failure to deal with the succession of the American South.

Which choice most effectively combines the sentences at the underlined portion?

(A) Buchanan, being the 15th President of the United States, serving
(B) Buchanan, the 15th President of the United States, served
(C) Buchanan was the 15th President of the United States and served
(D) Buchanan the 15th President of the United States: served

5) Brazil is the fifth largest country in the <u>world, it covers</u> nearly half of the South American continent.

(A) NO CHANGE
(B) world by covering
(C) world, covering
(D) world covers

6) The Bill and Melinda Gates Foundation's 45-billion-dollar endowment comes largely from the <u>charity's founders,</u> Bill and Melinda Gates.

(A) NO CHANGE
(B) charities founder's,
(C) charity's founder's,
(D) charities' founders,

7) <u>Because</u> they are often only visible in men, Adam's apples, which are lumps of cartilage that surround people's voice boxes, exist in both men and women.

(A) NO CHANGE
(B) Lest
(C) Unless
(D) Although

8) In Disney's 1940 animated film *Pinocchio*, the Blue Fairy famously advises the puppet protagonist Pinocchio to "Let your <u>conscious</u> be your guide."

(A) NO CHANGE
(B) conscientious
(C) conscience
(D) confines

9) Arabic calligraphy has <u>also religious and artistic</u> significance, making calligraphers among the most valued artists in Islamic societies.

(A) NO CHANGE
(B) neither religious nor artistic
(C) both religious plus artistic
(D) both religious and artistic

10) In the Middle Ages, prosthetic limbs <u>were often made</u> of heavy materials, such as iron or steel.

(A) NO CHANGE
(B) made
(C) should often be made
(D) was often made

11) <u>When</u> he played an important role in America's fight for independence from England, Benjamin Franklin is probably more famous for being a philosopher, scientist, and inventor.

(A) NO CHANGE
(B) Whether
(C) Because
(D While

12) Although it may seem like a product of modern times, bowling can actually trace its roots back to ancient Egypt. <u>Ancient Romans also had their own variation of the game.</u>

Which choice provides evidence that best supports the claim made in the previous sentence?

(A) NO CHANGE
(B) Even in the ancient Roman Empire some 2,000 years ago, Roman soldiers developed their own variation of the game.
(C) Archaeological findings from Egypt dating back to 3200 BCE reveal balls made of leather and organic materials, and even some made out of porcelain and plastic.
(D) Many of our modern traditions and practices can trace their roots back to ancient Egypt.

13) <u>Perspective</u> applicants should make sure to contact the admissions office before submitting their completed forms.

(A) NO CHANGE
(B) Expecting
(C) Prosperous
(D) Prospective

14) Based on their DNA sequence alone, chimpanzees are <u>the most closely related</u> animals to human beings.

(A) NO CHANGE
(B) the mostly related, closest
(C) the closest
(D) the most close, related

15) <u>To be known</u> about the life of the ancient Greek philosopher Socrates is largely inferred from the writings of Plato.

(A) NO CHANGE
(B) Knowing
(C) What is known
(D) How we know

☑	1		4		7		10		13	
	2		5		8		11		14	
	3		6		9		12		15	

15 ~ 13	12 ~ 10	9 ~ 7	6 ~ 0
EXCELLENT	VERY GOOD	GOOD	NEEDS WORK

CHAPTER 2

1) After being dismissed from his post as the Archbishop of Salzburg's organist, a young Wolfgang Amadeus Mozart <u>had moved</u> to Vienna and worked as a free-lance musician.

(A) NO CHANGE
(B) moves
(C) moved
(D) was moving

2) <u>Nathaniel Owings was a prolific architect. He</u> oversaw dozens of construction projects during his forty-year career.

Which choice most effectively combines the sentences at the underlined portion?

(A) Nathaniel Owings (prolific architect)
(B) Being prolific, architect Nathaniel Owings
(C) Nathaniel Owings being a prolific architect, he
(D) A prolific architect, Nathaniel Owings

3) Water is present on the sun's surface in the form of vapor, <u>which scientists</u> have observed gathering over some relatively cool sunspots.

(A) NO CHANGE
(B) scientists
(C) where scientists
(D) when scientists

4) There are five transcontinental countries with territory in both Europe and <u>Asia. They are Azerbaijan,</u> Georgia, Kazakhstan, Russia, and Turkey.

Which choice most effectively combines the sentences at the underlined portion?

(A) Asia: Azerbaijan,
(B) Asia, being Azerbaijan,
(C) Asia; these are Azerbaijan,
(D) Asia, and the countries are Azerbaijan,

5) Assyrian medical texts outline teeth-cleaning procedures from 3000 BCE, <u>and toothpicks from about the same time have been discovered in present-day Iraq.</u>

The author wants to add an element of humor to the sentence. Which choice best accomplishes this goal?

(A) NO CHANGE
(B) making dental checkups as ancient as they are reviled.
(C) and the ancient Greek physician Hippocrates also made dental-hygiene recommendations.
(D) making dental hygiene at least as ancient as writing itself.

6) Although many literary scholars consider Charles Brockden Brown the first important American novelist, <u>though few people read his works</u> anymore.

(A) NO CHANGE
(B) but few people read his works
(C) and his works are not widely read
(D) his works are not widely read

7) The Yellowstone Caldera, a 34- by 45-mile caldera located in Yellowstone National Park, is evidence of the <u>land's regional geological history of volcanoes.</u>

(A) NO CHANGE
(B) geological history of the region, which involves volcanoes.
(C) region's volcanic geological history.
(D) volcanic geological history of the region's land.

8) Supplying nearly 22 percent of the world's rice, <u>of the world's rice exporters, Thailand is the second largest.</u>

(A) NO CHANGE
(B) as an exporter of rice, Thailand is the second largest in the world.
(C) Thailand is the second largest exporter of rice in the world.
(D) the second largest exporter of rice in the world is Thailand.

9) <u>Before ushering</u> in the era of aviation, the Wright Brothers established themselves as skilled bicycle manufacturers and repairmen.

(A) NO CHANGE
(B) Because they ushered
(C) Unless they ushered
(D) Whether ushering

10) While Anthony Burgess is best known as the <u>writers</u> of *A Clockwork Orange* and *Earthly Powers,* he also produced over 250 pieces of music.

(A) NO CHANGE
(B) author
(C) novelists
(D) creators

11) Some species of lizards, frogs, fish, and lampreys have one or more parietal eyes atop <u>its</u> heads; these "eyes" cannot discern images, but they can sense changes in light.

(A) NO CHANGE
(B) there
(C) they're
(D) their

12) While working as a traveling salesman, Duncan Hines <u>compiled notes that he gathered on restaurants</u> across the country, eventually publishing them in the 1935 book *Adventures in Good Eating.*

(A) NO CHANGE
(B) compiled notes on restaurants
(C) compiled notes on places to eat (restaurants)
(D) collected and compiled notes on restaurants

13) Because their fabric import businesses became <u>successful</u> to buy Mercedes Benz cars, some female merchants in the West African nation of Togo are known as "Nana Benz."

(A) NO CHANGE
(B) so successful
(C) successful enough
(D) enough successful

14) The Great Fire of London, which raged for four days in September of 1666, <u>was destroying upwards of</u> 13,000 houses in the overcrowded, medieval city.

(A) NO CHANGE
(B) destroys in excess of
(C) has destroyed more than
(D) destroyed over

15) The metalloid tellurium is used as a coloring agent for ceramics and <u>in the production of</u> glass fibers for telecommunications.

(A) NO CHANGE
(B) producing
(C) a produced
(D) for the producing

☑	1		4		7		10		13	
	2		5		8		11		14	
	3		6		9		12		15	

15 ~ 13	12 ~ 10	9 ~ 7	6 ~ 0
EXCELLENT	VERY GOOD	GOOD	NEEDS WORK

CHAPTER 2

1) The St. Petersburg-Tampa Airboat Line, although only operational for four months in 1914, <u>being</u> the first ever commercial passenger airline.

(A) NO CHANGE
(B) were
(C) are
(D) was

2) In 2010 dozens of 6-million-year-old marine mammal fossils were discovered in Chile's Atacama <u>Desert: determining</u> that the animals died after interacting with a toxic algal bloom.

(A) NO CHANGE
(B) Desert; with researchers determining
(C) Desert; researchers have determined
(D) Desert, having determined

3) Arteriosclerosis, <u>forms plaque on the arteries,</u> causes circulatory problems that may lead to heart attack and stroke.

(A) NO CHANGE
(B) plaque on the arteries is formed,
(C) which forming plaque on the arteries,
(D) the formation of plaque on the arteries,

4) Until the late 1990s, San Francisco's Golden Gate Bridge was the tallest suspension bridge in the <u>world. Its towers reach</u> 746 feet above the water.

Which choice most effectively combines the sentences at the underlined portion?

(A) world, with towers reaching
(B) world; towers that reach
(C) world, yet its towers reach
(D) world, the reach of its towers being

5) Misty Copeland, <u>which dances</u> combines expressiveness with precision, is one of the best-known ballerinas in the United States.

(A) NO CHANGE
(B) it was his dancing
(C) who danced
(D) whose dancing

6) During the Jacobite rising of 1745, Charles Edward Stuart rallied Scottish Highland clansmen to help him reclaim the British throne. <u>When Charles arrived in Scotland, most British forces were in continental Europe fighting in the War of the Austrian Succession.</u>

Which choice most effectively tells the reader the outcome of the Jacobite rising?

(A) NO CHANGE
(B) Within a year, the British Army had suppressed the uprising and Charles had fled for France.
(C) Much of the financing for the Jacobite rising came from French banker George Walters.
(D) Charles sailed to Scotland on a captured British warship filled with weapons for the uprising.

7) In 1947 Congress passed the 22nd Amendment, which stipulates that a U.S. president may serve for <u>a maximum of at most two terms.</u>

(A) NO CHANGE
(B) a maximum of two.
(C) a maximum of two terms.
(D) a maximum time period of two terms.

8) Robert Johnson was an early 20th century musician whom many <u>ponder over</u> the finest blues artist of all time.

(A) NO CHANGE
(B) contemplate
(C) deliberate on
(D) consider

9) Ian Fleming became one of the most successful authors in England after the publication of *Casino Royale*, the first book in the James Bond series.

(A) NO CHANGE
(B) *Royale* being the first book in the James Bond series.
(C) *Royale*, in the James Bond series it is the first book.
(D) *Royale*, this is the first book in the James Bond series.

10) Since the mid-20th century, sensitive radio telescopes are being used to detect the cosmic microwave background (CMB), which is radiation left over from an early stage in the development of the universe.

(A) NO CHANGE
(B) will be used to have detected
(C) have been used to detect
(D) having been used in detecting

11) Due to convergent evolution, Old World and New World vultures share physical and dietary similarities. They are not closely related and belong to different taxonomic families.

Which choice most effectively combines the sentences at the underlined portion?

(A) similarities, yet they are
(B) similarities, being
(C) similarities, so they are
(D) similarities; they are

12) Pompeii is just one of five Roman towns destroyed during the eruption of Mount Vesuvius in 79 CE, the others are Stabiae, Oplontis, Boscoreale, and Herculaneum.

(A) NO CHANGE
(B) others being Stabiae, Oplontis, Boscoreale, and Herculaneum.
(C) other ones called Stabiae, Oplontis, Boscoreale, and Herculaneum.
(D) others; Stabiae, Oplontis, Boscoreale, and Herculaneum.

13) If the largest known star were placed in the center of our solar system, its surface would extend beyond the orbit of Jupiter.

(A) NO CHANGE
(B) was placed in the center of our solar system, its
(C) were to be placed in the center of our solar system, it's
(D) was to be placed in the center of our solar system, it's

14) For his performance as a corrupt Los Angeles police officer in the 2002 film *Training Day*, the Academy Award for Best Actor was received by Denzel Washington.

(A) NO CHANGE
(B) the Best actor in a Leading Role Academy Award was received by Denzel Washington.
(C) receiving the Academy Award for Best Actor in a Leading Role was Denzel Washington.
(D) Denzel Washington received the Academy Award for Best Actor.

15) The North American bison became the first official mammal of the United States when President Obama signed the National Bison Legacy Act into law in 2016.

(A) NO CHANGE
(B) where
(C) if
(D) whom

☑	1		4		7		10		13	
	2		5		8		11		14	
	3		6		9		12		15	

15 ~ 13	12 ~ 10	9 ~ 7	6 ~ 0
EXCELLENT	VERY GOOD	GOOD	NEEDS WORK

1) Mount St. Helens <u>lying</u> dormant for over 100 years before its powerful eruption on May 18, 1980.

   (A) NO CHANGE
   (B) lays
   (C) had lain
   (D) laid

2) Kuala Lumpur is not only Malaysia's most populous city, <u>but it is as well</u> the country's capital.

   (A) NO CHANGE
   (B) but it is also
   (C) and it is
   (D) being too

3) <u>Southern California receives sparse rainfall and has a large population. Southern</u> California must import most of its water from the Colorado River.

   Which choice most effectively combines the sentences at the underlined portion?

   (A) Receives sparse rainfall and with a large population, Southern
   (B) With rain sparsely falling and highly populated, Southern
   (C) Although receiving sparse rainfall and having a large population, Southern
   (D) Because of sparse rainfall and a large population, Southern

4) Five of the solar system's planets are visible from Earth without the aid of a <u>telescope: Mercury,</u> Venus, Mars, Jupiter, and Saturn.

   (A) NO CHANGE
   (B) telescope: they are Mercury,
   (C) telescope; Mercury,
   (D) telescope, being Mercury,

5) In television and film, Batman's nemesis the Joker has been played by <u>several prestigiously acclaimed actors,</u> including Caesar Romero, Jack Nicholson, and Heath Ledger.

   (A) NO CHANGE
   (B) several prestigious actors,
   (C) several prestigious, acclaimed actors,
   (D) numerous prestigious actors of acclaim,

6) The words "kayak" and "racecar" are <u>palindromes; due to the fact that</u> they are read the same backwards and forwards.

   (A) NO CHANGE
   (B) palindromes, so as a result
   (C) palindromes
   (D) palindromes because

7) <u>The Sargasso Sea is located in the middle of the Atlantic Ocean. Because the sea does</u> not connect to any land masses, it is called "The Sea Without a Shore."

   Which choice most effectively combines the sentences at the underlined portion?

   (A) Because the Sargasso Sea, which is located in the middle of the Atlantic Ocean, does
   (B) The Sargasso Sea is located in the middle of the Atlantic Ocean and does
   (C) Located in the middle of the Atlantic Ocean, the Sargasso Sea does
   (D) The Sargasso Sea, because it is located in the middle of the Atlantic Ocean, does

8) In August 2016 Rio de Janeiro, Brazil became the first South American city to <u>store</u> the Olympic Games.

   (A) NO CHANGE
   (B) have
   (C) embrace
   (D) host

9) Early civilizations tended to form in regions with arable soil, sufficient rainfall, <u>the climates were mild,</u> and populations already engaged in agriculture.

(A) NO CHANGE
(B) climates being mild,
(C) climates mildly,
(D) mild climates,

10) Tornadoes have occurred in every U.S. <u>state. they</u> most commonly occur in the central U.S.

Which choice most effectively combines the sentences at the underlined portion?

(A) state, seeing as they
(B) state, although they
(C) state, as a matter of fact they
(D) state; indeed, they

11) Kohl is an ancient form of mascara that is usually created by pulverizing the mineral stibnite into a charcoal-colored powder. <u>It is illegal to ship kohl into the United States because the substance has not been approved by the Food and Drug Administration.</u>

Which choice provides information that most effectively explains why ancient people used kohl?

(A) NO CHANGE
(B) At times, kohl becomes contaminated with lead, which can increase a wearers use of lead poisoning.
(C) The ancient Egyptians, who were among the first to wear kohl, believed it protected eyes from disease and sunlight.
(D) Kohl use has been recorded in South Asia, the Middle East, and much of Northern and Western Africa.

12) In 1898 the French government was quietly convicting a Jewish military officer of treason based on flimsy evidence when author Emile Zola <u>had drawn</u> public attention to the government's unjust actions by publishing the essay "J'accuse," or "I accuse."

(A) NO CHANGE
(B) drew
(C) was drawing
(D) would draw

13) Approximately ninety percent of people are right-handed, ten percent are left-handed, and only about one percent is <u>ambidextrous, meaning they can</u> use both their right and left hands skillfully.

(A) NO CHANGE
(B) ambidextrous, these people can
(C) ambidextrous; and able to
(D) ambidextrous—the ability to

14) The fossilized remains of dire wolves reveal that they possessed larger skulls and stockier builds than <u>a gray wolf.</u>

(A) NO CHANGE
(B) do gray wolves.
(C) that of gray wolves.
(D) that of a gray wolf.

15) Rachel Carson's 1962 book *Silent Spring* highlighted the many dangers of treating crops with the pesticide DDT, leading to a decrease in <u>it's</u> use.

(A) NO CHANGE
(B) its
(C) their
(D) which they

☑	1		4		7		10		13	
	2		5		8		11		14	
	3		6		9		12		15	

15 ~ 13	12 ~ 10	9 ~ 7	6 ~ 0
EXCELLENT	VERY GOOD	GOOD	NEEDS WORK

1) Some species of North American cicadas <u>dwells</u> underground for periods of 13 or 17 years, emerging for just a few weeks at the end of their life cycle to reproduce.

(A) NO CHANGE
(B) dwell
(C) has dwelt
(D) dwelling

2) In 1947 <u>Norwegian adventurer, Thor Heyerdahl, and five companions attempted</u> to sail a small wooden raft called *Kon Tiki* from South America to Polynesia to prove that Pre-Columbian Americans could have reached Polynesia by sea.

(A) NO CHANGE
(B) Norwegian adventurer Thor Heyerdahl and five companions, attempted
(C) Norwegian adventurer Thor Heyerdahl and five companions attempted
(D) Norwegian adventurer (Thor Heyerdahl) and five companions attempted

3) Robert Todd Lincoln, the eldest son of Abraham Lincoln, <u>studied law at Harvard in 1864,</u> serving as secretary of war under President Garfield and as minister to Great Britain under President Benjamin Harrison.

Which choice most effectively sets up the information that follows?

(A) NO CHANGE
(B) was late in enlisting in the Union Army during the Civil War,
(C) lived in Chicago for most of his adult life,
(D) enjoyed a successful political career,

4) The radiocarbon dating of stone tools and mastodon bones that were discovered at an underwater excavation site in Florida <u>reveals that humans</u> migrated to the Americas at least 14,500 years ago.

(A) NO CHANGE
(B) reveal that humans
(C) reveals when human's
(D) revealing when humans

5) An insightful writer about ordinary life, <u>and Alice Munro was filling</u> her short stories with the customs and speech of the Canadian plains.

(A) NO CHANGE
(B) Alice Munro filled
(C) because Alice Munro filled
(D) Alice Munro who filled

6) <u>Because</u> Texas has many man-made lakes, the state's only large natural lake is Caddo Lake, which sits on the border of Texas and Louisiana.

(A) NO CHANGE
(B) After
(C) Provided that
(D) Although

7) The Pulitzer Prize in Letters is among the <u>highest awards for literary</u> given in the United States.

(A) NO CHANGE
(B) highest literary awards
(C) awards that is the highest literary
(D) highest awarding for literature

8) The stylized piano compositions of 19th century Polish musician Frédéric Chopin are strongly <u>associated with</u> Romanticism and Nationalism.

(A) NO CHANGE
(B) associates of
(C) associated towards
(D) associates with

9) In 1974 *The Philosophical Review* published Thomas
Nagel's essay "What is it like to be a bat?", which
<u>vows</u> that objective accounts of others' perspectives
are impossible because each individual experiences
the world subjectively.

(A) NO CHANGE
(B) decrees
(C) contends
(D) confesses

10) <u>Sir Arthur C. Clarke was an influential science
fiction writer. He</u> famously claimed, "Magic's just
science we don't understand yet."

Which choice most effectively combines the
sentences at the underlined portion?

(A) Because Arthur C. Clarke was an influential
science fiction writer, he
(B) Arthur C. Clarke, being an influential science
fiction writer,
(C) Influential science fiction writer Arthur C.
Clarke
(D) An influential science fiction writer was Arthur
C. Clarke, who

11) To reach Temple Cave, the largest of Malaysia's
Batu Caves, <u>they</u> must climb 272 steps.

(A) NO CHANGE
(B) one
(C) he
(D) who

12) Television writers <u>Eileen Heisler and DeAnn Heline</u>
successful comedy series *The Middle* follows their
similarly successful work on *Murphy Brown* and
Rosanne.

(A) NO CHANGE
(B) Eileen Heisler's and DeAnn Heline's
(C) Eileen Heislers and DeAnn Helines'
(D) Eileen Heisler and DeAnn Heline's

13) Most, if not all, educators believe that everyone <u>are
inherently capable</u> of learning.

(A) NO CHANGE
(B) are of inherent capability
(C) is inherently capable
(D) are capable inherently

14) There are more trees on Earth than <u>there are stars in
the Milky Way Galaxy.</u>

(A) NO CHANGE
(B) numerous stars in the Milky Way Galaxy.
(C) the number of stars there are in the Milky Way
Galaxy.
(D) that of stars in the Milky Way Galaxy.

15) Weighing over 2,000 pounds, the extinct North
American short-faced bear was one of the largest
mammalian land predators, <u>although none remain
today.</u>

(A) NO CHANGE
(B) and was quite massive.
(C) that ate meat.
(D) DELETE the underlined portion, and place a
period after "predators."

✓	1		4		7		10		13	
	2		5		8		11		14	
	3		6		9		12		15	

15 ~ 13	12 ~ 10	9 ~ 7	6 ~ 0
EXCELLENT	VERY GOOD	GOOD	NEEDS WORK

1) If a court case is dismissed "with prejudice," it is dismissed permanently and cannot <u>be brought</u> back to court.

(A) NO CHANGE
(B) bring
(C) be bringing
(D) have brought

2) For the Maori people of New Zealand, intricate patterns tattooed on an individual's face <u>assign</u> his or her tribe, family background, and status; the patterns are considered sacred.

(A) NO CHANGE
(B) depict
(C) signify
(D) signpost

3) Unemployment rates in the United States during the Great Depression were the highest in the nation's history, <u>which exceeded</u> 23 percent in 1932.

(A) NO CHANGE
(B) where they exceeded
(C) exceeded
(D) exceeding

4) Professional runner Dean Karnazes is probably best known for having run 350 miles <u>over the course of</u> nearly 81 sleepless hours.

(A) NO CHANGE
(B) through a course
(C) coursing through
(D) over of course

5) During the American Revolutionary War, a sixteen-year-old Sybil Ludington rode 40 miles on horseback to alert <u>soldier</u> of her father's volunteer army about incoming British troops.

(A) NO CHANGE
(B) members
(C) the troop
(D) minuteman

6) In the United States, a product's packaging must tell consumers what <u>they contain.</u>

(A) NO CHANGE
(B) it contains.
(C) its containing.
(D) there containing.

7) <u>Oscar Wilde was a devout classics scholar. His literature is peppered</u> with references to Hellenistic culture and mythology.

Which choice most effectively combines the sentences at the underlined portion?

(A) Oscar Wilde's literature, a devout classics scholar, is peppered
(B) The literature of Oscar Wilde, a devout classics scholar, is peppered
(C) As a devout classics scholar, the literature of Oscar Wilde is peppered
(D) A devout classics scholar's literature is that of Oscar Wilde, which is peppered

8) The cattle population of Texas is higher than <u>Nebraska.</u>

(A) NO CHANGE
(B) the one in Nebraska.
(C) that of Nebraska.
(D) of Nebraska.

9) The eyes of animals are subject to all of the various disorders <u>that affect human vision.</u>

(A) NO CHANGE
(B) affecting humans.
(C) affecting them of humans.
(D) that human vision is affected.

10) The Warsaw Radio Mast, a 2,120-foot radio tower, was the tallest structure ever built until <u>2010; the</u> 2,722-foot Burj Khalifa was completed in Dubai.

(A) NO CHANGE
(B) 2010 and the
(C) 2010 at which time the
(D) 2010, when the

11) Although Daniel never studied and hardly paid attention in class, he never received anything less than an "A" on a calculus test. "I just don't understand how you're so good at <u>math?" his</u> friend Andrew said to him.

(A) NO CHANGE
(B) math." His
(C) math," his
(D) math…" his

12) Founded in 1875, <u>in Cincinnati, Ohio is Hebrew Union College, the oldest existing Jewish seminary in the United States.</u>

(A) NO CHANGE
(B) being the oldest existing Jewish seminary in the United States is Hebrew Union College in Cincinnati, Ohio.
(C) a Jewish seminary called Hebrew Union College in Cincinnati, Ohio is the oldest existing Jewish seminary in the United States.
(D) Hebrew Union College in Cincinnati, Ohio is the oldest existing Jewish seminary in the United States.

13) After months of deliberation, the city council <u>reflected</u> Mr. Hornby's proposal to renovate the public library.

(A) NO CHANGE
(B) excepted
(C) incepted
(D) accepted

14) A photon of light emitted from the surface of the Sun takes <u>approximately eight minutes</u> to reach Earth.

(A) NO CHANGE
(B) about approximately eight minutes
(C) approximately eight minutes of traveling
(D) about eight minutes and it travels

15) <u>Jefferson Davis was President of the Confederate States of America during the American Civil War. Before his presidency, Davis</u> served as a U.S. Representative and Senator from Mississippi as well as the Secretary of War under President Pierce.

Which choice most effectively combines the sentences at the underlined portion?

(A) Jefferson Davis was President of the Confederate States of America during the American Civil War; before all this happened, he
(B) Before becoming President of the Confederate States of America during the American Civil War, Jefferson Davis
(C) President of the Confederate States of America during the American Civil War, Jefferson Davis also (before his presidency)
(D) Jefferson Davis, before he becomes the President of the Confederate States of America during the American Civil War,

☑	1		4		7		10		13	
	2		5		8		11		14	
	3		6		9		12		15	

15 ~ 13	12 ~ 10	9 ~ 7	6 ~ 0
EXCELLENT	VERY GOOD	GOOD	NEEDS WORK

1) American <u>writer</u> Edgar Allan Poe and Nathaniel Hawthorne were both interested in the darker aspects of the human soul.

(A) NO CHANGE
(B) wordsmith
(C) authors
(D) novelist's

2) <u>The art critic had a son,</u> William Pène du Bois wrote and illustrated children's books, his best known work being *The Twenty-One Balloons.*

(A) NO CHANGE
(B) He was the son of an art critic,
(C) The art critic having a son,
(D) The son of an art critic,

3) As the least massive planet in the solar system, Mercury's surface gravity is just 38 percent of Earth's surface gravity. <u>Thus, a person who weighs 150 pounds on Earth would weigh 57 pounds on Mercury.</u>

The writer wants to provide a statistic that supports the information in the previous sentence. Which choice best accomplishes this goal?

(A) NO CHANGE
(B) The surface gravity of Venus, however, is 91 percent of Earth's surface gravity.
(C) Moreover, Mercury is the closest planet to the Sun.
(D) The planet is named for the Roman messenger god, who is called "Hermes" in Greek mythology.

4) About 300 million years ago, the seven continents that exist today were joined into one <u>supercontinent, that is called</u> "Pangea."

(A) NO CHANGE
(B) supercontinent, called
(C) supercontinent, it is called
(D) supercontinent called

5) <u>The Cambodian temple-complex of Angkor Wat was constructed in the 12th century. It</u> is the largest religious monument in the world.

Which choice most effectively combines the sentences at the underlined portion?

(A) Constructed in the 12th century, the Cambodian temple-complex of Angkor Wat
(B) Because the Cambodian temple-complex of Angkor Wat was constructed in the 12th century, it
(C) In the 12th century the Cambodian temple-complex Angkor Wat was constructed, so it
(D) The Cambodian temple-complex of Angkor Wat was constructed in the 12th century while it

6) Belief in spontaneous generation, whereby certain organisms could arise from nonliving matter, persisted until the 19th century, when it <u>is disproven</u> by the experiments of Louis Pasteur.

(A) NO CHANGE
(B) was disproven
(C) disproves
(D) could disprove

7) Before Australian musician Sia Furler found international success with her single "Chandelier," she wrote songs for many pop artists, including <u>Rihanna, Beyoncé, and the pop artist Brittney Spears.</u>

(A) NO CHANGE
(B) Rihanna, the artist Beyoncé, and also Brittney Spears.
(C) Rihanna, Beyoncé, and Brittney Spears.
(D) artists Rihanna, Beyoncé, Brittney Spears.

8) Tofu, which is processed from soybeans, <u>are</u> high in protein and can be used as a meat substitute.

(A) NO CHANGE
(B) being
(C) be
(D) is

9) A giraffe's tongue is almost black in color, <u>something most people notice when they watch the animal feed by stripping leaves from branches at the zoo.</u>

Which choice provides the most relevant details explaining why giraffes have black tongues?

(A) NO CHANGE
(B) probably to protect it from being sunburned during the many hours the animal spends feeding each day.
(C) and the animal is the tallest extant land animal on the planet.
(D) and it can measure up to 20 inches, its length helping the animal reach the leaves of high-up branches.

10) In 1989, Cahomy Thipyaso of Thailand was found guilty of corporate fraud and subsequently <u>given</u> the longest prison sentence ever handed down, 141,078 years.

(A) NO CHANGE
(B) giving
(C) to give
(D) had given

11) The ancient Aztecs played a ball game called *ullamaliztli*, in which two opposing teams tried to get a heavy rubber ball through a hoop without <u>enabling</u> the ball to touch the ground.

(A) NO CHANGE
(B) allocating
(C) allowing
(D) authorizing

12) Cryptozoologists search for supposedly extinct or folkloric <u>creatures, the</u> field is considered a pseudoscience because it relies on second-hand accounts and anecdotal evidence.

(A) NO CHANGE
(B) creatures and the
(C) creatures; the
(D) creatures while

13) Daria spent the weeks before her trip to Mexico <u>sweeping up</u> her Spanish-speaking skills by reviewing her old textbooks from Spanish class.

(A) NO CHANGE
(B) brushing up on
(C) dusting
(D) vacuuming up

14) Dionysus, the Greek God of revelry, wine, and theater, is often depicted holding a pinecone-topped, <u>covered in ivy</u> staff called a "thyrsus."

(A) NO CHANGE
(B) with ivy covering it
(C) being ivy-covered
(D) ivy-covered

15) Evidence that the Sahara desert began drying out in about 4000 BCE includes prehistoric humans' rock paintings showing <u>less hippos</u> and more camels.

(A) NO CHANGE
(B) fewer hippos
(C) least hippos
(D) lesser hippos

☑	1		4		7		10		13	
	2		5		8		11		14	
	3		6		9		12		15	

15 ~ 13	12 ~ 10	9 ~ 7	6 ~ 0
EXCELLENT	VERY GOOD	GOOD	NEEDS WORK

CHAPTER 2

1) During the 19th century, the average height of a wealthy Englishman was significantly greater than <u>those of a poor Englishman.</u>

(A) NO CHANGE
(B) that of a poor Englishman.
(C) a poor Englishman.
(D) averages for poor Englishmen.

2) <u>If</u> over 70 percent of the Earth's surface is covered in water, only about 1 percent of that water is accessible and potable.

(A) NO CHANGE
(B) Because
(C) Despite
(D) Although

3) <u>The naming of the element Lawrencium for Ernest O. Lawrence,</u> the inventor of the cyclotron.

(A) NO CHANGE
(B) Ernest O. Lawrence named the element Lawrencium,
(C) Ernest O. Lawrence's name is the origin of the element Lawrencium,
(D) The element Lawrencium was named for Ernest O. Lawrence,

4) Treating wood with creosote, a preservative formed from distilled tars, <u>helps it</u> resist moisture and decay.

(A) NO CHANGE
(B) help it
(C) help them
(D) helps them

5) <u>There was a time once when it was</u> a large whaling port, New London, Connecticut is now home to the United States Coast Guard Academy.

(A) NO CHANGE
(B) Having at one time been
(C) Being at one time
(D) Once

6) Although wild gorillas abandon their sleeping nests after one night's use, researchers can gather a great deal of information from <u>them.</u>

(A) NO CHANGE
(B) the gorillas.
(C) the nests.
(D) it.

7) Many works of science fiction and fantasy offer commentary on real-world political and social situations. <u>In 2013 Solomon Northrop's 1853 autobiography *Twelve Years a Slave* was made into a critically acclaimed film.</u>

Which choice contains information that best supports the information in the sentence above?

(A) NO CHANGE
(B) For instance, Joe Halderman's 1974 science fiction novel *The Forever War* was heavily influenced by the author's experiences while serving in the U.S. armed forces during the Vietnam War.
(C) Some of the most influential science fiction authors of the 20th century include Isaac Asimov, Philip K. Dick, and Ursula Le Guin.
(D) Moreover, J.R.R. Tolkien's *Lord of the Rings* trilogy shaped the landscape of epic fantasy for decades after its publication, and is still praised today for its memorable characters and detailed, nuanced world-building.

8) Under the pen name Dr. Seuss, American author Theodore Geisel wrote 46 children's <u>books, many</u> of which are still widely read today.

(A) NO CHANGE
(B) books; many
(C) books and many
(D) books, and many

9) Each year, Columbia University awards twenty-one Pulitzer Prizes for achievements in journalists, literature, and musical composition.

(A) NO CHANGE
(B) doing journalism,
(C) journalism,
(D) a journalist,

10) Spanish explorer Juan Rodrigo Cabrillo was the first European to explore the California coast. He landed two ships in San Diego Bay and claimed the land for Spain in 1542.

Which choice most effectively combines the sentences at the underlined portion?

(A) Because he was a Spanish explorer, Juan Rodrigo Cabrillo was the first European to explore the California coast, and he landed
(B) A Spanish explorer, Juan Rodrigo Cabrillo being the first European to explore the California coast, landed
(C) Spanish explorer, Juan Rodrigo Cabrillo, and the first European to explore the California coast, landed
(D) Spanish explorer Juan Rodrigo Cabrillo, the first European to explore the California coast, landed

11) Lying south of Amman, Jordan, during Roman times the ancient city of Petra was one of the centers of Arab culture.

(A) NO CHANGE
(B) the ancient city of Petra was one of the centers of Arab culture during Roman times.
(C) one of the centers of Arab culture during Roman times was the ancient city of Petra.
(D) one of Arab culture's centers was the ancient city of Petra during Roman times.

12) The *caste system is a social* structure that once dominated Indian society wherein occupation and status are inherited from one's parents.

(A) NO CHANGE
(B) *system*: a social
(C) *system*, being a social
(D) *system*, it is a social

13) Foods labeled "low-fat" may seem healthier than their full-fat counterparts. Manufacturers of "low-fat" foods often replace the fats with unhealthy amounts of sugar.

Which choice most effectively combines the sentences at the underlined portion?

(A) counterparts; manufacturers
(B) counterparts, so manufacturers
(C) counterparts, but manufacturers
(D) counterparts, since manufacturers

14) Although the early efforts of playwright Tennessee Williams failed to achieve critical or commercial success, he sheltered his place as one of the 20th century's greatest playwrights with *The Glass Menagerie* and *A Streetcar Named Desire*.

(A) NO CHANGE
(B) secured
(C) shielded
(D) appropriated

15) The candidate's involvement in an embezzlement scandal had an adverse effect on his overall popularity and jeopardized his chances of winning the upcoming election.

(A) NO CHANGE
(B) an averse
(C) an inverse
(D) a universal

☑	1		4		7		10		13	
	2		5		8		11		14	
	3		6		9		12		15	

15 ~ 13	12 ~ 10	9 ~ 7	6 ~ 0
EXCELLENT	VERY GOOD	GOOD	NEEDS WORK

1) The fangtooth fish, named for its large, needle-like teeth, is one of the deepest-dwelling sea creatures, <u>had</u> been found at depths of about 16,000 feet.

(A) NO CHANGE
(B) has
(C) have
(D) having

2) In 2016 a team of Australian engineers developed the most efficient solar cells to <u>date. The</u> 11-square-inch cells are able to convert 34.5 percent of the sun's energy to electricity without the use of mirrors or other concentrators.

Which choice most effectively combines the sentences at the underlined portion?

(A) date; the
(B) date, yet the
(C) date, if the
(D) date, whereas the

3) Individuals with O negative blood are considered universal <u>donors, their</u> red blood cells can be received by any blood type.

(A) NO CHANGE
(B) donors: their
(C) donors yet their
(D) donors, moreover, their

4) Many of the fruits and vegetables consumed by humans are the results of millennia of artificial selection. <u>Although wild bananas are fairly small and have many seeds, they still have an outer casing that must be peeled away.</u>

Which choice provides an example that best supports the information in the previous sentence?

(A) NO CHANGE
(B) Although it may surprise many Americans, mangoes are actually the most consumed fruit in the world.
(C) The world's largest green cabbage was grown by John Evans in 1998; it weighed an astounding 76 pounds.
(D) In fact, corn was developed from a type of grass called teosinte in North America starting about 10,000 years ago.

5) <u>Sharks, rays, and a chimera are</u> the only extant groups of cartilaginous fish.

(A) NO CHANGE
(B) Sharks, rays and the chimera is
(C) Sharks, rays, and chimera are
(D) Sharks, rays, and chimera is

6) The ancient Greek philosopher and mathematician Pythagoras is one of the first known vegetarians, as <u>he and his pupils</u> abstained from consuming meat for moral and ethical reasons.

(A) NO CHANGE
(B) his pupils and him
(C) himself and his pupils
(D) his pupils plus himself

7) The city of Cincinnati, Ohio is named in honor of Roman statesman Lucius Quinctius Cincinnatus, who was elected dictator when Rome needed strong military leadership, and who <u>avoided</u> his position once the empire had been secured and stabilized.

(A) NO CHANGE
(B) abdicated
(C) discarded
(D) disowned

8) <u>Those of Switzerland consume</u> more chocolate per capita than any other country in the world.

(A) NO CHANGE
(B) The people of Switzerland consume
(C) Switzerland consumes
(D) In Switzerland is consumed

9) The majority of Facebook's revenue <u>is generated through</u> advertisements, which secured the company over $17 billion in 2015.

(A) NO CHANGE
(B) generates by means of
(C) has a generation of
(D) is generations by which

10) Flynn's room was immaculate: his clothes neatly folded in his dresser, <u>with a freshly vacuumed carpet,</u> and his desk dusted and free of clutter.

(A) NO CHANGE
(B) just having vacuumed his carpet,
(C) he had just vacuumed his carpet,
(D) his carpet freshly vacuumed,

11) American hip hop artist Chancelor Bennet, better known by his stage name Chance the Rapper, has achieved <u>being critically and commercially successful</u> despite not being signed to a major record label.

(A) NO CHANGE
(B) critical, commercial success
(C) critically and commercial success
(D) critical and commercial success

12) Some <u>has claimed</u> that elephants are the only land mammals that cannot jump, yet rhinoceroses, hippopotamuses, and sloths are also unable to jump.

(A) NO CHANGE
(B) have claimed
(C) claiming
(D) claims

13) <u>Priests, of the ancient Celtic people, in Northern Europe</u> were called "Druids," a name which some scholars translate as "knowing oak trees."

(A) NO CHANGE
(B) Priests of the ancient Celtic people, in Northern Europe,
(C) Priests of the ancient, Celtic people, in Northern Europe,
(D) Priests of the ancient Celtic people in Northern Europe

14) In the Academy Award winning film *Amadeus*, renowned composer Wolfgang Amadeus Mozart is physically and psychologically destroyed by rival composer Antonio <u>Salieri. Mozart</u> likely died from a fever.

Which choice most effectively combines the sentences at the underlined portion?

(A) Salieri, so really, Mozart
(B) Salieri, but in reality, Mozart
(C) Salieri, proving that Mozart
(D) Salieri because Mozart

15) In 2013 Pfizer grossed over 4.7 billion dollars in global sales, making <u>it</u> the top earning pharmaceutical company in the world.

(A) NO CHANGE
(B) themselves
(C) them
(D) one

☑	1		4		7		10		13	
	2		5		8		11		14	
	3		6		9		12		15	

15 ~ 13	12 ~ 10	9 ~ 7	6 ~ 0
EXCELLENT	VERY GOOD	GOOD	NEEDS WORK

10 min. 34   34   34   34   34

CHAPTER 2

1) The mosquito-borne Zika virus causes flu-like symptoms in most victims, but it may cause microcephaly (Microcephaly is a condition characterized by abnormal smallness of the head.) in babies born to mothers affected by the virus.

(A) NO CHANGE
(B) (microcephaly) abnormal smallness (of the head) in
(C) microcephaly: (abnormal smallness of the head) in
(D) microcephaly (abnormal smallness of the head) in

2) Alligators are fast swimmers and can move surprisingly quickly on land in short bursts. They spend most of their time lying in wait so they can ambush unsuspecting prey.

Which choice most effectively combines the sentences at the underlined portion?

(A) bursts, spending
(B) bursts, but they spend
(C) bursts, when they spend
(D) bursts, in fact spending

3) Members of the art movement known as Dadaism, which arose in central Europe during the early 20th century, attempted to subvert the capitalist and nationalist sentiments that they believed incited World War I.

(A) NO CHANGE
(B) which arising
(C) who arose
(D) whom arising

4) The monkey deity Hanuman, who helps Lord Rāma defeat the evil Rāvana in the epic *Ramayana*, is regarded as representations of loyalty and selflessness.

(A) NO CHANGE
(B) a symbol
(C) figures
(D) the characterizations

5) Poet and novelist Hilda Doolittle was among the leading female figures in Imagism, a style of poetry that declined the expansiveness of Romantic poetry in favor of conciseness.

(A) NO CHANGE
(B) forgot
(C) rejected
(D) shunned

6) An alloy is a metal that is formed by combining two or more metallic elements. One example of an alloy is brass, which made of copper and zinc.

The author wants to elaborate on the information in the previous sentence by explaining the function(s) of alloys. Which choice best accomplishes this goal?

(A) NO CHANGE
(B) Base metals, such as zinc and copper, are commonplace whereas precious metals, such as silver and gold, are rarer and more valuable.
(C) Of all pure metals, tungsten has the highest melting point, which is above 6,100 degrees Fahrenheit.
(D) Often, alloys are manufactured because they are stronger or more resistant to corrosion than elemental metals.

7) There are a number of environmental conditions that may cause the green flash phenomenon, wherein a brief flash of green light follows a sunset or precedes a sunrise.

(A) NO CHANGE
(B) Their are
(C) There is
(D) Their is

8) In 1800 until 1865, it is estimated that up to 100,000 slaves escaped the Southern United States via a secret network of homes called the "Underground Railroad."

(A) NO CHANGE
(B) Between 1800 and 1865,
(C) From 1800 and 1865,
(D) The years 1800 until 1865,

9) The peregrine falcon can reach speeds upwards of 200 miles per hour when diving for prey, making them the fastest animal on Earth.

(A) NO CHANGE
(B) themselves
(C) him
(D) it

10) If baseball is traditionally cited as "America's favorite pastime," many will argue that professional football is a more popular and beloved spectator sport.

(A) NO CHANGE
(B) Although
(C) Because
(D) Provided that

11) The Dead Sea is like the Great Salt Lake is uninhabitable for all but a few life forms.

(A) NO CHANGE
(B) Like the Dead Sea,
(C) Although the Dead Sea is like
(D) It is like the Dead Sea,

12) For centuries, industrial and agricultural activities have released excessive carbon dioxide into the atmosphere, about a quarter of which is absorbed by the ocean. As the ocean's carbon dioxide levels increase, its pH decreases, a process known as *ocean acidification*.

Which choice most effectively combines the sentences at the underlined portion?

(A) ocean; as
(B) ocean, yet as
(C) ocean because as
(D) ocean, seeing as

13) First receiving attention for his surrealistic portraits, recognition came to Jackson Pollock later for his innovative abstract expressionist murals, which he created by dripping liquid paint directly onto canvas.

(A) NO CHANGE
(B) his innovative abstract expressionist murals brought Jackson Pollock recognition later,
(C) Jackson Pollock was later recognized for his innovative abstract expressionist murals,
(D) Jackson Pollock's innovative abstract expressionist murals brought him recognition later,

14) After juries acquitted defendants in several high-profile American court trials in the 1990s, a Massachusetts judge, Hiller B. Zobel, said that the jury system being the way of courts reaching verdicts was "asking the ignorant to use the incomprehensible to decide the unknowable."

(A) NO CHANGE
(B) juries were essentially
(C) that relying on juries for verdicts was
(D) that using juries to come to a verdict of guilty or not guilty meant

15) Sumo wrestling develops in Japan centuries ago, during the Edo Period (1603 – 1863), and is the country's oldest sport.

(A) NO CHANGE
(B) has developed
(C) is developing
(D) developed

☑	1		4		7		10		13	
	2		5		8		11		14	
	3		6		9		12		15	

15 ~ 13	12 ~ 10	9 ~ 7	6 ~ 0
EXCELLENT	VERY GOOD	GOOD	NEEDS WORK

CHAPTER 2

1) Mexico City, the capital of Mexico, is pumping so much water from its underground aquifers that everything in the city <u>sink</u> several inches each year.

(A) NO CHANGE
(B) are sinking
(C) is sinking
(D) would be sinking

2) <u>Harlequin-type ichthyosis is a rare genetic disease. Those</u> affected are born with thin skin that cracks instead of folds, which allows pathogens to enter the body more easily.

Which choice most effectively combines the sentences at the underlined portion?

(A) A rare genetic disease, harlequin-type ichthyosis causes those
(B) Harlequin-type ichthyosis, a rare genetic disease, and those
(C) Harlequin-type ichthyosis is a rare genetic disease, so those
(D) Harlequin-type ichthyosis is a rare genetic disease; those

3) In United States law, <u>an individual</u> who feels that he or she has been wrongly imprisoned or is being kept under inhumane conditions may request that a court review the circumstances of the imprisonment by filling out a writ of *habeas corpus.*

(A) NO CHANGE
(B) individuals
(C) people
(D) the people

4) According to archaeological evidence, the area around Lake Neuchatel in western Switzerland <u>being inhabited</u> for about 13,000 years.

(A) NO CHANGE
(B) is inhabited
(C) has habitation
(D) has been inhabited
(E) having had inhabitation

5) Riding horses at full gallop while turning around in their saddles to shoot arrows backward <u>were hallmarks</u> of the ancient Parthians.

(A) NO CHANGE
(B) was a hallmark of
(C) hallmarked
(D) were hallmarking

6) <u>After working as machinists on a farm,</u> John and Horace Dodge decided to start their own automobile manufacturing company in 1914.

(A) NO CHANGE
(B) They worked as machinists on a farm and after,
(C) Working as machinists on a farm, afterwards
(D) They worked as machinists on a farm,

7) In William Shakespeare's play King Lear, the king banishes his youngest daughter, Cordelia, because she makes <u>less pronouncements</u> of her love for him than her sisters do.

(A) NO CHANGE
(B) less of a pronouncement
(C) littler pronouncements
(D) fewer pronouncements

8) While the populations of both China and India exceed one billion, the population of China is greater than <u>that of India.</u>

(A) NO CHANGE
(B) India.
(C) in India.
(D) the number of Indians.

9) It is estimated that <u>about 100 African elephants are illegally killed in the wilderness each and every day</u> simply so that their tusks can be turned into decorative objects.

(A) NO CHANGE
(B) wilderness-roaming elephants are killed, illegally, up to 100 daily in Africa
(C) poachers kill about 100 wild African elephants every day
(D) elephant killings happen daily

10) Each time you recall a past event, you are remembering the version of the event that you last <u>recalled; not</u> the event itself.

(A) NO CHANGE
(B) recalled, not
(C) recalled not
(D) recalled so not

11) Calling someone a "Neanderthal" is often meant as an insult, implying that the person is unintelligent or uncivilized. However, <u>Neanderthals lived throughout modern-day Europe, and likely had contact with modern humans for thousands of years.</u>

Which choice most effectively refutes the claim made in the sentence above?

(A) NO CHANGE
(B) Neanderthals are believed to have died off about 30,000 to 40,000 years ago, either because of climate change or through interactions with modern humans.
(C) based on fossil evidence, Neanderthals were, on average, larger than modern humans.
(D) archaeological evidence suggest that Neanderthals created tools, used fire, and maintained complex social systems.

12) Although many geologists maintain <u>when the Grand Canyon formed</u> by the flow of the Colorado River about 6 million years ago, some argue that it formed up to 17 million years ago.

(A) NO CHANGE
(B) the Grand Canyon forming
(C) that the Grand Canyon was formed
(D) that the Grand Canyon, having formed

13) September of 1975 must have been a difficult month for former President Gerald Ford, <u>who</u> faced two assassination attempts that month, both of which occurred in California.

(A) NO CHANGE
(B) he
(C) whom
(D) which

14) When the lewd, frequently <u>abusive</u> sitcom It's *Always Sunny in Philadelphia* first aired on a shoestring budget in 2005, few would have guessed that it would go on to become one of the longest running comedy shows of all time.

(A) NO CHANGE
(B) offensive
(C) hostile
(D) incursive

15) Located in Busan, South Korea, the Buddhist temple Beomeosa was established over 1,300 years ago, although <u>many of its original and earliest structures were destroyed</u> during the Japanese invasion in the 16th century.

(A) NO CHANGE
(B) many of its original structures were destroyed
(C) many were destroyed
(D) many of its original structures were destroyed and ruined

☑	1		4		7		10		13	
	2		5		8		11		14	
	3		6		9		12		15	

15 ~ 13	12 ~ 10	9 ~ 7	6 ~ 0
EXCELLENT	VERY GOOD	GOOD	NEEDS WORK

1) Just as "Bollywood" refers to India's Hollywood-like film industry, "Nollywood" <u>refers to Nigeria's Hollywood-like film industry.</u>

(A) NO CHANGE
(B) refers to Nigeria's.
(C) refers to those in Nigeria.
(D) refers to Nigeria.

2) Many science fiction films and television shows depict space battles that are filled with a cacophony of laser fire and <u>explosions. No</u> sound can travel in the near-perfect vacuum of outer space.

Which choice most effectively combines the sentences at the underlined potion?

(A) explosions: no
(B) explosions, so no
(C) explosions, yet no
(D) explosions; indeed, no

3) George Washington owned more than 100 slaves throughout his life. <u>Paradoxically,</u> he privately opposed slavery, claiming in a letter to a friend, "There is not a man living who wishes more sincerely than I do, to see a plan adopted for the abolition of slavery."

(A) NO CHANGE
(B) Of course,
(C) For this reason,
(D) Conclusively,

4) In the aftermath of the San Francisco earthquake of 1989, <u>the Red Cross operates out of</u> an emergency headquarters in Santa Cruz, set up a temporary "tent city" for the homeless.

(A) NO CHANGE
(B) the Red Cross operated out of
(C) the Red Cross, operating out of
(D) the Red Cross, to operate out of

5) You can always see <u>bolts of lightning</u> strike before you hear the thunder it produces because light travels faster than sound.

(A) NO CHANGE
(B) lightning's bolts
(C) the bolts that lightning produces
(D) a bolt of lightning

6) Octopuses in captivity have been known to figure out ways of escaping their tanks, sometimes <u>sneaking</u> into neighboring tanks to feed on the organisms contained within.

(A) NO CHANGE
(B) sneak
(C) they sneak
(D) they have been known to sneak

7) The film scores of American composer John Williams, which include *Star Wars*, *Jaws*, *Indiana Jones*, and three of the *Harry Potter* films, <u>being</u> among cinema's most recognizable.

(A) NO CHANGE
(B) which are
(C) are
(D) is

8) Before France and Spain sided with the United States during the American Revolutionary War in 1778 and 1779 <u>respectively,</u> both countries supplied American troops with arms, ammunition, and other supplies.

(A) NO CHANGE
(B) receptively,
(C) respectfully,
(D) responsively,

9) American historian Arthur Schlesinger won the Pulitzer Prize for Biography or Autobiography in 1966 for *A Thousand Days: John F. Kennedy in the White House*, an <u>excuse for</u> the Kennedy administration from 1960 to 1963.

(A) NO CHANGE
(B) account of
(C) definition of
(D) decision by

10) Andrew Lloyd Webber's musical *The Phantom of the Opera* has been performed on Broadway more than <u>the others.</u>

(A) NO CHANGE
(B) any other musical in history.
(C) the performance of others.
(D) the history of musical theater.

11) A pioneer of the free verse poetic form, Walt Whitman served as a nurse during the Civil War, worked as journalist, and <u>traveling across the United States.</u>

(A) NO CHANGE
(B) traveled across the United States.
(C) who traveled across the United States.
(D) he had traveled across the United States.

12) <u>Former President Theodore Roosevelt was born with severe asthma. At the age of 11 he began a vigorous exercise regime that</u> virtually eliminated the symptoms of his illness.   D

Which choice most effectively combines the sentences at the underlined portion?

(A) Born with severe asthma, at the age of 11 former President Theodore Roosevelt began a vigorous exercise regime and it
(B) Having begun a vigorous exercise regime at the age of 11, Theodore Roosevelt, who was born with severe asthma, found that it
(C) At the age of 11, although he was born with severe asthma, former President Theodore Roosevelt found that a vigorous exercise regime
(D) Born with severe asthma, former President Theodore Roosevelt began a vigorous exercise regime at the age of 11 that

13) <u>The short life of a housefly seldom (over a month) consists</u> of four stages: egg, larva, pupa, and adult.

(A) NO CHANGE
(B) The short life (of a housefly), seldom over a month, consists
(C) The (short life of) a housefly, which is seldom over a month, consists
(D) The short life of a housefly (seldom over a month) consists

14) <u>Whereas professional swimmers are often fairly tall, professional divers are usually relatively short.</u> For instance, American swimmer Michael Phelps is 6 feet 4 inches tall, yet his arm span measures 6 feet 7 inches.

Which sentence provides general information that most effectively sets up the information that follows it?

(A) NO CHANGE
(B) Professional swimmers are often taller than the population at large.
(C) The arm span of the average man is equal to his height, but many professional swimmers have longer-than-average arm spans.
(D) An individual's arm span is measured as the distance from the tip of one middle finger to the tip of the other when his or her arms are outstretched at ninety degree angles.

15) Aquatic mammals, such as <u>dolphins and whales,</u> get all the fresh water their bodies need through the metabolic breakdown of food.

(A) NO CHANGE
(B) the dolphin and whales,
(C) dolphins and the whale,
(D) dolphins or whales,

✓	1		4		7		10		13	
	2		5		8		11		14	
	3		6		9		12		15	

15 ~ 13	12 ~ 10	9 ~ 7	6 ~ 0
EXCELLENT	VERY GOOD	GOOD	NEEDS WORK

CHAPTER 2

1) Robert Clifton Weaver, <u>the African American who was the first one</u> to head a federal department, was Secretary of Housing and Urban Development from 1966 to 1968 under President Lyndon Johnson.

(A) NO CHANGE
(B) was the first African American
(C) the first African American
(D) firstly the African American

2) When Igor Stravinsky's ballet *The Rite of Spring* premiered in 1913, its avant-garde music and choreography as well as its pagan themes nearly <u>incited</u> a riot among audience members.

(A) NO CHANGE
(B) persuaded
(C) swayed
(D) fostered

3) Sunlight is essential to human health: the energy from sunlight's UVB rays <u>convert</u> a type of cholesterol stored in the skin to vitamin D.

(A) NO CHANGE
(B) is converting
(C) are converting
(D) converts

4) The Korean dish called *gimbap* consists of sliced vegetables or meat covered in steamed <u>rice. These ingredients are</u> wrapped in dried seaweed and served in bite-sized slices.

Which choice most effectively combines the sentences at the underlined portion?

(A) rice is
(B) rice; being
(C) rice and they are
(D) rice, all of which is

5) The acquittal of four Los Angeles police officers of the use of excessive force in the arrest of black American Rodney King sparked a series of riots in Los Angeles County that resulted in 55 deaths, <u>casualties of over 2,000,</u> and nearly $1 billion in property damage.

(A) NO CHANGE
(B) over 2,000 casualties,
(C) casualties upwards of 2,000,
(D) over 2,000 people were casualties,

6) Claims that Betsy Ross designed and sewed the first American flag are <u>doubted because they are baffling,</u> as there is no reliable documentation that Ross met with any of the revolution's leaders regarding the flag's design or creation.

(A) NO CHANGE
(B) doubts,
(C) dubious,
(D) undoubtedly baffling in nature,

7) A body of relatively shallow and still water <u>that is separated</u> from the sea by a sandbank or reef is called a "lagoon."

(A) NO CHANGE
(B) where there is separation
(C) which, being separated,
(D) having been separated

8) Although there are over 7 billion people alive today, humans are far from the most numerous animal species on the planet. In fact, <u>the smallest mammal species are the Etruscan shrew and a type of bat found in Thailand.</u>

Which choice most effectively supports the topic introduced in the first sentence?

(A) NO CHANGE
(B) the world's population of humans has more than doubled since 1970.
(C) As of 2016, the International Union for the Conservation of Nature (IUCN) has identified over 41,000 species whose populations are threatened.
(D) it has been estimated that there are from 1 to 2 million ants for every human.

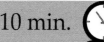
9) The Frisians are an ethnic group who inhabit some of the coastal regions of the Netherlands and Germany. Their language is more closely related to contemporary English than any other language.

Which choice most effectively combines the sentences at the underlined portion?

(A) The language of the Frisians, an ethnic group who inhabit some of the coastal regions of the Netherlands and Germany, is
(B) The Frisians, who speak their own language and who inhabit some of the coastal regions of the Netherlands and Germany, are
(C) Inhabiting some of the coastal regions of the Netherlands and Germany, the language of the Frisians is
(D) The Frisians inhabit some of the coastal regions of the Netherlands and Germany; they are an ethnic group, their language being

10) Shakespeare's use of soliloquy, wherein a character speaks his or her thoughts aloud, will allow audiences to better understand a character's psyche and inner turmoil.

(A) NO CHANGE
(B) allows
(C) had allowed
(D) is allowing

11) Charlemagne, King of the Franks and the first Holy Roman Emperor, stood over six feet tall, making him much taller than the height of the average man from his era.

(A) NO CHANGE
(B) greater in terms of height than the average male of his time.
(C) taller than the average male of his time.
(D) more than an average man from his era.

12) The only elements that are (liquids at room temperature) approximately 72 degrees Fahrenheit are mercury and bromine.

(A) NO CHANGE
(B) liquids (at room temperature) approximately 72 degrees Fahrenheit, are mercury and bromine.
(C) liquids at room temperature, which is approximately 72 degrees Fahrenheit, are (mercury and bromine).
(D) liquids at room temperature (approximately 72 degrees Fahrenheit) are mercury and bromine.

13) Located on the back of the foot and just above the ankle, the Achilles tendon is named for the legendary Greek warrior Achilles, who was invulnerable accept for the area around the aforementioned tendon.

(A) NO CHANGE
(B) except
(C) expect
(D) inspect

14) It has often been noted that some groups of animals have strange names: a group of geese is a "gaggle," a group of crows a "murder," and a group of frogs an "army" or a "colony." This naming system can be traced to Medieval Europe, where aristocratic hunters developed a complex hunting vocabulary, which included species-specific names for groups of animals.

(A) NO CHANGE
(B) "colony": this
(C) "colony," so this
(D) "colony," interestingly, this

15) The presence of a tumor on an individual's pituitary gland may trigger excessive growth hormone production, this leads to gigantism in children and acromegaly in adults.

(A) NO CHANGE
(B) production, leading
(C) production leads
(D) production to lead

☑	1		4		7		10		13	
	2		5		8		11		14	
	3		6		9		12		15	

15 ~ 13	12 ~ 10	9 ~ 7	6 ~ 0
EXCELLENT	VERY GOOD	GOOD	NEEDS WORK

1) Ernest Hemingway spent much of the 1920s living in Paris, where he socialized with some of the most <u>veritable</u> artists of the 20th century, including James Joyce, Gertrude Stein, and F. Scott Fitzgerald.

(A) NO CHANGE
(B) haughty
(C) influential
(D) protruding

2) When injured, many plants secrete a viscous liquid called *resin*, which covers and seals a wound to <u>protect them from</u> invasive organisms.

(A) NO CHANGE
(B) protect it from
(C) protect them with
(D) protect it with

3) <u>Among</u> Native Americans from the Great Sioux Nation, boys as young as ten were expected to participate in bison hunts.

(A) NO CHANGE
(B) Whereby
(C) In order that
(D) DELETE underlined portion.

4) In 2015 India <u>exports</u> over 10.2 million tons of rice, overtaking Thailand as the world's largest exporter of rice.

(A) NO CHANGE
(B) was exporting
(C) having exported
(D) exported

5) <u>Chile's and Argentina's shared borders are</u> the longest in the world, and the two countries' populations mirror each other by having high average incomes and levels of education.

(A) NO CHANGE
(B) The borders of Chile's and Argentina's are
(C) Chile and Argentina, the border that is between them is just about
(D) The border that separates Chile and Argentina is one of

6) Bruce Springsteen's 1982 album <u>*Nebraska* is his darkest release to date. Most</u> of the album's songs chronicle tragedies in the lives of blue-collar workers, criminals, and social outcasts.

Which choice most effectively combines the sentences at the underlined portion?

(A) *Nebraska*: his darkest release to date, and most
(B) *Nebraska* is his darkest release to date, as most
(C) *Nebraska* being his darkest release to date because most
(D) *Nebraska* as his darkest release to date; in fact, most

7) More than 80 percent of Australians live within 30 miles of the <u>coast, and the country's largest coastal city is Sydney, which has a population of nearly 5 million.</u>

Which choice most effectively outlines why the majority of Australians live in coastal regions?

(A) NO CHANGE
(B) coast, and Australia's famous beaches attract millions of tourists each year.
(C) coast because the country's interior is a nearly uninhabitable, arid, desert-like environment.
(D) coast, yet the country's interior is still sparsely populated.

8) In 2015 the solar power capacity of China surpassed <u>that of Germany,</u> making China the largest market for both photovoltaics and solar thermal energy.

(A) NO CHANGE
(B) those in Germany,
(C) Germany,
(D) the Germans,

9) Some linguists and language researchers predict that: 90 percent, of the approximately 7,000 languages spoken in the world today, will be extinct by the year 2050.

(A) NO CHANGE
(B) that: of the approximately 7,000 languages spoken in the world today, 90 percent
(C) that 90 percent of the approximately 7,000 languages spoken in the world today
(D) that 90 percent—of the approximately 7,000 languages spoken in the world today

10) The writings of early 20th century feminist Charlotte Perkins Gilman are discussing the struggles of American women in the home and in society at large.

(A) NO CHANGE
(B) is discussing
(C) discusses
(D) discuss

11) Ford Motor Company manufactured about 15 million Model Ts from 1908 to 1927. This is one of the longest production runs in automotive history.

Which choice most effectively combines the sentences at the underlined portion?

(A) 1927, one
(B) 1927, it is one
(C) 1927—having been one
(D) 1927; among one

12) The powerful force is exerted by some tsunamis—often referred to as "tidal waves"—that they have been known to destroy entire cities.

(A) NO CHANGE
(B) The force is powerful
(C) How powerful the force is
(D) So powerful is the force

13) His writing was in an era when public taste favored satirical tales, Sinclair Lewis' *Main Street* was for years an extremely popular novel in the United States.

(A) NO CHANGE
(B) Written in an era
(C) He wrote in an era
(D) An era of writing

14) All mammals have hair on their bodies during some period of their lives. Therefore, certain mammals, such as whales and dolphins, lose this hair shortly before or after birth.

(A) NO CHANGE
(B) Moreover,
(C) However,
(D) Likewise,

15) An American inventor and the son of escaped slaves, Lewis Latimer served in the Union Navy during the Civil War, patenting an improved method for light bulb production, and created the patent drawings for many of Alexander Graham Bell's telephones.

(A) NO CHANGE
(B) patented an improved method for producing light bulbs,
(C) an improved method for producing light bulbs was patented by him,
(D) light bulb production was improved because of a patent of his,

☑	1		4		7		10		13	
	2		5		8		11		14	
	3		6		9		12		15	

15 ~ 13	12 ~ 10	9 ~ 7	6 ~ 0
EXCELLENT	VERY GOOD	GOOD	NEEDS WORK

CHAPTER 2

1) Salmon lay their eggs in gravel beds, <u>which is where the eggs sit</u> for three months before hatching.

(A) NO CHANGE
(B) where the eggs sit
(C) this is where the eggs sit
(D) it is here that the eggs sit

2) Although English has become a *lingua franca* in much of the world, it is not expected to <u>surpass</u> Mandarin as the most spoken language in the world anytime soon.

(A) NO CHANGE
(B) bypass
(C) excel
(D) upstage

3) Measurements of rivers from around the world have revealed that the length of an S-shaped curve in a river <u>is generally equal in length to about six times the river's width.</u>

(A) NO CHANGE
(B) is usually measured to be equal to about six time the river's width.
(C) is usually equal to about six times the river's width, in general.
(D) is generally equal to about six times the river's width.

4) After the Associated Press published articles that led to the rescue of thousands of people enslaved by fishing <u>companies it won</u> the Pulitzer Prize for Public Service.

(A) NO CHANGE
(B) companies: it won
(C) companies. It won
(D) companies, it won

5) Canning involves heating food that has been placed in a sealable container; the heat kills any micro-organisms that cause food spoilage and <u>is forcing</u> air from the container, so a vacuum seal is formed when the container cools.

(A) NO CHANGE
(B) force
(C) forces
(D) will force

6) Charon is a figure from Greek mythology <u>whose responsibility is to ferry</u> the recently deceased across the mythical rivers Styx and Acheron, which divide the world of the living from the world of the dead.

(A) NO CHANGE
(B) whom has the responsibility of ferrying
(C) who's responsibility it is to ferry
(D) in which the responsibility is to ferry

7) Domestication is the process by which a wild species of animal is selectively bred to produce a new species that lives symbiotically with <u>humans. Taming</u> is the process of changing the behavior of an individual wild animal.

Which choice most effectively combines the sentences at the underlined portion?

(A) humans, so taming
(B) humans and taming
(C) humans, whereas taming
(D) humans, which means that taming

8) Contrary to popular belief, the vast majority of Dubai's wealth comes from real estate, aviation, and <u>tourism, not</u> from oil reserves.

(A) NO CHANGE
(B) tourism: not
(C) tourism; not
(D) tourism, yet not

9) <u>The First Great Awakening was a religious revival from the 1730s to the 1740s. At this time,</u> the number of Americans who regularly attended church increased dramatically.

Which choice most effectively combines the sentences at the underlined portion?

(A) During the First Great Awakening, a religious revival from the 1730s to the 1740s,
(B) A religious revival, the First Great Awakening, which lasted from the 1730s to the 1740s, was a time when
(C) Lasting from the 1730s to the 1740s was the First Great Awakening, a religious revival in which
(D) In the 1730s and the 1740s a religious revival called the First Great Awakening occurred, and so

10) Historical records indicate that the Roman Emperor Caligula was cruel, petty, and mentally unstable. <u>During his reign, he ordered the construction of two aqueducts in Rome.</u>

Which choice provides an example that effectively supports the claim made in the first sentence?

(A) NO CHANGE
(B) His distrust of the Roman Senate inspired him to make some senators his personal servants, while others were forced to run alongside his chariot.
(C) Philo of Alexandria claimed that, during the first seven months of Caligula's rule, he was universally beloved and admired.
(D) Caligula was assassinated in 41 CE as a result of a conspiracy involving many high-profile Romans.

11) The basic premise behind the Arab story collection *One Thousand and One Nights* is that a woman named Scheherazade is able to save her own life because she tells stories so <u>good.</u>

(A) NO CHANGE
(B) well.
(C) favorable.
(D) better.

12) Humans' potential to feel disgusted may have evolved in us so that we became <u>adverse</u> to substances that could spread disease.

(A) NO CHANGE
(B) averted
(C) advertised
(D) averse

13) Although coal, petroleum, and natural gas remain the most common sources of energy, non-conventional energy sources such as solar, wind, and geo-thermal are becoming <u>increased in popularity.</u>

(A) NO CHANGE
(B) increasing popular.
(C) increasingly popular.
(D) popular at an increase.

14) Penguins may look ungainly on land and <u>flying is impossible for them,</u> yet their streamlined bodies and strong, flipper-like wings allow them to streak through the water at speeds of up to 25 miles per hour.

(A) NO CHANGE
(B) have the inability to fly,
(C) be unable to fly,
(D) being incapable of flight,

15) Willem de Kooning's <u>abstract impressionist painting *Interchange*</u> is one of the most expensive work of art ever sold; it was purchased in 2015 for $300 million.

(A) NO CHANGE
(B) abstract, impressionist, painting *Interchange*
(C) abstract impressionist painting, *Interchange*,
(D) abstract, impressionist, and painting, *Interchange*,

☑	1		4		7		10		13	
	2		5		8		11		14	
	3		6		9		12		15	

15 ~ 13	12 ~ 10	9 ~ 7	6 ~ 0
EXCELLENT	VERY GOOD	GOOD	NEEDS WORK

1) <u>Because</u> humans have been using naturally occurring plastics for over 3,000 years, the first fully synthetic plastic was not invented until the early 20th century.

(A) NO CHANGE
(B) Though
(C) If
(D) When

2) In 1983, <u>with thirty-two years old,</u> Sally Ride became the first American woman in space, and she remains the youngest American astronaut to have traveled to space.

(A) NO CHANGE
(B) she was thirty-two,
(C) when aged thirty-two years,
(D) at the age of thirty-two,

3) If a golfer's <u>errant</u> shot sends the ball toward others, the golfer is expected to yell "fore," a term used to *fore*warn others of an approaching ball.

(A) NO CHANGE
(B) errand
(C) irate
(D) arrogant

4) In 1965 American actress Ruby Dee became the first black woman to perform leading roles in the American Shakespeare <u>Festival, Dee portrayed</u> Kate in *The Taming of the Shrew* and Cordelia in *King Lear*.

(A) NO CHANGE
(B) Festival, portraying
(C) Festival, portrayals of
(D) Festival; by portraying

5) <u>James Watt invented the steam engine. He also</u> formulated a conversion between the pulling capacity of a draft horse and a steam engine's power, giving rise to the term "horsepower."

Which choice most effectively combines the sentences at the underlined portion?

(A) James Watt, the man who invented the steam engine, also
(B) Inventing the steam engine, James Watt also
(C) The steam engine was invented by James Watt; Watt also
(D) Steam engine inventor James Watt was the one who also

6) A giant tortoise named Jonathan <u>maybe</u> the oldest living terrestrial animal; biologists estimate that he is approximately 183 years old.

(A) NO CHANGE
(B) be
(C) may be
(D) perhaps being

7) The more precise a doctor's instructions, <u>with ease a patient follows them.</u>

(A) NO CHANGE
(B) easily they are followed by a patient.
(C) more easily a patient follows them.
(D) the easier they are for a patient to follow.

8) Wim Hof is known as "the Iceman" for his ability to withstand extreme <u>cold; holding</u> 21 world records, including one for longest amount of time spent fully immersed in ice.

(A) NO CHANGE
(B) cold: holds
(C) cold; he holds
(D) cold, held by him are

9) American author Nathanial Hawthorne published his popular short stories collection *Twice-Told Tales* in two <u>volumes, one of which</u> was released in 1837 and the other in 1842.

(A) NO CHANGE
(B) volumes, the one which
(C) volumes, so one that
(D) volumes, with one

10) Renowned rock climber Alex Honnold wedged his fingers into the <u>nearly inconceivable</u> fissure in the smooth rock face and hoisted himself a couple of feet closer to the edge of the bluff.

(A) NO CHANGE
(B) nearly imperceptible
(C) virtually impermeable
(D) virtually implausible

11) An avid reader from a young age, Augusta Baker went on to become an influential librarian, literary consultant, and <u>writing</u> extensively about representations of African Americans in children's literature.

(A) NO CHANGE
(B) as an author she wrote
(C) she was writing
(D) author, writing

12) Even after being separated from the body for upwards of an hour, the arms of an octopus <u>remain responsive to external stimuli</u> and are capable of moving away from perceived danger.

(A) NO CHANGE
(B) respond to things
(C) retain the ability to respond to external environmental stimuli
(D) are responsive to external stimuli from their outside environment

13) The population of the black rhinoceros has experienced a sharp decline in recent decades. <u>Other species of rhinoceros, such as the Sumatran and Javan rhino, are on the brink of extinction.</u>

Which choice most effectively supports the information in the first sentence?

(A) NO CHANGE
(B) The black rhinoceros is a solitary animal, only congregating in groups during mating.
(C) In the late 1960s its population was estimated at around 70,000, while fewer than 6,000 exist in the wild today.
(D) Black rhinoceroses are known for their extreme aggression, and both males and females will engage in potentially deadly fights.

14) The village children dubbed the old willow the "Hexing Tree" because it had an eerie resemblance to a witch. A haggard witch's face peered out from the bark of the gnarled trunk, and its <u>extending branches</u> snagged passersby with long, seeking fingers.

The author would like to attribute human qualities to the description of the tree. Which choice would most effectively accomplish this goal?

(A) NO CHANGE
(B) grasping limbs
(C) long limbs
(D) thin, extended branches

15) The 1955 film *Blackboard Jungle* was the first Hollywood production to feature a rock 'n roll <u>soundtrack. The soundtrack delighted</u> younger audiences while scandalizing some concerned parents.

Which choice most effectively combines the sentences at the underlined portion?

(A) soundtrack; delighting
(B) soundtrack, which delighted
(C) soundtrack: to the delight of
(D) soundtrack, it was delightful to

☑	1		4		7		10		13	
	2		5		8		11		14	
	3		6		9		12		15	

15 ~ 13	12 ~ 10	9 ~ 7	6 ~ 0
EXCELLENT	VERY GOOD	GOOD	NEEDS WORK

CHAPTER 3

Mastering
Writing & Language

The world of the future is in our making. Tomorrow is **now**.
— Eleanor Roosevelt

Refer to the passage below to answer questions 1 – 5.

A successful marketing slogan is a catchy short phrase or sentence that consumers memorize and associate with a particular brand. Marketing slogans became ubiquitous with the advent of the household radio in the 1920s.

[1] One of the earliest products to be mass-marketed on radio and television was a laundry soap called "Rinso." [2] From the 1920s to the early 1950s, **1** their slogans were: "Rinso white, Rinso bright," and "Rinso contains sodium, the *sunlight* ingredient." [3] The soap contained sodium silicate, which has especially fine particles that are less likely to get trapped in cloth than **2** the sodium carbonate used in other soaps. [4] Because the sodium silicate particles rinse out of fabric easily, **3** it may leave fabric colors brighter, suggesting the vibrancy of sunlight. [5] The brand's marketers realized that facts and logical associations were irrelevant—the slogan simply had to associate Rinso with clean laundry drying under a cloudless sky. **4**

Ultimately, many of the longest lived slogans use ordinary words **5** and factual statements. As was the case for Rinso, an effective slogan may simply need to have a certain sound or create a desirable mental image.

───── ★ ─────

1

(A) NO CHANGE
(B) they're
(C) its
(D) it's

2

(A) NO CHANGE
(B) the particles of sodium carbonate used
(C) sodium that was used
(D) the types of sodium used

3

(A) NO CHANGE
(B) we
(C) using it
(D) they

4

Where is the most logical place in this paragraph to add the following sentence?

Thus, it is clear that the connection between "sodium" and "sunlight ingredient" requires mental acrobatics.

(A) After sentence 2
(B) After sentence 3
(C) After sentence 4
(D) After sentence 5

5

(A) NO CHANGE
(B) such as vocabulary that even young children can comprehend.
(C) despite the competition's use of technical jargon.
(D) that create vivid, lasting associations in the minds of consumers.

Refer to the passage below to answer questions 1 – 5.

While the nightingale is known for its sweet song, the goose for its boisterous honk, and **1** ravens for their raspy caws, the woodpecker's signature sound is that of hammering. Indeed, woodpeckers arduously spend their days gripping tree trunks, propping themselves with stiff tail feathers, squarely facing the wood, and attacking it.

Most species of woodpecker use their strong beaks to pierce tree bark. Then, their long, sticky tongues reach in and grab unlucky beetles, termites, ants, **2** or they retrieve insect larvae. Woodpeckers also peck out cavities in the wood that are big enough for them to roost in at night. It is fair to say that woodpeckers are noisy and destructive, **3** and that they seem to be injurious to trees. Their incessant drilling controls harmful insect infestations in trees and creates cozy homes that other birds and small mammals can use later.

Because its head functions as miniature jack-hammer, the woodpecker has evolved a number of protective physical features. **4** Its brain **5** is relatively small and encased snugly in a skull that is thick and a little spongy. The woodpecker also has special eyelids and nostril-covers to shield it from flying wood chips, so one might say that it has a built-in helmet and goggles.

───────────── ★ ─────────────

1

(A) NO CHANGE
(B) ravens for their raspy caws; the woodpecker's
(C) the raven for its raspy caw, the woodpecker's
(D) the raven for its raspy caw; the woodpecker's

2

(A) NO CHANGE
(B) or the larvae belonging to the insects.
(C) and the larvae's of insects.
(D) or insect larvae.

3

Which choice most effectively sets up a contrast in the paragraph and is consistent with the information that follows?

(A) NO CHANGE   *annoyance*
(B) and the truth is, some people consider them to be a nuisance.
(C) but they also provide indispensable ecological maintenance.
(D) and they seem to harm ecological relationships.

4

At this point, the writer is considering adding the following sentence:

A woodpecker minimizes rotational force—the force that causes most concussions—by positioning itself at a 90-degree angle to the surface it is pecking.

Should the writer make this addition here?

(A) Yes, because it maintains the passage's focus on the relationship between biology and physics.
(B) Yes, because it explains a behavior that is referred to in the next sentence.
(C) No, because it interrupts the paragraph's focus on physical features.
(D) No, because it does not take into account other types of force on woodpecker skulls.

5

(A) NO CHANGE
(B) is small for their size
(C) is smaller than other birds'
(D) is comparatively smaller

☑	1		2		3		4		5	

Refer to the passage below to answer questions 1 – 5.

American hero Harriet Tubman is best known for her work on the Underground Railroad in the mid-19th century. An escaped slave herself, she repeatedly sneaked back to the South—where slavery was legal—to help small groups of slaves escape to freedom in the North. However, Tubman's greatest victory is less well known: during the American Civil War, Tubman helped plan a raid that **1** freed hundreds of slaves in a single night.

The northern Union Army employed Tubman at its island base off the coast of South Carolina. **2** The lay of the land was unfamiliar; she was provided with excellent informants: hundreds of escaped slaves in refugee camps at the island base. Tubman learned about nearby plantations from recently escaped slaves, even hiring some to return as scouts. She learned that the southern states' Confederate Army only lightly guarded the marshy mainland, probably not expecting northerners to brave the **3** diseased marshes.

On the night of June 1, 1863, Tubman accompanied a river raid by Union forces that included 300 African American soldiers. In three steam-powered boats, Union forces traveled up the Combahee River. **4** They targeted a few large plantations. They carried away stores of rice and cotton and burned buildings. Most importantly, they helped 727 slaves scramble on board. **5**

──────── ★ ────────

1

(A) NO CHANGE
(B) won everlasting fame.
(C) moved to new territory.
(D) helped many slaves.

2

(A) NO CHANGE
(B) As for Tubman, she was unfamiliar with the lay of the land:
(C) Tubman being unfamiliar with the lay of the land,
(D) Although Tubman was unfamiliar with the lay of the land,

3

(A) NO CHANGE
(B) disease-ridden
(C) disease riding
(D) infested-with-disease

4

Which choice most effectively combines the underlined sentences?

(A) Stores of rice and cotton were carried away, whereas a few large plantations were targeted.
(B) Carrying away stores of rice and cotton, they targeted a few large plantations and burned buildings.
(C) They burned buildings and carried away stores of rice and cotton, having targeted a few large plantations.
(D) Targeting a few large plantations, they burned buildings and carried away stores of rice and cotton.

5

The writer is considering ending the passage with the following sentence:

Many of the men freed in the raid later served in the Union Army.

Should the writer add this information here?

(A) Yes, because it adds relevant information regarding the overall impact of the raid.
(B) Yes, because it illustrates an important and widespread recruitment strategy used by the Union Army.
(C) No, because it fails to focus on Tubman's specific military accomplishments.
(D) No, because it fails to explain how the raid affected the Confederate Army.

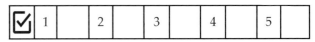

Refer to the passage below to answer questions 1 – 5.

From time to time, we all need to escape from the stress and monotony of work. Even the most diligent worker daydreams about taking time off. **1** Therefore, vacations are often more work than the jobs that we are paid to do.

As a rule, vacations require a great deal of planning to be fully enjoyed. In order to make the most of our vacations, it is best to be prepared. **2** We must choose a destination that matches our interests and budget, make any reservations **3** necessary, research the hours and accessibility of any nearby attractions. Too often, planning a vacation takes up more time than the vacation itself.

4 Even minor oversights—forgetting to check the weather, patch the spare tire, pack the tent poles, bring the phone charger—can make vacations difficult. Without meticulous and thoughtful planning, a vacation may prove to be as stressful an experience as any encountered in the workplace. It is not surprising that more and more people are using time off to take a "staycation," a vacation in which we stay right where we are most **5** comfortable; at home.

———————— ★ ————————

1

(A) NO CHANGE
(B) Coincidentally,
(C) In reality,
(D) Regardless,

2

The writer is considering deleting the previous sentence. Should the writer make this change?

(A) Yes, because it does not logically follow the previous sentence.
(B) Yes, because it contains information that is redundant.
(C) No, because it is supports the main argument about planning.
(D) No, because it serves as a transition to the points that follow.

3

(A) NO CHANGE
(B) necessary, researching
(C) necessary, and research
(D) necessary. We research

4

Which choice most effectively sets up the examples that follow the underlined portion?

(A) NO CHANGE
(B) It is little things
(C) With even the best planning
(D) Major concerns

5

(A) NO CHANGE
(B) comfortably at home.
(C) comfortable, at home!
(D) comfortable: at home.

| ☑ | 1 | | 2 | | 3 | | 4 | | 5 | |

Refer to the passage below to answer questions 1 – 5.

The four-humor theory was a popular way to explain human psychology from ancient times to the 19th century. **1** According to this theory, personal characteristics are determined by four humors (fluids). These fluids are in the human body: blood, yellow bile, black bile, and phlegm. All four were thought to be present in each person in unique combinations, shaping an individual's personality, temperament, and even **2** their destiny.

3 Depending on which humor was believed to be present in the greatest amount in an individual, his or her personality had certain characteristics. Those in whom blood **4** is dominant had sanguine, or cheerful and vivacious, personalities. Those in whom yellow bile played the preponderant role had choleric, or irritable and restless, personalities. Those ruled by black bile were serious and analytical, and tended toward sadness. Finally, those with the highest proportion of phlegm had phlegmatic—calm, peaceful, sometimes even apathetic—personalities.

It was considered ideal to keep all the humors in balance as much as possible. Indeed, having too much of a particular humor build up in the body was thought to cause most physical and mental illnesses, as well as bad moods. Physicians often prescribed blood-letting from particular veins, or medicines that made a patient vomit, **5** as methods of "curing" imbalances.

─────── ★ ───────

1

Which choice most effectively combines the underlined sentences?

(A) Blood, yellow bile, black bile, and phlegm determine personal characteristics, according to the theory about the four humors.
(B) The theory says that personal characteristics are determined by four humors in the human body, blood, yellow bile, black bile, and phlegm.
(C) Personal characteristics are determined by blood, yellow bile, black bile, and phlegm, all four of which are present in the body, according to the theory of the four humors.
(D) According to the theory, fluid "humors" — blood, yellow bile, black bile, and phlegm — determine personal characteristics.

2

(A) NO CHANGE
(B) your
(C) there
(D) his or her

3

At this point, the writer is considering adding the following sentence.

In much the same way, the four elements of Chinese astrology (fire, wood, earth, and water) are each associated with a natural season. Each humor was associated with a season, an element, and a body organ.

Should the writer make this addition here?

(A) Yes, because it explains beliefs associated with the humors.
(B) Yes, because it provides cultural context for the discussion.
(C) No, because it blurs the focus on the humors' effects on personality.
(D) No, because it implies that the Chinese also based their beliefs on the four humors.

4

(A) NO CHANGE
(B) is dominant will have
(C) was dominant had
(D) was dominant have

5

Which conclusion best supports the paragraph's claim?

(A) NO CHANGE
(B) most likely causing patients more harm than good.
(C) thinking the process would reduce inflammation.
(D) or special diets.

	1		2		3		4		5	

Refer to the passage below to answer questions 1 – 5.

For more than half a century, groups of Harvard University students have **1** found jobs with campus businesses. In 1960, a freshman named Oliver Koppell mimeographed and assembled a 25-page travel guide to Europe. **2** Focus: youthful interests and bargain prices. He handed out copies to students traveling to Europe. He then **3** persuaded, an organization of student-run businesses, to help him set up a guidebook company. For several years, Koppell spearheaded production of *Let's Go: the Student Guide to Europe*. He paid Harvard students to travel during their summer vacations, reporting about hotels, restaurants, and sights.

[1] Nevertheless, Harvard students continued the legacy. [2] Koppell himself graduated and went on to a career in New York state politics. [3]By the early 1970s, major publishers were buying rights to the books. [4] Let's Go began expanding its titles with guides to individual countries in Europe, such as *Let's Go: Italy*. [5] By the mid-1980s, it was publishing a dozen or more **4** differentiated titles every year. [6] That number grew as the company began publishing guides for specific cities, as well as for countries on other continents. Today, Let's Go, still produced by students at Harvard University, offers not only books but also mobile apps for travelers. **5**

───────────────── ★ ─────────────────

1

Which choice most effectively introduces the topic of the passage?

(A) NO CHANGE
(B) gone to Europe every summer.
(C) learned about publishing.
(D) published guides for budget travel.

2

(A) NO CHANGE
(B) His focus:
(C) Its focus was
(D) Information including

3

(A) NO CHANGE
(B) persuaded: an organization of student-run business,
(C) persuaded an organization of student-run businesses
(D) persuaded an organization, of student-run businesses,

4

(A) NO CHANGE
(B) different
(C) distinguishable
(D) differential

5

To make this paragraph most logical, sentence 2 should be placed

(A) before sentence 1.
(B) where it is now.
(C) after sentence 3.
(D) after sentence 6.

| ☑ | 1 | | 2 | | 3 | | 4 | | 5 | |

Refer to the passage below to answer questions 1 – 5.

Most people have drawers, cupboards, or boxes of things that they never use. These are things they feel they should get rid of, but they procrastinate. They worry that later, they may want the old clothes, buttons, paper clips, unmatched socks, birthday cards, baseball mitts, pipe-cleaner art from first grade, and outdated technological devices. They may just not know how to get rid of them. Of course, **1** some items can be given away or recycled, but an often-overlooked alternative is to reuse the items artistically. **2**

Indeed, many contemporary artists have used ordinary "junk" to build sculptures and craft collages. For example, at the airport in Sacramento, California, artist Brian Goggin has created two giant pillars made of 700 old suitcases and chests. The pillars appear to rest precariously on luggage **3** carts, and they appear to hold up the roof. Travelers waiting to claim their own luggage may be inspired to imagine all the travelers who once owned the suitcases, and how they managed to **4** loose them.

However, it does not take a professional artist to create art from junk. Quilters, for example, have long used old scraps of cloth to make stunning new designs. Ultimately, so-called "useless" **5** items have much more potential than many of us realize.

———————★———————

1

Which choice most closely follows the pattern that has been established in the paragraph?

(A) NO CHANGE
(B) they can give away or recycle some items,
(C) it is possible to give away or recycle many items,
(D) donations and recycling are not to be ruled out,

2

The writer is considering deleting the previous sentence. Should the writer make this change?

(A) Yes, because it introduces a topic that is not explained.
(B) Yes, because it adds information that is already obvious in the passage.
(C) No, because reinforces the information in the previous sentence.
(D) No, because it links the paragraph to the information that follows.

3

(A) NO CHANGE
(B) carts. They
(C) carts, yet they also
(D) carts, which

4

(A) NO CHANGE
(B) lose
(C) let
(D) loss

5

(A) NO CHANGE
(B) items'
(C) item's
(D) item

Refer to the passage below to answer questions 1 – 5.

Among the organelles, the separate functional parts found inside animal cells, are lysosomes. They are often referred to as the "digestive organs" of cells because their function in cells is similar to **1** that of the liver, kidneys, and intestines in human bodies. Compared to other organelles, **2** lysosomes are relatively small, indeed minute. They measure between 0.1 and 1.0 micrometers. (One micrometer is one-millionth of a meter.) But their small size belies their crucial role: waste removal. **3** Additionally, lysosomes recycle the obsolete parts of the cell itself, breaking them down to their components so **4** they can be reassembled into new structures. Lysosomes can also take on important roles if the cell becomes damaged. **5** Moreover, lysosomes help repair the cellular damage by sealing the wound.

─────────── ★ ───────────

1

(A) NO CHANGE
(B) the liver's, kidneys,' and intestines'
(C) these of the liver, kidneys, and intestines
(D) the liver, kidneys, and intestines

2

(A) NO CHANGE
(B) lysosomes are, indeed, relatively small and minute.
(C) lysosomes are relatively small.
(D) small lysosomes.

3

At this point, the writer is considering adding the following sentence.

Lysosomes are responsible for digesting and destroying the remnants of invasive foreign substances, such as viruses and bacteria.

Should the writer make this addition here?

(A) Yes, because it helps explain how lysosomes remove waste from cells.
(B) Yes, because it adds relevant background information about cell invasion.
(C) No, because it blurs the paragraph's focus on lysosomes' size.
(D) No, because it merely reformulates information from previous sentences.

4

(A) NO CHANGE
(B) the materials
(C) all of it
(D) the lysosomes

5

(A) NO CHANGE
(B) As such,
(C) Under these circumstances,
(D) DELETE the underlined portion.

| ☑ | 1 | | 2 | | 3 | | 4 | | 5 | |

Refer to the passage below to answer questions 1 – 5.

Americans often pride themselves on [1] their independent thinking. [2] Thus, it may surprise many to learn that studies over the past six decades have revealed that individuals regularly conform to the opinions of those around them.

Solomon Asch, a pioneer in the field of social psychology, is particularly known for his 1950s studies on the effects that group pressure has upon individuals. In his studies, volunteers sat together around a table. [3] They were shown two white cards. One depicted a vertical line they were told was "standard length." The other card showed three different vertical lengths. One by one, subjects were asked to say which line on the second card matched the "standard length" depicted on the first card. The process was repeated a number of times with different cards.

However, the group was not what it seemed; one [4] random person, who was positioned to answer last, was the only true subject of the experiment. The other volunteers were actually following directions that Asch had given them privately before the experiment. Acting on Asch's instructions, the group unanimously named a line that was incorrect during some rounds. In many instances, the subject went along with the group instead of trusting his or her own senses. Of all the subjects, 75 percent conformed to the group at least once. While that seems high, it is also important to note that 95 percent of the subjects defied the majority at least once. [5]

———————— ★ ————————

1

(A) NO CHANGE
(B) their thinking autonomously and independently.
(C) their independently thinking.
(D) their ability to think autonomously.

2

Which choice best links the claim in the previous sentence to the information that follows it?

(A) NO CHANGE
(B) Thus, it is appropriate that
(C) In keeping with this belief, many social psychologists agree that
(D) DELETE the underlined portion, and capitalize "Individuals."

3

Which choice most effectively combines the underlined sentences?

(A) Being told that the vertical line on a card was "standard length," they looked at two white cards.
(B) Researchers showed the group a white card with a standard-length vertical line, and they were shown the other card.
(C) They were shown two white cards; a vertical line on the first card was described as "standard length."
(D) They were shown two white cards, one who depicted a vertical line of so-called "standard length."

4

(A) NO CHANGE
(B) unconscious
(C) clueless
(D) unwitting

5

The writer wants a conclusion that offers a criticism of Asch's 1950s studies. Which choice best accomplishes this goal?

(A) Asch later went on to study what kinds of factors increase the willingness of subjects to yield to group pressure.
(B) Today, scholars cast doubt on the studies' reliability and validity in the "real world," but Asch's studies nevertheless raised interesting questions about human behavior.
(C) To this day, Asch ranks among the most cited psychologists.
(D) Asch's studies were so significant that they are described in most textbooks for social psychology courses at the college level at American institutions.

| ✓ | 1 | | 2 | | 3 | | 4 | | 5 | |

Refer to the passage below to answer questions 1 – 5.

Velvet, a soft, cushiony fabric, **1** may make some people feel like kings and queens. The earliest velvet fabrics were indeed precious and costly, laboriously fashioned out of the threads produced by silkworms. Nowadays, velvet can also be manufactured from cotton as well as from synthetic **2** materials, such as, polyester and nylon.

One method of velvet production requires a special loom that creates two face-to-face layers of fabric simultaneously. The layers are connected by loops of thread or yarn. **3** The loops are then sliced apart using a sharp blade, resulting in two tufted-thread surfaces. The densely packed strands that stick up from the face of the fabric are its "pile," which comes from the Latin word *pilus*, meaning "hair."

Although velvet's origins remain unclear, the fabric first shows up in historical records at the court of Harun al-Rashid in 8th century Baghdad, where it was introduced by Kashmiri merchants. Gradually making its way to Europe via the Silk Road, **4** the elite classes and church leaders there embraced velvet with great enthusiasm. Its warmth, elegance, and vibrancy have long made it perfect for showy clothing and furnishings. **5** Inevitably, several Italian cities specialized in producing the luxurious fabric from the 12th to the 18th centuries.

———————— ★ ————————

1

Which choice provides the most appropriate introduction to the passage?

(A) NO CHANGE
(B) has long been associated with wealth and elegance.
(C) has an interesting history.
(D) is a time-consuming undertaking.

2

(A) NO CHANGE
(B) materials, such as polyester, and nylon.
(C) materials—such as polyester and nylon.
(D) materials such as polyester and nylon.

3

(A) NO CHANGE
(B) Afterward, they slice them apart
(C) This is followed by slicing
(D) The loops being sliced apart

4

(A) NO CHANGE
(B) where it was enthusiastically embraced by elite classes and church leaders.
(C) enthusiastic embracing of it was the response from the elite classes and church leaders.
(D) velvet was enthusiastically embraced by the elite classes and church leaders.

5

(A) NO CHANGE
(B) Somewhat surprisingly,
(C) As such,
(D) Consequently,

Refer to the passage below to answer questions 1 – 5.

Contrary to popular belief, ears are good for more than getting pierced and holding earbuds in place. The vestibular system, **1** a location found in the inner ear, helps the body regulate balance and stabilize vision. The system is named for the Latin word *vestibulum*, which describes the chamber between an entrance and an interior door of a building.

2 We can see a system with three curved, fluid-filled tubes joined at right angles. When the head moves in a certain direction, gravity causes the fluid in the tubes to settle at the lowest point. Sensory hair cells that line each tube bend in the direction of the moving fluid, and stimulate nerves to signal the brain.

Each of the three circular tubes **3** specialize in a different type of directional **4** information. Namely, these are up-and-down, side-to-side, or tilted. Signals from the vestibular system interact primarily with ocular structures to help control eye movement, and with various muscle groups that **5** allows us to stay upright and move around without falling.

———————— ★ ————————

1

(A) NO CHANGE
(B) within
(C) located in
(D) found to be in

2

Which choice results in the most effective transition between the previous paragraph and the information that follows?

(A) NO CHANGE
(B) Deep within each ear sits
(C) The "chambers" are essentially
(D) The vestibular system, which helps stabilize the vision, has

3

(A) NO CHANGE
(B) specializes in
(C) specialize at
(D) specializes at

4

Which choice most effectively combines the sentences at the underlined portion?

(A) information, so
(B) information; including
(C) information that is
(D) information:

5

(A) NO CHANGE
(B) allowed us
(C) is allowing us
(D) allow us

☑ | 1 | | 2 | | 3 | | 4 | | 5 | |

CHAPTER 3

Refer to the passage below to answer questions 1 – 5.

The tasks assigned to wildlife biologists are as interesting as they are varied. Their jobs generally involve scouring forests, deserts, swamps, or prairies for information regarding a particular habitat and its respective animal and plant populations. Regardless of where he or she works, **1** a wildlife biologist's main goals include to learn about wild animals and improving the health of their habitats. Fundamentally, wildlife biologists serve as the human population's eyes and ears in uninhabited areas. **2**

Although the majority of their funding comes from government agencies, wildlife biologists can find work in any number of organizations. Most wildlife biologists are employed by national, state, or county agencies, but many also work with universities, nonprofit conservation groups, **3** and additionally with private consulting firms.

A typical day in the life of a wildlife biologist varies based on his or her research priorities. A day might be spent netting birds and placing bands on their legs before releasing them, so that data can be collected on their migratory patterns and life spans. Another day might involve live-trapping small mammals to check weight and health. Another typical task might be to **4** ascertain inventory of the flora in a specified area, and to collect water samples to take back to a laboratory. While many days may involve hiking, boating, or even flying in helicopters, **5** others involve filming or photographing wildlife.

———————————★———————————

1

(A) NO CHANGE
(B) a wildlife biologist's main goals include learning
(C) wildlife biologists' main goals include to learn
(D) wildlife biologists' main goals include learning

2

The writer is considering deleting the previous sentence. Should the sentence be kept or deleted?

(A) Kept, because it reinforces the information in the paragraph.
(B) Kept, because it introduces an important new topic.
(C) Deleted, because it contradicts the main proposition in the passage.
(D) Deleted, because it undermines the significance of wildlife biologists.

3

(A) NO CHANGE
(B) and
(C) not to mention
(D) moreover

4

(A) NO CHANGE
(B) ascertaining inventory
(C) take inventory
(D) taking inventory

5

The writer would like to conclude the passage with contrasting yet realistic information. Which choice most effectively accomplishes this goal?

(A) NO CHANGE
(B) others are spent indoors, analyzing data and writing reports.
(C) most wildlife biologists still choose not to work on weekends.
(D) they really can be said to have a satisfying career.

✓	1		2		3		4		5	

Refer to the passage below to answer questions 1 – 5.

England's Industrial Revolution nearly stalled half a century before it began. Factories required machinery (a **1** blueprint of industrial productivity), and machinery had to be forged from iron. However, by the end of the 1600s, iron smelters in England were running out of fuel. England itself lacked enough forests and lumber to supply smelters with the charcoal they needed, and charcoal was too costly to import in large quantities.

As the 18th century dawned, an Englishman named Abraham Darby was experimenting. **2** He knew that malted grains were roasted using coke, a fuel made from coal. He decided to borrow the idea. He set up a smelting facility next to a river in a coal-mining area, and built powerful coke furnaces. Darby's business was the first **3** to be producing high-quality iron using inexpensive fuel. Without such iron, the Industrial Revolution would have been stymied.

Years later, as industrialization was gaining momentum, Darby's grandson, Abraham Darby III, took over the company. Darby III hired a designer **4** and, in 1779 constructed a picturesque cast-iron bridge over the River Severn. It was the first iron bridge in the world; visitors were astounded at its thinness, as bridges had always been made of thick stone or wood. The Iron Bridge still stands in Shropshire, **5** England it is now a UNESCO World Heritage Site and a popular tourist destination.

────────── ★ ──────────

1

(A) NO CHANGE
(B) restriction of
(C) prerequisite for
(D) perquisite for

2

At this point, the writer is considering adding the following information.

Darby had been an apprentice at a malt mill.

Should the writer make this addition here?

(A) Yes, because it provides a specific example of Darby's work experience.
(B) Yes, because it explains how Darby gained crucial knowledge.
(C) No, because it interrupts the flow of the paragraph with irrelevant information.
(D) No, because it raises the topic of malt milling which is not explained.

3

(A) NO CHANGE
(B) when producing
(C) by producing
(D) to produce

4

(A) NO CHANGE
(B) and—in 1779—
(C) and in 1779
(D) and (in 1779)

5

(A) NO CHANGE
(B) England. It is now
(C) England, it is now
(D) England, which it is now

	1		2		3		4		5	

Refer to the passage below to answer questions 1 – 5.

A generic feature of all beaches—be they sandy or rocky, sunny or cloudy—is the sound of waves crashing against the shoreline. Yet most waves first form far out at sea, and the original force behind most waves is wind, not water. **1** First thing's first, wind pushes on water, passing energy from air molecules to water molecules; the energy travels through water in the form of a wave. When waves lap against **2** the shore the energy pushes the water up.

[1] A wave must expend energy to climb up the shore. [2] Once depleted of energy, the water succumbs to gravity and falls back into the ocean. [3] The flow of water away from shore is called the "undertow," because the water slides under the next swell, towing sand and debris with it. [4] Wide, flat beaches spread out the force of the wave, causing a gentle undertow. [5] Waves hitting cliffs or short, steep beaches will fall back with much more force. **3**

Unlike undertow, rip currents are usually temporary. They **4** would occur when a trough of some kind forms. For example, a sandbar may form offshore, trapping water between the sandbar and the beach. Trapped water spills out to sea at the lowest spot in the sandbar, like bath water pouring down a drain. The strong funnel-like current near that spot is called a "rip current." It can pull hapless swimmers out beyond the sandbar. **5**

───────── ★ ─────────

1

Which choice best maintains the tone established in the passage?

(A) NO CHANGE
(B) Obviously,
(C) Most waves start when
(D) With awe-inspiring power,

2

(A) NO CHANGE
(B) the shore, the energy
(C) the shore, so the energy
(D) the shore then the energy

3

Where is the most logical place in the paragraph to add the following sentence?

More energy passes into the water, and it is heaved up to hit the beach again.

(A) Before sentence 1
(B) After sentence 1
(C) After sentence 3
(D) After sentence 4

4

(A) NO CHANGE
(B) are occurring
(C) will occur
(D) occur

5

Which choice most clearly and cohesively concludes the paragraph?

(A) However, undertows and rip currents are not the only currents that form near a shoreline.
(B) In fact, it is estimated that over 80 percent of beach rescues by lifeguards are the result of rip currents.
(C) I was once caught in a rip current, but a lifeguard saw that I was in trouble and came to help me.
(D) Gravity is also the driving force behind the currents of rivers.

☑	1		2		3		4		5	

CHAPTER 3

Refer to the passage below to answer questions 1 – 5.

In many cultures, languages are manipulated to form coded speech or writing. Sometimes these coded languages follow simple rules and are meant to be playful. For example, the English language game called "Pig Latin" requires moving the first consonant sound of each word to the end of the word, which then receives an "ay" suffix. Thus, **1** "hello" becomes "ellohay," and the phrase "see you tomorrow" becomes "eesay ouyay omorrowtay."

2 Fake forms of Latin have been used to comedic effect for centuries. Speakers of Cebuano in the Philippines have a language game called "*Kinabayo,*" which means "horse language." The game requires repeating every vowel sound after inserting "g" and "d" consonants. So, the word "ani-a" becomes "agadanigidiagada." The **3** editions make the language sound like galloping horses.

Of course, many secret languages **4** are not meant to be playful. *Nushu* is a written script once used among the women of Jiangyong County, located in China's Hunan Province. It consisted of 600 to 700 characters that represented the sounds of a local dialect. No boys or men knew how to read it. Cultural expectations for **5** women being housebound and to have bound feet meant that they had few opportunities to communicate with friends after marriage. *Nushu* was a means of private expression in letters, painted fans, and embroidery.

———————— ★ ————————

1

The writer is considering deleting the underlined portion of the sentence. Should the writer make this change?

(A) Yes, because it would make the examples that follow more logical.
(B) Yes, because it would maintain the passage's focus on phrases.
(C) No, because it illustrates the importance of greetings in any language.
(D) No, because it provides a relevant and concise example.

2

Which of the following sentences provides the best transition from paragraph 1 to paragraph 2?

(A) NO CHANGE
(B) Although the most commonly spoken language in the Philippines is Filipino, the island nation is home to over 100 languages.
(C) However, Pig Latin is not recognized as an official language anywhere in the world.
(D) As with the "ay" sound in Pig Latin, many language games require speakers to add sounds.

3

(A) NO CHANGE
(B) auditions
(C) admissions
(D) additions

4

Which choice most effectively sets up the example that follows?

(A) NO CHANGE
(B) have many more rules.
(C) are not named after animals.
(D) become too confusing over time and are forgotten.

5

(A) NO CHANGE
(B) women to be housebound and having feet bound
(C) women's housebound and bound feet
(D) women to be housebound and to have bound feet

| ☑ | 1 | | 2 | | 3 | | 4 | | 5 | |

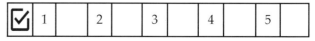

Refer to the passage below to answer questions 1 – 5.

-- 1 --

Music can often help people get work done, according to research. A number of studies have looked at the effects of music on workers. One clear finding is that when a job is simple and repetitive, as in assembly-line work **1** music has a marked effect on productivity. **2** In studies, people who listened to music while doing mundane work were happier and more productive than people who did not. This was especially true if the music was in a major key.

-- 2 --

Music on headphones can also help to block out *external* noise. **3** Not every sound may be blocked by it, but it should dull any nearby conversations. Thus, music can provide a method of curbing unnecessary gossip and eavesdropping in a workplace.

-- 3 --

Moreover, researchers suggest listening to familiar music when concentrating on a task. Doing so ensures that the brain does not focus on the novelty of unfamiliar lyrics or rhythms in the music.

-- 4 --

When it comes to cognitively taxing work, music can sometimes **4** get more concentration. For example, when workers use headphones, they are better able to manage *internal* emotional distractions: they can choose soothing rhythms when they are worried, upbeat music when they are tired, and so on.

Question 5 asks about the passage as a whole.

──────────── ★ ────────────

1

At this point, the writer wants to add a second example of a simple, repetitive job. Which choice would be most effective for this purpose?

(A) or data entry,
(B) or copyediting,
(C) or car sales,
(D) or party planning,

2

(A) NO CHANGE
(B) Doing mundane work while listening to music, people were happier and more productive than people who did not, in studies.
(C) In studies, compared to people who did not listen to music, people who listened to music while doing mundane work reported better moods and more productivity.
(D) In studies, doing mundane work, more was accomplished by people who listened to music than people who did not, and music-listeners reported better moods.

3

(A) NO CHANGE
(B) The music may not block every sound,
(C) Not every sound will get blocked,
(D) Not all noise,

4

Which choice best maintains the tone established in the passage?

(A) NO CHANGE
(B) bump up
(C) improve
(D) fix

5

To make the passage most logical, paragraph 4 should be placed

(A) where it is now.
(B) before paragraph 1.
(C) before paragraph 2.
(D) before paragraph 3.

☑ | 1 | | 2 | | 3 | | 4 | | 5 | |

Refer to the passage below to answer questions 1 – 5.

In the mid-1800s, archaeologists first discovered fossil remains of Neanderthals, **1** a type of hominid. The name "Neanderthal" comes from that first discovery in Germany, in the *Neander* Valley. But before this important paleontological discovery, the name "Neander" was associated in the public mind with music, not fossils.

The valley is named after Joachim Neander, a teacher, songwriter, and theologian. Neander **2** did not own the valley, but he lived near it in Düsseldorf during the 1670s. Neander taught Latin, but he was constantly in conflict with leaders at the school where he taught. After only five years, he quit and moved away, and unfortunately died shortly thereafter. But it was said that his frequent walks in the valley had **3** inspired Neander to write dozens of beautiful hymns. during his time there.

Neander lived more than a century after the Protestant Reformation began in Europe. As such, his goal was to make church music accessible to common people. His lyrics are in German rather than Latin, and he used familiar folk tunes **4** in addition. Long after his death, his works remained popular; Johann Sebastian Bach even based one of his chorale cantatas on one of **5** his hymns. In 1850, the valley was officially named for him. Six years later, the first fossils were found there, and Neander's name became attached to an entire branch of hominids.

───────── ★ ─────────

CHAPTER 3

1

(A) NO CHANGE
(B) a subspecies of people, but not people like you and me.
(C) an extinct subspecies of hominid.
(D) an intriguing species.

2

The writer is considering deleting the underlined portion of the sentence. Should the writer make this change?

(A) Yes, because its tone does not match that of the rest of the passage.
(B) Yes, because it distracts from the passage's focus on Neanderthals.
(C) No, because it helps clarify Neander's relationship with the valley.
(D) No, because it contradicts information that comes later in the paragraph.

3

(A) NO CHANGE
(B) forced
(C) exhilarated
(D) invigorated

4

Which choice best supports the claim made in the previous sentence?

(A) NO CHANGE
(B) that people could easily memorize and sing.
(C) which extolled the beauty of the valley.
(D) to cement his artistic legacy.

5

(A) NO CHANGE
(B) their
(C) Bach's
(D) Neander's

| ✓ | 1 | | 2 | | 3 | | 4 | | 5 | |

Refer to the passage below to answer questions 1 – 5.

The young heroes and heroines in classic children's stories often misbehave. The monkey in H.A. Rey's *Curious George* series paints pictures on a stranger's walls in one story and **1** lives with the Man with the Yellow Hat. Eloise, the protagonist of Kay Thompson's *Eloise Takes a Bawth*, spills so much **2** water playing in the tub, that she floods a ballroom on a lower floor. And in the book *Where the Wild Things Are*, by Maurice Sendak, the main character Max dreams about an imaginary land where he makes the rules and does whatever he wants to do.

3 Simply put, it is ironic that the target audience—children—know more about rules and proper behavior than the character does. **4** Nevertheless, when reading such stories, children can feel "big" because they realize that the character is misbehaving. When they get to assume the role of the responsible adult, children nearly always find the role reversal to be humorous. In *Don't Let the Pigeon Drive the Bus*, readers become the voice of responsibility, as they must keep a pesky pigeon from commandeering a bus. Preschool audiences laugh at **5** the pigeon, who is relentless, even as they repeatedly tell him "No!" And yet, as with other mischievous characters, the pigeon remains lovable even when breaking the rules and having a tantrum. No doubt many children find reassurance in such stories.

———————★———————

1

Which of the following examples is most consistent with the pattern established in the rest of the paragraph?

(A) NO CHANGE
(B) and accidentally steals a handful of helium balloons in another.
(C) and saves a baby bear that becomes stuck in a tree in another.
(D) learns to read the alphabet in another.

2

(A) NO CHANGE
(B) water, playing in the tub, that
(C) water, playing in the tub that
(D) water playing in the tub that

3

Which choice most effectively sets up the information that follows?

(A) Such stories engage children using dramatic irony.
(B) Some parents refuse to read such books to their young children.
(C) The characters are not always children; they can be animals.
(D) In fact, well-behaved characters can be boring.

4

(A) NO CHANGE
(B) Regardless,
(C) Moreover,
(D) However,

5

(A) NO CHANGE
(B) the relentless pigeon,
(C) the persistent pigeon's relentlessness,
(D) the pigeon, relentless as he is,

☑	1		2		3		4		5	

Refer to the passage below to answer questions 1 – 5.

Sometimes, people need help solving their problems, especially if they do not know where to turn for support. Social workers, in the broadest sense, are professional helpers. They assess needs and then suggest ways to meet them. Social workers can be found in a huge variety of settings. A hospital social worker might help **1** a patient, discharged, sign up for Meals on Wheels. A social worker in an urban area might run a group home for adolescents, **2** engage in advocacy for homeless people, or coordinate an emergency response to an earthquake. **3**

Licensed clinical social workers (LCSW) can provide counseling that is similar to **4** that provided by psychological therapists. LCSWs, however, are more likely to focus on helping their clients make practical changes to their personal environments.

Thus, whereas a therapist may talk with a patient about his or her job, an LCSW might help a patient seek a new and better job. A psychologist and a LCSW might also take differing approaches when helping a teenager **5** whom is failing classes. A psychologist might focus on the teen's self-defeating thoughts regarding school. A LCSW might touch on those thoughts but also suggest that the student's parents offer incentives for good grades. The two approaches are both aimed at helping patients solve problems and feel better.

★

CHAPTER 3

1
(A) NO CHANGE
(B) a patient being discharged
(C) a patient,
(D) a patient and

2
(A) NO CHANGE
(B) do advocacy
(C) advocate
(D) speak

3
The writer wants to link the first paragraph with the ideas that follow. Which choice best accomplishes this goal?

(A) Thus, social workers tackle both long-standing and emergency situations.
(B) Social workers are a major part of modern American society's safety net.
(C) However, a social worker without an advanced degree tends to earn very little.
(D) Overall, social workers focus on improving the systems surrounding individuals.

4
(A) NO CHANGE
(B) psychological therapists.
(C) those by psychological therapists.
(D) psychology.

5
(A) NO CHANGE
(B) which is
(C) who is
(D) whose

	1		2		3		4		5	

Refer to the passage below to answer questions 1 – 5.

Placing a hand on a windowpane tells us that glass is solid, but some people have claimed that glass is actually a liquid. Glass does have some liquid-like properties. In fact, chemists describe glass as **1** neither solid or liquid. They call glass an "amorphous solid."

Most matter **2** is subject to certain principles. In a liquid state, its molecules move around, constantly breaking and reforming bonds with each other. When it cools, the molecules that comprise it lose energy and form more stable bonds, wherein they attach to each other in repeating three-dimensional patterns. For example, when water freezes into ice, its molecules lose the energy needed to move around in a liquid state and **3** would have been bonded in hexagonal structures. Conversely, when ice is warmed to its melting point, the molecular bonds break apart and the molecules are free to move around in a liquid state.

Glass behaves differently. Hot liquid glass cools so fast that its molecules do not have time to attract each other and form geometrical patterns. Without the energy provided by heat, **4** there is less vibration. Like in a liquid, the particles are disorganized, **5** but like a solid, their movements nearly stop. The molecules in glass can theoretically flow into a more organized formation—but only over many eons.

───────────── ★ ─────────────

1

(A) NO CHANGE
(B) not solid, but also not liquid.
(C) neither solid nor liquid.
(D) either solid, nor liquid.

2

Which choice most effectively sets up the information that follows?

(A) NO CHANGE
(B) in life forms combines states of gases, liquids, and solids.
(C) makes an orderly transition from a liquid to a solid state.
(D) has a definite and predictable "freezing point."

3

(A) NO CHANGE
(B) bonded
(C) are going to bond
(D) become bonded

4

(A) NO CHANGE
(B) the vibrating atoms slow down.
(C) there are fewer vibrations.
(D) a sense of calm descends on the atoms.

5

(A) NO CHANGE
(B) but like in a solid,
(C) but, like solids,
(D) but as in liquids and solids alike,

☑	1		2		3		4		5	

Refer to the passage below to answer questions 1 – 5.

When it comes to job security, not all professions are created equal. Some businesses sink at the first sign of recession while others sail through unscathed. People looking for **1** invulnerable employment sectors might do well to ask themselves: what goods and services cannot be mistaken for luxuries?

Even in a recession, people of all ages still need health care and pharmaceutical services. Students still need backpacks and pencils. Car owners still need car insurance and towing services, **2** and homeowners still need plumbers and trash collectors. Analysts call these sorts of businesses, products, and services "static."

[1] Some businesses even flourish during recessions. [2] Trade schools and graduate schools often experience increased enrollment during economic slumps. [3] The reason **3** for this is that during these times, unemployed people return to school to learn new skills, while some students decide to "wait out" the downturn by staying in school. [4] Not surprisingly, repair services thrive as people get things fixed instead of buying new—thus the **4** phrase, "Renovators hire when builders fire." **5**

────── ★ ──────

1

Which choice best maintains the metaphor established in the previous sentence?

(A) NO CHANGE
(B) a business that can weather any storm
(C) benign opportunities
(D) prudent areas of inquiry

2

Which choice gives a second supporting example that is most similar to the example already in the sentence?

(A) NO CHANGE
(B) and charities still need donations.
(C) and some people might begin to take the bus instead of driving.
(D) because unfortunately, car accidents still happen.

3

(A) NO CHANGE
(B) can be said to be that
(C) for it is that
(D) is that

4

(A) NO CHANGE
(B) phrase "renovators hire when builders fire…"
(C) phrase. "Renovators hire when builders fire."
(D) phrase; "renovators hire when builders fire…"

5

To improve the cohesion and flow of this paragraph, the writer wants to add the following sentence.

The underemployed also patronize businesses that help them economize in one way or another.

The sentence would most logically be placed after

(A) sentence 1.
(B) sentence 2.
(C) sentence 3.
(D) sentence 4.

Refer to the passage below to answer questions 1 – 5.

The 2015 film *Embrace of the Serpent* is set against the backdrop of the "rubber boom" in the Amazon rainforests of Colombia. At the turn of the 20th century, industrialists rushed to collect natural rubber from throughout the Amazon; their brutal treatment of native tribes caused untold suffering and death. **1** Colombian filmmaker Ciro Guerra wanted *Embrace of the Serpent* to tell a fictional tale about lost cultures from the point of view of the indigenous people, transporting viewers into their world.

For background, Guerra studied the diaries of two white scholars who traveled in the region. **2** Their's are some of the only written records of the now-lost cultures the film depicts. Drawing inspiration from the diaries, Guerra creates a dual plot in which two scholars, separated by over three decades, **3** seek the help of the same indigenous shaman, who is the only surviving member of his tribe. Each scholar enlists the shaman to help him find a sacred plant, **4** and the film uses different actors for the young and old shaman.

Prior to filming, Guerra took the script to some current-day Amazonians and asked them to translate parts of it into their languages. Guerra later said that the indigenous translators suggested many cultural details **5** that ultimately transformed the script.

———————————— ★ ————————————

1

At this point, the writer is considering adding the following sentence.

At the time, rubber came only from liquid latex, which was tapped from the trunks of wild rubber trees.

Should the writer make this addition here?

(A) Yes, because it supports the passage's claim about the causes of the rubber boom.
(B) Yes, because it explains a process that is relevant to the passage.
(C) No, because it makes a claim that is not supported in the passage.
(D) No, because it distracts from the paragraph's focus on the film.

2

(A) NO CHANGE
(B) Theirs are
(C) There's
(D) There's are

3

(A) NO CHANGE
(B) seeks help
(C) seek the helps
(D) seek help

4

Which choice best completes the description of the film's plot?

(A) NO CHANGE
(B) specifically the "yakruna," a fictional hallucinogenic plant.
(C) and both scholars, the first one a German and the second an American, travel through the Amazon.
(D) and their journeys intertwine as the characters cope with loss, insanity, friendship, and betrayal.

5

The writer wants to conclude the passage by showing that the Amazonians' suggestions influenced Guerra's creative decisions. Which choice best accomplishes this goal?

(A) NO CHANGE
(B) such as names of plants and sacred chants.
(C) while translating into four or five separate languages.
(D) for the fictional tribe of the shaman character.

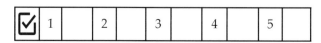

Refer to the passage below to answer questions 1 – 5.

Some psychological researchers suggest that people **1** <u>who suffer from loneliness</u> may benefit from training in social perceptiveness. In other words, some chronically lonely people may be unable to form relationships because they misread other peoples' tones, expressions, and social cues, so their responses may strike others as **2** <u>wrong.</u>

In 2015, Megan Knowles of Franklin and Marshall College led a team of researchers to explore a more nuanced picture of chronic loneliness. Researchers recruited volunteers and assessed their levels of loneliness. All volunteers were then tested on their sensitivity to expressed emotions. **3** <u>It was</u> to identify emotions in either images of faces or audio tapes of spoken words.

Before beginning the task, volunteers read a brief introduction explaining the objective. Researchers found that when the introduction said that the task measured academic skills, lonely people performed the same as or better than non-lonely people. **4** <u>But when "measuring of social skills," according to the task's introduction, it meant a lower score for the lonely people.</u> Researchers suggested that many chronically lonely people are perfectly capable of interpreting emotional cues. **5** <u>In fact,</u> when they interact with others, they may "choke under pressure," or experience performance anxiety that undercuts their ability.

———————————— ★ ————————————

1

Which choice provides the most appropriate introduction to the passage?

(A) NO CHANGE
(B) who feel certain ways
(C) without a support network
(D) complaining of relationship problems

2

(A) NO CHANGE
(B) menacing.
(C) unfriendly.
(D) unapproachable.

3

(A) NO CHANGE
(B) In the test, which was
(C) They were impelled
(D) They were asked

4

Which choice most closely matches the stylistic pattern established in the previous sentence?

(A) NO CHANGE
(B) Saying in the introduction that the test measured social skills had the opposite effect, with lonely people less able to succeed.
(C) Compared to others, however, the lonely people got a worse score when the introduction said that it measured social skills.
(D) But when the introduction said that it measured social skills, the lonely people performed worse than the others.

5

(A) NO CHANGE
(B) Hence,
(C) However,
(D) At the same time,

1		2		3		4		5	

Refer to the passage below to answer questions 1 – 5.

Although many consider them simple passages that connect one part of a building to another, **1** the hallway has long been central to Western architecture, serving to simultaneously divide **2** spaces, and link them together. Nearly three millennia ago, at the onset of Europe's Iron Age, long, rectangular "mead halls" housed lords, ladies, and their attendants. Over time, smaller rooms were partitioned within or built adjacent to these large mead halls. Gradually, a mead hall might have transformed into what is today considered a hallway.

Since their **3** progress, hallways have proven socially and architecturally influential. One of their largest social impacts has been providing privacy; hallways allow people to walk past rooms instead of through them. **4** Structurally, hallways provide access for piping and ventilation systems. Their walls also offer essential interior support for the weight of the building. **5** Consequently, interior hallways may be the safest places within a building during extreme weather such as tornadoes. Hallways, it is plain, could not be more central to building design.

———————— ★ ————————

1
(A) NO CHANGE
(B) a hallway has
(C) the hallway had
(D) hallways have

2
(A) NO CHANGE
(B) spaces, for they link
(C) spaces and to link
(D) spaces as a way to link

3
(A) NO CHANGE
(B) invention,
(C) growth,
(D) development,

4

The writer is considering deleting the underlined sentence. Should the sentence be kept or deleted?

(A) Kept, because it provides a transition between the social and structural functions of hallways.
(B) Kept, because it references the historical information provided in the first paragraph.
(C) Deleted, because it takes the focus of the passage away from Iron Age architecture.
(D) Deleted, because it contradicts a claim made later in the paragraph.

5

Which choice provides the most logical introduction to the sentence?

(A) NO CHANGE
(B) Significantly,
(C) When necessary,
(D) DELETE the underlined portion, and begin the sentence with "Interior."

| ☑ | 1 | | 2 | | 3 | | 4 | | 5 | |

Refer to the passage below to answer questions 1 – 5.

The blisters on my feet felt raw. The others were far ahead of me; looking up at the slope, I could see their brightly colored, aluminum-frame backpacks bobbing along the switchback trail. We were mostly above the tree line, although at the end of this particular switchback, a gnarled little pine tree clung to a rocky **1** outcropping. I longed to sit down and lean on it. **2** Rooted in a crevice among the rocks, I noticed, hesitating near the pine, a patch of columbine blossoms. Their long yellow spurs and lacy leaves seemed to sprout impossibly from the unyielding granite. This morning, I would have taken a photo, but after the day's grueling hike, I was too tired to harbor enthusiasm.

I bade farewell to pine and blossom, and resumed my trek. After what felt like an eternity, I looked up to see only sky above the next switchback. I trudged up and over the **3** crest. It was a wide, unpeopled rock plain, scraped out of the mountain by glaciers. It was too high for trees, but filled with flat boulders, pure lakes, grass-choked brooks. **4** I reached the tents and unbuckled my pack, letting it thump to the ground. Then—I felt weightless. I sprang back to the trail to look at the vast mountain canyons **5** from where we were, catching my breath as I absorbed the breathtaking view.

───────── ★ ─────────

1

(A) NO CHANGE
(B) outgrowth.
(C) offshoot.
(D) cornerstone.

2

(A) NO CHANGE
(B) I noticed, hesitating near the pine, rooted in a crevice among the rocks, a patch of columbine blossoms.
(C) Hesitating near the pine, I noticed a patch of columbine blossoms rooted in a crevice among the rocks.
(D) A patch of columbine blossoms rooted in a crevice among the rocks, hesitating near the pine, I noticed.

3

(A) NO CHANGE
(B) crest; it was
(C) crest into
(D) crest and there was

4

At this point, the writer is considering adding the following sentence.

> I could see my parents, aunts, uncles, and cousins making camp.

Should the writer make this addition here?

(A) Yes, because it explains the narrator's determination to reach the destination.
(B) Yes, because it provides relevant details about the narrator's age and social context.
(C) No, because it interrupts a description about the valley above the crest.
(D) No, because it introduces a new topic that goes unexplained.

5

(A) NO CHANGE
(B) which we had come up for,
(C) from which we had come,
(D) where we had been coming up there,

✓	1		2		3		4		5	

CHAPTER 3

Continuous effort - not strength or intelligence - is the key **to unlocking our potential**.

— Winston Churchill

CHAPTER **4**

Mastering
Writing & Language

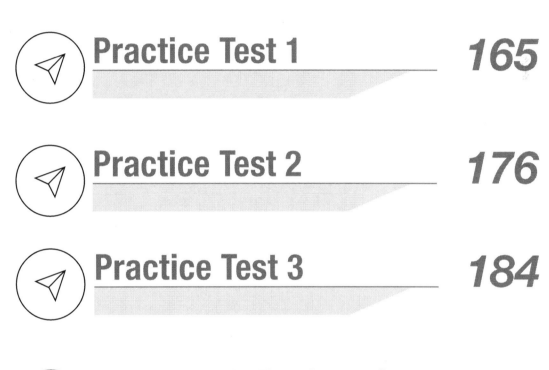

Writing and Language Test Scoring Guide

Number correct on the SAT Writing and Language Test: _____
(Raw Score)

The practice tests in this book will give you a good impression of how well you will do on the official SAT. Find a quiet place where you will not be interrupted and set a timer for 35 minutes. When you have completed the practice test or the time is up, check your answers and count how many you answered correctly; that is your raw score. Next, convert your raw score to a scaled score using the KALLIS scoring guide chart.

The Redesigned SAT composite (overall) score ranges from 400 to 1600, which does not include the optional Essay portion. The Writing and Language portion of the test contributes one-fourth of the composite score. Thus, it is possible to score anywhere from 100 to 400 on the Writing and Language portion.

Remember that there is no penalty for wrong answers on the Redesigned SAT. Only correct answers will contribute toward a test taker's score; incorrect and unmarked answers will have no effect. Therefore, never leave a question blank, even if you must guess.

Raw Score	Scaled Score
44	400
43	390
42	380
41	370
40 – 38	360
37	350
36	340
35 – 34	330
33 – 32	320
31	310
30 – 28	300
27 – 26	290
25 – 24	280
23 – 22	270
21	260
20	250
19	230 – 240
18	220
17	210
16	200
15	190
14	180
13	170
12	160
11	150
10	140
9	130
8	120
7	110
6 – 1	100

SAT Practice Test
Answer Sheet

Remove (or photocopy) this answer sheet and use it to complete the SAT Practice Test.
See the answer key and explanations following the test when finished.

Start with number 1 for each section.
If a section has fewer questions than answer spaces, leave the extra spaces blank.

1. Ⓐ Ⓑ Ⓒ Ⓓ   12. Ⓐ Ⓑ Ⓒ Ⓓ   23. Ⓐ Ⓑ Ⓒ Ⓓ   34. Ⓐ Ⓑ Ⓒ Ⓓ
2. Ⓐ Ⓑ Ⓒ Ⓓ   13. Ⓐ Ⓑ Ⓒ Ⓓ   24. Ⓐ Ⓑ Ⓒ Ⓓ   35. Ⓐ Ⓑ Ⓒ Ⓓ
3. Ⓐ Ⓑ Ⓒ Ⓓ   14. Ⓐ Ⓑ Ⓒ Ⓓ   25. Ⓐ Ⓑ Ⓒ Ⓓ   37. Ⓐ Ⓑ Ⓒ Ⓓ   #right in
4. Ⓐ Ⓑ Ⓒ Ⓓ   15. Ⓐ Ⓑ Ⓒ Ⓓ   26. Ⓐ Ⓑ Ⓒ Ⓓ   38. Ⓐ Ⓑ Ⓒ Ⓓ   Section 2
5. Ⓐ Ⓑ Ⓒ Ⓓ   16. Ⓐ Ⓑ Ⓒ Ⓓ   27. Ⓐ Ⓑ Ⓒ Ⓓ   39. Ⓐ Ⓑ Ⓒ Ⓓ
6. Ⓐ Ⓑ Ⓒ Ⓓ   17. Ⓐ Ⓑ Ⓒ Ⓓ   28. Ⓐ Ⓑ Ⓒ Ⓓ   40. Ⓐ Ⓑ Ⓒ Ⓓ
7. Ⓐ Ⓑ Ⓒ Ⓓ   18. Ⓐ Ⓑ Ⓒ Ⓓ   29. Ⓐ Ⓑ Ⓒ Ⓓ   41. Ⓐ Ⓑ Ⓒ Ⓓ
8. Ⓐ Ⓑ Ⓒ Ⓓ   19. Ⓐ Ⓑ Ⓒ Ⓓ   30. Ⓐ Ⓑ Ⓒ Ⓓ   42. Ⓐ Ⓑ Ⓒ Ⓓ   #wrong in
9. Ⓐ Ⓑ Ⓒ Ⓓ   20. Ⓐ Ⓑ Ⓒ Ⓓ   31. Ⓐ Ⓑ Ⓒ Ⓓ   43. Ⓐ Ⓑ Ⓒ Ⓓ   Section 2
10. Ⓐ Ⓑ Ⓒ Ⓓ   21. Ⓐ Ⓑ Ⓒ Ⓓ   32. Ⓐ Ⓑ Ⓒ Ⓓ   44. Ⓐ Ⓑ Ⓒ Ⓓ
11. Ⓐ Ⓑ Ⓒ Ⓓ   22. Ⓐ Ⓑ Ⓒ Ⓓ   33. Ⓐ Ⓑ Ⓒ Ⓓ

1. Ⓐ Ⓑ Ⓒ Ⓓ   12. Ⓐ Ⓑ Ⓒ Ⓓ   23. Ⓐ Ⓑ Ⓒ Ⓓ   34. Ⓐ Ⓑ Ⓒ Ⓓ
2. Ⓐ Ⓑ Ⓒ Ⓓ   13. Ⓐ Ⓑ Ⓒ Ⓓ   24. Ⓐ Ⓑ Ⓒ Ⓓ   35. Ⓐ Ⓑ Ⓒ Ⓓ
3. Ⓐ Ⓑ Ⓒ Ⓓ   14. Ⓐ Ⓑ Ⓒ Ⓓ   25. Ⓐ Ⓑ Ⓒ Ⓓ   37. Ⓐ Ⓑ Ⓒ Ⓓ   #right in
4. Ⓐ Ⓑ Ⓒ Ⓓ   15. Ⓐ Ⓑ Ⓒ Ⓓ   26. Ⓐ Ⓑ Ⓒ Ⓓ   38. Ⓐ Ⓑ Ⓒ Ⓓ   Section 2
5. Ⓐ Ⓑ Ⓒ Ⓓ   16. Ⓐ Ⓑ Ⓒ Ⓓ   27. Ⓐ Ⓑ Ⓒ Ⓓ   39. Ⓐ Ⓑ Ⓒ Ⓓ
6. Ⓐ Ⓑ Ⓒ Ⓓ   17. Ⓐ Ⓑ Ⓒ Ⓓ   28. Ⓐ Ⓑ Ⓒ Ⓓ   40. Ⓐ Ⓑ Ⓒ Ⓓ
7. Ⓐ Ⓑ Ⓒ Ⓓ   18. Ⓐ Ⓑ Ⓒ Ⓓ   29. Ⓐ Ⓑ Ⓒ Ⓓ   41. Ⓐ Ⓑ Ⓒ Ⓓ
8. Ⓐ Ⓑ Ⓒ Ⓓ   19. Ⓐ Ⓑ Ⓒ Ⓓ   30. Ⓐ Ⓑ Ⓒ Ⓓ   42. Ⓐ Ⓑ Ⓒ Ⓓ   #wrong in
9. Ⓐ Ⓑ Ⓒ Ⓓ   20. Ⓐ Ⓑ Ⓒ Ⓓ   31. Ⓐ Ⓑ Ⓒ Ⓓ   43. Ⓐ Ⓑ Ⓒ Ⓓ   Section 2
10. Ⓐ Ⓑ Ⓒ Ⓓ   21. Ⓐ Ⓑ Ⓒ Ⓓ   32. Ⓐ Ⓑ Ⓒ Ⓓ   44. Ⓐ Ⓑ Ⓒ Ⓓ
11. Ⓐ Ⓑ Ⓒ Ⓓ   22. Ⓐ Ⓑ Ⓒ Ⓓ   33. Ⓐ Ⓑ Ⓒ Ⓓ

Writing & Language Test 1

35 MINUTES, 44 QUESTIONS

Turn to Section 2 of your answer sheet to answer the questions in this section.

Cockroach Robots

The word "robot" comes from the Czech word *robota*, which means "hard work." Not all automated machines that are doing hard work fit the definition of robot, however. In general, robots have the ability to adapt to situations using information that they collect. For example, if a space robot bumps into a rock on a distant planet, it can gather visual information, search its database for appropriate algorithms, and adapt them by setting variables. It "plans" an adaptive behavior by putting the algorithms in an appropriate sequence. **2** Forthwith, it appears to be making decisions about how to proceed. This adaptive behavior allows the robot in the example above to "decide" to navigate around, rather than into, the rock.

Because adaptive robots can be used to accomplish many tasks, the science of robotics is developing quickly in many directions. One branch is creating software bots; another is exploring new ways to use conventional mechanical robots. **3** Then there is a branch of robotics inspired by biological organisms. Researchers in the field of "soft robotics" use relatively soft materials, such as silicon, plastic, or rubber, to create bio-inspired robots that can interact with an environment in much the same way as some living organisms. Robots have been modeled on the **4** octopus for example, and on everyone's favorite swarming insect: the cockroach.

1

(A) NO CHANGE
(B) machines with hard-working automation
(C) hard-working automated machines
(D) automated machines work hard to

2

(A) NO CHANGE
(B) Straightaway,
(C) All things considered,
(D) For this reason,

3

(A) NO CHANGE
(B) In parallel, scientists are
(C) There is interest in being
(D) Some scientists have even been

4

(A) NO CHANGE
(B) octopuses, for example and
(C) octopus for examples and
(D) octopus, for example, and

Scientists say that cockroach-like robots **5** <u>would be serving</u> many purposes. After a natural disaster or a mine collapse or the like, these robots may be able to get through rubble, locate survivors, and evaluate the rubble's stability. They could also be used to diagnose problems in pipes or to clean up toxic spills in hard-to-reach areas. **6**

Russian engineers at Immanuel Kant Baltic Federal University announced in 2015 that they had created a 10-cm robot that can run 30 cm per second. **7** <u>One-third</u> as fast as real cockroaches. The artificial cockroaches may be slow, but they can carry up to 10 grams of weight, enough for light-weight surveillance equipment.

8 Bio-mechanists at the University of California at Berkeley have studied how real cockroaches squeeze through tight spaces. Professor Robert Full and graduate student Kaushik Jayarim made tiny clear tunnels with ceilings **9** <u>lower.</u> They found that cockroaches could continue moving at full speed even when their bodies were compressed by more than half, and emerge unharmed. In such a situation, **10** <u>they</u> are able to splay their legs out to the side and scoot on their bellies. The researchers concluded that cockroaches need to have just enough friction so that their splayed legs can "find purchase," or have something to push against.

Full and Jayarim designed a cockroach-sized robot that can similarly splay its legs and move quickly through tight spots. The researchers say their robot should pave the way to more arthropod-inspired robot development, because not only are insects malleable and **11** <u>strong but they</u> have appendages that could be adapted for different tasks.

—————————— ★ ——————————

5

(A) NO CHANGE
(B) would have been serving
(C) could someday serve
(D) could have served

6

At this point, the writer is thinking of adding the following sentence:

> Essentially, scientists are just beginning to imagine the potential uses of automated bugs.

Should the writer make this addition here?

(A) Yes, because it provides a larger context for the preceding points.
(B) Yes, because it summarizes the examples in the paragraph.
(C) No, because it fails to maintain the passage's focus on useful applications of the technology.
(D) No, because it undermines the main claim about disaster response in the paragraph.

7

(A) NO CHANGE
(B) That speed is only one-third
(C) A mere one-third
(D) Which is one-third

8

Which choice most effectively establishes the main topic of the paragraph?

(A) Other scientists are focusing on making cockroach robots that are agile.
(B) Scientists say that cockroach abilities are nothing short of amazing.
(C) You may have wondered how cockroaches have gotten into a closed room.
(D) Other countries, naturally, want to keep up with the Russians.

9

(A) NO CHANGE
(B) at small intervals.
(C) at gradually lower heights.
(D) that were increasingly accommodating.

10

(A) NO CHANGE
(B) most of them
(C) researchers
(D) real cockroaches

11

(A) NO CHANGE
(B) strong, they
(C) strong, but they also
(D) strong and they

Separate and Not Equal

On the Tuesday before Thanksgiving in 1951, at an African-American high school in Kinston, North Carolina, a student made a routine announcement over the intercom explaining that one of the girls had lost a red pocketbook; [12] the student asks that anyone who found it to bring it to the office. Suddenly, to the astonishment of school staff, all 720 students stood up and walked out the front door of the school.

Most of the students knew that the announcement about the red pocketbook was the signal for a well-planned public protest. No adults knew of the plan. The students' main grievance was that their gymnasium had burned down, and [13] rebuilding was ignored by the school board. The school's basketball and volleyball teams had no place to practice or play games, putting them at a competitive disadvantage. Meanwhile, the school district provided the nearby whites-only high school with top-notch facilities and equipment.

Socio-economic disparities like the one described above were common in the 1950s and before. In spite of the long and passionate struggle to integrate American schools, the goal had not and still has not been reached. [14] The 1950s did mark the beginning of change, however, when African-American students themselves began calling attention to blatant inequities in legally segregated schools.

The Kinston protest [15] may have been inspired by a protest that occurred in Farmville, Virginia earlier that year. In Farmville, the high school that was open to African Americans had a leaky roof and inadequate heating. It was severely overcrowded; [16] students were wedged in. Yet the district's only response to this overcrowding was to provide three tar-paper shacks.

★

12

(A) NO CHANGE
(B) and that anyone who
(C) the student asked anyone who
(D) they said that whoever

13

(A) NO CHANGE
(B) the school board was not taking action to rebuild it.
(C) the problem was being ignored by the school board.
(D) rebuilding was not happening by the school board.

14

At this point, the writer wants to add specific information that supports the previous sentence. Which choice offers a relevant and accurate interpretation of the data in the chart that follows the passage?

(A) Most U.S. schools are still predominantly one group or another for every group except Asians.
(B) Only 8.3 percent of white students attend schools with a majority of black students, while 27.6 percent of black students attend schools with a majority of white students.
(C) About half of black and Latino students in the U.S. still attend predominantly black or Latino schools.
(D) There are more schools in the U.S. that have predominantly white enrollment than there are schools that are predominantly attended by any other group.

15

(A) NO CHANGE
(B) compared with
(C) precisely corresponded to
(D) happened due to

16

Which choice provides information that best supports the claim made in this sentence?

(A) NO CHANGE
(B) textbooks were those that had been discarded by the whites-only school.
(C) some classes were even held in parked school buses.
(D) space per person was just too limited.

A quiet, studious 11th-grader who was the first to risk speaking out in Farmville. Barbara Rose Johns was the daughter of a farmer, but she was also the niece of a Civil Rights activist, the Rev. Vernon Johns. Spurred by something a teacher said, Barbara Johns began a discrete recruitment of friends to her cause.

[1] Hence, one day a student called the school's front office and notified the principal about an emergency in town involving students. [2]There was no truth to the report, but it did lure the principal away. A forged memo was delivered to all classes, announcing an unscheduled assembly. [3] The classes went to the assembly hall to find Barbara Johns on stage. [4] Understanding the gravity of the situation, Johns asked the teachers to leave. [5] She then encouraged students to join her on a strike, saying, "Don't be afraid; just follow us out."

The 450 Farmville students did go on strike that day. Eventually, the National Association for the Advancement of Colored People (NAACP) supported their cause, who became part of the lawsuit that led to the Supreme Court's landmark 1954 decision in Brown v. the Board of Education. The decision declared that segregated schools are "inherently unequal" and therefore unconstitutional.

Racial Composition of School Attended by Average Student of Each Race, 2011-12

Percent Race in Each School	Racial Composition of School Attended by Average			
	White Student	Black Student	Asian Student	Latino Student
% White	72.5%	27.6%	38.9%	25.1%
% Black	8.3%	48.8%	10.7%	10.9%
% Asian	3.9%	3.6%	24.5%	4.7%
% Latino	11.8%	17.1%	22.1%	56.8%
% Other	3.5%	2.9%	3.8%	2.5%

Note: Other represents students who identified as Native American or Multiracial.

Source: U.S. Department of Education, National Center for Education Statistics, Common Core of Date(CCD), Public Elementary/Secondary School Universe Survey Date, *2011-12* Gary Orfield, Erica Frankenberg, "Brown at 60: Great Progress, a Long Retreat and an Uncertain Future," Civil Rights Project, May 15, 2014

★

17

(A) NO CHANGE
(B) which was
(C) that was
(D) was

18

(A) NO CHANGE
(B) disparate
(C) discreet
(D) discordance

19

Which choice most effectively combines the sentences at the underlined portion?

(A) away; in the interval, a
(B) away, because a
(C) away—although a
(D) away, when a

20

(A) NO CHANGE
(B) saying, not to "be
(C) saying "Don't be
(D) saying "don't be

21

To improve the cohesion and flow of this paragraph, the writer wants to add the following sentence:

   In Farmville, protesting the status quo carried real risks to one's family or oneself.

The sentence would most logically be placed before

(A) sentence 1.
(B) sentence 2.
(C) sentence 4.
(D) sentence 5.

22

(A) NO CHANGE
(B) which
(C) whereby
(D) whom

Workplace Monitoring

[1]

"Big Data" is the understated term for the vast amount of information that can be collected, stored, and used in the digital age. Big Data has revolutionized daily life, even **23** the workplace. Managers now have access to countless methods of monitoring **24** employees that includes via cameras, microphones, infrared sensors, and thermometers. Employees' computer activity can even be tracked and analyzed by employers.

[2]

And **25** while it may seem incredibly uncomfortable to be monitored, the practice has the potential to benefit everyone at a workplace. Data can help managers make rational and fair decisions rather than going on gut feelings, **26** which has a boomerang effect. In that case, employees may be more energetic and efficient, strengthening the company as a whole. Using data to provide optimal working conditions may indirectly improve a company's earnings. A study by Massachusetts Institute of Technology (MIT) found that companies that rely on data of all kinds most heavily tend to experience the highest profits. Data injects a healthy dose of "what we know" instead of "what we think" into company policy.

[3]

Employees will be likely to embrace monitoring at work if it is done in a transparent manner, and not for the purpose of evaluating individual job performance. People being monitored should understand **27** a company purposes. One example would be to determine the ideal time of day to hold meetings. Another may be to **28** evaluate the effectiveness of certain types of computer keyboards. Ideally, an outside company collects results and keeps individual data anonymous. One company commissioned a study in which sensors were placed in employee nametags to learn how often employees at a call center talked with colleagues. When that information was compared with individual productivity, the data indicated that interactive employees were actually more productive. As a result, the company established group break times, and found that job performance at the call center rose across the board.

───────── ★ ─────────

23

(A) NO CHANGE
(B) experiences in the workplace.
(C) desks in the typical office.
(D) cubicles and conference rooms.

24

(A) NO CHANGE
(B) an employee that include
(C) the employee, which includes
(D) employees, including

25

The writer is thinking of deleting the underlined portion. Should the writer make this change?

(A) Yes, because it undermines the main claim about potential benefits of monitoring.
(B) Yes, because it adds details that are not relevant to the topic of the paragraph.
(C) No, because it introduces an important argument in support of monitoring.
(D) No, because it acknowledges the main counter-argument to monitoring.

26

Which choice provides information that best supports the point developed in this paragraph?

(A) NO CHANGE
(B) helping them see business opportunities clearly.
(C) and could also improve working conditions.
(D) DELETE the underlined portion, and place a period after "gut feelings."

27

(A) NO CHANGE
(B) companies
(C) company's
(D) companies'

28

The writer wants to provide a second example of how data from employee monitoring can improve working conditions. Which choice would best accomplish this goal?

(A) NO CHANGE
(B) determine which employees work the fastest.
(C) understand why the air conditioning is malfunctioning.
(D) prevent customers from shoplifting merchandise.

[4]

Some large corporations unwisely monitor individual data for performance evaluation, supported by the notion that honest feedback leads to self-improvement. Employers may micro-manage workers by tracking their levels of concentration, their average transaction times, the success of their projects, and so on. Some companies even provide constant rankings of employees from <u>**29** employees who are most successful down to employees who are least successful.</u> Such use of Big Data creates a level of competition and anxiety that many employees <u>**30** really hate.</u> They may feel very little enthusiasm about going to work every day to be monitored.

[5]

Historically, Google has supported its workers' needs at the workplace on the theory that doing so reduces <u>**31** turnover and</u> the associated costs. Google continuously analyzes data about how to make its workers and workplaces more productive. **32** <u>Their</u> innovations include diner-style booths for cozy creative meetings, bicycles for getting around company buildings, and "nap capsules." **33**

───────── ★ ─────────

29

(A) NO CHANGE
(B) those who are most successful to those who are least successful.
(C) most successful ones on down.
(D) most successful to least.

30

Which choice best maintains the tone established in the paragraph?

(A) NO CHANGE
(B) may find untenable.
(C) do not want to deal with.
(D) cannot even deal with.

31

(A) NO CHANGE
(B) turnover; also
(C) turnover, and
(D) turnover,

32

(A) NO CHANGE
(B) They're
(C) Its
(D) It's

Think about the previous passage as a whole as you answer question 33.

33

To make the passage more logical, paragraph 4 should be placed

(A) where it is now.
(B) before paragraph 1.
(C) before paragraph 2.
(D) after paragraph 5.

Comic poet

In 1930, a young man named Ogden Nash was working as a manuscript reader for a publisher in New York City. He often amused himself and his coworkers by writing a humorous rhyming comment on a slip of paper, crumpling the paper up and tossing [34] them to another desk.

One day, Nash wrote a poem in which an office worker confesses to irresistible spring fever. It begins, "I sit in an office at 2244 Madison Avenue / And say to myself You have a responsible job, havenue?..." He submitted the poem to the prestigious *New Yorker* magazine, [35] which to his astonishment accepted it.

[1] The poem launched Nash's career as a poet. [2] Nash was hired to work at the *New Yorker*, and within a year, he had published a book of his poems—the first of many. [3] Critics [36] and the public alike loved his work. [4] Nash offered bold insights, delivered in uneven lines that contained clever misspellings and elisions in order to rhyme. [5] Yet they became part of the canon of popular culture. People could never forget lines such as, "If called by a panther, / Don't anther." [37]

Nash's career coincided with the start of the Great Depression [38] of the1930s. When many Americans lost their savings and their jobs. Nash's silliness provided some distraction, but at the same time he did not [39] fear pointed social commentary. For example, in "Bankers Are Just Like Anybody Else, Except Richer," he protests: "Most bankers dwell in marble halls, / Which they get to dwell in because they encourage deposits and discourage withdrawals," and succeed because they only lend money to the already rich: "And all the vice-presidents nod their heads in rhythm, / And the only question asked is do the borrowers want the money sent or do they want to take it withm..."

★

34

(A) NO CHANGE
(B) them to other desks.
(C) it to another desk.
(D) coworkers the paper.

35

A) NO CHANGE
(B) which, to his astonishment,
(C) which, to his astonishment
(D) which to his astonishment,

36

Which choice results in a sentence that best supports the point developed in this paragraph?

(A) NO CHANGE
(B) unanimously praised and
(C) and New York office workers
(D) DELETE the underlined portion.

37

The writer wants to add the following sentence to the paragraph:

In 1935, a New York Times Book Review writer commented that Nash's poems were "fundamentally and magnificently unsound."

The best placement for the sentence is immediately

(A) before sentence 1.
(B) before sentence 2.
(C) after sentence 3.
(D) after sentence 4.

38

(A) NO CHANGE
(B) of the 1930s. So, many
(C) of the 1930s: many
(D) of the 1930s, when many

39

(A) NO CHANGE
(B) encounter
(C) attempt to produce
(D) shy away from

40 But for the most part, ordinary life was Nash's preferred subject matter. Nash lived with his wife and two **41** daughters, whom were often the subjects of his dry wit. "A man could be granted to live a dozen lives, / And he still wouldn't understand daughters and wives," Nash opined in one poem. **42**

Nash's classic children's book *The Tale of Custard the Dragon* takes a humorous stab at those who **43** boast and swagger and ran from real danger. One braggart mouse in the story "strategically mouse-holes" when faced with real danger. The classic theme amuses both children and adults. Yet Nash was not arrogant, and he always included himself in the world that he critiqued. Generally, he called himself a "worsifier," a pun on the word "versifier." Nash **44** was featured on a U.S. postage stamp three decades after his death in 1971.

—————————— ★ ——————————

40

Which choice results in the most effective transition to the information that follows in the paragraph?

(A) NO CHANGE
(B) In other words,
(C) By the same token,
(D) For this reason,

41

(A) NO CHANGE
(B) daughters, who
(C) daughters to whom
(D) daughters, which

42

The writer is considering adding the following information.

> In another he describes parenting adolescents: "Their eyes signal What's cooking? at you, / And lips hiss, Shush, Daddy, everybody's looking at you!..."

Should the writer make this addition here?

(A) Yes, because it elaborates on the paragraph's primary claim.
(B) Yes, because it provides relevant biographical information.
(C) No, because it shifts the focus of the paragraph.
(D) No, because it is not explained in the context of the paragraph.

43

(A) NO CHANGE
(B) boast, who swagger and run
(C) boast and swagger, and yet run
(D) boasted, swaggered, and ran

44

The writer wants a conclusion that emphasizes the longevity of Nash's career. Which choice best accomplishes this goal?

(A) NO CHANGE
(B) continued writing and publishing for more than 40 years until
(C) appeared on many comic radio and television programs before
(D) was called America's "best known producer of humorous poetry" at the time of

Writing & Language Test 2

 35 MINUTES, 44 QUESTIONS

Turn to Section 2 of your answer sheet to answer the questions in this section.

DIRECTIONS

Each of the following passages is accompanied by approximately 11 questions. Some questions will require you to revise the passages in order to improve coherence and clarity. Other questions will require you to correct grammatical errors. Passages may be accompanied by graphs, charts, or tables that you must consider when making revisions. For most questions, you may select the "NO CHANGE" option if you believe that portion of the passage is clear, concise, and grammatically correct as is.

Within the passages, highlighted numbers followed by underlined text indicate which part of the text corresponds with each question. Bracketed numbers [1] indicate sentence number. These bracketed numbers are only relevant to problems that require you to add or rearrange sentences in a paragraph.

Genes and Sports

Is it possible to say who will **1** <u>win</u> a sport based on studying individual players' DNA? Probably not; most geneticists doubt that genes will ever become the only factor in predicting athletic success. **2** <u>We are born with</u> natural advantages or disadvantages in sports. *The Sports Gene*, by David Epstein, details many such cases where particular physical traits make a difference. A short person with long, thin legs has an advantage in long-distance running, because he or she will have a longer stride and less weight to carry **3** <u>than other runners.</u> People with relatively long arms obviously have an edge in reaching for the ball in basketball, tennis, and water polo. Petite competitors in gymnastics will be better able launch their own weight into back flips. **4** <u>Even the willingness to train and practice may be an inheritable trait.</u>

———————— ★ ————————

1

Which choice provides the most appropriate introduction to the passage?

(A) NO CHANGE
(B) excel at
(C) conquer
(D) be rewarded by

2

Which choice most logically follows the previous sentence?

(A) NO CHANGE
(B) In the first place it is clear that we each have
(C) No one denies that our inherited traits give us
(D) Science aside, people clearly grasp

3

(A) NO CHANGE
(B) than other runners'.
(C) than those of other runners.
(D) than other runners do.

4

Which choice includes an example that effectively concludes the list of competitive advantages?

(A) NO CHANGE
(B) Hand-eye coordination is also important in many sports.
(C) Regardless, all athletes must be in peak physical shape to compete professionally.
(D) Some famous athletes have children who follow in their parent's footsteps.

However, lifestyle also has an enormous impact on athletic development. For example, at first glance, 5 it would seem that Kenyans and Ethiopians have some special gene for long-distance running, as they dominate the sport. One group especially dominates—the Kalenjin tribe of Kenya. Researchers point out that, although the Kalenjin population does tend to have long, thin legs, there are also environmental factors that contribute to their prowess at running. For example, they live at high altitudes, so their bodies are adjusted to using oxygen efficiently. 6

The most hotly debated genetic profiling issue in professional sports involves predicting 7 weather players are more prone to injuries. Barcelona, Spain's professional soccer team, the Barcelona Football Club, has been actively attempting to predict 8 its players risk of injury and probable time to heal. Team doctors reportedly test players to identify genes that control the production of collagen, 9 the main component in the body's connective tissues. They hypothesize that an athlete who naturally produces more collagen will have more resilient tendons and ligaments, and will be able to repair torn tissue quickly.

Genetic researchers have indeed identified gene variants that correlate with a tendency for tendon and ligament 10 injuries. Despite that, the researchers caution that the science for predicting connective tissue injuries is still rudimentary. Genes represent probabilities, not certainties, geneticists say, and the probabilities are often quite small. Thousands of genes may be involved in producing a given characteristic. Genes respond to environmental cues, such as what a person eats or how he or she trains. In addition, personal factors such as age and gender help determine a characteristic such as injury recovery time. 11

——————————— ★ ———————————

5

(A) NO CHANGE
(B) it will seem like
(C) it seemed like
(D) it used to seem like

6

At this point, the writer wants to further reinforce the paragraph's claim about lifestyle contributing as well as genes. Which choice most effectively accomplishes this goal?

(A) A staple of Kalenjin people's diet is boiled cornmeal and greens, occasionally with meat, and fermented milk.
(B) Kalenjin homes are widely scattered, so children often must travel a number of miles on foot to get to school and back every day.

(C) Kalenjin children are expected to help with family chores, including taking care of their little sisters or brothers and herding goats or cattle close to home.
(D) The Kalenjin, living in the fertile Rift Valley, are relatively prosperous compared to some other Kenyan ethnic groups.

7

(A) NO CHANGE
(B) whether
(C) which
(D) witch

8

(A) NO CHANGE
(B) it's players'
(C) its players'
(D) their players'

9

Which choice offers the most relevant detail?

(A) NO CHANGE
(B) which makes up 30 percent of the protein in the human body.
(C) which can become dry and brittle with a diet high in sugar.
(D) which is sometimes applied to wounds to speed healing.

10

Which choice most effectively combines the sentences at the underlined portion?

(A) injuries, they caution that
(B) injuries, but they say that
(C) injuries with
(D) injuries; and still,

11

Which choice most clearly ends the passage with a restatement of the writer's primary claim?

(A) Overall, genes may not have as much of an effect on athletic performance as we have thought.
(B) Nevertheless, sports science and genetics are converging at a fast pace.
(C) In short, the science of genetics may never be able to explain or predict who will become a star athlete.
(D) It is fair to say that the Barcelona Football Club may be using data that will not actually help.

Fashion Revolutions

During the 19th century, British and American women were influenced by the culture surrounding Britain's Queen Victoria. Extreme emphasis was placed on respectability, which at the time [12] meant that women were required to go to extreme lengths to dress in a socially accepted manner, covering themselves from head to toe. Thus, women faced barriers to any kind of activity, even walking, because of their [13] own clothes: a tight corset squeezing the waist and rib cage, layers of petticoats, stockings, a draping dress with huge sleeves, tight shoes, and a hat pinned to the hair. That began to change, however, when several women became celebrities [14] —international celebrities— by pioneering comfortable exercise clothing.

Bicycles for men were popular during the 1890s, but many people thought it was scandalous for a woman to ride one. [15] Therefore, it was surprising when, in Boston in 1894, a 23-year-old married mother of three, Annie Kopchovsky, announced that she [16] will ride a bicycle around the world. She said that she was doing it to win a bet.

Kopchovsky and her husband did not have the means to finance the trip, so she arranged to start out with $100 from the Londonderry Lithia Spring Water Company in return for attaching an advertisement on her bicycle. She agreed to change her public moniker to "Annie Londonderry" [17] to please the company. Some historians credit her with inventing the very idea of corporate sponsorship for sports.

★

12

(A) NO CHANGE
(B) translated to the idea that women should take care to wear bulky clothing so that they did not cause people to criticize them.
(C) called for molding and cloaking the female body.
(D) dictated what kind of clothing women should wear inside and outside of the home in order to maintain respectability.

13

(A) NO CHANGE
(B) own clothes. A tight
(C) own clothes; a tight
(D) own clothes: a tight

14

Which choice most effectively sets up a contrast in the sentence and is consistent with the information in the rest of the passage?

(A) NO CHANGE
(B) —and pariahs—
(C) and earned money
(D) DELETE the underlined portion

15

Which choice results in the most effective transition to the information that follows?

(A) NO CHANGE
(B) Nevertheless,
(C) Yet
(D) Moreover,

16

(A) NO CHANGE
(B) was going to ride
(C) will be riding
(D) had been planning to ride

17

Which choice results in a sentence that best supports the point developed in the paragraph?

(A) NO CHANGE
(B) pretend to be an owner of
(C) out of personal gratitude toward
(D) to further promote

Londonderry had to quickly learn how to ride a bike. She then departed from Boston with fanfare, wearing a dress with full skirts. [18] Reportedly, by the time she reached Chicago, she wanted to quit. But she decided to continue—in the opposite direction, with a lighter bicycle, and with bloomers (billowing pants) instead of skirts.

Londonderry's bloomers shocked the public. Nevertheless, Londonderry eventually pared down further by donning a men's tighter-fitting riding costume (still covered to the wrists and ankles.)

[1] Media attention followed Londonderry as she took a steamship to many cities around the world, riding her bike at each stop. [2] She became quite fit by riding everywhere she stopped; she often won bicycle races organized in her honor. [3] Throughout the year-long trip, Londonderry earned money through advertising and giving talks about her travels. [4] She denounced corsets, and demonstrated that [19] they could dress comfortably and still be respectable. [20]

About a decade later, the fashion revolution spread to swimwear. A typical Victorian woman's swimming suit was a flannel dress, petticoats, and stockings, all of which [21] harnessed any attempt at actual swimming. Enter Annette Kellermann, an Australian competitive swimmer. She began thrilling U.S. audiences in 1907 with underwater ballet performances in large glass tanks. She wore a close-fitting swimming costume, eventually shortening it above the knees. In spite of being arrested for indecency in Boston, Kellermann [22] persisted in wearing it. She even started selling a line of swimming suits like the one she wore, which became known as "Annette Kellermanns."

———————————— ★ ————————————

18

At this point, the writer is considering adding the following information.

> A support carriage followed, and she and her crew camped or slept at homes of supporters along the way.

Should the writer make this addition here?

(A) Yes, because it describes an important logistical factor in the journey.
(B) Yes, because it sets up financing the tour as a main topic.
(C) No, because it undermines the emphasis on an independent achievement.
(D) No, because it fails to describe the carriage or its occupants.

19

(A) NO CHANGE
(B) everyone
(C) women
(D) her audiences

20

To improve the cohesion and flow of the paragraph, the writer wants to add the following sentence.

> Eventually she landed in California and continued her celebrated quest by riding to Chicago.

The sentence would most logically be placed

(A) before sentence 1.
(B) after sentence 2.
(C) after sentence 3.
(D) after sentence 4.

21

(A) NO CHANGE
(B) distracted
(C) detained
(D) hindered

22

Which choice most effectively sets up the example that follows?

(A) NO CHANGE
(B) advocated the benefits of swimming.
(C) continued her aquatic performances.
(D) began appearing in silent films.

Airline Pilot Careers

Airline passengers may not give much thought to the pilots who fly their planes. After all, passengers rarely see their pilots. When feeling restless, [23] passengers may irrationally blame pilots for how long the flight is taking. When the plane lands safely, they may declare that the pilots are brilliant. But the actual people serving as pilots remain something of a mystery.

[24] There are more than 100,000 working pilots in the U.S. The most obvious benefit to working for an airline is getting to travel. Pilots may have enough of a layover at destinations for sightseeing, and [25] pilots and families often receive free or reduced-price tickets to fly on the airline. A second basic benefit is that pilots' schedules [26] would offer many days off to spend at home between flights. Thirdly, and perhaps most importantly, many pilots love flying. They enjoy experiencing stunning views of sunsets, sunrises, clouds, stars, sea, and land.

Nonetheless, there are significant challenges in a typical piloting career. Pilots get bored on long flights just like the passengers do, but unlike the passengers, pilots' opportunities for sleeping and reading may be limited or nonexistent. Sometimes a layover between [27] flights are too short for adequate rest. They may be away from their families for days at a time.

Of course, provided that pilots are [28] patient, it gets better. They achieve the seniority to get the best assignments and schedules. Hence, pilots have a disincentive to apply for new jobs at other airline companies, [29] because they would have to start over at the bottom of the seniority ranking.

★

23

(A) NO CHANGE
(B) pilots may be irrationally blamed
(C) pilots may get the blame (irrationally)
(D) blame goes to pilots

24

Which choice most effectively establishes the main topic of the paragraph?

(A) NO CHANGE
(B) Clearly, airline pilots have important responsibilities to their passengers.
(C) People become airline pilots for several reasons.
(D) Pilots love flying airplanes.

25

(A) NO CHANGE
(B) their families and them
(C) families of theirs
(D) they and their families

26

(A) NO CHANGE
(B) may offer
(C) are offering
(D) have offered

27

(A) NO CHANGE
(B) one flight and another are
(C) a flight is
(D) flights is

28

Which choice most effectively combines the sentences at the underlined portion?

(A) patient; they
(B) patient, it will
(C) patient, they can
(D) patient, and they

29

The writer is considering deleting the underlined portion and adding a period after "companies." Should the writer make this change?

(A) Yes, because it merely reformulates a point that is already adequately explained.
(B) Yes, because it fails to explain the information that precedes it in the sentence.
(C) No, because it serves as a transitional point for the next paragraph.
(D) No, because it elaborates on a key point in the paragraph.

The biggest challenge, however, is that the airline business **30** <u>is a volatile one with a thin profit margin.</u> Not only does the price **31** <u>of fuel fluctuate, earnings are</u> sensitive to economic trends. Consequently, airline pilots' jobs and salaries also tend to be volatile, and most pilots experience furloughs—periods of unpaid leave—during their career. Some veteran pilots recommend that new pilots have a back-up career plan.

The U.S. Bureau of Labor Statistics predicts that jobs for airline and commercial pilots will increase by an average amount in the coming years, **32** <u>perhaps by about 5 percent a year.</u> Young people considering the career should know that airlines require pilots to have a four-year college degree, various licenses and certificates, and thousands of hours of flight time. Most would-be pilots take one of two paths. One route is to serve as a pilot in the military. **33** <u>Others</u> attend flight school and work for several years as a commercial pilot, flying helicopters or small planes for tasks such as firefighting or crop dusting.

US AIRLINE INDUSTRY NET PROFIT MARGINS

1950-2004

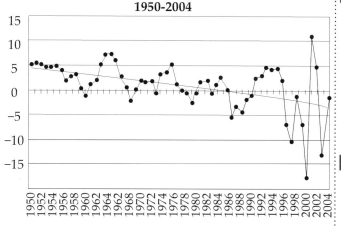

From a presentation by Charles E. Schlumberger, principal air transport specialist for the World Bank, as reported in the *Business Insider*, "Airlines have a small profit margin," June 2012.

★

30

Which choice offers an accurate interpretation of the data that is displayed on the graph?

(A) NO CHANGE
(B) has increasingly volatile profit margins.
(C) experiences many periods of low revenue.
(D) is currently unable to sustain steady growth.

31

(A) NO CHANGE
(B) of fuel fluctuate, in addition earnings are
(C) of fuel fluctuate, but earnings are also
(D) fluctuate—fuel earnings being

32

Which choice most effectively supports the claim made in this sentence?

(A) NO CHANGE
(B) and many children dream of becoming pilots.
(C) though such predictions can be hard to support.
(D) and flying remains the safest means of travel.

33

Which choice most closely matches the stylistic pattern established by the previous sentence?

(A) NO CHANGE
(B) Alternatives include the option to
(C) The other is to
(D) Instead some may choose to

Tulsidas

Around the same time that William Shakespeare was composing sonnets and plays in England, another of the world's greatest writers 34 had created timeless classics in Uttar Pradesh, India: Goswami Tulsidas.

Hindus consider Tulsidas a saint. Among his devotional works is the epic poem-song *Ramcharitmanas*, which means "The Lake of the Deeds of Rama." It is a retelling of ancient stories about the Hindu deity, Rama. The lengthy poem usually fills up around 600 pages. It narrates battles, adventures, 35 and romances. Goodness triumphs over evil.

Ramcharitmanas is not familiar to most people outside of India, at least partly because it is very difficult to translate from the original Hindi dialect 36 properly. For example, it loses compelling effects such as multiple alliterative "t-t-t-t" sounds to describe a battle. Many of its subtle shades of meaning become lost in translation, such as the more than two dozen different terms that translate into English only as "lotus." 37 But over the centuries, the poem has been a core text of Indian culture.

Tulsidas was an ascetic and a teacher in the late 16th century. He became part of a movement to make the Hindu religion 38 more about common people. Until then, Hindu sacred texts had not been translated from the ancient language of Sanskrit, and thus only learned scholars could read 39 what they contained. Tulsidas retold the stories in musical rhymed verse, in Awadhi, a dialect of Hindi that most people in the region spoke.

――――――★――――――

34

(A) NO CHANGE
(B) would have created
(C) was creating
(D) had been creating

35

Which choice most effectively combines the sentences at the underlined portion?

(A) romances, and the triumph of good over evil.
(B) romances, and good over evil.
(C) romances—thus, goodness over evil.
(D) and romance and good, winning over evil.

36

Which choice most effectively sets up the examples that follow?

(A) NO CHANGE
(B) because its plot is complicated and its narrator changes.
(C) due to its extraordinary length.
(D) without losing its poetic power and nuance.

37

The writer is considering revising the underlined sentence to read:

> But over the centuries, the poem has remained immensely popular among those of the Hindu faith, serving as a core text of Indian culture.

Should the writer make this change here?

(A) Yes, because it establishes the relationship between religious and secular cultures in India.
(B) Yes, because it describes the poem's continuing influence on Indian culture, as set up by the beginning of the paragraph.
(C) No, because it fails to provide specific information about the poem's popularity in Indian society.
(D) No, because it misinterprets information from the earlier paragraph.

38

Which choice most effectively establishes the main topic of this paragraph?

(A) NO CHANGE
(B) more important for
(C) more accessible to
(D) less demanding of

39

(A) NO CHANGE
(B) that they
(C) which was
(D) things they

CHAPTER 4

It is likely that Tulsidas 40 mainly thought of the *Ramcharitmanas* primarily as a script to be acted out. He helped initiate the practice of *Ramlila*, folk theater adaptations of the work. These free outdoor reenactments continue to take place annually in many towns and villages in Northern India. They strictly follow the poem, at the same time welcoming spontaneous audience participation.

Every evening over the course of 10 or more days features a different episode of the story, with plots that the audience 41 knows to speak of. The audience knows when to act as rowdy guests at a wedding, when to cheer or jeer, and when to sing. Some audience members bring their own drums and finger cymbals. Some bring their own copies of the *Ramcharitmanas* and sing along with the narration. 42 Vividly colored sets and costumes, processions through town, fireworks, food stalls and fairs add to the excitement.

[1] The most famous traditional Ramlila takes place in the town of Ramnagar in the Varanasi district. [2] Episodes are staged in the nearby forests, temples, and villages. [3] For a whole month, the whole town serves as a set. [4] Even in heavy rain, the audience and actors walk between different scene locations, sometimes for miles. [5] The final evening's 43 episode, in which a giant effigy of a demon, is burned, draws more than a million people. 44

──────────── ★ ────────────

40

(A) NO CHANGE
(B) thought of the *Ramcharitmanas* as a script to mainly be acted out.
(C) thought of the *Ramcharitmanas* mainly as a script to be acted out.
(D) thought mainly of the *Ramcharitmanas* as a script to be acted out, primarily.

41

(A) NO CHANGE
(B) froze in memory.
(C) learned a lesson.
(D) knows by heart.

42

The writer wants to convey an enthusiastic yet factual attitude. Which choice best accomplishes this goal?

(A) NO CHANGE
(B) Truly gorgeous
(C) Unbelievably bright
(D) Overly adorned

43

(A) NO CHANGE
(B) episode, in which a giant effigy of a demon is burned,
(C) episode in which a giant effigy of a demon is burned,
(D) episode in which a giant effigy of a demon is burned

44

To make the paragraph more logical, sentence 3 should be placed

(A) before sentence 1.
(B) after sentence 1.
(C) after sentence 4.
(D) after sentence 5.

Writing & Language Test 3

 35 MINUTES, 44 QUESTIONS

Turn to Section 2 of your answer sheet to answer the questions in this section.

DIRECTIONS

Each of the following passages is accompanied by approximately 11 questions. Some questions will require you to revise the passages in order to improve coherence and clarity. Other questions will require you to correct grammatical errors. Passages may be accompanied by graphs, charts, or tables that you must consider when making revisions. For most questions, you may select the "NO CHANGE" option if you believe that portion of the passage is clear, concise, and grammatically correct as is.

Within the passages, highlighted numbers followed by underlined text indicate which part of the text corresponds with each question. Bracketed numbers [1] indicate sentence number. These bracketed numbers are only relevant to problems that require you to add or rearrange sentences in a paragraph.

Family Leave

Competitive employers in both the public and private sector have started to offer **1** <u>better health benefits</u> that make them more attractive to job applicants. When it comes to maternity leave, for example, some large tech companies now provide a full year. In 2016, the U.S. Department of Defense (DOD) announced that it was doubling the paid maternity leave for women in the armed forces from six weeks to 12 weeks. The DOD said that the leave would not only improve **2** <u>mother's and babies</u> health, but would also appeal to young women who think that they may later want to have children while maintaining their careers. Thus, **3** <u>it</u> may attract more female applicants and help to retain women who are already serving.

While an increase in maternity leave helps many employees, caring for *adult* relatives is also a pressing concern. Changes in the economic structure and

---
★ ---

1

Which choice provides the most appropriate introduction to the passage as a whole?

(A) NO CHANGE
(B) more flexible family-leave policies
(C) longer maternity leave
(D) more positions to women

2

(A) NO CHANGE
(B) mother's and baby's
(C) mother-and-baby
(D) mothers' and babies'

3

(A) NO CHANGE
(B) they
(C) each
(D) some

demographics of the U.S. **4** <u>created</u> conflicts between work and home like never before. **5** Government initiatives have tried to help workers cope. Since 1993, federal law has required companies that employ 50 people or more to offer at least 12 weeks of unpaid "family" leave. This refers to childbirth or a serious illness of a close family member. Yet as most employees either work for smaller companies or cannot afford to take unpaid leave, the law **6** <u>does little to help millions of people.</u>

[1] For example, it is estimated that at least 3.6 million people between the ages of 18 and 24 help to care for an ill, disabled, or elderly family member, while around 2.4 million grandparents are the primary caregivers of their grandchildren. [2] People in "Generation X"—around the ages of 36 to 51 in 2016—sometimes call themselves the "sandwich generation" because they feel squeezed between the responsibilities of caring for **7** <u>there</u> aging parents and raising their children. [3] If a spouse also becomes ill or disabled, Gen X-ers may find themselves in a "club sandwich" situation, where they are caring for three generations at once. [4] But when it comes to family leave, the need is **8** <u>omnipotent.</u> [5] Hence, a grandmother may need to stay home from work with a sick grandchild; a teenager may need time off work to take a grandparent to the doctor. **9**

The total number of people in the U.S. caring for adult family members is estimated at about 66 million—29 percent of the population. Nearly two in three of these are also employed. If care-giving needs conflict with work **10** <u>schedules, care giving</u> most likely takes precedence. Caregivers may have to reduce their hours, use up vacation and sick leave, or quit their jobs. If they are not able to contribute to retirement funds, **11** <u>they may have to work into their old age.</u>

---------------- ★ ----------------

4

(A) NO CHANGE
(B) have created
(C) were creating
(D) used to create

5

At this point, the writer is considering adding the following information.

Members of the outsized generation known as the Baby Boomers are beginning to hit their 70s, developing more health issues associated with old age.

Should the writer make this addition here?

(A) Yes, because it helps explain who the Baby Boomers are.
(B) Yes, because describes the growing demands on the health care industry.

(C) No, because it fails to connect with the paragraph's focus on workers needing more family leave.
(D) No, because it introduces information about retirees that is inaccurate based on the passage.

6

The writer wants to link the second paragraph to the information that follows. Which choice best accomplishes this goal?

(A) NO CHANGE
(B) creates a new standard in the labor force.
(C) has only negative impacts on the economy.
(D) mainly benefits smaller companies.

7

(A) NO CHANGE
(B) they're
(C) theirs
(D) their

8

(A) NO CHANGE
(B) universal.
(C) incomprehensible.
(D) ordinary.

9

To make the paragraph more logical, sentence 1 should be placed

(A) where it is now.
(B) after sentence 2.
(C) after sentence 3.
(D) after sentence 4.

10

(A) NO CHANGE
(B) schedules—care giving
(C) schedules care giving
(D) schedules: care giving

11

The writer wants a conclusion that conveys a significant social impact of the problem discussed in the sentence. Which choice best accomplishes this goal?

(A) NO CHANGE
(B) their outlook may become quite gloomy.
(C) they risk placing a financial burden on the next generation.
(D) will have to go back to work eventually.

Tensile Strength

My friend and I contemplated the ramp before us. **[12] It appeared to have been made by a child with too much access to plastic tape.** It **[13] lead** temptingly into an entryway just above eye-level.

We were at the Ruben H. Fleet Science Center in San Diego, curious yet a little dubious about a step-in exhibit called "Taping Shape." Engineers and artists—presumably adults—had taped up what looked like snow tunnels in the air. They had started with some kind of scaffolding, and wrapped layers of clear packaging tape in curving directions around it, creating smooth surfaces. They had taped diagonally, creating a dizzying effect as floors became ceilings. **[14] Plastic shrink wrap was the final touch** to make everything soft and springy. They had increased the allure by aiming colored lights at the semi-transparent walls, bathing the rounded passageways with pinks, greens, and blues. Even more enticing, **[15] we could sit down inside.**

A small sign near the entrance directed us take off our shoes, but there were no indications of a weight limit, and no prohibitions on running or jumping inside, as many shoeless people seemed to be doing at the moment. Could **[16] me and my friend** really enter without tearing the **[17] tape and falling through it?**

———————— ★ ————————

12

At this point, the writer is considering deleting the underlined sentence. Should the sentence be kept or deleted?

(A) Kept, because it illustrates a reason for the writer's doubtful attitude.
(B) Kept, because it establishes a link between children and the exhibit.
(C) Deleted, because it fails to explain the key role of tape in the exhibit.
(D) Deleted, because it introduces an idea that goes unexplained.

13

(A) NO CHANGE
(B) leaded
(C) left
(D) led

14

Which choice maintains the sentence pattern already established in the paragraph?

(A) NO CHANGE
(B) They had finished it off with plastic shrink wrap
(C) Finishing it off, there was plastic shrink wrap
(D) Next, they add plastic shrink wrap

15

Which choice provides the detail that most effectively helps the reader visualize the exhibit?

(A) NO CHANGE
(B) it would not take too long to go through it.
(C) one of the exits consisted of a long, soft slide.
(D) the ramp was textured so that people wouldn't slip.

16

(A) NO CHANGE
(B) my friend and me
(C) I and my friend
(D) my friend and I

17

(A) NO CHANGE
(B) tape, and falling through it?
(C) tape. And falling through it?
(D) tape; falling through it?

[18] Apparently the exhibit's creators were confident that the tape's tensile strength was adequate to hold us up. "Tensile strength" refers to the ability of a material to resist being pulled apart. For example, suppose a boat is tied to a [19] dock. How much would the boat have to pull on the rope in order to break it, say from wind? The total force needed to break the rope is the measure of that rope's tensile strength.

If a boat [20] will be pulling on a rope, the rope's fibers would likely stretch in length. Up to a certain point, if the wind stopped blowing on the boat, the rope would spring back to its previous form. But the point where stronger force permanently stretched the rope would be its "elastic limit." Continuing to pull on the rope with increasing force would quickly stretch it so much as to weaken it, so that even less force would break it. That point of maximum stress on the rope before it weakened and broke is its "ultimate tensile strength." Naturally, [21] depending on the material used, the more force it can absorb, and the higher the rope's tensile strength will be.

Later I learned that some packaging tapes have tensile strengths of 35 pounds per inch. If my foot coming down on the tape floor covered about 20 square inches, then I could weigh 700 pounds before falling through one layer. In this case, the multiple layers of tape dispersed the weight, increasing the tensile strength of the surface even more. [22]

DOUBLE-BRAIDED ROPE (POLYESTER)

Diameter (inches)	Tensile Strength (pounds)
3/16	1,400
1/4	2,350
5/16	3,850
3/8	5,100
7/16	7,000
1/2	10,100

———————— ★ ————————

18

(A) NO CHANGE
(B) Supposedly
(C) Possibly
(D) Probably

19

Which choice most effectively combines the sentences at the underlined portion?

(A) dock; how much would, say, the wind, have to pull on the rope before the boat broke it?
(B) dock, but strong winds cause the boat to strain against the rope.
(C) dock and the rope is being stretched by the wind for it is blowing on the boat.
(D) dock but is straining, due to the effects of the wind, and may break away from the rope.

20

(A) NO CHANGE
(B) was pulling
(C) has been pulling
(D) were pulling

21

Which choice offers an accurate interpretation of the data in the chart?

(A) NO CHANGE
(B) with a longer rope,
(C) the thicker a rope is,
(D) the more synthetic materials that are used to make a rope,

22

Which choice most clearly reinforces the point developed throughout the passage?

(A) In the end, our curiosity overcame our concern, because we wanted to see the interior.
(B) Therefore, just like boats, we were able to successfully put strain on the plastic tape.
(C) Thus, although the plastic tape looked thin and weak, we found that it easily supported us.
(D) We entered the exhibit, not even straining the tape beyond its elastic limit.

Romance Languages

Are the Romance languages more *romantic* than others? Do they contain more loving expressions? More compliments? **23** The answer is, "Probably not"; the name indicates only that they are, at least in part, derived from Latin, the language of ancient *Rome*.

Romance languages **24** have interesting characteristics. The Romance family includes French, Romanian, Italian, Spanish, and Portuguese; it is one of the largest language families, **25** with nearly a billion speakers worldwide. Each of the Romance languages originated from the spoken language of the Romans—Vulgar Latin. In modern English, the word "vulgar" means "rude" or "inappropriate," but the term "Vulgar Latin" is derived from the term for "common," *vulgaris*. It refers to the everyday, informal language spoken by ancient Romans.

The Roman Empire encompassed much of Central and Western Europe as well as portions of North Africa, the Middle East, and **26** in what is now Turkey. In each of these regions, Romans imposed aspects of their own culture and language. Over the course of centuries, the Latin spoken in many conquered regions, especially in Central and Western Europe, evolved into entirely new languages. Although mapping the evolution of a language family **27** is a hugely large and complex task, the development of the Romance languages can be boiled down to a few key factors.

——————— ★ ———————

23

At this point the writer wants to add a third example that corresponds with the previous examples. Which choice would best accomplish this goal?

(A) More flowery terms of endearment?
(B) More candle-lit dinners?
(C) More pronouns for "you," "me," and "us"?
(D) More formal expressions?

24

Which choice provides the most appropriate introduction to the Romance languages?

(A) NO CHANGE
(B) fit under an academic umbrella known as "Romance Studies."
(C) comprise a language family; as with all siblings, they share some characteristics.
(D) such as Spanish, French, and Portuguese are spoken around the globe.

25

Which choice best supports the claim made in this sentence?

(A) NO CHANGE
(B) and has existed for over two thousand years.
(C) larger than the Germanic language family.
(D) and is a subgroup of the Indo-European language family.

26

(A) NO CHANGE
(B) what is now Turkey.
(C) at modern-day Turkey.
(D) over Turkish lands.

27

(A) NO CHANGE
(B) is highly complex,
(C) is a task that is not easily undertaken,
(D) has many hugely complex aspects to it,

For one, Vulgar Latin itself underwent many linguistic changes over the centuries of Roman rule. Thus, a population conquered by Rome in the third century BCE would have been exposed to a different "version" of Latin than a population that was conquered 500 years later. **28** Latin was also the primary language of the clergy.

The extent of Roman presence in a region also **29** affected the development of Romance **30** languages. Some regions experienced Roman settlement and intense contact with Romans and their language, while other conquered regions were mostly left alone. In areas of complete Roman domination, Vulgar Latin may have largely replaced local languages, **31** since areas of less Roman contact retained more of their native languages.

[1] **32** Rome's crash in the fifth and sixth centuries CE left populations throughout Europe relatively isolated. [2] By the tenth century CE, the Vulgar Latin dialects that developed in the Roman Empire had evolved into distinct languages. [3] The development of national identity in later centuries deepened these distinctions, and the spread of Romance-language literature led to increased standardization of languages. [4] The various versions of Vulgar Latin were consolidated into the languages now recognized as Romance languages. **33**

———————★———————

28

The writer is considering deleting the underlined sentence. Should the sentence be kept or deleted?

(A) Kept, because it explains the key role that the clergy played in promoting Latin.
(B) Kept, because it provides relevant information about the diffusion of Latin.
(C) Deleted, because it fails to show the link between the clergy and Romance language development.
(D) Deleted, because it prematurely introduces information that is discussed later in the passage.

29

(A) NO CHANGE
(B) effected
(C) was affected by
(D) was effected by

30

Which choice most effectively combines the sentences at the underlined portion?

(A) languages, some
(B) languages and some
(C) languages some
(D) languages; some

31

(A) NO CHANGE
(B) unless
(C) whereas
(D) given that

32

Which choice best maintains the tone established in the paragraph?

(A) NO CHANGE
(B) Rome basically ending
(C) Taking care of Roman territory stopped
(D) The disintegration of the Roman Empire

33

To improve the flow of this paragraph, the writer wants to add the following sentence.

Many of these groups were influenced by disparate languages of new immigrants or new conquerors.

The sentence would most logically be placed

(A) before sentence 1.
(B) before sentence 2.
(C) before sentence 3.
(D) before sentence 4.

Urban parks

34 There is more park revitalization recently. After World War II, the populations of cities generally declined, and parks tended to be a low priority for many of them. However, starting in the 2000s, the trend reversed, with young Americans beginning to move back to city centers. City planners and real estate developers began realizing that greenery and open space are people-magnets. Shops and restaurants near parks draw more customers; homes near parks sell for higher prices. Some cities estimate that parks **35** generate 5 percent of their income. Higher property values mean that cities can collect higher property taxes. **36** Public parks are increasingly seen **37** as necessary infrastructure, not a luxury. Even Nevada's Las Vegas Strip, the stretch of road that overwhelms the senses with its gigantic glitzy hotels and casinos, recently made room for a small park with desert trees.

★

34

The writer is considering revising the underlined information to read

Nationwide, appreciation of urban parks is gaining ground.

Should the writer make this change?

(A) Yes, because it sets up the main topic of global change.
(B) Yes, because it introduces the paragraph's focus on a trend in the United States.
(C) No, because it fails to introduce the role of local governments in the change.
(D) No, because blurs the paragraph's focus on money generated by parks.

35

Which choice offers an accurate interpretation of the chart?

(A) NO CHANGE
(B) are 5 percent of a typical property's value.
(C) make up an average 5 percent of cities' budgetary expenses.
(D) raise surrounding property values by an average of 5 percent.

36

At this point, the writer wants to add specific information that supports the main topic of the paragraph. Which choice most effectively adds accurate and relevant information based on the chart?

(A) Washington, D.C.'s parks increase its income by about $7 million annually.
(B) Washington, D.C. has many parks, leading to nearly $24 billion in property values.
(C) The nation's capitol even raises more than $1 billion in tax income from parks.
(D) Typical cities can expect to raise their tax income by about 0.58 percent with more parks.

37

Which choice most effectively sets up the example that follows?

(A) NO CHANGE
(B) as more important than other uses for land.
(C) as a crucial challenge to older, industrial cities.
(D) as an urgent priority for suburbs as well as urban centers.

Open space also offers 38 all kinds of advantages. Parks can improve both physical and mental health. Green spaces for exercise and relaxation can help people combat obesity, asthma, and anxiety. Some physicians are even dispensing information 39 about parks nearby to their patients. Parks may also provide habitats for insects, birds and other animals. Parks may deter crime in a neighborhood by encouraging law-abiding residents rather than criminals to use outdoor areas. And during rainstorms, 40 floods may be prevented because they absorb water. Most importantly, plants reduce heat and air pollution; Madrid, Spain has announced plans to virtually cover itself in greenery to cool down.

[1] Planners in densely populated cities around the world have had to get creative about where to squeeze in parks among the skyscrapers. [2] One place they have looked is at the skyscrapers themselves. [3] Landscaped paths known as "linear parks" have also become popular. [4] Singapore actively promotes "skyrise greenery," meaning lush gardens on rooftops and terraced buildings. [5] Paris, France and New York City have turned old aerial railroad tracks into walkways high off the ground. [6] The aerial walkway in New York, called the "High Line," has become one of the city's top tourist attractions. Someday there may be linear parks below ground as well; one well-publicized proposal in London was to create a linear mushroom garden in an unused mail tunnel. 41

Cities have also sought new ways to use existing resources for recreation. For example, in some river ports, river barges 42 being converted into floating skateboard or parks. Ottawa, the capital city of Canada, opens a frozen canal in its downtown area for ice skating in winter. Sometimes even the places that seem 43 not likely prove to be highly popular. The desert city of Henderson, Nevada noticed that a large number of migrating birds (and bird-watchers) were visiting its wastewater reclamation ponds. Henderson decided that the ponds could serve a dual purpose. The city designated the ponds as a 44 "bird-viewing preserve."

Amount of Increase to Property Value Attributed to City Parks in Washington, D.C.

Total value of properties in D.C. within 500 feet of parks	$23,977,160,000
Assumed average value of a nearby park	5 percent
Total property value that is attributable to parks in D.C.	$1,198,858,025
Annual residential tax rate in D.C.	0.58 percent
D.C.'s annual property tax capture due to parks	$6,953,377

Data from "Measuring the Economic Value of a City Park System," a report by Trust for Public Land in 2009

38

The writer wants to convey a positive attitude, but still maintain the formal tone of the passage. Which choice best accomplishes this goal?

(A) NO CHANGE
(B) many intangible benefits.
(C) other really great perks--in an indirect way.
(D) indescribable returns on investment.

39

(A) NO CHANGE
(B) nearby to their patients about parks.
(C) to their patients about nearby parks.
(D) about parks to their patients nearby.

40

(A) NO CHANGE
(B) floods may flow elsewhere
(C) parks may prevent floods
(D) floods may rise

41

To make the paragraph more logical, sentence 4 should be placed

(A) before sentence 2.
(B) before sentence 3.
(C) after sentence 5.
(D) after sentence 6.

42

(A) NO CHANGE
(B) having been converted
(C) have been converted
(D) converting to

43

(A) NO CHANGE
(B) least likely.
(C) less likely
(D) unlikely

44

(A) NO CHANGE
(B) Bird-Viewing Preserve.
(C) (bird-viewing preserve).
(D) bird-viewing preserve.

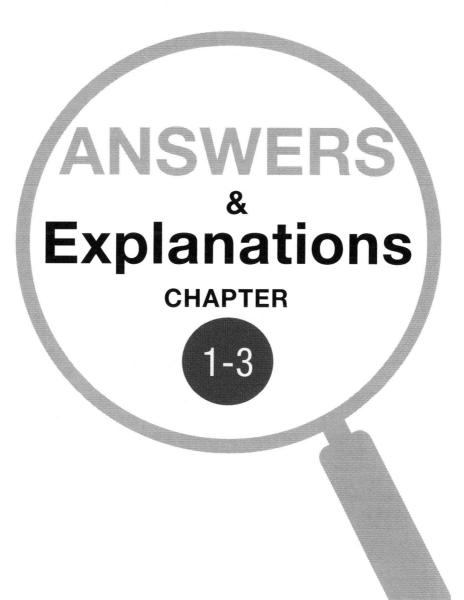

ANSWERS
&
Explanations
CHAPTER
1-3

Chapter 1 : Answers & Explanations

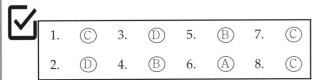

Topic 1 - 2

1. Ⓒ	3. Ⓓ	5. Ⓑ	7. Ⓒ
2. Ⓓ	4. Ⓑ	6. Ⓐ	8. Ⓒ

1) **C**
Choice (C) is correct because the underlined portion refers to and must agree with the plural subject of the sentence, "friends and family members," making the third-person plural verb form "exchange" correct.

2) **D**
Choice (D) is correct; the subject of the sentence must be singular ("a sister") to agree in number with the pronoun "her" that refers to the subject later in the sentence. Moreover, the underlined verb must agree with a third-person singular subject ("a sister"), which the third-person singular verb form "gives" does.

3) **D**
Choice (D) is correct because the verb in the underlined portion refers to and must agree with the singular noun "the Netherlands," making the third-person singular verb form "celebrates" correct.

4) **B**
Choice (B) is correct; the underlined noun phrase "street festivals" must be plural because it is not preceded by an article, so it cannot be singular. Moreover, the underlined verb must agree with the plural noun phrase "street festivals," making the third-person plural verb form "abound" correct.

5) **B**
Choice (B) is correct because the verb in the underlined portion refers to and must agree with the singular noun "the Bahamas," making the third-person singular verb form "has" correct.

6) **A**
Choice (A) is correct because the underlined verb refers to and must agree with the plural subject of the sentence, "Junkanoo parades," making the third-person plural verb form "create" correct.

7) **C**
Choice (C) is correct because the verb in the underlined portion refers to and must agree with the plural phrase "a number of encyclopedic resources," making the third-person plural verb form "are" correct.

8) **C**
Choice (C) is correct because the verb in the underlined portion refers to and must agree with the book title and singular subject of the sentence, *"501 Must-Be-There Events,"* making the third-person singular verb form "provides" correct.

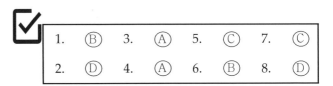

Topic 3 - 4

1. Ⓑ	3. Ⓐ	5. Ⓒ	7. Ⓒ
2. Ⓓ	4. Ⓐ	6. Ⓑ	8. Ⓓ

1) **B**
Choice (B) is correct because the underlined verb phrase refers to and must agree with the plural subject of the sentence "People in Japan's Ryukyu islands," making the third-person plural verb form "tend" correct.

2) **D**
Choice (D) is correct because the underlined verb refers to and must agree with the singular indefinite pronoun subject "everything," making the third-person singular verb form "is" correct.

3) **A**
Choice (A) is correct because the underlined verb refers to and must agree with the singular indefinite pronoun "anyone," making the third-person singular verb form "is" correct.

4) **A**
Choice (A) is correct because the underlined verb must agree with the plural noun "genes," making the third-person plural verb form "make" correct.

5) 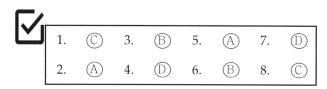 C

Choice (C) is correct because the underlined verb phrase refers to and must agree with the plural subject of the sentence "people," making the third-person plural verb form "enjoy" correct.

6) 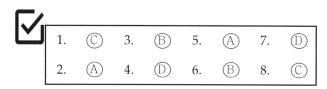 B

Choice (B) is correct because the verb in the underlined portion refers to and must agree with the singular indefinite pronoun "something," making the third-person singular verb form "is" correct.

7) 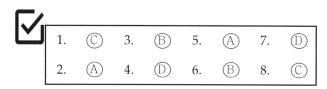 C

Choice (C) is correct because the singular subject, "each," must agree with the third-person singular verb form "relies." Other choices contain an incorrect verb form.

8) 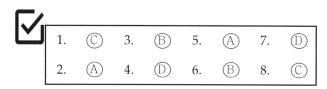 D

Choice (D) is correct because the verb in the underlined portion refers to the singular pronoun "either," so the third-person singular verb form "serves" is correct.

Topic 5 - 6

| 1. | Ⓐ | 3. | Ⓒ | 5. | Ⓐ | 7. | Ⓑ |
| 2. | Ⓓ | 4. | Ⓐ | 6. | Ⓑ | 8. | Ⓓ |

1) 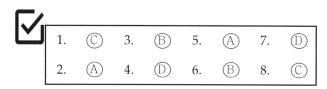 A

Choice (A) is correct because the underlined verb refers to and must agree with the plural subject of the sentence, "The stories," making the third-person plural verb form "are" correct.

2) 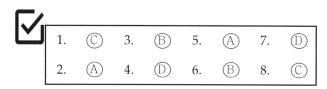 D

Choice (D) is correct because the underlined portion refers to and must agree with the singular gerund subject of the sentence, "describing," so the third-person singular verb form "is" and the singular noun "a hallmark" are correct.

3) 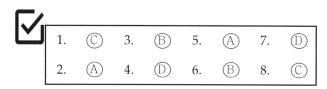 C

Choice (C) is correct because the verb in the underlined portion refers to the singular infinitive subject of the sentence, "To create," making the third-person singular verb form "is" correct.

4) 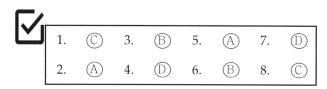 A

Choice (A) is correct because the verb in the underlined portion refers to the singular gerund "tolerating," making the third-person singular verb form "is" correct.

5) 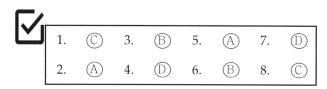 A

Choice (A) is correct because the underlined portion refers to and must agree with the singular gerund "stopping," so the third-person singular noun form "is" and the singular verb phrase "a compelling idea" are correct.

6) 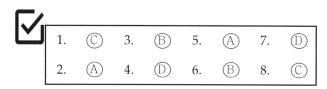 B

Choice (B) is correct because the verb in the underlined portion refers to the plural subject of the sentence, "members," making the third-person plural verb form "have" correct.

7) 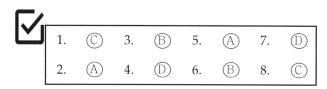 B

Choice (B) is correct because the verb in the underlined portion refers to and must agree with the gerund "demonstration," making the third-person singular verb form "is" correct.

8) 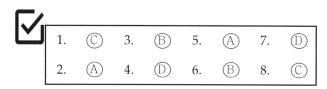 D

Choice (D) is correct because the verb in the underlined portion refers to and must agree with the plural noun phrase "systems of thought," making the third-person plural verb form "categorize" correct.

Topic 7 - 8

| 1. | Ⓒ | 3. | Ⓑ | 5. | Ⓐ | 7. | Ⓓ |
| 2. | Ⓐ | 4. | Ⓓ | 6. | Ⓑ | 8. | Ⓒ |

1) 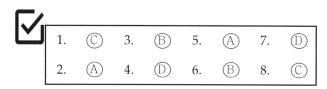 C

Choice (C) is correct because both "roommate's" and "my" show possession over "window."

2) 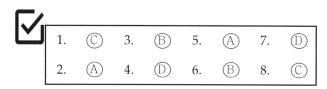 A

Choice (A) is correct because the underlined adjective refers to "dorm" and shows possession over "pervasive odor," so the singular possessive adjective "its" is correct.

3) ➡ B
Choice (B) is correct because the underlined adjective shows possession over "roommate," making the possessive adjective "my" correct. Moreover, the narrator's roommate shows possession over "resourceful use of incense," so the singular possessive "roommate's" is correct.

4) ➡ D
Choice (D) is correct because the underlined adjective refers to the singular noun phrase "dining hall" and shows possession over "menu," making the singular possessive adjective "its" correct.

5) ➡ A
Choice (A) is correct because the underlined adjective refers to "some of the other freshmen" and shows possession over "rooms," so the possessive adjective "whose" is correct. Because "rooms" and "freshmen" are not showing possession over anything, they do not need apostrophes.

6) ➡ B
Choice (B) is correct because the underlined adjective refers to the singular noun "a friend" and shows possession over "hair," making the singular possessive adjective "her" correct.

7) ➡ D
Choice (D) is correct; the underlined singular noun phrase shows possession over "food," making the singular possessive "dining hall's" correct.

8) ➡ C
Choice (C) is correct; the first word in the underlined portion refers to the singular noun "a theater," making the singular possessive adjective "its" correct. Additionally, "Orson Welles'" must have an apostrophe at the end to indicate possession over *Citizen Kane*. Since "Welles" already ends in an "s," it is correct to add only an apostrophe

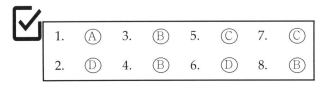

Topic 9 - 10

☑
| 1. | Ⓐ | 3. | Ⓑ | 5. | Ⓒ | 7. | Ⓒ |
| 2. | Ⓓ | 4. | Ⓑ | 6. | Ⓓ | 8. | Ⓑ |

1) ➡ A
Choice (A) is correct because the underlined verb refers to and must agree with the singular subject of the sentence, "cuisine," making the third-person singular verb form "combines" correct.

2) ➡ D
Choice (D) is correct because "millennia" is a measurable period of time, so the term must be preceded by an adjective that goes with countable nouns, which "few" does. The adjectives "little" and "small" do not work because they relate to size, not time.

3) ➡ B
Choice (B) is correct because "porridge" is uncountable. It can be plural if preceded by an adjective of quality, as in "types of porridges," but when not preceded by an adjective, or when

preceded by an adjective of quantity, as in "two bowls of porridge," "porridge" must remain singular, so (A) is correct because "porridge" and "it" (the pronoun that refers to "porridge" in the sentence) are both singular.

4) ➡ B
Choice (B) is correct; the sentence implies that there was *a lack of* wheat flour in the Americas until the 1860s. Choice (B) best clarifies this absence while effectively modifying the uncountable noun "wheat flour." Although (A) and (C) make sense in the sentence, (A) is incorrect because "a lot" is avoided in formal English writing, and (C) is incorrect because "a little" implies the *presence* of wheat flour rather than *a lack of* it.

5) ➡ C
Choice (C) is correct because the noun "versions" is countable, and the adjective "many" effectively describes countable nouns.

6) ➡ D
Choice (D) is correct because the pronoun in the underlined portion refers to the singular noun "Election Cake," making third-person singular pronoun "it" correct.

7) ➡ C
Choice (C) is correct because the underlined portion refers to two nouns in the sentence: traveling, and transporting (both gerunds in this sentence.) Thus, the plural, past-tense verb "were" is appropriate.

8) ➡ B
Choice (B) is correct; "dough" and "fish" are uncountable nouns, and because they are not preceded by any adjectives, they must both be

singular. Although choice (D) makes both "dough" and "fish" singular, it is incorrect because it does not maintain subject-verb agreement: the verb form "is" does not agree in number with the plural noun "balls."

Topic 11 - 12

1.	Ⓐ	3.	Ⓓ	5.	Ⓐ	7.	Ⓒ
2.	Ⓒ	4.	Ⓓ	6.	Ⓑ	8.	Ⓒ

1) ➡ A
Choice (A) is correct because the underlined pronoun refers to the plural noun "people," making the plural pronoun "they" correct.

2) ➡ C
Choice (C) is correct because the underlined pronoun refers to the singular phrase "any of them," making the singular pronouns "him or her" correct.

3) ➡ D
Choice (D) is correct because the first word of the underlined portion is a pronoun that refers to the singular subject of the sentence, "insurance," making the singular pronoun "it" correct.

4) ➡ D
Choice (D) is correct because the underlined verb refers to and must agree with the singular noun phrase "a given client," making the third-person singular verb form "contributes" correct. Moreover, the underlined pronoun refers to the singular noun phrase "the pool of money," making the singular pronoun "it" correct.

5) ➡ A
Choice (A) is correct; the underlined portion is a prepositional phrase that begins with "for." All pronouns in a prepositional phrase must be in the objective case, making the objective pronoun "me" correct.

6) ➡ B
Choice (B) is correct because the underlined pronoun(s) refer to the singular noun "a client," making the singular pronouns "he or she" correct.

7) ➡ C
Choice (C) is correct because the underlined portion is a prepositional phrase that begins with "to." All pronouns in a prepositional phrase must be in the objective case, making the objective pronoun "whom" correct.

8) ➡ C
Choice (C) is correct because "you and I" act as the subject of the sentence, so they should both be in the subjective case. Choice (D) is also technically correct, but (C) is a better answer because it substitutes "each of us" instead of repeating "you and I."

Topic 13 - 14

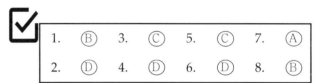

1.	Ⓑ	3.	Ⓒ	5.	Ⓒ	7.	Ⓐ
2.	Ⓓ	4.	Ⓓ	6.	Ⓓ	8.	Ⓑ

1) ➡ B
Choice (B) is correct because the pronouns in the underlined portion show possession over "job," making the possessive pronouns "yours or mine" correct.

2) ➡ D
Choice (D) is correct because the underlined portion must specify which of the three listed jobs Hunter liked most, which (D) accomplishes by specifying that "he liked catering best."

3) ➡ C
Choice (C) is correct because the underlined pronoun refers to "tutoring clients" and shows possession over "house," so the plural possessive pronoun "theirs" is correct.

4) ➡ D
Choice (D) is correct because it clearly states the relationship between "Chloe and Ben" and the "prancing horses." All other choices are incorrect because it is unclear whether "their" refers to "Ben and Chloe" or "the prancing horses."

5) ➡ C

Choice (C) is correct because the underlined portion must specify whether the narrator's dogs did not get along with one another, the neighbor's dogs did not get along with one another, or the narrator's dogs and the neighbor's dogs did not get along with one another, which (C) accomplishes by stating that "our dogs and his [dogs] did not get along."

6) ➡ D

Choice (D) is correct; the sentence differentiates the jobs assigned to two groups of people. The underlined portion must supply a possessive adjective ("their") and the noun to which the possessive adjective refers ("jobs"), making (D) correct. Choices (A) and (B) are incorrect because they do not specify *what* is being possessed. Choice (C) is incorrect because using "our" in the underlined portion would make the "ours" at the end of the sentence redundant.

7) ➡ A

Choice (A) is correct because the underlined pronoun refers to "My sister and I" and shows possession over "house," which is not stated in the sentence but implied by the sentence's context.

8) ➡ B

Choice (B) is correct because the pronouns "his" and "hers" show possession over the implied singular noun "order."

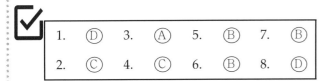

Topic 15 - 16

1. Ⓓ	3. Ⓐ	5. Ⓑ	7. Ⓑ
2. Ⓒ	4. Ⓒ	6. Ⓑ	8. Ⓓ

1) ➡ D

Choice (D) is correct because it is the clearest and most concise version of the underlined portion. All other choices are unnecessarily wordy.

2) ➡ C

Choice (C) is correct because it is the most concise version of the underlined portion. Choices (A) and (B) are incorrect because they contain redundancies, as "small," "short," and "tiny" all

mean the same thing in the context of the sentence. Choice (D) is incorrect because it is implied that "shorter" refers to length, making the term "in length" unnecessary.

3) ➡ A

Choice (A) is correct because "the science of manipulating matter at the molecular level" is an appositive that describes "nanotechnology," and the appositive must be separated from the rest of the sentence using a pair of commas.

4) ➡ C

Choice (C) is correct because "university" and "industry" act as titles that describe different types of "nanotechnologists," and no commas should separate the word "nanotechnologists" from its titles.

5) ➡ B

Choice (B) is correct because it is the clearest and most concise version of the underlined portion. Choice (A) is incorrect because it contains a redundancy: "attach" and "connect" are synonyms. Choice (C) is incorrect because it contains convoluted phrasing, as the relationship between "particles" and "dissolved" is unclear. Choice (D) is incorrect because it is an unnecessarily wordy rephrasing of (B).

6) ➡ B

Choice (B) is correct because it is the clearest and most concise version of the underlined portion. Choice (A) is incorrect because it is unnecessarily wordy; choices (C) and (D) are incorrect because they do not specify *into whom* the particles are injected.

7) ➡ B

Choice (B) is correct because it is the clearest and most concise version of the underlined portion. Choice (A) and (C) are incorrect because they are unnecessarily wordy and repeat information found later in the sentence; choice (D) is incorrect because it does not specify *what type* of cells bond to the nanoparticles.

8) ➡ D

Choice (D) is correct because it is the clearest and most concise version of the underlined portion, and because it does not contain any unnecessary punctuation. Choice (A) and (C) are incorrect because they place a comma between the subject and verb of the sentence. Choice (B) is incorrect because it does not specify *what* is destroyed by the nanoparticles.

Topic 17 - 18

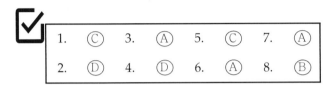

1. Ⓒ   3. Ⓐ   5. Ⓒ   7. Ⓐ
2. Ⓓ   4. Ⓓ   6. Ⓐ   8. Ⓑ

1) ➡ C

Choice (C) is correct; the sentence compares the sizes of Russia and Canada to the sizes of every other nation in the world, so the underlined adjective should be superlative. Moreover, the underlined adjective, "large," is a single-syllable word, so it should have the "-est" ending, making "largest" correct.

2) ➡ D

Choice (D) is correct; the sentence compares the size, wealth, and population density of Monaco to the size, wealth, and population density of every other nation in the world, so the underlined adjectives should be superlative. Because "rich" is a single-syllable word, it should have the "-est" ending; "crowded" is a two-syllable word, so it should be preceded by "most," making "richest and most crowded" correct.

3) ➡ A

Choice (A) is correct; the sentence compares the population of China to the population of India, so the underlined adjective should be comparative. Because "populous" is a three-syllable word, it should be preceded by "more."

4) ➡ D

Choice (D) is correct; the sentence compares the median age in Africa to the worldwide median age, so the underlined adjective should be comparative. Because "low" is a single-syllable word, it should have the "-er" ending.

5) ➡ C

Choice (C) is correct; the sentence compares how idyllic the Seychelles are to how idyllic every other

nation is, so the underlined adjective should be superlative. Because "idyllic" is a three-syllable word, it should be preceded by "most."

6) ➡ A

Choice (A) is correct; the sentence discusses the differing opinions regarding which out of all the Seychelles' beaches is the *most beautiful*, so the underlined portion should be superlative. Because "soft," "white," and "clear" are all single-syllable words, they should all have the "-est" ending.

7) ➡ A

Choice (A) is correct; the sentence compares the amount of rain received by Meghalaya to the amount of rain received in every other part of the world, so the underlined portion should be superlative. Although "rainy" is a two-syllable word, it should change its "y" to an "i" and add the "-est" ending. Generally, two-syllable words ending in "y" take the "-est" ending.

8) ➡ B

Choice (B) is correct; the underlined portion compares the amount of precipitation received by the Dry Valleys to the amount of precipitation received by every other part of the world, so the superlative term "least" is correct.

Topic 19 - 20

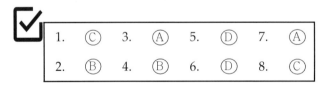

1. Ⓒ   3. Ⓐ   5. Ⓓ   7. Ⓐ
2. Ⓑ   4. Ⓑ   6. Ⓓ   8. Ⓒ

1) ➡ C

Choice (C) is correct because the participial phrase "founded in 1960" that describes "The music label Motown" must be separated from the rest of the sentence with a pair of commas.

2) ➡ B

Choice (B) is correct because it places the noun being modified, "Berry Gordy," directly after the participial phrase that modifies it, "Working at the time on one of the many automobile assembly lines in the city of Detroit."

3) 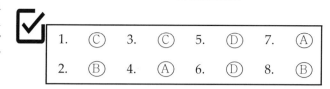► A

Choice (A) is correct because the relative clause beginning with "that" adds essential information to the sentence, so it should not be separated from the rest of the sentence with commas. All other choices are incorrect because they are unclear or they over-punctuate.

4) ► B

Choice (B) is correct because it places the noun being modified, "Gordy," directly after the participial phrase that modifies it, "Borrowing $800 from family members."

5) ► D

Choice (D) is correct because the relative clause beginning with "that" adds essential information to the sentence, so it should not be separated from the rest of the sentence with commas. All other choices are incorrect because they over-punctuate, and/or because they use the present participle "recording" where the past participle "recorded" is needed.

6) ► D

Choice (D) is correct because the participial phrase "schooled in poise and charm" that describes "Motown groups" must be separated from the rest of the sentence with a pair of commas. All other choices change the intended meaning.

7) ► A

Choice (A) is correct because the relative clause beginning with "who" adds essential information to the sentence, so it should not be separated from the rest of the sentence with commas. Choices (B) and (C) are incorrect because they over-punctuate, and choice (D) is incorrect because it uses the conjunction "and" where the sentence calls for a relative pronoun.

8) ► C

Choice (C) is correct because it creates a clear, active-voice sentence. Choice (A) is incorrect because "Becoming 'crossover hits'" does not clearly modify a noun, so it is a dangling modifier. Choices (B) and (D) are incorrect because they do not clarify what the "crossover hits" were, making the sentence unclear.

Topic 21 - 22

| 1. | Ⓒ | 3. | Ⓒ | 5. | Ⓓ | 7. | Ⓐ |
| 2. | Ⓑ | 4. | Ⓐ | 6. | Ⓓ | 8. | Ⓑ |

1) ► C

Choice (C) is correct because the sentence provides a general fact about the naming of leaders, making the simple present tense verb form "is" correct.

2) ► B

Choice (B) is correct; the sentence describes actions taken by leaders in the past, and the verbs in the underlined portion must maintain the same tense as the first verb of the sentence, "were." Thus, the simple past-tense verb forms "built" and "gave" are correct.

3) ► C

Choice (C) is correct because the sentence describes a situation in which one event was occurring, "Europe was embracing new ways of thinking," when another event began "Peter the Great came to power." The past progressive clearly establishes that one event was interrupted by or coincided with another event, making "was embracing" correct.

4) ► A

Choice (A) is correct; the sentence describes events that occurred in the past, and the verbs in the underlined portion must maintain the same tense as the first verb of the sentence, "transformed." Thus, the simple past-tense verb form "remained" is correct.

5) ► D

Choice (D) is correct; the sentence describes events that occurred in the past, and the verbs in the underlined portion must maintain the same tense as the first verb of the sentence, "went." Thus, the simple past-tense verb phrase "could study" is correct. Note that "could" is the irregular past-tense form of "can."

6) ► D

Choice (D) is correct because the underlined verb phrase refers to historians *today*, indicating that the verb should be present tense, making the simple present tense verb form "applaud" correct.

7) ➡ A

Choice (A) is correct because the sentence describes events that occurred in the past, so the simple past-tense verb phrase "were designed" is correct.

8) ➡ B

Choice (B) is correct because the sentence describes a situation that will continue to occur in the future, so the future tense verb phrase "will never… agree" is correct.

Topic 23 - 24

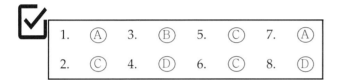

1.	Ⓐ	3.	Ⓑ	5.	Ⓒ	7.	Ⓐ
2.	Ⓒ	4.	Ⓓ	6.	Ⓒ	8.	Ⓓ

1) ➡ A

Choice (A) is correct because it uses the present perfect tense with "not" to show that a certain event—the narrator taking Abnormal Psychology in this case—has yet to occur.

2) ➡ C

Choice (C) is correct; because it is not important *who* added the Computational Biology major, the underlined sentence must take the passive voice ("been"), and because the major was added to the university at an unspecified time in the past, the present perfect tense ("has") is appropriate.

3) ➡ B

Choice (B) is correct; when forming a conditional statement that uses perfect-tense verbs, the "If" clause of the conditional should take a past perfect verb form, and the "then" (result) clause should take a conditional verb ("would," "could," "should") followed by a present perfect verb form, making the verb phrase "would have had" correct.

4) ➡ D

Choice (D) is correct because the sentence predicts that most students will change their college majors at an unspecified point before a specified point (the time they finish college). Thus, using the future perfect tense "will…have changed" is correct.

5) ➡ C

Choice (C) is correct; because it is important to specify *who* offers the Introduction to Sociology

class, the underlined portion must take the passive voice, making "is offered" the correct choice.

6) ➡ C

Choice (C) is correct; because William made his decision at some point prior to the action of the sentence, the present perfect tense is appropriate, making "has decided" correct.

7) ➡ A

Choice (A) is correct; the clause "Neftali had already decided that she wanted to become a teacher" occurred sometime before Neftali "finished kindergarten." The past perfect tense is appropriate when describing something that occurred before some past point in time, making "had already decided" correct.

8) ➡ D

Choice (D) is correct; because it is implied that most people have never considered philosophy lucrative, the underlined portion can take the passive voice, making "has never been considered" correct.

Topic 25 - 26

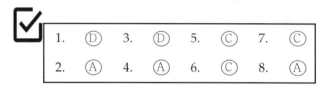

1.	Ⓓ	3.	Ⓓ	5.	Ⓒ	7.	Ⓒ
2.	Ⓐ	4.	Ⓐ	6.	Ⓒ	8.	Ⓐ

1) ➡ D

Choice (D) is correct because the sentence speculates on the outcome of an altered history, making the past perfect conditional verb forms "had not been" and "would not have been" correct.

2) ➡ A

Choice (A) is correct because the sentence provides a hypothetical yet possible situation in the past, making the past tense verb forms "wanted" and "could move" correct.

3) ➡ D

Choice (D) is correct because the underlined portion of the sentence speculates on the outcome of an altered history, making the past perfect conditional verb forms "had not" and "may have been" correct.

4) ➡ A

Choice (A) is correct because the sentence describes a factual, present-tense conditional statement, so the present-tense form "bites" and the future tense verb form ""will regurgitate" are correct.

5) ➡ C

Choice (C) is correct because the sentence describes a universal truth given a set of circumstances, making the present- and future-tense verb forms "occupy" and "will be bitten" correct.

6) ➡ C

Choice (C) is correct; the sentence describes a situation that is impossible (the population of Eurasia and North Africa in the 1300s being known), making the subjunctive mood correct. Thus, the subjunctive verb forms "were" and "would be" correct.

7) ➡ C

Choice (C) is correct because the sentence is a declarative sentence, so a normal verb form is appropriate, making "was" correct.

8) ➡ A

Choice (A) is correct because the underlined portion of the sentence speculates on the outcome of an altered history, making the past perfect conditional verb forms "would have" and "had" correct.

Topic 27 - 28

☑

| 1. | ⓒ | 3. | Ⓐ | 5. | Ⓓ | 7. | Ⓐ |
| 2. | Ⓑ | 4. | ⓒ | 6. | Ⓓ | 8. | ⓒ |

1) ➡ C

Choice (C) is correct because formal English writing does not use contractions, so the uncontracted verb form "is not attempting" is correct. Moreover, an adverb should come between the auxiliary verb and the participle/base verb, making "is not primarily attempting" correct. Choice (A) is incorrect because it uses a contraction ("isn't") and a double negative; choice

(B) is incorrect because it uses a contraction and awkward phrasing; choice (D) is incorrect because of a misplaced adverb that changes the meaning of the sentence.

2) ➡ B

Choice (B) is correct because the adverb "cleverly" describes the past participle "contrived," so the adverb should go before the term that it modifies, making "cleverly contrived film sequences" correct.

3) ➡ A

Choice (A) is correct because the underlined portion refers to photographs that should, or "ought to" fit, but do not. Thus, the modal verb "ought to" is correct because the sentence implies possibility, and (A) is the only choice that does so. All other choices imply certainty, which changes the meaning of the sentence.

4) ➡ C

Choice (C) is correct because the adverb "well" describes to what extent the "artist holds viewers' attention." Because the adverb "well" describes the entire phrase, "holds viewers' attention," the adverb should come at the end of the clause, making "holds viewers' attention well" correct.

5) ➡ D

Choice (D) is correct because the adverb "suddenly" describes the verbs "sing" and "scream," so it should come immediately before the verbs, making "might suddenly sing—or scream" correct.

6) ➡ D

Choice (D) is correct because formal English writing does not use contractions, so the uncontracted verb form "would not be" is correct.

7) ➡ A

Choice (A) is correct; the adverb "Surprisingly" describes the phrase "splatters of color suggest." Because the adverb modifies the entire phrase, it should immediately before the phrase, making "Surprisingly, splatters of color suggest" correct.

8) ➡ C

Choice (C) is correct because the adverb "nearly" modifies the phrase "all of their assumptions about gravity," so it should come immediately before the phrase it describes, making "nearly all of the assumptions" correct.

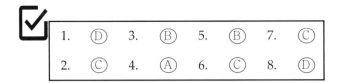
| 1. | Ⓓ | 3. | Ⓑ | 5. | Ⓑ | 7. | Ⓒ |
| 2. | Ⓒ | 4. | Ⓐ | 6. | Ⓒ | 8. | Ⓓ |

1) ➡ D

Choice (D) is correct; the sentence implies that the increase in athletic shoe sales is "a result of several factors." Choice (D) most clearly and concisely conveys this idea by phrasing the underlined portion as a dependent clause.

2) ➡ C

Choice (C) is correct because the sentence contains an independent clause followed by a dependent clause. When a dependent clause comes after an independent clause, a comma is optional but not necessary to separate the two clauses, making (C) correct.

3) ➡ B

Choice (B) is correct because the sentence contains an independent clause followed by a dependent clause. When a dependent clause comes after an independent clause, a comma is optional but not necessary. Furthermore, the conjunction "although" does not need to be separated from the rest of the phrase, and it does not need to be preceded by a conjunction (as is the case with "yet"in choice (D)).

4) ➡ A

Choice (A) is correct because the sentence contains a dependent clause followed by an independent clause. When a dependent clause comes first, it must be followed by a comma, making (A) correct.

5) ➡ B

Choice (B) is correct because the conjunction "though" begins a dependent clause. Although the comma between the two clauses is not necessary, it provides a pause in the middle of a long sentence and is therefore an appropriate stylistic choice. No comma is necessary after the conjunction "though."

6) ➡ C

Choice (C) is correct; the sentence contains an independent clause followed by a conditional statement. The independent clause should be separated from the conditional statement with either a semicolon or a period to show that it is a complete thought. The dependent clause

beginning with "if" must be separated from the rest of the sentence using a comma, making (C) the only acceptable choice.

7) ➡ C

Choice (C) is correct because the sentence conveys contrast: previous decades did not have much "athleisure" fashion; the 2010s saw a growth in "athleisure" fashion. The only choice that conveys contrast is the subordinate conjunction "whereas," making (C) correct.

8) ➡ D

Choice (D) is correct because the sentence contains a dependent clause followed by an independent clause. When a dependent clause comes first, it must be followed by a comma, making (D) correct.

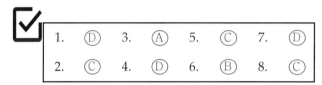
| 1. | Ⓓ | 3. | Ⓐ | 5. | Ⓒ | 7. | Ⓓ |
| 2. | Ⓒ | 4. | Ⓓ | 6. | Ⓑ | 8. | Ⓒ |

1) ➡ D

Choice (D) is correct because sentences contain related, non-contrasting information, so they can be combined into one sentence using a comma plus the coordinating conjunction "and."

2) ➡ C

Choice (C) is correct because the sentences contain contrasting information: A man-of-war looks like a jellyfish; it is actually a colony of small animals. The conjunction "but" conveys contrast, and a comma plus a conjunction effectively join two sentences, making (C) correct.

3) ➡ A

Choice (A) is correct because the clause "it shoots water out of its body to rocket backwards" provides a description of "jet propulsion," and a colon effectively separates a piece of information from a definition or description of that information.

4) ➡ D

Choice (D) is correct; the two sentences provide facts about icefish blood, and the relationship between the facts is self-evident and requires no transition words or conjunctions for clarification. Thus, a semicolon effectively joins the two sentences.

5) ➡ C

Choice (C) is correct; the relative pronoun "where" introduces a relative clause that refers to a place, "coral reefs." Because the relative clause modifies the noun phrase that comes before but is not grammatically essential, it should be separated from the rest of the sentence with a comma, making (C) correct.

6) ➡ B

Choice (B) is correct because the correlative conjunctions "as well as" connect "20 or more walking legs" to "two more." Although both (B) and (C) use the correct correlative conjunctions, (C) is incorrect because it over-punctuates; it is unnecessary to put a comma after the phrase "as well as."

7) ➡ D

Choice (D) is correct because a phrase beginning with "both" will generally follow the pattern "both x and y," which only (D) does effectively.

8) ➡ C

Choice (C) is correct because the relative pronoun "which" introduces a relative clause that refers to "complicated songs." Because the relative clause adds non-essential information, it should be separated from the rest of the sentence with a comma, making (C) correct.

Topic 33 - 34

☑

| 1. | Ⓑ | 3. | Ⓒ | 5. | Ⓓ | 7. | Ⓑ |
| 2. | Ⓓ | 4. | Ⓓ | 6. | Ⓐ | 8. | Ⓒ |

1) ➡ B

Choice (B) is correct; the sentence compares Great Britain's establishment of an emergency phone number to United States' establishment of an emergency phone number. In the underlined portion, the verb "did" can effectively replace the phrase "established a universal emergency telephone number," making (B) correct.

2) ➡ D

Choice (D) is correct because the listed actions must maintain parallel structure. The first action in the list establishes a "verb-first" word pattern that the other two listed items must maintain, which (D) does: "has stopped" and "has been" maintain the list's parallel word pattern.

3) ➡ C

Choice (C) is correct; in order to be logical, the sentence must compare whether one method (compression of the chest) or another method (mouth-to-mouth resuscitation) would be more effective for an untrained person to perform. Choices (A), (B), and (D) create confusion about whether the untrained person is giving or receiving the first aid.

4) ➡ D

Choice (D) is correct because the underlined verb form must maintain parallel structure with the infinitive verb "to look." Thus, it makes sense to say that people should "look around and assess safety risks," making (D) the correct choice.

5) ➡ D

Choice (D) is correct; the underlined portion must match the word pattern established by the phrase "that people call," which choice (D), "that they avoid," does.

6) ➡ A

Choice (A) is correct because the underlined portion must maintain the noun phrase word pattern established by the first item of the list, which (A) does: both "heat stroke" and "heart attack" are noun phrases.

7) ➡ B

Choice (B) is correct because the underlined portion must match the "gerund-first" word pattern established by "*Going* into shock," which "not *being* able to pump" does effectively. Although (D) also maintains this word pattern, it creates a awkwardly phrased, unclear sentence, making it less effective than (B).

8) ➡ C

Choice (C) is correct because it is the clearest version of the underlined portion. Choice (B) is incorrect because it does specify *what* a victim's legs need to be higher than. Choices (A) and (D) are incorrect because the victim's legs are part of the victim, so the underlined portion needs to specify *what part* of the victim his or her legs need to be higher than.

Topic 35 - 36

1.	Ⓑ	3.	Ⓐ	5.	Ⓒ	7.	Ⓓ
2.	Ⓑ	4.	Ⓒ	6.	Ⓑ	8.	Ⓐ

1) ➡ B
Choice (B) is correct because a colon effectively separates a piece of information from a definition of or elaboration on that information. In the sentence, the phrase "rodents, birds, lizards, and insects" is an elaboration on the term "prey that is too small to share" that precedes it in the sentence.

2) ➡ B
Choice (B) is correct; the sentence consists of two independent clauses that discuss how and why cats seem aloof, and the relationship between the facts is self-evident and requires no transition words or conjunctions for clarification. Thus, a semicolon effectively joins the two clauses.

3) ➡ A
Choice (A) is correct because the relationship between the two clauses is one of separate yet related ideas that do not need conjoining, so a semicolon effectively connects them. Choice (B) is incorrect because the second clause is a different idea, not an elaboration on the first.

4) ➡ C
Choice (C) is correct because the underlined portion forms part of a complex list (some of the listed elements use commas), so semicolons must separate the listed elements from one another.

5) ➡ C
Choice (C) is correct because the underlined portion is a participial phrase that modifies the subject of the sentence, "cats," and the participial phrase should be separated from the rest of the sentence with a comma.

6) ➡ B
Choice (B) is correct because all of the information in the underlined portion is essential to the meaning of the sentence, so it should not be separated from the rest of the sentence with any punctuation. Other choices are incorrect because they over-punctuate.

7) ➡ D
Choice (D) is correct because the clause that begins with "a person whose legs..." elaborates on the previous information in the sentence, and a dash effectively separates the elaboration from the "person" it describes.

8) ➡ A
Choice (A) is correct; the sentence consists of two independent clauses that discuss how cats show affection differently than do dogs, and the relationship between the facts is self-evident and requires no transition words or conjunctions for clarification. Thus, a semicolon effectively joins the two clauses.

Topic 37

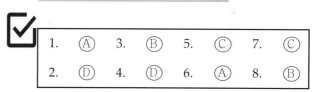

1.	Ⓐ	3.	Ⓑ	5.	Ⓒ	7.	Ⓒ
2.	Ⓓ	4.	Ⓓ	6.	Ⓐ	8.	Ⓑ

1) ➡ A
The correct choice is (A) because it conveys the sense that the film's plot is based upon a particular concept, which matches the meaning of "principle."

2) ➡ D
Choice (D) is correct because the relative clause "whose book of..." describes the writer via his book. "Who's" and "who is" would state that the writer _is_ the book.

3) ➡ B
Choice (B) is the correct choice because the sentence describes a situation ("robots are programmed to obey humans") and the special case that changes the situation ("_except_ when doing so may harm other humans.") The other answers do not make sense.

4) ➡ D
The correct answer is (D) because logically, the writer can explore a noun—as in, the _effects_ of such programming. It would not make sense to explore "to affect," a verb.

5) ➡ C

The correct answer is (C) because it shows possession: the humans' life experiences (*their* life experiences.)

6) ➡ A

Choice (A) is correct because the verb phrase "lose control over" means "fail to maintain control over," which fits the sentence logically.

7) ➡ C

The sentence is discussing how the robotic organisms feel, and *averse* is the only choice referring to an emotion or opinion; thus, the correct answer is (C).

8) ➡ B

Choice (B), "past," is correct because the word must describe "events," so it must be an adjective or noun. The word "passed" is a past-tense verb, i.e., "The rocket passed the moon."

Topic 38

1.	Ⓐ	3.	Ⓐ	5.	Ⓑ	7.	Ⓐ
2.	Ⓑ	4.	Ⓐ	6.	Ⓑ	8.	Ⓑ

1) ➡ A

Choice (A) is correct; the main topic of the passage is the effects of video games on teens' social and cognitive development. The underlined sentence frames, or provides context, for the main topic by pointing out how popular video games are among teens.

2) ➡ B

Choice (B) is correct because the sentence presents a counter-argument (adults worry that video games have a negative effect on teen development), which is followed by the passage's main claim that video games do not negatively affect teens.

3) ➡ A

Choice (A) is correct; the claim that "video games can inspire…social learning" is supported throughout paragraph 2 using statistical evidence. Thus, the sentence at number 3 introduces the paragraph's main argument.

4) ➡ A

Choice (A) is correct because the sentence at number 4 provides statistical evidence that supports the main claim of paragraph 2, that "video games can inspire…social learning."

5) ➡ B

Choice (B) is correct because the sentence at number 5 provides additional statistical evidence and explanation that supports the main claim of paragraph 2, that "video games can inspire… social learning."

6) ➡ B

Choice (B) is correct; the main claim of paragraph 3 is that, on average, teens play a wide variety of video games that enhance imagination and critical thinking skills. Because the claim at number 6 states the opposite, that "video games involve nothing but repetitive gun violence," we can infer that it is presenting a counter-argument that will be dispelled by the information that follows.

7) ➡ A

Choice (A) is correct; the two sentences that follow the sentence at number 7 explain how video games "enhance imagination and thinking skills." Thus, we can infer that the sentence at number 7 serves to set up examples.

8) ➡ B

Choice (B) is correct because the sentence at number 8 tells the reader why "playing the role of a hero" in a video game interests people, so it provides an explanation for the information in the previous sentence.

Topic 39

1.	Ⓑ	3.	Ⓑ	5.	Ⓐ	7.	Ⓐ
2.	Ⓑ	4.	Ⓐ	6.	Ⓑ	8.	Ⓑ

1) ➡ B

Choice (B) is correct; the sentence containing the underlined portion explains how the name "flying squirrel" is slightly misleading because flying squirrels technically "leap" rather than "fly." Thus, the phrase "Despite the name" effectively introduces the sentence by indicating that the name is misleading.

2) ➡ B
Choice (B) is correct; the part of the sentence after the underlined portion provides a reason that flying squirrels can leap from tree to tree. The phrase "because of" effectively introduces a reason or an effect, making (B) correct.

3) ➡ B
Choice (B) is correct because the added sentence provides information that compares a flying squirrel's method of gliding to "the physics of a paper airplane." Because the added sentence elaborates on information in sentence 2, it should come immediately after sentence 2.

4) ➡ A
Choice (A) is correct; sentence 2 discusses where the flying squirrel originated, and sentence 1 builds on this discussion by describing how flying squirrels spread across the world. Sentence 2 should come before sentence 1 because it makes sense to describe a creature's evolutionary origins before explaining the creature's proliferation.

5) ➡ A
Choice (A) is correct because mentioning a "tree trunk" effectively explains how a flying squirrel's gliding could be dangerous—it implies that the squirrel could fly into the tree trunk and injure itself.

6) ➡ B
Choice (B) is correct because the underlined portion adds relevant, non-redundant information about how a flying squirrel safely glides from tree to tree.

7) ➡ A
Choice (A) is correct because it effectively concludes an explanation of how flying squirrels land on trees. Choice (B) is incorrect because it discusses how flying squirrels glide, which deviates from the paragraph's focus on flying squirrels' landing techniques.

8) ➡ B
Choice (B) is correct; paragraphs 1 and 3 discuss the mechanics of flying squirrel gliding and landing, whereas paragraph 2 provides some general information about flying squirrel evolution. Usually, general information should come before specifics, so paragraph 2 should be placed before paragraph 1.

Chapter 2: Answers & Explanations ——————

✓
1.	Ⓐ	4.	Ⓑ	7.	Ⓑ	10.	Ⓑ	13.	Ⓐ
2.	Ⓐ	5.	Ⓓ	8.	Ⓒ	11.	Ⓓ	14.	Ⓒ
3.	Ⓓ	6.	Ⓒ	9.	Ⓑ	12.	Ⓑ	15.	Ⓐ

1) ➡ A
Concept(s) Tested: Modifiers
Choice (A) is correct because the underlined portion modifies "activity," so the participle (modifier) form of "to lead" is appropriate here.

2) ➡ A
Concept(s) Tested: Concision/Style
Choice (A) is correct because it is the most concise version of the underlined portion, and it maintains the direct, academic tone of the rest of the sentence.

3) ➡ D
Concept(s) Tested: Verb Tense.
Choice (D) is correct because it agrees with the plural subject, "species," and because the inclusion of "can" emphasizes the organisms' ability to survive in extreme environments.

4) ➡ B
Concept(s) Tested: Verb Tense.
Choice (B) is correct because colons introduce lists and other elaboration or explanations.

5) ➡ D
Concept(s) Tested: Subordinate conjunction and pronoun use.
Choice (D) is correct; the conjunction "because of" shows that the downtown is recognizable *as a result of* its iconic structures. The pronoun "its" refers to the singular noun phrase "New York City's downtown."

6) ➡ C
Concept(s) Tested: Combining sentences
Choice (C) is correct because the second sentence defines "fast day," so it can follow the term "fast day" as an appositive, a phrase that describes a noun and is separated from the rest of a sentence using commas.

7) ➡ B
Concept(s) Tested: Syntax

Choice (B) is the correct choice because the conjunction "so" is the most effective way to link the action of "keeping records" to the *reason* for the action "stored…for posterity."

8) ➡ C
Concept(s) Tested: Modifier placement
Choice (C) is correct because it places the noun being modified, "Lanercost Priory," directly after the phrase that modifies it, "Located near Naworth castle in Northern England."

9) ➡ B
Concept(s) tested: Commonly confused words
Choice (B) is correct because it shows who the "fossilized remains" belong to. The contraction "who's simply means, "who is", and does not show ownership.

10) ➡ B
Concept(s) tested: Pronouns
Choice (B) is correct because the pronoun "they" can be used to denote objects, such as "tablet computers".

11) ➡ D
Concept(s) tested: Verb Tense
Choice (D) is correct because the sentence should be in the present tense since "psychotherapy" is practiced currently. Furthermore, the verb should be singular, since the subject is "the goal," and "is" is a singular verb form.

12) ➡ B
Concept(s) tested: Relative clauses
Choice (B) is the correct choice because it shows that the "compound leaves and fragrant white flowers" belong to the "locust tree." "Whose" is wrong because it makes the leaves and flowers seem like they possess the trait of reaching "heights of eighty feet," rather than the tree.

13) ➡ A
Concept(s) tested: Punctuation
Choice (A) is correct because no comma is needed in this appositive phrase to denote a pause.

14) ➡ C
Concept(s) tested: Transition words
Choice (C) is correct because "nonetheless" reflects contrast, which makes sense when contrasting the positive associations of the color yellow ("bright, happy, warm, and…holy") with its negative associations ("illness or…danger").

15) ➡ A
Concept(s) tested: Concision/syntax
Choice (A) is correct because it tells us the subject first, "Klinefelter's syndrome", and then goes on to describe its characteristics, "two or more chromosomes", and "sterility", using commas to separate ideas.

Grammar Skills Practice 2

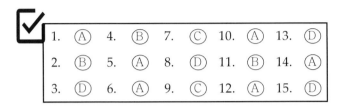

1. Ⓐ	4. Ⓑ	7. Ⓒ	10. Ⓐ	13. Ⓓ
2. Ⓑ	5. Ⓐ	8. Ⓓ	11. Ⓑ	14. Ⓐ
3. Ⓓ	6. Ⓐ	9. Ⓒ	12. Ⓐ	15. Ⓓ

1) ➡ A
Concept(s) tested: Subject-verb agreement
Choice (A) is correct; the underlined verb refers to and must agree with the singular subject of the sentence, "The state of Washington," so the third-person singular verb form "contributes" is correct.

2) ➡ B
Concept(s) tested: Relative clauses
Choice (B) is correct; the underlined portion introduces grammatically essential information that refers to "family dynamic." The relative pronouns "that" effectively connects "family dynamic" to "the one…the most," the phrase that describes "family dynamic."

3) ➡ D
Concept(s) tested: Precision
Choice (D) is correct because "to garner" is to gather or collect, especially information or approval. In this case the subject *gathers* attention from "the scientific community."

4) ➡ B
Concept(s) tested: Combining sentences
Choice (B) is correct because it combines both sentences concisely without unnecessary words or punctuation. Other choices are unnecessarily wordy and/or contain convoluted phrasing.

5) ➡ A
Concept(s) tested: Modifiers/syntax
Choice (A) is correct because it correctly identifies the participants as "unsuspecting," meaning they are the ones being surprised. Choice (B) conveys the same information, but is incorrect because it is unnecessarily wordy, and choice (C) and (D) use the wrong participle form: calling the participants "unsuspected" changes the meaning of the sentence.

6) ➡ A
Concept(s) tested: Within-sentence punctuation
Choice (A) is correct; a pair of commas is needed to separate the non-essential phrase "though now… and medicine" from the rest of the sentence, and the use of the conjunction "though" effectively conveys contrast.

7) ➡ C
Concept(s) tested: Conventional expressions
Choice (C) is correct because the idiom "in the face of danger" refers to an encountering of immediate danger; it makes sense to say that bitter enemies can bond when they encounter immediate danger.

8) ➡ D
Concepts tested: Comparisons/ correlative conjunctions
Choice (D) is correct because it clearly indicates that the quickness of the traits' evolution is being compared to itself for emphasis: it was surprising that it was as fast as it was.

9) ➡ C
Concept(s) tested: Possessive pronouns/commonly confused words
Choice C is correct because "the Spanish government" is a singular entity, and the singular possessive pronoun "its" refers to the Spanish government's possession of "territory."

10) ➡ A
Concept(s) tested: Concision
Choice (A) is correct because it is the clearest and most concise version of the underlined portion. All other choices contain redundancies: "forbidden" and "banned" are synonyms, and there is no need to put "there" immediately after "Italy."

11) ➡ B
Concept(s) tested: Appositive phrases
Choice (B) is correct because the underlined information is an appositive phrase that describes the subject of the sentence, "Hannibal Barca," so it must be separated from the rest of the sentence with a pair of commas.

12) ➡ A
Concept(s) tested: Subordinate conjunction use
Choice (A) is correct because the conjunction "while" correctly shows a relationship of contrast. The contrast in this sentence is between "advanced for its time in the 15th century" and "actually based on 2nd century knowledge."

13) ➡ D

Concept(s) tested: Correlative conjunctions

Choice (D) is correct because whenever the preposition "from" is followed by two options, the preposition "to" must come between the two options.

14) ➡ A

Concept(s) tested: Combining sentences

Choice (A) is correct because the two sentences provide facts about the origins of soccer, but the relationship between the facts is self-evident and requires no transition words or conjunctions for clarification. Thus, a semicolon effectively joins the two sentences.

15) ➡ D

Concept(s) tested: Concision

Choice (D) is correct because "by the body's digestive system" is unneeded. The meaning of the sentence is still clear without the underlined passage, and extra explanation would be redundant.

Grammar Skills Practice 3

1. Ⓐ	4. Ⓓ	7. Ⓐ	10. Ⓒ	13. Ⓑ
2. Ⓑ	5. Ⓒ	8. Ⓑ	11. Ⓑ	14. Ⓓ
3. Ⓓ	6. Ⓒ	9. Ⓒ	12. Ⓐ	15. Ⓓ

1) ➡ A

Concept(s) tested: Subject-verb agreement
Choice (A) is correct because the underlined verb must agree with the plural subject, "Salmon." The simple present tense is appropriate because the verb describes a regular, ongoing occurrence.

2) ➡ B

Concept(s) tested: Subject-verb agreement/relative clauses

Choice (B) is correct because the underlined portion introduces a relative clause that refers to "The outer layer of the eye," making the relative pronoun "which" appropriate. The underlined verb also refers to the singular subject "The outer layer of the eye," making the third-person singular verb form "includes" correct.

3) ➡ D

Concept(s) tested: Noun agreement
Choice (D) is correct because a noun that follows the phrase "among the..." is plural, making the plural noun "pastimes" the only acceptable choice.

4) ➡ D

Concept(s) tested: Appositive phrases

Choice (D) is correct because the underlined portion introduces a description of the preceding noun, "Earl Biggers," so it makes sense to make the description an appositive phrase by beginning it with the article "an." (Note: appositive phrases always begin with an article, and are separated from the rest of a sentence with a comma/commas.)

5) ➡ C

Concept(s) tested: Precision

Choice (C) is correct because "well over three decades after" implies a continuity over time, and "to remain" means "to continue to possess a particular quality or role." The other choices incorrectly imply that another album is "the best-selling album of all time."

6) ➡ C

Concept(s) tested: Concision

Choice (C) is correct because "raising" already implies that the one being raised will be "nurtured" and "cared for," making the latter two terms redundant, and "raising" the correct answer.

7) ➡ A

Concept(s) tested: Providing evidence

Choice (A) is correct; the first part of the sentence introduces the topic of the sentence, the writing of the *Epic of Gilgamesh.* Only (A) provides information relevant to the writing of the epic.

8) ➡ B

Concept(s) tested: Coordinate conjunction use

Choice (B) is correct because there is a difference between snakes that are merely poisonous and those that "can kill a human with a single bite." Only "and" acknowledges this, and a comma is necessary to separate the two independent clauses in the sentence.

9) ➡ C

Concept(s) tested: Subordinate conjunction use

Choice (C) is correct because "since then" conveys the passage of time, and it fits the syntax of the sentence. Although "after" also denotes the passage of time, its meaning would be ambiguous in the context of the sentence.

10) ➡ C

Concept(s) tested: Combining sentences

Choice (C) is correct because it is the only choice that effectively shows contrast: the sentence contrasts the U.S.'s hesitancy to send troops into combat in WWII battles to its willingness to support certain countries during WWII.

11) ➡ B
Concept(s) tested: Rhetorical style
Choice (B) is correct because the question asks for a hyperbole or exaggeration, and "that spider was bigger than my head" is a perfect example of exaggeration, as no spider is that large.

12) ➡ A
Concept(s) tested: Within-sentence punctuation
Choice (A) is correct; the underlined portion introduces a participial phrase that modifies *"gestation period."* The comma is necessary to indicate that "measured" modifies the preceding clause, not just the word "develop," which would not make sense.

13) ➡ B
Concept(s) tested: Syntax
Choice (B) is correct because the underlined portion is part of the subject, and as such, cannot be a conjunction like "since" or "still."

14) ➡ D
Concept(s) tested: Parallel structure
Choice (D) is correct because the underlined portion must maintain a past-tense verb pattern, which only (D) does: past-tense verb ("directed and starred") + prepositional phrase ("in several films").

15) ➡ D
Concept(s) tested: Logical comparison/precision
Choice (D) is correct because the sentence contrasts "modern individuals" and those that fit a stereotype of Eskimos. Choice (A) is incorrect grammatically, while choices (B) and (C) are vague and confusing. Only choice (D) suits the writer's purpose with the appropriate adjective ("stereotypical") and with quotation marks to show that the term "Eskimo" may be inaccurate.

Grammar Skills Practice 4

☑
1. Ⓐ	4. Ⓓ	7. Ⓒ	10. Ⓑ	13. Ⓒ
2. Ⓓ	5. Ⓑ	8. Ⓑ	11. Ⓐ	14. Ⓑ
3. Ⓒ	6. Ⓐ	9. Ⓓ	12. Ⓓ	15. Ⓐ

1) ➡ A
Concept(s) tested: Conventional expressions

Choice (A) is correct because when someone completes an action, they are said to have "carried it out." In this case the action "carried out" was a failed assassination attempt.

2) ➡ D
Concept(s) tested: Subject-verb agreement
Choice (D) is correct because the underlined portion must contain the main verb of the sentence, and the third-person plural verb form "are" agrees with the subject "large portions."

3) ➡ C
Concept(s) tested: Within-sentence punctuation
Choice (C) is correct because a colon effectively separates a piece of information from a definition of or elaboration on that information. In the sentence, the list "dramatic lighting, startling realism, and vibrant textures" is an elaboration on the "artist's strengths" mentioned earlier in the sentence.

4) ➡ D
Concept(s) tested: Modifiers
Choice (D) is correct because "remarkable" is used to describe the noun "resistance," so "remarkable" must be an adjective that precedes the noun it describes, making the phrase "remarkable resistance" correct.

5) ➡ B
Concept(s) tested: Combining sentences
Choice (B) is correct; the second sentence focuses on Erik's activities in Greenland, so it makes sense to turn the second sentence into a relative clause that refers to "Greenland," making the relative pronoun "where" appropriate.

6) ➡ A
Concept(s) tested: Within-sentence punctuation
Choice (A) is correct because the nouns "1994 film" act as a title to *"Pulp Fiction,"* and no commas should separate them. However, a comma is necessary after *Pulp Fiction* to separate the dependent clause ("Since...Fiction") from the independent clause ("Samuel...films").

7) ➡ C
Concept(s) tested: Precision
Choice (C) is correct because "to transmit" means "to pass on from one person or place to another." This fits the description of "radio broadcast" which is passed from one location to another. "transport" does not fit in this case because one cannot physically transport a "radio broadcast."

8) ➡ B
Concept(s) tested: Rhetorical style
Choice (B) is correct because "sarcasm" is saying one thing while meaning the opposite. The question states that Jordan is "feeling woefully unprepared," so we can infer that he means the opposite when he says, "this should be easy," making choice (B) is appropriate.

9) ➡ D
Concept(s) tested: Conjunction use
Choice(D) is correct; the participle "during" cannot introduce a new clause. The subordinate conjunction "when," however, can introduce a clause and conveys the same meaning, making it the correct choice.

10) ➡ B
Concept(s) tested: Subject-verb agreement/verb tense, mood, and voice
Choice (B) is correct; the underlined verb must agree with the sentence's subject, *Titus Andronicus*," and it must express the "literary present" (the present tense is used to recount events in literature, even though the literature itself was written in the past). Therefore, the present-tense, third-person singular verb form "tells" is correct.

11) ➡ A
Concept(s) tested: Conjunction use
Choice (A) is correct because "if" designates possibility. There is only a possibility of olives being edible if they are brined. Only (A) correctly communicates this.

12) ➡ D
Concept(s) tested: Pronoun clarity
Choice (D) is correct because the underlined portion must specify which of the three males in the sentence "hoped that the expedition would help establish an overland route," and only (D) provides a specific name.

13) ➡ C
Concept(s) tested: Logical comparison
Choice (C) is correct; the sentence compares Hemingway's writing style to the *writing style* of any *other* 20th century author. The other choices compare the writing style to authors, or fail to include Hemingway in "20th century authors."

14) ➡ B
Concept(s) tested: Parallel structure
Choice (B) is correct because the underlined portion must match the word pattern established by the other listed noun ("a dictionary...artistic

sense). Choice (B) effectively lists all items as nouns, and shows that these nouns are qualities that a good reader *has*, or *possesses*.

15) ➡ A
Concept(s) tested: Combining sentences
Choice (A) is correct because the subject, "Ansel Adams's photographs" comes first, followed by their description. The sentence's verbs also agree in tense, all being in the present, since Adam's photographs can still be viewed. In addition, (A) properly emphasizes the main point about the photographs portraying the American West by placing it at the end.

Grammar Skills Practice 5

☑
1. Ⓒ	4. Ⓐ	7. Ⓐ	10. Ⓑ	13. Ⓒ
2. Ⓑ	5. Ⓓ	8. Ⓓ	11. Ⓐ	14. Ⓑ
3. Ⓒ	6. Ⓒ	9. Ⓑ	12. Ⓓ	15. Ⓐ

1) ➡ C
Concept(s) Tested: Subordinate conjunction use
Choice (C) is correct because the sentence compares the time it takes for the sun's light to reach Earth to the time it takes for the same light to reach Pluto. The conjunction "whereas" is the most appropriate choice for expressing comparison.

2) ➡ B
Concept(s) Tested: Possessive nouns
Choice (B) is correct because the article "a" that precedes the underlined portion indicates that "colony" should be singular. "Colony" also shows possession over the plural noun "eggs," so "colony" should end with 's.

3) ➡ C
Concept(s) Tested: Precision/conventional expression
Choice (C) is correct because "to coin a term" is an English idiom meaning "to invent a new word or phrase," which makes sense in the context of the sentence.

4) ➡ A
Concept(s) Tested: Combining sentences
Choice (A) is correct; the conjunction "because" links a cause to its effect. In the sentence, the *cause* is Venus' proximity to Earth and its being

highly reflective, while the *effect* is its brightness in the night sky.

5) ➡ D
Concept(s) Tested: Modifier placement
Choice (D) is correct because it places the noun being modified, "the Erie Canal," directly after the phrase that modifies it, "Opened in 1825." Other choices are ambiguous about what exactly was opened in 1825.

6) ➡ C
Concept(s) Tested: Subject-verb agreement
Choice (C) is correct; the underlined portion must contain the main verb of the sentence (as the sentence does not otherwise have one), and (C) includes the verb "was," which agrees in person and number with the sentence subject, "The Grand Canyon."

7) ➡ A
Concept(s) Tested: Correlative conjunctions
Choice (A) is correct because a phrase beginning with "between" will always follow the pattern "between *x* and *y.*" Choice (B) incorrectly phrases this correlative conjunction, and choice (C) and (D) are incorrect because it does not make sense to characterize interactions between two people as being "within" the individuals.

8) ➡ D
Concept(s) Tested: Parallel structure
Choice (D) is correct because the underlined portion must follow the same "each + singular noun + verb" word pattern established by "each U.S. penny costs," which (D) does: "each + singular noun (U.S. nickel) + verb (costs)."

9) ➡ B
Concept(s) Tested: Logical comparison
Choice (B) is correct; the sentence compares "the average annual salary of a physician" to the average salary of a registered nurse. Because "the average annual salary" is singular, the singular pronoun "that" effectively replaces "the average salary" in the underlined portion.

10) ➡ B
Concept(s) Tested: Combining sentences
Choice (B) is correct because it is the clearest and most concise version of the underlined portion. Choice (A) is incorrect because it does not provide a subject for the second independent clause; choices (C) and (D) are incorrect because they are unnecessarily wordy.

11) ➡ A
Concept(s) Tested: Relative clauses/Pronoun person and number

Choice (A) is correct because the underlined portion introduces a relative clause that refers to the plural noun "the folk stories," so the relative pronoun "which" effectively introduces this clause, and the plural personal pronoun "they" effectively refers to "animated films."

12) ➡ D
Concept(s) Tested: Concision
Choice (D) is correct because it provides the clearest and most concise version of the underlined portion. All other choices are unnecessarily wordy.

13) ➡ C
Concept(s) Tested: Comparisons
Choice (C) is correct because in the sentence, the effectiveness of only two actions is being weighed: moving fuel and dousing with water. Thus it is correct to indicate which action is *more effective.*

14) ➡ B
Concept(s) Tested: Commonly confused words/ Pronoun person and number
Choice (B) is correct because the underlined pronoun refers to the singular noun "Mount Krakatoa" and shows possession over "cataclysmic eruption," making the singular possessive pronoun "its" the correct choice.

15) ➡ A
Concept(s) Tested: Combining sentences
Choice (A) is correct because the second sentence provides a description of *The Story of the Vivian Girls,* so it makes sense to combine the sentences, turning the second sentence into a relative clause that refers to and describes *The Story of the Vivian Girls.* Other choices awkwardly position the word "expansive," emphasizing it and creating a redundancy.

Grammar Skills Practice 6

1. Ⓑ	4. Ⓒ	7. Ⓓ	10. Ⓑ	13. Ⓐ
2. Ⓓ	5. Ⓒ	8. Ⓒ	11. Ⓐ	14. Ⓓ
3. Ⓐ	6. Ⓐ	9. Ⓑ	12. Ⓓ	15. Ⓒ

1) ➡ B
Concept(s) Tested: Concision/syntax
Choice (B) is correct because it is the clearest and

most concise version of the underlined portion. Choice (A) is incorrect because it does not specify that hydrogen is the "lightest and most abundant" of; choices (C) and (D) are incorrect because they are unnecessarily wordy.

2) ➡ D
Concept(s) Tested: Subject-verb agreement/ Parallel structure
Choice (D) is correct because the underlined verb refers to and must agree with the singular noun phrase "the word *sushi*," and it must maintain the same tense as the present-tense verb "means," making the third-person singular verb form "refers" correct.

3) ➡ A
Concept(s) Tested: Within-sentence punctuation
Choice (A) is correct because all of the information in the underlined portion is essential to the meaning of the sentence, so it should not be separated from the rest of the sentence with any punctuation. Other choices are incorrect because they over-punctuate.

4) ➡ C
Concept(s) Tested: Appositive phrases
Choice (C) is correct because it uses an appositive phrase followed by a comma to describe the subject of the sentence, "Winslow Homer." Choice (A) is incorrect because it creates a run-on sentence. Choice (B) could serve as a title if it were not followed by a comma. (D) results in an awkward sentence.

5) ➡ C
Concept(s) Tested: Subject-verb agreement
Choice (C) is correct because the underlined verb/ verb phrase refers to and must agree with the sentence's singular subject "The North American passenger pigeon," making the third-person singular verb phrase "was driven" correct.

6) ➡ A
Concept(s) Tested: Verb tense, mood, and voice
Choice (A) is correct because the sentence describes a general scientific process, making the simple present tense appropriate. Moreover, the underlined verb must agree in tense with the other verb of the sentence, "is," making the present-tense form "arise" correct.

7) ➡ D
Concept(s) Tested: Verb tense, mood, and voice/ subject-verb agreement
Choice (D) is correct; the underlined verb clearly refers to "The first transcontinental flight," so

the inclusion of "it" in choices (B) and (C) is unnecessary, making these choices incorrect. Moreover, the sentence describes an event "in 1911," making the simple past tense verb for "occurred" appropriate.

8) ➡ C
Concept(s) Tested: Parallel structure/items in a list
Choice (C) is correct because each listed item maintains the same plural noun word pattern, each listed noun is separated from other listed nouns using commas, and the conjunction "and" separates the last two listed items.

9) ➡ B
Concept(s) Tested: Subordinate conjunction use
Choice (B) is correct because the sentence is a conditional statement (also called an "If...then" statement). Conditional statements generally begin with "If," making (B) the most appropriate choice.

10) ➡ B
Concept(s) Tested: Precision
Choice (B) is correct because "to associate" one thing with another is to link or connect the two things, and it makes sense to say, "fortune cookies are generally *linked with* Chinese food."

11) ➡ A
Concept(s) Tested: Combining sentences
Choice (A) is correct because the second sentence elaborate on New Amsterdam, so it makes sense to combine the sentences, turning the second sentence into a relative clause that refers to and elaborates on New Amsterdam. Moreover, (A) provides an active-voice clause

12) ➡ D
Concept(s) Tested: Concision
Choice (D) is correct because it is the only choice that avoids redundancy.

13) ➡ A
Concept(s) Tested: Subordinate conjunction use
Choice (A) is correct because the underlined portion must express a relationship of time to show that Hall was in high school *at the time* that she established a company. Only "when" establishes this relationship of time, making (A) correct.

14) ➡ D
Concept(s) Tested: Combining sentences
Choice (D) is correct because it clearly and concisely restructures the second sentence into a participial phrase that modifies "sequoia trees."

Other choices are incorrect because they are unnecessarily wordy.

15) ➡ C
Concept(s) Tested: Conventional expressions
Choice (C) is correct because the phrase "contrary to popular belief" is an English idiom the comes before a statement that opposes most people's beliefs, which fits the context of the sentence. Other choices are incorrect because they do not properly phrase this idiom.

Grammar Skills Practice 7

✓
1. Ⓐ	4. Ⓒ	7. Ⓓ	10. Ⓐ	13. Ⓒ
2. Ⓑ	5. Ⓓ	8. Ⓐ	11. Ⓐ	14. Ⓒ
3. Ⓑ	6. Ⓒ	9. Ⓑ	12. Ⓓ	15. Ⓑ

1) ➡ A
Concept(s) Tested: Noun agreement
Choice (A) is correct because the underlined noun phrase refers to the creations of automobile manufacturers, so the underlined portion should be plural to match the number of "Many automobile manufacturers," making "electric automobiles" the only acceptable choice.

2) ➡ B
Concept(s) Tested: Providing evidence
Choice (B) is correct because it provides an example of a location where lightning strikes many times each year, further disproving the myth presented in the first sentence. (A) is incorrect because individuals may have been in different places each time they were struck.

3) ➡ B
Concept(s) Tested: Subordinate conjunction use
Choice (B) is correct because the sentence presents a contrast: The Declaration of Independence was finalized in July of 1776; the document was not signed until August of 1776. Although the conjunction "while" often denotes a relationship of time, it can also denote contrast, making it the best choice.

4) ➡ C
Concept(s) Tested: Participial phrase
Choice (C) is correct because the underlined portion introduces a phrase that modifies "Legal disputes." Participial phrases effectively modify nouns/noun phrases, so the underlined portion should introduce

the phrase using the present participle "involving."

5) ➡ D
Concept(s) Tested: Logical comparison
Choice (D) is correct; the sentence compares the time it takes to travel from Glasgow to London by bus to the time it takes to travel from those same locations by train. At the underlined portion, "it does" effectively replaces the phrase "it takes to travel," making (D) the most effective choice.

6) ➡ C
Concept(s) Tested: Correlative conjunctions
Choice (C) is correct because the term "not only" must always be followed by the term "but also," making (C) the only acceptable answer.

7) ➡ D
Concept(s) Tested: Within-sentence punctuation
Choice (D) is correct because all of the information provided in the underlined portion is grammatically necessary to the sentence, so no punctuation is necessary to separate any of it. Also, the participle "found" modifies the word directly preceding "diamonds," so no comma is needed for clarity.

8) ➡ A
Concept(s) Tested: Transition words
Choice (A) is correct because the second sentence contrasts information in the first sentence: billions of species have lived on earth; less than one percent of all species are alive today. The transition word "however" effectively conveys this contrast.

9) ➡ B
Concept(s) Tested: Pronoun clarity
Choice (B) is correct because the underlined portion must specify which of the two males in the sentence "picked up the guitar," and only (B) provides a specific name.

10) ➡ A
Concept(s) Tested: Syntax
Choice (A) is correct because the phrase "wheat and barley" serves as the subject of the sentence, and therefore should not be preceded by a relative or personal pronoun, as is the case with all other choices.

11) ➡ A
Concept(s) Tested: Rhetorical Style
Choice (A) is correct; understating something means making it seem smaller or less important than it is. In choice (A), the Hawaiian is understating the coldness of the water by claiming that it is only "a bit colder" than he is used to, though Arctic waters are certainly much colder than a Hawaiian

would be accustomed to.

12) ➡ D
Concept(s) Tested: Subject-verb agreement
Choice (D) is correct because the underlined verb must agree with the plural subject "the only... objects," which the third-person plural verb form "are" does.

13) ➡ C
Concept(s) Tested: Concision
Choice (C) is correct because it is the clearest and most concise version of the underlined portion. Choices (A) and (D) contain redundancies: "confirmed" and "established" are synonyms, as are "oldest" and "most ancient." Choice (B) includes the unnecessary conjunction "and."

14) ➡ C
Concept(s) Tested: Parallel structure
Choice (C) is correct because the underlined portion must maintain the same word pattern as the previously mentioned qualities. Since the other listed qualities are nouns or noun phrases, the underlined portion must also be a noun, making "perseverance" the correct choice.

15) ➡ B
Concept(s) Tested: Combining sentences
Choice (B) is correct because the second sentence qualifies information in the first sentence: The fall of the Berlin Wall was the symbolic end of the Soviet Union; it officially dissolved two years later. The use of "but" in choice (B) effectively conveys this clarification.

Grammar Skills Practice 8

1. Ⓓ	4. Ⓐ	7. Ⓐ	10. Ⓓ	13. Ⓑ
2. Ⓓ	5. Ⓑ	8. Ⓑ	11. Ⓐ	14. Ⓒ
3. Ⓐ	6. Ⓐ	9. Ⓒ	12. Ⓑ	15. Ⓐ

1) ➡ D
Concept(s) Tested: Subject-verb agreement
Choice (D) is correct because the underlined portion must act as the main verb of the sentence, and it must agree with the plural subject, "Most works." Only the third-person plural verb form "were" meets both these qualifications.

2) ➡ D
Concept(s) Tested: Modifier placement

Choice (D) is correct because it places the noun being modified, "The Grand Canal of China," directly after the phrase that modifies it, "Completed in the early 7th century CE." Other choices create confusion about what was completed in the 7th century.

3) ➡ A
Concept(s) Tested: Combining sentences
Choice (A) is correct because it results in the clearest and most concise sentence. It immediately introduces the subject, "Sharks" and the main verb "have ruled," and does not contain unclear or redundant phrasing.

4) ➡ A
Concept(s) Tested: Precision
Choice (A) is correct because "diverse" means "having a large amount of variety," and it makes sense to say, "Orchids are the family of flowering plant *with the largest amount of variety."*

5) ➡ B
Concept(s) Tested: Pronoun person and number
Choice (B) is correct because both pronoun in the underlined portion refer to the singular subject, "The massive sperm whale," so the underlined pronouns must also be singular. Moreover, the second underlined pronoun shows possession over "time," so the singular possessive pronoun "its" is appropriate.

6) ➡ A
Concept(s) Tested: Concision
Choice (A) is correct because it is the clearest and most concise version of the underlined portion. Choice (B) does not specify *what* Monroe achieved, and choices (C) and (D) contain redundancies: "international," "everywhere," and "worldwide" are all synonyms.

7) ➡ A
Concept(s) Tested: Conventional expression
Choice (A) is correct because, when referencing something created, such as works of art, the preposition "over" means "more than," which fits the context of the sentence more appropriately than the other choices.

8) ➡ B
Concept(s) Tested: Parallel structure
Choice (B) is correct because the underlined portion must maintain the same plural noun word pattern established by the previously listed animals. Only "koalas" maintains this plural noun structure.

9) ➡ C
Concept(s) Tested: Combining sentences
Choice (C) is correct; the conjunction "because" links an effect to its cause. In the sentence, the *effect* is that Pickett's art style is called naïve art ("naïve" means "innocent, or lacking experience"), while the *cause* is that his style ignores formal conventions.

10) ➡ D
Concept(s) Tested: Correlative conjunctions
Choice (D) is correct because in a comparison where the word "as" is followed by the quality being compared ("environmentally devastating" in the sentence), another "as" must always come immediately after the quality.

11) ➡ A
Concept(s) Tested: Parallel structure
Choice (A) is correct because the underlined portion must maintain the same "adjective + noun" word pattern established by the previously listed resources, which only (A) does: "adjective (abundant) + water supplies (noun)."

12) ➡ B
Concept(s) Tested: Noun agreement
Choice (B) is correct because the underlined portion refers to a group of people called "scribes." Thus, the underlined noun/noun phrase must also describe a group of people, which only "members of society" does. Other choices are incorrect because they describe objects or concepts.

13) ➡ B
Concept(s) Tested: Conventional expressions
Choice (B) is correct because the underlined portion forms part of the English idiom "required by law." Thus, the preposition "by" always pairs with "law" in this context, making the other choices inaccurate.

14) ➡ C
Concept(s) Tested: Within-sentence punctuation
Choice (C) is correct because a non-essential phrase ("one of the oldest known board games") must be separated from the rest of the sentence by a *pair* of commas, parentheses, or dashes, and only (C) uses a punctuation pair. Other choices use inconsistent punctuation marks fail to use a plural noun for "games," both of which are grammatically incorrect.

15) ➡ A
Concept(s) Tested: Subordinate conjunction use
Choice (A) is correct because the second part of the sentence limits the statement in the first part of the sentence. The use of "although" in choice (A)

effectively conveys this limitation: all of the plays may be considered great, but some are thought to be greater than others.

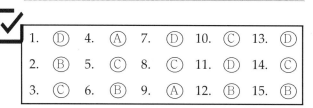

Grammar Skills Practice 9

✓				
1. Ⓓ	4. Ⓐ	7. Ⓓ	10. Ⓒ	13. Ⓓ
2. Ⓑ	5. Ⓒ	8. Ⓒ	11. Ⓓ	14. Ⓒ
3. Ⓒ	6. Ⓑ	9. Ⓐ	12. Ⓑ	15. Ⓑ

1) ➡ D
Concept(s) Tested: Noun agreement
Choice (D) is correct because the underlined noun must be plural in order to match the plural subject ("the gravitational forces") that it refers to, making "causes of" the only acceptable choice.

2) ➡ B
Concept(s) Tested: Logical comparison
Choice (B) is correct because the sentence compares the size of one of the Cyclades islands to the sizes of all other Cyclades islands. When one thing is compared two or more other things, the comparative adjective ("large" in this case) must end in "-est" to express the superlative degree, making "largest" correct.

3) ➡ C
Concept(s) Tested: Precision
Choice (C) is correct because "to exceed" is to be greater than in size or number, and it makes sense to say, "The population of California...*is greater than* 38 million people."

4) ➡ A
Concept(s) Tested: Combining sentences
Choice (A) is correct because it clearly and concisely restructures the sentences by turning the first sentence into an appositive phrase that describes the Copts' origins.

5) ➡ C
Concept(s) Tested: Subordinate conjunction use
Choice (C) is correct because the second part of the sentence contrasts with the first part. The use of "although" in choice (C) establishes this relationship.

6) ➡ B
Concept(s) Tested: Conventional expression
Choice (B) is correct because it is the only choice

that correctly phrases "to put something in perspective," which is an English idiom that means "to realize the significance of something."

7) ➤ D
Concept(s) Tested: Providing evidence
Choice (D) is correct because it is the only choice that discusses the consequences of "dangerous defects in Ford Pinto fuel systems," and therefore provides the best elaboration on the information in the first sentence.

8) ➤ C
Concept(s) Tested: Combining sentences
Choice (C) is correct; the second sentence explains how eyebrows "keep sweat and rain out of" eyes, and "as" can show that the second clause elaborates on the first, making it the correct choice. Other choices are incorrect because they misrepresent the relationship between the two sentences.

9) ➤ A
Concept(s) Tested: Within-sentence punctuation
Choice (A) is correct because only one comma is necessary in this sentence to separate the two independent clauses. All other choices contain too many commas, making the sentence unnecessarily choppy.

10) ➤ C
Concept(s) Tested: Subject-verb agreement
Choice (C) is correct because the underlined portion must contain the sentence's main verb, which must agree with the subject of the sentence, "Norman Rockwell." The relationship between the subject and the verb is easier to determine if one ignores the appositive phrase "an American illustrator," and reads the sentence as "Norman Rockwell...is best known..." From this, we can determine that (C) is correct.

11) ➤ D
Concept(s) Tested: Conventional expressions
Choice (D) is correct; the underlined portion forms part of the phrase "It took Apollo 11...4 days and 7 hours *to reach* the moon." The phrase "it took *x amount of time*" is always followed by an infinitive verb ("to reach" in this case), making (D) the only appropriate choice.

12) ➤ B
Concept(s) Tested: Subject-verb agreement
Choice (B) is correct because the underlined verb phrase refers to the singular subject, "The... franchise," making the third-person singular verb phrase "was created" the most appropriate choice.

13) ➤ D
Correct Choice: D
Concept(s) Tested: Subject-verb agreement
Choice (D) is correct because the underlined verb must agree with the singular subject of the sentence, "the...combination," making the third-person singular verb form "is" correct.

14) ➤ C
Concept(s) Tested: Concision
Choice (C) is correct because it is the clearest and most concise version of the underlined portion. Choices (A) and (D) are redundant, as "customer," "clientele," and "patron" are all synonyms. Choice (B) is unclear, as it does not specify who "they" refers to.

15) ➤ B
Concept(s) Tested: Verb tense, mood, and voice
Choice (B) is correct because "would" + the perfect tense can express a course that is desired but not taken (i.e. "I *would have called*, but I lost your number."). With the word "rather," it can express a desire to have made a different choice in the past (taking the elevator in this case).

Grammar Skills Practice 10

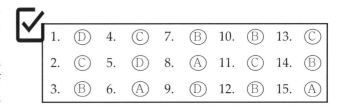

1.	D	4.	C	7.	B	10.	B	13.	C
2.	C	5.	D	8.	A	11.	C	14.	B
3.	B	6.	A	9.	D	12.	B	15.	A

1) ➤ D
Concept(s) Tested: Within-sentence punctuation
Choice (D) is correct; the two sentences can become two joined independent clauses connected with a semicolon because their relationship is self-explanatory.

2) ➤ C
Concept(s) Tested: Conventional expressions
Choice (C) is correct because "at the age of" is an English idiom used when providing a person's age. Choice (D) is incorrect because it creates a run-on sentence, and choices (A) and (B) are incorrect because they contain awkward or unclear phrasing.

3) ➤ B
Concept(s) Tested: Pronoun persons and number/

possessive nouns

Choice (B) is correct because the pronoun in the underlined portion refers to the plural noun phrase "most students" and shows possession over "undergraduate degrees," making the plural possessive pronoun "their" appropriate. Moreover, "degrees" must be plural to agree with "most students," and it does not possess anything in this sentence.

4) ➡ C

Concept(s) Tested: Subordinate conjunction use

Choice (C) is correct; the conjunction "because of" links a cause to its effect. In the sentence, the *cause* is a "comfortable climate, excellent beaches, and luxury hotels," while the *effect* is its Acapulco's popularity as a tourist destination.

5) ➡ D

Concept(s) Tested: Concision

Choice (D) is correct because it is the clearest and most concise version of the underlined portion. All other choices contain redundancies, as "group," "categorize," and "classify" all have approximately the same meaning.

6) ➡ A

Concept(s) Tested: Providing evidence

Choice (A) is correct because it is the only choice that tell the reader what percent of the world's population consumes insects, and proves that "the majority of the world's population consumes insects," thus fully addressing the question. While choice (C) implies that much of the world eats insects, it is not as clear as (A), making it incorrect.

7) ➡ B

Concept(s) Tested: Subject-verb agreement

Choice (B) is correct because "grows" acts as the main verb of the sentence and agrees with the subject, "the *carambola*." Thus, no pronoun (as in choice (A)), conjunction (as in (B)), or participle (as in (D)), is necessary here, making (B) the only acceptable choice.

8) ➡ A

Concept(s) Tested: Modifiers

Choice (A) is correct because the modifier in the underlined portion modifies the verb phrase "is associated," so the underlined modifier must be an adverb (a modifier that describes a verb or another modifier). Only (A) contains the adverb "strongly," making it the correct choice.

9) ➡ D

Concept(s) Tested: Correlative conjunctions

Choice (D) is correct; when the term "both" is followed by two options, the conjunction "and" must always separate the options from one another.

10) ➡ B

Concept(s) Tested: Parallel structure

Choice (B) is correct because the underlined portion must maintain the same "present participle + noun + prepositional phrase" as "causing a sensation in the United States," and only (B) does so: "present participle (heralding) + noun (the decline) + prepositional phrase (of the silent film era)."

11) ➡ C

Concept(s) Tested: Relative clauses

Choice (C) is correct because the underlined pronoun introduces a relative clause that refers to *"quoits"* and shows possession over "origins," making the possessive relative pronoun "whose" correct.

12) ➡ B

Concept(s) Tested: Participial phrases

Choice (B) is correct because the participial phrase, "earning him the nickname" refers to "Lon Chaney" and his actions in the preceding clause. When a participial phrase modifies a group of words, it needs to be set apart by a comma to avoid confusion.

13) ➡ C

Concept(s) Tested: Parallel structure

Choice (C) is correct; the underlined portion must maintain the word pattern established by the previously listed steps, both of which begin with present participles. Only choice (C) begins with a present participle, maintaining the list's parallel structure.

14) ➡ B

Concept(s) Tested: Participial phrases

Choice (B) is correct; when a term (*"Arizuma"* in this case) is followed by its definition or translation, it is generally appropriate to follow the term with a comma and the participle "meaning," or the relative clause "which means." Thus, "meaning" is the only acceptable choice

15) ➡ A

Concept(s) Tested: Combining sentences

Choice (A) is correct because the two sentences contain contrasting information: Bruce Lee was born in San Francisco; he grew up in Hong Kong. The use of "but" in choice (A) effectively conveys this contrast.

☑

1.	Ⓑ	4.	Ⓓ	7.	Ⓓ	10.	Ⓑ	13.	Ⓓ
2.	Ⓑ	5.	Ⓓ	8.	Ⓒ	11.	Ⓒ	14.	Ⓐ
3.	Ⓒ	6.	Ⓐ	9.	Ⓐ	12.	Ⓑ	15.	Ⓓ

1) ➡ B
Concept(s) Tested: Noun Agreement
Choice (B) is correct because the underlined portion modifies "different patterns," a countable noun. "Many" is appropriate for countable nouns.

2) ➡ B
Concept(s) Tested: Combining sentences
Choice (B) is correct because it states the relationship between Hassium and other radioactive elements (that they decay over time) without redundancy or unclear phrasing. It also properly emphasizes the important point of the sentence—that Hassium decays—by placing it last.

3) ➡ C
Concept(s) Tested: Verb tense, mood, and voice
Choice (C) is correct because the infinitive "to eliminate" acts adverbially to show that ants "join together" in order to eliminate "other nearby ant species."

4) ➡ D
Concept(s) Tested: Logical comparison
Choice (D) is correct; the sentence compares the computers of the present to the computers of the past. Because "computers" is plural, the plural pronoun "those" effectively replaces "computers" in the underlined portion.

5) ➡ D
Concept(s) Tested: Precision
Choice (D) is correct because "to propose" means "to present an idea to others," and it makes sense in the context of the sentence that a biologist would present an idea regarding evolution.

6) ➡ A
Concept(s) Tested: Within-sentence punctuation
Choice (A) is correct because the sentence contains two independent clauses (ideas that could act as complete sentences) that present closely related information, and a semicolon alone can separate two clauses whose relationship is self-explanatory.

7) ➡ D
Concept(s) Tested: Concision
Choice (D) is correct because "to precede" is "to come before" or "herald," making all choices but (D) redundant.

8) ➡ C
Concept(s) Tested: Syntax
Choice (C) is correct because within the clause it follows conventional word order: subject-verb-adjective. Hence, "the vast majority of Earth's oceans" (subject) "remain" (verb) "uncharted" (adjective/participle).

9) ➡ A
Concept(s) Tested: Parenthetical elements
Choice (A) is correct because parentheses are often used to separate grammatically non-essential information from the rest of a sentence. Other choices are unnecessarily wordy (choice (B)), over-punctuated (choice (C)), or under-punctuated (choice (D)).

10) ➡ B
Concept(s) Tested: Subordinate conjunction use
Choice (B) is correct because the conjunction "because" links an effect to its cause. In the sentence, the *effect* is the Greeks "limited knowledge of human anatomy," while the *cause* is not practicing human dissection.

11) ➡ C
Concept(s) Tested: Subject-verb agreement
Choice (C) is correct because the verb "consists" agrees with the third-person singular subject "The diet of the Greenland shark."

12) ➡ B
Concept(s) Tested: Modifier placement
Choice (B) is correct because it places the noun being modified, "the Great Lakes," directly after the phrase that modifies it, "Located on the Canada-United States border."

13) ➡ D
Concept(s) Tested: Possessive determiner
Choice (D) is correct because the pronoun at the underlined portion shows possession over the phrase "waking hours," and it refers to the plural noun "chimpanzees," making the plural possessive pronoun "their" appropriate.

14) ➡ A
Concept(s) Tested: Conventional expressions
Choice (A) is correct because the phrase "mass consumption" can mean "the purchase of goods by many people," which makes sense in the context of the sentence; other choices fail to

convey the same meaning.

15) 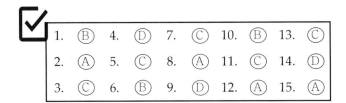 D
Concept(s) Tested: Noun agreement
Choice (D) is correct because the noun at the underlined portion refers to the singular noun "Delhi," and "metropolitan area" is the only singular answer choice.

Grammar Skills Practice 12

☑
1. Ⓑ	4. Ⓓ	7. Ⓒ	10. Ⓑ	13. Ⓒ
2. Ⓐ	5. Ⓒ	8. Ⓐ	11. Ⓒ	14. Ⓓ
3. Ⓒ	6. Ⓑ	9. Ⓓ	12. Ⓐ	15. Ⓐ

1) B
Concept(s) Tested: Subordinate conjunction use/ Possessive nouns
Choice (B) is correct because the conjunction "While" shows that multiple names for the sand dollar exist at the same time in different places. Moreover, the plural noun "Americans" agrees with plural nouns "New Zealanders" and "South Africans."

2) A
Concept(s) Tested: Phrases
Choice (A) is correct because the phrase describes the museum's collection by beginning with the participle "including." Choice (B) and (C) offer verb forms of "include," which do not make sense in context. Choice (D) would create an independent clause by adding a subject ("these"), but (D) fails to connect the clause correctly with a semicolon

3) C
Concept(s) Tested: Parallel structure
Choice (C) is correct because the underlined portion must maintain parallel wording to the previous phrase, "crocodiles have pointed"; the "-ed" ending of "rounded" maintains this parallel structure.

4) D
Concept(s) Tested: Concision
Choice (D) is correct because "last" and "final" convey the same meaning, making (A) redundant, while (B) and (C) are convoluted and contain too many prepositional phrases. Thus, only choice (D) conveys the information concisely and clearly.

5) C
Concept(s) Tested: Verb tense, mood, and voice
Choice (C) is correct because the sentence is in the past tense (referring to events that occurred around 1905), making "played" the correct verb form.

6) B
Concept(s) Tested: Conventional expressions
Choice (B) is correct because a person is said to "retire from" a profession. Other choices fail to convey the same meaning and make the sentence unclear.

7) C
Concept(s) Tested: Modifier placement
Choice (C) is correct because it places the noun being modified, "FORTRAN," directly after the phrase that modifies it, "One of the first computer programming languages." Other choices would create confusion about what was "one of the first programming languages."

8) A
Concept(s) Tested: Within-sentence punctuation
Choice (A) is correct because the nouns "Nike co-founder" act as a title to "Philip Knight," and no commas should separate an individual from his or her title. Moreover, there is no reason to separate a subject and a verb when the verb ("paid") comes immediately after the subject ("Philip Knight").

9) D
Concept(s) Tested: Parallel structure
Choice (D) is correct because the underlined portion must be a noun to maintain the parallel structure of the phrase "began his…activism and involvement in…."

10) B
Concept(s) Tested: Noun agreement
Choice (B) is correct because the underlined portion must be plural to effectively refer to the plural noun "orcas."

11) C
Concept(s) Tested: Logical comparison
Choice (C) is correct because the sentence is comparing "the scientific accomplishments of Edison" to the scientific accomplishments of Tesla. Since "accomplishments" is plural, it can be substituted by the plural pronoun "those," as in choice (C).

12) ➡ A
Concept(s) Tested: Combining sentences
Choice (A) is correct because the two sentences contain contrasting information: Claudius was considered incompetent; now he is regarded as competent. The use of "yet" in choice (A) effectively conveys this contrast.

13) ➡ C
Concept(s) Tested: Precision
Choice (C) is correct because "to assemble" a sea craft is "to build" it, which makes sense in the context of the sentence. The other choices are terms used for bringing together, people not objects.

14) ➡ D
Concept(s) Tested: Pronoun person and number
Choice (D) is correct because the underlined pronoun refers to the plural noun "black holes," so the pronoun must also be plural. Moreover, the pronoun acts as the subject of the clause, so the subjective plural pronoun "they" is appropriate here.

15) ➡ A
Concept(s) Tested: Combining sentences
Choice (A) is correct because it immediately establishes the subject of the sentence, "Stephen Crane," and its use of "although" establishes a contrast between Crane's short life and his lasting literary legacy.

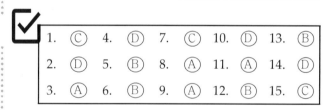

Grammar Skills Practice 13

✓

1.	C	4.	D	7.	C	10.	D	13.	B
2.	D	5.	B	8.	A	11.	A	14.	D
3.	A	6.	B	9.	A	12.	B	15.	C

1) ➡ C
Concept(s) Tested: Transition words
Choice (C) is correct because the phrase "in fact" serves to introduce information that will strengthen a previous claim, which describes the relationship between the two sentences.

2) ➡ D
Concept(s) Tested: Conventional expressions
Choice (D) is correct because something that commemorates a person is said to be "in honor of" that person. Other choices do not convey the same sense of commemoration.

3) ➡ A
Concept(s) Tested: Within-sentence punctuation
Choice (A) is correct because a colon effectively separates a piece of information from a definition of or elaboration on that information. In the sentence, the phrase "compact and spongy" is an elaboration on the "two types of tissue" mentioned earlier

4) ➡ D

Concept(s) Tested: Syntax

Choice (D) is correct because it is the clearest version of the sentence; it maintains the active voice, and structures the sentence using the easy-to-follow "subject-verb-object" format.

5) ➡ B
Concept(s) Tested: Verb tense, mood, and aspect
Choice (B) is correct because the simple present tense describes general facts such as the one in the sentence.

6) ➡ B
Concept(s) Tested: Concision
Choice (B) is correct because the phrases "up to" and "as much as" convey the same meaning, so any choices that contain both are redundant. Moreover, it is implied that the weight described is an orangutans total weight, making the phrases "a total of" and "in total" totally unnecessary.

7) ➡ C
Concept(s) Tested: Words in context
Choice (C) is correct because "to originate" is "to begin," and it makes sense in the context of the sentence to say that the trait of red hair *began* in Iran.

8) ➡ A
Concept(s) Tested: Logical comparison
Choice (A) is correct because the sentence demonstrates one way that sharks are unlike fish. Thus, the noun "sharks" must come immediately after the phrase "Unlike fish" to show that sharks are being compared to fish.

9) ➡ A
Concept(s) Tested: Syntax/adverbs and auxiliary verbs
Choice (A) is correct because a colon effectively separates a piece of information from a definition or description of that information. In the sentence, "holy basil, Thai basil, and lemon basil" are descriptions of the "three types of basil" mentioned previously.

10) ➡ D

Concept(s) Tested: Noun agreement

Choice (D) is correct because the underlined noun phrase refers to the singular noun "Ohaguro," so the underlined portion must also be singular, making the phrase "a Japanese custom" correct.

11) ➡ A

Concept(s) Tested: Commonly confused words

Choice (A) is correct because "to immigrate" is "to settle permanently in a foreign country." The verb "immigrate" is always followed by the preposition "to."

12) ➡ B

Concept(s) Tested: Subject-verb agreement

Choice (B) is correct because the sentence describes a general process; general processes take simple present tense verbs. Moreover, the underlined verb must agree with the gerund "cutting." Gerunds are always singular, so the correct answer is the present tense, third-person singular verb "damages."

13) ➡ B

Concept(s) Tested: Syntax

Choice (B) is correct because it provides a subject-verb pattern. (A) and (C) do not contain main verbs, and (D) is unnecessarily wordy.

14) ➡ D

Concept(s) Tested: Correlative conjunctions

Choice (D) is correct because in a comparison where the word "as" is followed by the quality being compared ("linguistic diversity" in the sentence), another "as" must always come immediately after the quality.

15) ➡ C

Concept(s) Tested:

Choice (C) is correct; a metaphor relates two seemingly unrelated concepts, and in choice (C) the poet relates his genius to an empty well.

Grammar Skills Practice 14

☑
1.	Ⓓ	4.	Ⓐ	7.	Ⓑ	10.	Ⓐ	13.	Ⓓ
2.	Ⓓ	5.	Ⓑ	8.	Ⓓ	11.	Ⓒ	14.	Ⓒ
3.	Ⓑ	6.	Ⓒ	9.	Ⓐ	12.	Ⓐ	15.	Ⓒ

1) ➡ D

Concept(s) Tested: Conventional expressions

Choice (D) is correct because a person is said to be "deficient in" something, so the other prepositions do not make sense in the context of the sentence.

2) ➡ D

Concept(s) Tested: Combining sentences

Choice (D) is correct because the two sentences provide facts about uric acid, but the relationship between the facts is self-evident and requires no transition words or conjunctions for clarification. Thus, a semicolon effectively joins the two sentences.

3) ➡ B

Concept(s) Tested: Within-sentence punctuation

Choice (B) is correct because the nouns "Retired professional tennis player" act as a title to "Jennifer Capriati," and no commas should separate an individual from his or her title.

4) ➡ A

Concept(s) Tested: Verb tense, mood, and voice

Choice (A) is correct because the underlined verb must agree in number with the plural noun "crabs," and because the sentence describes a process that began sometime in the past and continues today, making the perfect aspect (*"have* remained") correct.

5) ➡ B

Concept(s) Tested: Relative clauses

Choice (B) is correct because the underlined portion refers to "the concept of zero as a numeral," making "which" the best choice because it is a relative pronoun (so it refers to the preceding information) that refers to non-human nouns/noun phrases.

6) ➡ C

Concept(s) Tested: Correlative conjunctions

Choice (C) is correct because the term "not only" must always be followed by the term "but also," making (C) the only acceptable answer.

7) ➡ B

Concept(s) Tested: Conventional expressions

Choice (B) is correct because to say that a rivalry "flares up" is an English idiom. (A) is not correct because it uses the wrong tense, as the rivalry occurred over a century ago, making the present perfect tense incorrect.

8) ➡ D

Concept(s) Tested: Parallel structure

Choice (D) is correct because the first part of the sentence establishes the word pattern "Poe is...

known *for his poems.*" Thus, the second part of the sentence must maintain this pattern by claiming that Poe was "famous *for his...criticisms.*"

9) 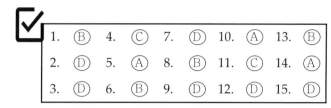 A

Concept(s) tested: Commonly confused words
Choice A is correct because "can drastically reduce" accurately describes what happens to the noun it precedes, "symptoms" with "can" included to keep the element of possibility.

10) A

Concept(s) Tested: Precision
Choice (A) is correct because an "ailment" is an illness, and it makes sense to say that numerous illnesses would have contributed to Fitzgerald's death.

11) C

Concept(s) Tested: Conventional expressions
Choice (C) is correct; when an idea "derives from" something, the idea is garnered from or influenced by that something. It makes sense to say that the "concept of the Hulk *was inspired by "Frankenstein."* Because the preposition "from" always follows "derived," (C) is correct.

12) A

Concept(s) Tested: Syntax
Choice (A) is correct because we can infer that a "Hoover wagon refers to" a type of automobile, so the correct choice places the phrase "a Depression-era automobile" as close to the phrasal verb "refers to" as possible to clarify this relationship.

13) D

Concept(s) Tested: Precision
Choice (D) is correct because "to avoid" something is to prevent it from happening, which makes sense in the context of the sentence. Choice (A), "prevent from," is incorrect because it implies that the fuel can stop itself from igniting.

14) C

Concept(s) Tested: Within-sentence punctuation
Choice (C) is correct because a colon effectively separates a piece of information from a definition of or elaboration on that information. In the sentence, the noun "Tarzan" is an elaboration on the "one of the most enduring characters..." mentioned earlier in the sentence.

15) C

Concept(s) Tested: Within-sentence punctuation
Choice (C) is correct "money" is generally an uncountable noun, so it must be singular and paired with the modifier "less" rather than "fewer."

1.	Ⓑ	4.	Ⓒ	7.	Ⓓ	10.	Ⓐ	13.	Ⓑ
2.	Ⓓ	5.	Ⓐ	8.	Ⓑ	11.	Ⓒ	14.	Ⓐ
3.	Ⓓ	6.	Ⓑ	9.	Ⓓ	12.	Ⓓ	15.	Ⓓ

1) B

Concept(s) Tested: Concision
Choice (B) is correct because it is the only choice that does not include unnecessary pronouns ("that") and does not create a sentence fragment with unnecessary punctuation (the semicolon in choice (D)).

2) D

Concept(s) Tested: Subordinate conjunction use
Choice (D) is correct because the underlined conjunction must show that the relationship between the two clauses is one of time. Only "when" conveys such a relationship.

3) D

Concept(s) Tested: Conventional expressions
Choice (D) is correct because food items ("Vegetables" in this case) are conventionally said to be "sources of" nutrition ("essential vitamins").

4) C

Concept(s) Tested: Combining sentences
Choice (C) is correct because the two sentences contain contrasting information: people think Darwin coined a term; Herbert Spencer actually coined the term. The use of "but" in choice (C) effectively conveys this contrast.

5) A

Concept(s) Tested: Participial phrases
Choice (A) is correct because the participial phrase, "participating in footraces..." refers to "The Tarahumara." Separating the participial phrase from the rest of the sentence with a comma avoids confusion by showing that it modifies the subject, not the word that immediately precedes it ("running").

6) B

Concept(s) Tested: Noun agreement
Choice (B) is correct because a noun that follows the phrase "one of the..." must always be plural.

7) D

Concept(s) Tested: Combining sentences

Choice (D) is correct because the sentences both provide information about testing an egg's freshness, and the relationship between the facts is self-evident and requires no transition words or conjunctions for clarification. Thus, a semicolon effectively joins the two sentences.

8) ➡️ B
Concept(s) Tested: Correlative conjunctions
Choice (B) is correct because a phrase beginning with "between" will always follow the pattern "between x and y." Other choices include unnecessary words and/or punctuation.

9) ➡️ D
Concept(s) Tested: Parallel structure
Choice (D) is correct because the items listed before the underlined portion are all nouns ending in "-er," and only choice (D) maintains this pattern.

10) ➡️ A
Concept(s) Tested: Subject-verb agreement
Choice (A) is correct because the underlined verb must agree with the compound plural subject "New Jersey and Oregon." All other choices agree with third-person singular subjects, making (A) the correct choice.

11) ➡️ C
Concept(s) Tested: Precision
Choice (C) is correct because "to react" is to respond in a particular way to something, and it makes sense to say that the pupil will respond "to fluctuations in brightness."

12) ➡️ D
Concept(s) Tested: Parallel structure
Choice (D) is correct because the underlined verb must match the word pattern established by the phrase "known to use fire…" Thus, the infinitive form of "practice" continues the pattern established by the infinitive "to use."

13) ➡️ B
Concept(s) Tested: Concision
Choice (B) is correct because all other choices contain redundancies; claiming something is the "oldest" and "most ancient" is redundant, as is claiming that something is "written" and "recorded."

14) ➡️ A
Concept(s) Tested: Relative clauses/subject-verb agreement
Choice (A) is correct because the pronoun "which" effectively refers to the plural noun phrase

"nautical miles," and because the verb "are" agrees "nautical miles" in number.

15) ➡️ D
Concept(s) Tested: Modifier placement
Choice (D) is correct because it places the noun being modified, "the Taj Mahal complex," directly after the phrase that modifies it, "Completed in 1653." Other choices to clarify what was "completed in 1653."

Grammar Skills Practice 16

☑️

1.	Ⓑ	4.	Ⓓ	7.	Ⓒ	10.	Ⓑ	13.	Ⓒ
2.	Ⓒ	5.	Ⓓ	8.	Ⓓ	11.	Ⓐ	14.	Ⓓ
3.	Ⓐ	6.	Ⓐ	9.	Ⓑ	12.	Ⓒ	15.	Ⓑ

1) ➡️ B
Concept(s) Tested: Combining sentences
Choice (B) is correct; the conjunction "because" links an effect to its cause. In the sentence, the *effect* is that helium is called an "inert gas," while the *cause* of this naming is that "it does not burn or react…"

2) ➡️ C
Correct Choice: C
Concept(s) Tested: Concision
Choice (C) is correct because it is the clearest and most concise version of the underlined portion. Choices (A) and (B) are incorrect because they contain redundancies ("foremost," "premier," and "leading" are all synonyms), and (D) is incorrect because is does not clarify what Christie was the most of.

3) ➡️ A
Concept(s) Tested: Relative clauses
Choice (A) is correct because the underlined section refers to a location—"China"—and the relative pronoun "where" is appropriate when referencing location.

4) ➡️ D
Concept(s) Tested: Modifier placement
Choice (D) is correct because it places the noun being modified, "Arches National Park," directly after the phrase that modifies it, "Established in 1929."

5) ➡️ D
Concept(s) Tested: Logical comparison
Choice (D) is correct because the sentence compares two sources of Las Vegas's revenue.

Thus, the correct choice will include mention of "the revenue it [Las Vegas] generates…" making (D) correct.

6) 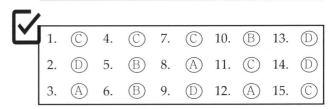 A
Concept(s) Tested: Precision
Choice (A) is correct because "to extend" is "to occupy or *stretch* to a specific area," and it makes sense that a highway would stretch from one location to another.

7) 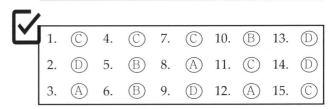 C
Concept(s) Tested: Subject-verb agreement/noun agreement
Choice (C) is correct because the verb in the underlined section must agree with the compound subject "Martin Luther King, Jr. and Malcolm X," making "are" the only appropriate choice.

8) 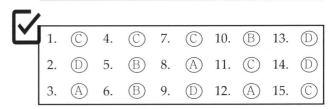 D
Concept(s) Tested: Verb tense, mood, and voice
Choice (D) is correct because based on the context and punctuation, it is clear that *Teacher Strategies* is the title of a book. Therefore, even though the title is plural, the book is a singular noun, and must agree with the verb, as in (the book) builds the case.

9) 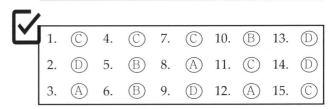 B
Concept(s) Tested: Combining sentences
Choice (B) is correct because it is the clearest, most concise version of the sentence. Choice (A) is a wordier version of (B), choice (C) is a sentence fragment, and the wording of choice (D) makes it unclear *how* cuckoos trick other birds "with eggs."

10) 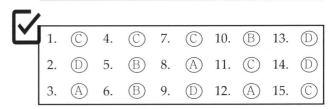 B
Concept(s) Tested: Subordinate conjunction use
Choice (B) is correct because the underlined conjunction must show that the relationship between the two clauses is one of time. Only "when" conveys such a relationship.

11) 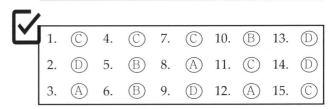 A
Concept(s) Tested: Commonly confused words
Choice (A) is correct because the verb "to affect" mean "to have an influence on," whereas "to effect" is "to achieve." It makes the most sense in the context of the sentence to claim that the hurricane *had an influence on* millions of people. Generally, "effect" is used as a noun that means "a result or consequence."

12) 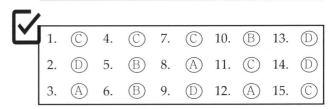 C
Concept(s) Tested: Parallel structure
Choice (C) is correct because the underlined portion must follow the "modifier + noun" word pattern established by the phrase "witty dialogue," and the only choice that does so is "tightly (modifier) constructed (modifier) plots (noun)."

13) 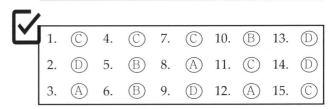 C
Concept(s) Tested: Subject-verb agreement
Choice (C) is correct because the verb at the underlined portion must agree with the plural noun "leaves," making "serve" the correct verb form. "That" is necessary to show that the information that follows refers to the aforementioned "leaves."

14) 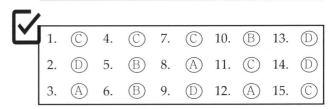 D
Concept(s) Tested: Syntax
Choice (D) is correct because the phrase "to break free" means "to escape," and it makes sense in the context of the sentence that "escape velocity" would be the speed needed to *escape* "Earth's gravitational pull."

15) 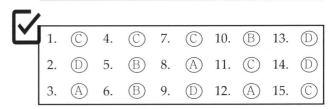 B
Concepts Tested: Correlative conjunctions
Choice (B) is correct because when two options come after the word "neither," the word "nor" must be placed between the two options.

Grammar Skills Practice 17

1.	Ⓒ	4.	Ⓒ	7.	Ⓒ	10.	Ⓑ	13.	Ⓓ
2.	Ⓓ	5.	Ⓑ	8.	Ⓐ	11.	Ⓒ	14.	Ⓓ
3.	Ⓐ	6.	Ⓑ	9.	Ⓓ	12.	Ⓐ	15.	Ⓒ

1) 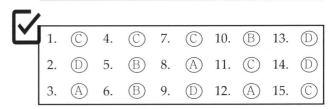 C
Concept(s) Tested: Subordinate conjunction use
Choice (C) is correct because the sentence presents a contrast: "the Pythagorean Theorem is often attributed…to Pythagoras," yet the theorem was likely "developed by one of his successors." The only choice that indicates contrast is "although."

2) 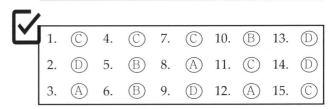 D
Concept(s) Tested: Subject-verb agreement
Choice (D) is correct because the underlined verb form must agree with the plural subject of the sentence, "Some species." The only choice that does so is "have."

3) ➡ A
Concept(s) Tested: Combining sentences
Choice (A) is correct because it clearly illustrates that Genoa is where jeans were first produced. Choice (B) and (C) are unnecessarily wordy, and choice (D) is a run-on sentence.

4) ➡ C
Concept(s) Tested: Precision
Choice (C) is correct because "to produce" is "to create or make" something, and it makes sense in the context of the sentence that pressing a piano key creates a tone, or sound. The other choices also mean "to create," but their meanings are limited to the creation of products, not sounds.

5) ➡ B
Concept(s) Tested: Within-sentence punctuation

Choice (B) is correct because it is the only choice that properly finishes the contrast set up by "while."

6) ➡ B
Concept(s) Tested: Pronoun clarity
Choice (B) is correct; the underlined pronoun refers the singular noun "an area," so the plural pronouns "ones" and "those" are incorrect. Moreover, "one" is correct because it clarifies that the sentence is discussing two areas, whereas use of "this" would confuse the issue.

7) ➡ C
Concept(s) Tested: End-of-sentence punctuation
Choice (C) is correct because a comma is used to punctuate the end of a quoted statement when the speaker is identified immediately after the quote.

8) ➡ A
Concept(s) Tested: Within-sentence punctuation
Choice (A) is correct because the nouns "Roman statesman" act as a title to "Cato the Elder," and no commas should separate an individual from his or her title. Moreover, no comma should separate a subject and a verb when the verb ("would end") comes immediately after the subject ("Cato the Elder").

9) ➡ D
Concept(s) Tested: Combining sentences
Choice (D) is correct because the second sentence limits information in the first sentence: *Voyager 1* has reached interstellar space; it will not encounter other systems. The use of "but" in choice (D) effectively conveys this limitation.

10) ➡ B
Concept(s) Tested: Providing evidence
Choice (B) is correct because it clearly states *why*

water bears are considered durable: they can survive a number of extreme conditions.

11) ➡ C
Concept(s) Tested: Commonly confused words
Choice (C) is correct because "respectively" means "in the order already mentioned," and it makes sense to say that Buda and Pest occupy the west and east banks of a river *in the order already mentioned.*

12) ➡ A
Concept(s) Tested: Conventional expressions
Choice (A) is correct because "to exact revenge" is an English idiom meaning "to execute a plan for revenge," which makes sense in the context of the sentence.

13) ➡ D
Concept(s) Tested: Pronoun person and number
Choice (D) is correct because the underlined pronoun refers to the singular noun phrase "The present-day territory of Texas," so the singular person pronoun "it" is correct.

14) ➡ D
Concept(s) Tested: Concision
Choice (D) is correct because the terms "widespread," "universal," and "pervasive" all have approximately the same meaning, so all choices that include more than one of these terms is redundant, making (D) the only acceptable choice.

15) ➡ C
Concept(s) Tested: Possessive nouns
Choice (C) is correct because the sentence refers to one country, and the correct way to show possession by a singular noun is to add 's to the end of the word.

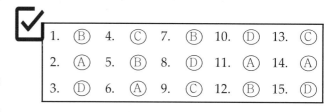

Grammar Skills Practice 18

1. Ⓑ	4. Ⓒ	7. Ⓑ	10. Ⓓ	13. Ⓒ
2. Ⓐ	5. Ⓑ	8. Ⓓ	11. Ⓐ	14. Ⓐ
3. Ⓓ	6. Ⓐ	9. Ⓒ	12. Ⓑ	15. Ⓓ

1) ➡ B
Concept(s) Tested: Subordinate conjunction use
Choice (B) is correct because the sentence provides contrasting information: potatoes grow underground, yet they are not roots. The only

choice that indicates contrast is "Despite."

2) ■➤ A
Concept(s) Tested: Precision
Choice (A) is correct because "abundant" means "plentiful," and it makes sense to say that water is "the body's most *plentiful* substance."

3) ■➤ D
Concept(s) Tested: Parallel structure
Choice (D) is correct because the underlined section must follow the same word pattern ("the college *has* a mascot") as the other items in the list. Only choice (D) has the same structure as the rest of the list.

4) ■➤ C
Correct Choice: C
Concept(s) Tested: Noun agreement
Choice (C) is correct because a noun that follows the phrase "among the most..." must always be plural, making the plural noun "methods" correct.

5) ■➤ B
Concept(s) Tested: Combining sentences
Choice (B) is correct because it effectively combines the sentences by turning the first sentence into a prepositional phrase that describes the subject of the sentence, Craco.

6) ■➤ A
Concept(s) Tested: Within-sentence punctuation
Choice (A) is correct; phrases beginning with "such as" are separated from the rest of the sentence with commas (unless the "such as" phrase is grammatically essential to the sentence, in which case no comma is necessary).

7) ■➤ B
Concept(s) Tested: Relative clauses
Choice (B) is correct because the subjective form "who" effectively refers to the noun "a Greek soldier." Choice (A) incorrectly uses the object pronoun "whom," while choices (C) and (D) create sentence fragments.

8) ■➤ D
Concept(s) Tested: Logical comparison
Choice (D) is correct; the sentence compares the surface temperatures of Mercury and Venus. Because "temperatures" is plural, the plural pronoun "those" effectively replaces "temperatures" in the underlined portion.

9) ■➤ C
Concept(s) Tested: Combining sentences
Choice (C) is correct because it is the most concise, grammatically correct version of the sentence.

Choice (A) fails to mention when Key wrote the poem, choice (B) creates a sentence fragment by incorrectly using a semicolon, and choice (D) is unnecessarily wordy.

10) ■➤ D
Concept(s) Tested: Conventional expressions
Choice (D) is correct because the phrase "when [it happened] *is* still debated" always uses "is."

11) ■➤ A
Concept(s) Tested: Within-sentence punctuation
Choice (A) is correct because the long dash functions to separate grammatically nonessential (nonrestrictive) information from the rest of a sentence. The other choices create either run-ons or sentence fragments.

12) ■➤ B
Concept(s) Tested: Verb tense, mood, and voice
Choice (B) is correct because the sentence describes a historical event, making the simple past tense ("destroyed") appropriate.

13) ■➤ C
Concept(s) Tested: Precision
Choice (C) is correct because "to encompass" can mean "to include or contain," and it makes sense to say, "Russia *includes/contains* nine contiguous time zones."

14) ■➤ A
Concept(s) Tested: Within-sentence punctuation/ modifiers
Choice (A) is correct because the list of adjectives "first feature-length animated film" does not require commas, as they function as cumulative adjectives (adjectives not separated by commas that must be in a particular order to make sense). A comma is appropriate after "film" because the film title is informative, but not grammatically necessary, and can therefore be separated from the rest of the sentence using a comma.

15) ■➤ D
Concept(s) Tested: Providing evidence
Choice (D) is correct because it clarifies why Scottish and Irish folk music sound similar: they were inspired by the same musical tradition.

1.	Ⓑ	4.	Ⓐ	7.	Ⓑ	10.	Ⓓ	13.	Ⓐ
2.	Ⓓ	5.	Ⓒ	8.	Ⓐ	11.	Ⓒ	14.	Ⓓ
3.	Ⓑ	6.	Ⓓ	9.	Ⓒ	12.	Ⓑ	15.	Ⓑ

1) ➡ B
Concept(s) Tested: Parallel structure
Choice (B) is correct because the underlined verb must match the word pattern established by the phrase, "he...*experimented* with numerous other crops," so the correct choice must end in "-ed" to match the aforementioned word pattern.

2) ➡ D
Concept(s) Tested: Relative clauses
Choice (D) is correct; the underlined pronoun refers to "boxes of Thin Mints" and introduces a relative clause that provides more information, so "which" is an appropriate relative pronoun here.

3) ➡ B
Concept(s) Tested: Subject-verb agreement
Choice (B) is correct because the underlined verb must agree in number and person with the third-person plural subject "Strong hind legs and a flexible spine," which only "allow" does.

4) ➡ A
Concept(s) Tested: Conjunction use
Choice (A) is correct because "for" can be used to introduce a purpose or goal. In the sentence, surfing "at a beach with no waves" is the goal, making "for" appropriate for introducing the phrase.

5) ➡ C
Concept(s) Tested: Combining sentences
Choice (C) is correct; when a comma plus "and" are used to join two independent clauses, it shows that the second clause is adding related information to the first clause. In the sentence, the second clause provides additional information about *soi dogs*, so joining the two ideas with "and" is appropriate

6) ➡ D
Concept(s) Tested: Combining sentences
Choice (D) is correct because the comma serves the same function here as a colon: it separates a piece of information from a definition of or elaboration

on that information. In the sentence, the phrase "physics and chemistry" is an elaboration on the "two fields" mentioned earlier in the sentence.

7) ➡ B
Concept(s) Tested: Correlative conjunctions/verb tense, mood, and voice
Choice (B) is correct; because dinosaurs are extinct, they must be referred to in the past tense, so "were" is the correct verb form. Moreover, the conjunction "whether" always pairs with "or," making (B) correct.

8) ➡ A
Concept(s) Tested: Combining sentences
Choice (A) is correct because the second sentence simply adds information about Earth's three-trillion trees, so making the second sentence into a relative clause effectively connects it to the information presented in the first sentence.

9) ➡ C
Concept(s) Tested: Noun agreement
Choice (C) is correct because the underlined noun must agree in number with the verb that comes after it ("do"). The noun must be third-person plural to agree with "do," so the correct choice must be the "instruments."

10) ➡ D
Concept(s) Tested: Modifier placement
Choice (D) is correct because it places the noun being modified, "American Arnold Palmer," directly after the phrase that modifies it, "Competing in the earliest televised golf tournaments."

11) ➡ C
Concept(s) Tested: Precision
Choice (C) is correct because "to develop" is "to spread and/or grow," and it makes sense to say that "Gothic architecture *grew and spread* in the 12th century," especially since artistic and cultural trends are often said to "develop."

12) ➡ B
Concept(s) Tested: Appositive phrases
Choice (B) is correct because the underlined information is separated from the rest of the sentence with a comma, and it consists of a phrase that describes the subject of the sentence, Joyce Carol Oates. Thus, the underlined phrase must be an appositive, which begins with an article ("a," "an," or "the") and contains a noun or noun phrase.

13) ➡ A
Concept(s) Tested: Concision
Choice (A) is correct because it clearly and concisely

presents the subject of the sentence, "Few blues artists." Other choices include unnecessary articles ("the") or verbs ("are").

14) ■■▶ D
Concept(s) Tested: Logical comparison
Choice (D) is correct because the sentence compares one type of insect sting to another. Because "the sting" is singular, the singular pronoun "that" effectively replaces "the sting" in the underlined portion.

15) ■■▶ B
Concept(s) Tested: Providing evidence
Choice (B) is correct because Newton's quote supports the statement "Scientific progress is cumulative." In Newton's quote, seeing further than others means making more scientific progress than past scientists, and "standing on the shoulders of giants" refers to having access to the knowledge gathered by his predecessors.

Grammar Skills Practice 20

1.	B	4.	B	7.	A	10.	D	13.	C
2.	D	5.	D	8.	C	11.	A	14.	A
3.	A	6.	C	9.	B	12.	D	15.	B

1) ■■▶ B
Concept(s) Tested: Appositive phrases
Choice (B) is correct because the underlined portion should introduce an appositive that describes the "assembly plant," which only (B) accomplishes.

2) ■■▶ D
Concept(s) Tested: Correlative conjunctions
Choice (D) is correct because a phrase beginning with "between" will always follow the pattern "between x and y."

3) ■■▶ A
Concept(s) Tested: Subject-verb agreement
Choice (A) is correct because the underlined verb refers to the third-person plural noun "the films," and only "include" agrees with a third-person plural noun.

4) ■■▶ B
Concept(s) Tested: Parallel structure
Choice (B) is correct because the underlined section must maintain the same word pattern as the phrase "increases heart rate"; (B) maintains

this pattern and is the most concise choice.

5) ■■▶ D
Concept(s) Tested: Transition words
Choice (D) is correct because the first sentence mentions one form of respiration, and the second sentence presents an alternative method. The adverb "instead" means "alternatively," which accurately identifies the relationship between sentence one and two.

6) ■■▶ C
Concept(s) Tested: Subordinate conjunction use
Choice (C) is correct; the conjunction "because of" links a cause to its effect. In the sentence, the *cause* is porous structure, while the *effect* is its ability to float in water.

7) ■■▶ A
Concept(s) Tested: Concision
Choice (A) is correct because it is the clearest, most concise version of the underlined section. Choice (A) does not contain enough information for the sentence to have meaning, and choices (C) and (D) are unnecessarily wordy.

8) ■■▶ C
Concept(s) Tested: Pronoun clarity
Choice (C) is correct because it indicates that the underlined pronoun refers to Albany ("the latter" means "the second of two things"). The other choices do not specify whether they refer to New York City or Albany.

9) ■■▶ B
Concept(s) Tested: Precision
Choice (B) is correct because "to consider" is to regard or to think of something in a certain way, and it makes sense to say that "*Don Quixote* is often *regarded/thought of* as the first modern novel."

10) ■■▶ D
Concept(s) Tested: Combining sentences
Choice (D) is correct because the two sentences contain contrasting information: "Christianity is the world's largest religion"; Islam is "the fastest growing religion." The use of "but" in choice (D) effectively conveys this contrast.

11) ■■▶ A
Concept(s) Tested: Providing evidence
Choice (A) is correct because it explains what part of a turtle's skeletal system the shell comprises.

12) ➡ D

Concept(s) Tested: Combining sentences

Choice (D) is correct; the conjunction "because" links an effect to its cause. In the sentence, the *effect* is that sorbitol "is a popular sugar substitute in diet foods," while the *cause* is its relatively low calorie count.

13) ➡ C

Concept(s) Tested: Transition words

Choice (C) is correct because "thus" introduces consequences and/or results, and the second sentence lists consequences of birds' reliance on head movement, a concept presented in the first sentence.

14) ➡ A

Concept(s) Tested: Commonly confused words

Choice (A) is correct because an "ascent" is a climb to the summit of a mountain. Although the other choices sound similar to "ascent," they have very different meanings that do not fit the context of the sentence.

15) ➡ B

Concept(s) Tested: Logical comparison

Choice (B) is correct because the sentence compares the financial success of McCartney to the financial success of Starr. Because "financial success" is singular, the singular pronoun "that" effectively replaces "financial success" in the underlined portion.

Grammar Skills Practice 21

1. Ⓐ	4. Ⓑ	7. Ⓓ	10. Ⓐ	13. Ⓒ
2. Ⓓ	5. Ⓐ	8. Ⓒ	11. Ⓑ	14. Ⓒ
3. Ⓒ	6. Ⓑ	9. Ⓒ	12. Ⓓ	15. Ⓑ

1) ➡ A

Concept(s) Tested: Parenthetical elements

Choice (A) is correct because a pair of parentheses is used to separate grammatically nonessential information from the rest of a sentence; the phrase "later renamed the Wildlife Conservation Society" is not essential to the sentence's grammatical structure, so the entire phrase should be set in parentheses.

2) ➡ D

Concept(s) Tested: Precision

Choice (D) is correct because "to overtake" something is to surpass or become more successful than it, and it makes sense to say that "the United States is set to surpass Saudi Arabia" in oil production.

3) ➡ C

Concept(s) Tested: Subject-verb agreement

Choice (C) is correct because the underlined verb refers to "marine plant life," which acts as a third-person singular noun. Only "consists" in choice (C) agrees with "marine plant life." Choice (B) is incorrect because " is...consisted" forms the passive-voice, whereas this sentence calls for an activee-voice verb form.

4) ➡ B

Concept(s) Tested: Providing evidence

Choice (B) is correct because it explains just how massive the sun actually is, providing direct support for the claim in sentence 1 that the sun is "the most massive object in the solar system."

5) ➡ A

Concept(s) Tested: Syntax/concision

Choice (A) is correct because "the country's largest island" acts as an appositive (a description beginning with "/an" or "the") of "Honshu," and an appositive should be separated from the term it describes with a comma.

6) ➡ B

Concept(s) Tested: Verb tense, mood, and voice

Choice (B) is correct because it uses a passive-voice structure (form of "to be" + verb) to clarify the relationship between salt and those who use it (salt "is used" by others, but salt itself does not "use" anything).

7) ➡ D

Concept(s) Tested: Pronoun person and number

Choice (D) is correct because the underlined pronoun refers to the singular noun "A politician." Since the gender of "a politician" is unknown, "he or she" is correct. Although it is a singular pronoun, "one" is incorrect because it is used to refer to a person *in general*, whereas in this sentence the referent is a specific type of person.

8) ➡ C

Concept(s) Tested: Subordinate conjunction use

Choice (C) is correct; when used in a sentence, the conjunction "although" indicates the sentence contains a contrast: "no sound can travel in... space," *yet* "television shows and films" include space noises.

9) ➡️ C

Concept(s) Tested: Correlative conjunctions/ parallel structure
Choice (C) is correct; when the term "both" is followed by two options, the conjunction "and" must always separate the options from one another. Additionally, "influenced" and "worked" must maintain the same word pattern (the "-ed" ending), so (C) maintains parallel structure.

10) ➡️ A

Concept(s) Tested: Combining sentences
Choice (A) is correct because it clearly and concisely states that Congress can override a veto. Choice (B) unnecessarily repeats "Congress," making it wordy, and choices (C) and (D) are run-on sentences.

11) ➡️ B

Concept(s) Tested: Noun agreement
Choice (B) is correct because the underlined term refers to the singular noun "troposphere," so the underlined term must also be a singular noun ("portion").

12) ➡️ D

Concept(s) Tested: Syntax/conventional expressions
Choice (D) is correct because "over the age of" is a conventional English expression that states that someone is older than a given age. Choice (A) is redundant ("over" and "above" have the same meaning), and (B) and (C) are incorrect because it is not conventional English to say that someone is "beyond" or "more than" an age.

13) ➡️ C

Concept(s) Tested: Combining sentences
Choice (C) is correct; the conjunction "so" connects a statement to an elaboration or consequence of that statement, and the statement, "a day [on Venus] takes longer than an entire year" is an elaboration on the first sentence.

14) ➡️ C

Concept(s) Tested: Subject-verb agreement
Choice (C) is correct because the underlined verb must agree with the plural subject "social media sites," which is only accomplished by "have."

15) ➡️ B

Concept(s) Tested: Modifier placement
Choice (B) is correct because it places the noun being modified, "Terry Pratchett's *Discworld*," directly after the phrase that modifies it, "Consisting of over 40 books."

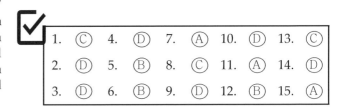

Grammar Skills Practice 22

1.	Ⓒ	4.	Ⓓ	7.	Ⓐ	10.	Ⓓ	13.	Ⓒ
2.	Ⓓ	5.	Ⓑ	8.	Ⓒ	11.	Ⓐ	14.	Ⓓ
3.	Ⓓ	6.	Ⓑ	9.	Ⓓ	12.	Ⓑ	15.	Ⓐ

1) ➡️ C

Concept(s) Tested: Modifiers
Choice (C) is correct because the underlined portion must modify the verb phrase "is known," so the adverb "best," used without any articles preceding it, is the best choice.

2) ➡️ D

Concept(s) Tested: Within-sentence punctuation
Choice (D) is correct because a comma is needed to separate "Pierre de Coubertin" from his description. Other choice either lack punctuation or are unnecessarily wordy.

3) ➡️ D

Concept(s) Tested: Verb tense, mood, and voice
Choice (D) is correct; the writer is making a claim about a current situation (results raise ethical dilemmas), and thus the claim must be about a future course of action. While (C) also offers a future tense, it muddles the meaning with a vague time frame.

4) ➡️ D

Concept(s) Tested: Concision
Choice (D) is correct because the terms "long" and "in length" are redundant, as are the terms "more than" and "upwards," making (D) the only non-redundant choice.

5) ➡️ B

Concept(s) Tested: Participial phrases
Choice (B) is correct; the underlined portion introduces a participial phrase that modifies the sentence's subject, "the Anglo-Zanzibar War." Because the war occurred in the past, the past participle "fought" correctly introduces the phrase.

6) ➡️ B

Concept(s) Tested: Providing evidence
Choice (B) is correct because the second sentence discusses the history of checkers, so it makes sense that the first sentence would clarify that the

game has ancient origins, which (B) does clearly and concisely.

7) ➡ A
Concept(s) Tested: Relative clauses
Choice (A) is correct; when a pronoun follows a preposition ("of" in this case"), the pronoun must be an object pronoun, not a subject or possessive pronoun. Because "whom" is the objective case of "who," (A) is correct.

8) ➡ C
Concept(s) Tested: Combining sentences
Choice (C) is correct because it clearly and concisely restructures the sentences by turning the first sentence into an appositive phrase. Choice (A) is incorrect because it is redundant, choice (B) breaks the sentence up too much with commas, and choice (D) contains awkward participle use ("being" and "forming").

9) ➡ D
Concept(s) Tested: Conventional expressions
Choice (D) is correct because "to pass something off" as genuine is to disguise or falsely represent something, which makes sense in the context of the sentence.

10) ➡ D
Concept(s) Tested: Correlative conjunctions
Choice (D) is correct because when two options come after the word "either," the word "or" must be placed between the two options.

11) ➡ A
Concept(s) Tested: Combining sentence
Choice (A) is correct because the information in the first sentence (Venus's "thick clouds" that reflect sunlight) are what make Venus the brightest object in the night sky. Joining the sentences by using the participle "making" clearly indicates cause and effect.

12) ➡ B
Concept(s) Tested: Subject-verb agreement
Choice (B) is correct; the underlined verb must agree in number with the singular subject, "The average NFL game." Moreover, since the sentence is stating a general fact, the verb should be in the simple present tense, making the present-tense, third-person singular verb "lasts" correct.

13) ➡ C
Concept(s) Tested: Participial phrases
Choice (C) is correct because the main verb of the sentence is "connects." Therefore, the underlined portion must describe the pipeline network, as is

only accomplished by the participle "totaling."

14) ➡ D
Concept(s) Tested: Combining sentences
Choice (D) is correct because a colon effectively separates a piece of information from a definition of or elaboration on that information. In the sentence, the titles "The Three Musketeers and The Count of Monte Cristo" provide descriptions of "some of fiction's most enduring works."

15) ➡ A
Concept(s) Tested: Precision/ conventional expressions
Choice (A) is correct; when discussing a state of chaos or disorder, the verb "sow" is generally followed by the noun "discord," which means "disagreement or conflict."

1. Ⓓ	4. Ⓓ	7. Ⓑ	10. Ⓐ	13. Ⓓ
2. Ⓑ	5. Ⓒ	8. Ⓐ	11. Ⓓ	14. Ⓑ
3. Ⓐ	6. Ⓑ	9. Ⓒ	12. Ⓒ	15. Ⓒ

1) ➡ D
Concept(s) Tested: Syntax/pronoun number and person
Choice (D) is correct because the information that follows "because" must contain a subject and a verb, and the pronoun subject must agree in number with its singular referent, "The sentence." Only choice (D) contains both singular pronoun subject and a verb.

2) ➡ B
Concept(s) Tested: Combining sentences
Choice (B) is correct because it clearly and concisely connects the information about the federal budget using a relative clause. Choices (A) and (D) form run-on sentences, and choice (C) is unnecessarily wordy.

3) ➡ A
Concept(s) Tested: Possessive nouns/subject-verb agreement
Choice (A) is correct because "Earth" is a singular noun showing possession over "surface," and singular nouns show possession by adding 's to the end of the word. Although choice (D) uses the correct possessive noun form, the term "many" is

plural, which does not agree with the verb "was" that follows.

4) ▶ D
Concept(s) Tested: Verb tense, mood, and voice
Choice (D) is correct; the verb in the underlined portion must be in the past tense because it refers to an event that occurred in the 12th century, and only (D), "began," is in the past tense.

5) ▶ C
Concept(s) Tested: Combining sentences
Choice (C) is correct because the two sentences contain closely related information, and a semicolon effectively separates two such clauses containing related ideas.

6) ▶ B
Concept(s) Tested: Transition words
Choice (B) is correct; the planets' formation on a flat, "disk-like" plane is *the reason* that the planets orbit on a shared plane now, making "For this reason" the most appropriate transition between the two statements.

7) ▶ B
Concept(s) Tested: Subordinate conjunction use
Choice (B) is correct because the sentence presents a contrast: "humans have been producing music" for millennia, yet "detailed musical notation" has only existed for a few centuries. The only choice that indicates contrast is "Although."

8) ▶ A
Concept(s) Tested: Noun agreement
Choice (A) is correct; the underlined noun must be singular because it refers to the singular noun "Diamond," and the only singular choice is (A), "material."

9) ▶ C
Concept(s) Tested: Verb tense, mood, and voice/ subject-verb agreement
Choice (C) is correct because the verb in the underlined portion must agree in number with the plural noun "species," which "have" does. While "are being observed" agrees in number with "species," it implies that the writer is referring to observations being made at this moment, which does not make sense in the sentence.

10) ▶ A
Concept(s) Tested: Within-sentence punctuation
Choice (A) is correct because the two sentences contain closely related information, and a semicolon effectively separates two such clauses containing related ideas.

11) ▶ D
Concept(s) Tested: Concision
Choice (D) is correct because the terms "anthropomorphic" and "human-like" are synonyms, as are "language" and "speech," so all choices except (D) contain redundancies.

12) ▶ C
Concept(s) Tested: Rhetorical styles
Choice (C) is correct; understating something means making it seem smaller or less important than it is. In choice (C), Daniel is understating the severity of the storm by referring to a hurricane as "a little bit windy."

13) ▶ D
Concept(s) Tested: Pronoun clarity
Choice (D) is correct because it indicates that the last person mentioned is the one who "kicks back" profit. Choice (A) is incorrect because "someone" must be replaced by a singular, not a plural pronoun as in "they." Choice (B) is incorrect because the gender of the person is not known. (C) is incorrect because it does not make sense to pair a definite article ("the") with an indefinite noun ("someone").

14) ▶ B
Concept(s) Tested: Precision
Choice (B) is correct because "dominant" means "most powerful," and it makes sense to say, "Wolves were once the *most powerful* predators in Great Britain."

15) ▶ C
Concept(s) Tested: Within-sentence punctuation
Choice (C) is correct because a comma is the only appropriate punctuation for connecting a dependent clause ("Even though...the body") to an independent clause ("the brain...receptors").

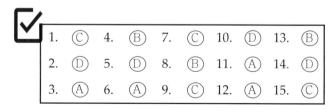

Grammar Skills Practice 24

1.	Ⓒ	4.	Ⓑ	7.	Ⓒ	10.	Ⓓ	13.	Ⓑ
2.	Ⓓ	5.	Ⓓ	8.	Ⓑ	11.	Ⓐ	14.	Ⓓ
3.	Ⓐ	6.	Ⓐ	9.	Ⓒ	12.	Ⓐ	15.	Ⓒ

1) ▶ C
Concept(s) Tested: Pronoun person and number/ parallel structure

Choice (C) is correct because the underlined portion must maintain the same word pattern as the phrase "*one drives* on the right side of the road."

2) ➡ D
Concept(s) Tested: Verb tense, mood, and voice
Choice (D) is correct because the simple past tense is the most appropriate verb form for relaying historical events, making "became" the best choice.

3) ➡ A
Concept(s) Tested: Combining sentences
Choice (A) is correct because is clearly and concisely combines the two sentences by using "that" to introduce a clause explaining the purpose of starfish legs. The other choices, though grammatically correct, are unnecessarily wordy.

4) ➡ B
Concept(s) Tested: Providing evidence
Choice (B) is correct because it continues the discussion of huntsman spiders' methods of finding prey.

5) ➡ D
Concept(s) Tested: Precision
Choice (D) is correct because "to determine" is to discover or deduce, usually as a result of research or calculation, and it makes sense to say, "John Snow *discovered*" the cause of a London cholera outbreak.

6) ➡ A
Concept(s) Tested: Parallel structure
Choice (A) is correct because the underlined portion must maintain the same word pattern established by the previously listed elements: "sedimentary rocks *form*," and "igneous rocks *form*." Only (A) uses the same word pattern.

7) ➡ C
Concept(s) Tested: Syntax
Choice (C) is correct because "a fourth state of matter" acts as an appositive (a description) of "plasma," and an appositive should be separated from the term it describes with a comma.

8) ➡ B
Concept(s) Tested: Logical comparison
Choice (B) is correct; the sentence compares U.S. military spending to the military spending of every other country. Because "military spending" is singular, the singular pronoun "that" effectively replaces "military spending" in the underlined portion.

9) ➡ C
Concept(s) Tested: Combining sentences
Choice (C) is correct because the two sentences contain contrasting information: "The common cold is usually associated with" one type of virus; it is actually caused by any one of over 200 viruses. The use of "yet" in choice (C) effectively conveys this contrast.

10) ➡ D
Concept(s) Tested: Precision
Choice (D) is correct because "to accurately reflect" is to reliably represent or demonstrate something, which makes sense in the context of the sentence.

11) ➡ A
Concept(s) Tested: Verb tense, mood, and voice/ Concision
Choice (A) is correct because in the context, it is most appropriate and concise to use the passive voice. The actual people doing the housing and displaying are not the main idea of the sentence. Moreover, it does not make sense to personify the museum, and in (B); nor is it precise to say that the museum's staff or directors "house" the artifacts themselves, as in (C) and (D).

12) ➡ A
Concept(s) Tested: Conventional expressions
Choice (A) is correct because the phrase "is best remembered" is always followed by the preposition "for" and a present participle. Only (A) maintains this structure by including the present participle "vaulting."

13) ➡ B
Concept(s) Tested: Relative clauses
Choice (B) is correct because the relative pronoun "which" is used to refer to non-human nouns, and in this sentence the underlined portion begins a relative clause that refers to *The Good Earth* (a non-human noun).

14) ➡ D
Concept(s) Tested: Transition words
Choice (D) is correct because the two sentences contain contrasting information: a barrel hold 42 gallons of oil; a "barrel only produces about 19 gallons of usable gasoline." The transition word "however" effectively conveys this contrast.

15) ➡ C
Concept(s) Tested: Precision/commonly confused words
Choice (C) is correct because the verb "to affect" mean "to influence or impact," whereas "to effect" is "to achieve." It makes the most sense in the context of the sentence to claim that the "oil spill… *impacted* over 8,000 animal species."

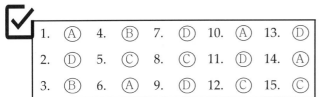

1. Ⓐ	4. Ⓑ	7. Ⓓ	10. Ⓐ	13. Ⓓ
2. Ⓓ	5. Ⓒ	8. Ⓒ	11. Ⓓ	14. Ⓐ
3. Ⓑ	6. Ⓐ	9. Ⓓ	12. Ⓒ	15. Ⓒ

1) **A**
Concept(s) Tested: Subject-verb agreement/verb tense, voice, and mood
Choice (A) is correct because the underlined verb must be in the past tense and must agree with the singular subject, "a herd." Moreover, because the herd of goats did not do the hiring, the sentence must be in the passive voice. Only "was hired" shows correct number, tense, and voice.

2) **D**
Concept(s) Tested: Conventional expressions
Choice (D) is correct because *"among the earliest"* is a common English idiom used to denote that something or someone is "one of the first" of something.

3) **B**
Concept(s) Tested: Restrictive clauses
Choice (B) is correct; the pronoun in the underlined section refers to "a species...of stingray." The relative pronouns "that" and "which" are used to refer to non-human objects, including animals, making (B) the most effective choice.

4) **B**
Concept(s) Tested: Combining sentences
Choice (B) is correct because it clearly and concisely restructures the sentences by turning the first sentence into an appositive phrase. Other choices are unnecessarily wordy, or contain incorrect punctuation.

5) **C**
Concept(s) Tested: Participial phrases
Choice (C) is correct because the underlined portion introduces a participial phrase that refers to Brazil; the phrase should begin with the present participle "covering." Moreover, a comma is needed before "covering" because participial phrases that are not right next to the word(s) they modify are separated from the rest of the sentence with a comma.

6) **A**
Concept(s) Tested: Possessive nouns
Choice (A) is correct because "the charity" is singular and shows possession over "founders." Founders, on the other hand, does not show possession over anything in the sentence.

7) **D**
Concept(s) Tested: Subordinate conjunction use
Choice (D) is correct because the sentence presents a contrast: Adam's apples "are often only visible in men," yet they "exist in both men and women." The only choice that indicates contrast is "Although."

8) **C**
Concept(s) Tested: Commonly confused words
Choice (C) is correct because a "conscience" is an internal moral and ethical guide, which makes sense in the context of the sentence. Although it sounds similar to "conscience," "conscious" is an adjective that means "aware" or "awake."

9) **D**
Concept(s) Tested: Correlative conjunctions
Choice (D) is correct; when the term "both" is followed by two options, the conjunction "and" must always separate the options from one another. Although choice (B) makes grammatical sense, it does not fit the context of the sentence: calligraphers are "valued artists in Islamic societies," so their art must have significance.

10) **A**
Concept(s) Tested: Verb tense, mood, and voice/ subject-verb agreement
Choice (A) is correct because the underlined verb refers to the plural noun "limbs" and must be in the past tense, since the sentence refers to the "Middle Ages." The only choice with a third-person plural, past tense verb form is (A).

11) **D**
Concept(s) Tested: Subordinate conjunction use
Choice (D) is correct because the sentence presents a contrast: Franklin was involved in American independence, yet he is better known "for being a philosopher, scientist, and inventor." Although the conjunction "while" often denotes a relationship of time, it can also denote contrast.

12) **C**
Concept(s) Tested: Providing evidence
Choice (C) is correct because it provides information that explains *how* archaeologists have traced bowling's origins to ancient Egypt— by finding physical evidence.

13) ➡ D

Concept(s) Tested: Commonly confused words
Choice (D) is correct because "prospective" means "potential" or "possible," and it makes sense to say, *Possible* applicants should…contact the admissions office." Although "perspective" sounds similar, it means "viewpoint" or "attitude."

14) ➡ A

Concept(s) Tested: Modifiers
Choice (A) is correct; for the sentence to make sense, "closely" must act as an adverb modifying the adjective "related," making all choices but (A) incoherent.

15) ➡ C

Concept(s) Tested: Syntax/Style
Choice (C) is correct; the underlined portion must serve as the subject of the sentence, and the phrase "What is known" forms the clearest subject.

Grammar Skills Practice 26

1. Ⓒ	4. Ⓐ	7. Ⓒ	10. Ⓑ	13. Ⓒ
2. Ⓓ	5. Ⓑ	8. Ⓒ	11. Ⓓ	14. Ⓓ
3. Ⓐ	6. Ⓓ	9. Ⓐ	12. Ⓑ	15. Ⓐ

1) ➡ C

Concept(s) Tested: Verb tense, mood, and voice
Choice (C) is correct because the sentence describes a one-time event that occurred in the past, making the simple past tense verb "moved" the best choice.

2) ➡ D

Concept(s) Tested: Combining sentences
Choice (D) is correct because it clearly and concisely restructures the sentences by turning the first sentence into an appositive phrase. Other choices are unnecessarily wordy.

3) ➡ A

Concept(s) Tested: Relative clauses
Choice (A) is correct; the pronoun in the underlined section refers to "vapor." The relative pronoun "which" refers to non-human objects ("vapor" in this case), making (A) the most effective choice. Choice (B) creates a run-on sentence, and choice (C) and (D) use incorrect relative pronouns to refer to "vapor."

4) ➡ A

Concept(s) Tested: Combining sentences

Choice (A) is correct because a colon effectively separates a piece of information from a definition of or elaboration on that information. In the sentence, "Azerbaijan, Georgia, Kazakhstan, Russia, and Turkey" provide elaboration on the "five transcontinental countries" mentioned earlier in the sentence.

5) ➡ B

Concept(s) Tested: Rhetorical strategies
Choice (B) is correct because the author adds humor (or attempts to, at least) by appealing to most people's dislike of the dentist, and comparing this intense dislike to the age of dentistry.

6) ➡ D

Concept(s) Tested: Conjunctions
Choice (D) is correct; the sentence begins with the conjunction "Although" to indicate that the sentence contains a contrast, so no other conjunction is necessary after the comma.

7) ➡ C

Concept(s) Tested: Concision
Choice (C) is correct because all other choices contain redundancies or wordiness.

8) ➡ C

Correct Choice: C
Concept(s) Tested: Modifier placement
Choice (C) is correct because the noun being modified, "Thailand," must come immediately after the phrase that modifies it, "Supplying nearly 22 percent of the world's rice." Other choices fail to show this relationship between the participial phrase and the subject of the sentence.

9) ➡ A

Concept(s) Tested: Subordinate conjunction use
Choice (A) is correct because the sentence contains a relationship of time, explaining what the Wright Brother did *prior to*, or *before*, they created the first airplane. The other choices fail to convey this relationship of time.

10) ➡ B

Concept(s) Tested: Noun agreement
Choice (B) is correct because the underlined noun refers to singular noun "Anthony Burgess," and "author" is the only singular answer choice.

11) ➡ D

Concept(s) Tested: Pronoun person and number/possessive pronouns
Choice (D) is correct because the underlined

pronoun refers to the plural noun phrase "Some species" and must therefore be plural. Additionally, the pronoun shows possession over "heads," so the correct choice is the plural possessive pronoun "their."

12) ➤ B
Concept(s) Tested: Concision
Choice (B) is correct because the terms "compiled," "gathered," and "collected" are synonyms, as are "restaurants" and "places to eat," so all choice except for (B) contain at least one redundancy.

13) ➤ C
Concept(s) Tested: Modifiers
Choice (C) is correct because in order for the sentence to make sense, it must indicate that the merchants became as successful as was necessary to pay for the cars. Thus, the adverb of degree, "enough," is called for. The pattern adjective ("successful")+ enough + infinitive ("to buy") must be used, as in choice (C).

14) ➤ D
Concept(s) Tested: Verb tense, mood, and voice
Choice (D) is correct because the sentence describes a one-time event that occurred in the past, making the simple past tense verb "destroyed" the best choice.

15) ➤ A
Concept(s) Tested: Parallel structure/conventional expressions
Choice (A) is correct; the underlined portion must follow the prepositional phrase word pattern established by "as a coloring agent for ceramics." The prepositional phrase "in the production of…" follows this word pattern, making it the correct choice. Although "for the producing" is also a prepositional phrase, "the producing" is not acceptable phrasing.

Grammar Skills Practice 27

1.	D	4.	A	7.	C	10.	C	13.	A
2.	C	5.	D	8.	D	11.	A	14.	D
3.	D	6.	B	9.	A	12.	B	15.	A

1) ➤ D
Concept(s) Tested: Verb tense, mood, and voice/ subject-verb agreement
Choice (D) is correct; the underlined verb must

agree with the singular subject of the sentence, "The St. Petersburg-Tampa Airboat Line," and the verb must be in the past tense because it refers to events from 1914. The verb "was" is correct because it agrees with a third-person singular subject and shows simple past tense.

2) ➤ C
Concept(s) Tested: Within-sentence punctuation
Choice (C) is correct because the semicolon effectively divides two independent clauses. Choices (A) and (D) fail to say who was determining how the animals died; choice (B) does not include an independent clause after the semicolon, which is awkward as well as grammatically incorrect.

3) ➤ D
Concept(s) Tested: Appositive phrases
Choice (D) is correct because the underlined information is separated from the rest of the sentence with a pair of commas, and it consists of a phrase that describes the subject of the sentence, arteriosclerosis. Thus, the underlined phrase must be an appositive, which begins with an article ("a," "an," or "the") and contains a noun or noun phrase.

4) ➤ A
Concept(s) Tested: Combining sentences
Choice (A) is correct because the preposition "with" clearly indicates that more information about the height of the Golden Gate Bridge follows, effectively combining the sentences.

5) ➤ D
Concept(s) Tested: Relative clauses/possessive pronouns
Choice (D) is correct because the pronoun at the underlined portion must refer to "Fred Astaire," introduce a description of Misty Copeland, and show possession over "dancing." Thus, the pronoun "whose" is correct.

6) ➤ B
Concept(s) Tested: Providing evidence
Choice (B) is correct because it explains that Charles lost the uprising and fled into exile, effectively concluding the description of the uprising.

7) ➤ C
Concept(s) Tested: Concision
Choice (C) is correct because it is the clearest and most concise answer. The terms "a maximum of" and "at most" are synonyms, and "time period"

and "terms" have the same meaning in the context of the sentence, so choices (A) and (D) contain redundancies. Choice (B) fails to offer a complete idea.

8) 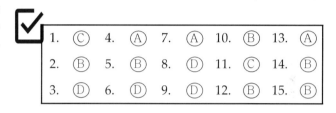 D
Concept(s) Tested: Precision
Choice (D) is correct because "to consider" is to regard or think of someone in a certain way, and it makes sense to say, "Robert Johnson is *regarded as* the finest blues artist."

9) 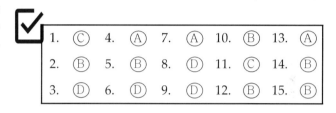 A
Concept(s) Tested: Appositive phrases
Choice (A) is correct because the underlined information is separated from the rest of the sentence with a comma, and it consists of a phrase that describes the noun *Casino Royale*. Thus, the underlined phrase must be an appositive, which begins with an article ("a," "an," or "the") and contains a noun or noun phrase.

10) 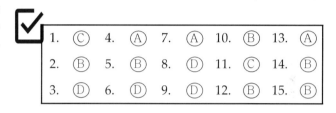 C
Concept(s) Tested: Verb tense, mood, and voice
Choice (C) is correct; the phrase "Since the mid-20th century" indicates that something started in the past and continues today. In cases such as this, the perfect-progressive aspect ("have been doing/have been done") is appropriate. Only choice (C) properly structures this aspect.

11) 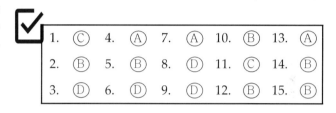 A
Concept(s) Tested: Combining sentences
Choice (A) is correct because the two sentences contain contrasting information: "Old World and New World vultures" look similar and eat similar things; "They are not closely related." The use of "yet" in choice (A) effectively conveys this contrast.

12) 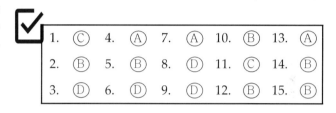 B
Concept(s) Tested: Syntax
Choice (B) is correct because "being" effectively connects the list of destroyed cities to the rest of the sentence. Choices (A) and (C) create run-on sentences, and choice (D) is incorrect because a semicolon separates two independent clauses, not a list from the rest of a sentence.

13) 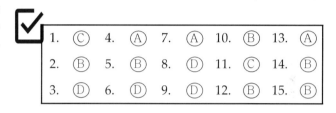 A
Concept(s) Tested: Verb tense, mood, and voice
Choice (A) is correct; the sentence presents a hypothetical situation (as indicated by the conjunction "if"), so the verb must be "were" to express the subjunctive mood. Moreover, the possessive pronoun "its" shows ownership over "surface," so any choices containing "it's" (a

contraction of "it is") are incorrect.

14) 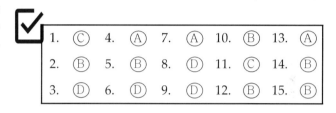 D
Concept(s) Tested: Modifier placement
Choice (D) is correct because it places the noun being modified, "Denzel Washington," directly after the phrase that modifies it, "For his performance...*Training Day*."

15) 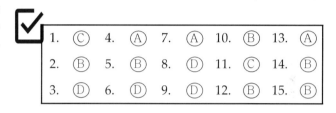 A
Concept(s) Tested: Subordinate conjunction use
Choice (A) is correct because the underlined conjunction must show that the relationship between the two clauses is one of time. Only "when" conveys such a relationship.

Grammar Skills Practice 28

✓

1. Ⓒ	4. Ⓐ	7. Ⓐ	10. Ⓑ	13. Ⓐ
2. Ⓑ	5. Ⓑ	8. Ⓓ	11. Ⓒ	14. Ⓑ
3. Ⓓ	6. Ⓓ	9. Ⓓ	12. Ⓑ	15. Ⓑ

1) 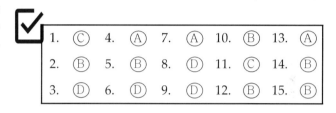 C
Concept(s) Tested: Verb tense, mood, and voice
Choice (C) is correct because the sentence describes a situation that began in the past (the 100-year-long dormancy of Mount St. Helens) and occurred until a particular point in the past (May 18, 1980). The past perfect aspect ("had" + past participle) shows that something began in the past, making (C) correct.

2) 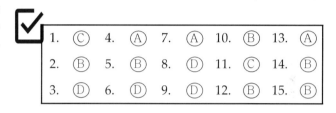 B
Concept(s) Tested: Correlative conjunctions
Choice (B) is correct because any time the phrase "not only" appears in a sentence, it must be followed by "but also," and only (B) effectively incorporates "but also" into the sentence.

3) 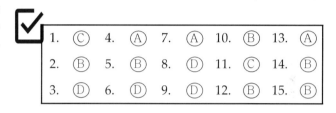 D
Concept(s) Tested: Combining sentences
Choice (D) is correct; "because of" shows the relationship between a cause and its effect. In this sentence, the *cause* is "sparse rainfall and a large population," and the *effect* is that water must be imported from the Colorado River, making "because of" an effective conjunction.

4) 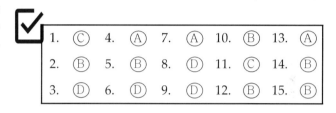 A
Concept(s) Tested: Within-sentence punctuation
Choice (A) is correct because a colon effectively separates a piece of information from a definition of or elaboration on that information. In the

sentence, the list of planets elaborates on the "Five...planets visible from Earth without the aid of a telescope" mentioned earlier in the sentence.

5) ➡ B
Concept(s) Tested: Concision
Choice (B) is correct; the terms "prestigious" and "acclaimed" are synonyms, so all choices that contain both are redundant, making (B) the most concise choice.

6) ➡ D
Concept(s) Tested: Subordinate conjunction use
Choice (D) is correct because in this context, "because" means *for the reason that*. It makes sense to say that the words are palindromes *for the reason that* they are read the same backwards and forwards. Choice (A) also expresses the relationship accurately, but it contains an unnecessary semicolon.

7) ➡ A
Concept(s) Tested: Combining sentences
Choice (A) is correct because it is the only choice that does not result in a run-on sentence, and because it clearly and concisely tells the reader where the Sargasso Sea is located.

8) ➡ D
Concept(s) Tested: Precision
Choice (D) is correct because "to host" is to receive others for a function or event, and it makes sense to say that Rio de Janeiro "will become the first South American country to *receive others for* the Olympic Games."

9) ➡ D
Concept(s) Tested: Parallel structure
Choice (D) is correct because the underlined portion must maintain the same "adjective + noun" word pattern as the other features in the list ("arable soil, sufficient rainfall"). Only choice (D) has this "adjective (mild) + noun (climates)" word pattern.

10) ➡ B
Concept(s) Tested: Combining sentences
Choice (B) is correct because the second sentence qualifies (provides an exception to) the information in the first sentence, and the use of of "although" in choice (B) effectively conveys this clarification.

11) ➡ C
Concept(s) Tested: Providing evidence
Choice (C) is correct because it provides reasons for kohl use: "it protected eyes from disease and

sunlight," so this choice "effectively explains why ancient people used kohl."

12) ➡ B
Concept(s) Verb tense, mood, and voice
Choice (B) is correct because the context and grammar call for using the simple past tense. The action is in the past and it interrupted an ongoing action in the past ("the French government was quietly convicting a Jewish military officer...").

13) ➡ A
Concept(s) Tested: Within-sentence punctuation/syntax
Choice (A) is correct because it clearly connects the description of ambidexterity to the rest of the sentence. Choice (B) is incorrect because it creates a run-on sentence. Choice (C) is incorrect because the phrase after the semicolon is not an independent clause. Choice (D) is incorrect because "an ability" must be a noun, and "ambidextrous" is an adjective ("ambidexterity" is the noun form).

14) ➡ B
Concept(s) Tested: Logical comparison
Choice (B) is correct because the sentence compares the physical characteristics of dire wolves and gray wolves. In the underlined portion, the verb "possessed" can be substituted by the verb "do," making (B) correct.

15) ➡ B
Concept(s) Tested: Pronoun person and number/possessive pronouns
Choice (B) is correct because the underlined pronoun refers to the singular noun "the pesticide" and shows possession over "use," making the singular possessive pronoun "its" the correct choice.

Grammar Skills Practice 29

☑
1. Ⓑ	4. Ⓐ	7. Ⓑ	10. Ⓒ	13. Ⓒ
2. Ⓒ	5. Ⓑ	8. Ⓐ	11. Ⓑ	14. Ⓐ
3. Ⓓ	6. Ⓓ	9. Ⓒ	12. Ⓓ	15. Ⓓ

1) ➡ B
Concept(s) Tested: Subject-verb agreement
Choice (B) is correct because the underlined verb must agree with the plural subject, "some

species," and only choice (B), "dwell," agrees with a third-person plural subject.

2) ➡️ C
Concept(s) tested: punctuation
Choice C is correct because "Norwegian adventurer" is "Thor Hyerdahl's" title, and nothing should separate n individual from their title. C is the only answer choice without unnecessary punctuation and separated titles.

3) ➡️ D
Concept(s) Tested: Providing evidence
Choice (D) is correct because after the underlined portion, the sentence discusses Robert Lincoln's political accomplishments, so it makes sense that the underlined portion mentions Lincoln's "successful political career."

4) ➡️ A
Concept(s) Tested: Subject-verb agreement/ possessive nouns
Choice (A) is correct because the verb in the underlined portion must agree with the third-person singular subject, "The radiocarbon dating...", making "reveals" the correct verb form. Moreover, "humans" is not showing possession in the sentence, and should be plural to show that more than one human made the migration.

5) ➡️ B
Concept(s) Tested: Syntax
Choice (B) is correct because the subject, "Alice Munro," should come immediately after the appositive phrase that describes it, "An insightful life," and the main verb of the sentence, "filled," should come immediately after the subject.

6) ➡️ D
Concept(s) Tested: subordinate conjunction use
Choice (D) is correct because the second part of the sentence qualifies (provides an exception to) information in the first part: Texas has many man-made lakes; it has only one large natural lake. The use of "although" in choice (D) effectively conveys this clarification.

7) ➡️ B
Concept(s) Tested: Modifiers/concision
Choice (B) is correct because it clearly and concisely tells the reader what kind of award the sentence is talking about: a prestigious ("highest") award that is related to literature ("literary").

8) ➡️ A
Concept(s) Tested: Verb tense, mood, and voice
Choice (A) is correct; the underlined portion is part of the verb phrase "are strongly associated with." Because "associated with" follows the verb "are,"

it must take the past participle form "associated," and the preposition "with" generally follows "associated."

9) ➡️ C
Concept(s) Tested: Precision
Choice (C) is correct because "to contend" is to make an assertion or claim about something, and it makes sense to say "Thomas Nagel's essay...*asserts* that objective accounts of others' perspectives are impossible."

10) ➡️ C
Concept(s) Tested: Combining sentences
Choice (C) is correct because it turns the first sentence into a title that describes Arthur C. Clarke, which clearly and concisely connects the two sentences.

11) ➡️ B
Concept(s) Tested: Pronoun person and number
Choice (B) is correct because the underlined pronoun is the subject of the sentence, and it does not refer to any specific, previously mentioned noun, but rather to "people in general." The most effective pronoun when referring to people in general is "one," so (B) is the correct choice.

12) ➡️ D
Concept(s) Tested: Possessive nouns
Choice (D) is correct because when a compound subject, such as the two writers in the sentence, both possess the same thing (in this case the comedy series), only one apostrophe is used.

13) ➡️ C
Concept(s) Tested: Subject-verb agreement
Choice (C) is correct because indefinite pronouns such as "everyone" are always singular. Only (C) offers a singular form of the verb ("is").

14) ➡️ A
Concept(s) Tested: Logical comparison
Choice (A) is correct because the sentence compares "trees" to "stars," and the only choice that creates a direct comparison between these two nouns is (A). Other choices compare "trees" to "the number of stars," or "numerous stars," which is illogical.

15) ➡️ D
Concept(s) Tested: Concision
Choice (D) is correct because "extinct" and "none remain today," "one of the largest" and "quite massive," and "predators" and "ate meat" are synonyms. Any choice that contains these redundancies is incorrect, so the underlined portion should be deleted.

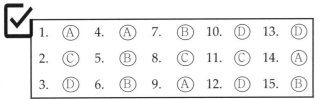

☑

1.	Ⓐ	4.	Ⓐ	7.	Ⓑ	10.	Ⓓ	13.	Ⓓ
2.	Ⓒ	5.	Ⓑ	8.	Ⓒ	11.	Ⓒ	14.	Ⓐ
3.	Ⓓ	6.	Ⓑ	9.	Ⓐ	12.	Ⓓ	15.	Ⓑ

1) ➡ A

Concept(s) Tested: Verb tense, mood, and voice
Choice (A) is correct because the underlined verb phrase must match the "form of 'to be' + past participle" structure of the previous verb "is dismissed," which only "be brought" does.

2) ➡ C

Concept(s) Tested: Precision
Choice (C) is correct because "to signify" means "to indicate." It makes sense to say that "the patterns tattooed on an individual's face indicate his or her tribe, …"

3) ➡ D

Concept(s) Tested: Participial phrases
Choice (D) is correct because the underlined portion introduces a participial phrase that modifies the subject of the sentence, "Unemployment rates." The phrase should therefore be introduced by the present participle "exceeding."

4) ➡ A

Concept(s) Tested: Conventional expressions
Choice (A) is correct because "over the course of" is an English idiom meaning "during a particular period of time," which makes sense in the context of the sentence.

5) ➡ B

Concept(s) Tested: Noun agreement
Choice (B) is correct; the underlined noun agrees with "volunteer army." Since an army consists of many individuals, the plural noun "members" is the correct choice.

6) ➡ B

Concept(s) Tested: Pronoun person and number
Choice (B) is correct; the underlined pronoun refers to the singular noun "a product's packaging." Because the pronoun at the underlined portion is not showing possession over anything, the singular pronoun "it" is the most appropriate choice.

7) ➡ B

Concept(s) Tested: Combining sentences
Choice (B) is correct; the appositive phrase "a devout classics scholar" must appear immediately before or after the noun it describes ("Oscar Wilde"), and only choice (B) effectively conveys this noun-appositive relationship.

8) ➡ C

Concept(s) Tested: Logical comparison
Choice (C) is correct; the sentence compares the cattle population of Texas to the cattle population of Nebraska. Because "cattle population" is singular, the singular pronoun "that" effectively replaces "cattle population" in the underlined portion.

9) ➡ A

Concept(s) Tested: Logical comparison
Choice (A) is correct because the sentence indicates that "The eyes of animals" and the eyes of humans are affected by the same disorders. Since "human vision" can effectively replace "the eyes of humans," choice (A) is correct.

10) ➡ D

Concept(s) Tested: Relative clauses
Choice (D) is correct; the underlined portion introduces a relative clause that refers to a phrase that references time ("until 2010"). Because the relative pronoun "when" is used to refer to time, (D) is the best, most concise choice.

11) ➡ C

Concept(s) Tested: End-of-sentence punctuation
Choice (C) is correct because a comma is used to punctuate the end of a quoted statement when the speaker is identified immediately after the quote.

12) ➡ D

Concept(s) Tested: Modifier placement/concision
Choice (D) is correct because it places the noun being modified, "Hebrew Union College," directly after the phrase that modifies it, "Founded in 1875." Although choice (C) also places the noun being modified directly after the modifying phrase, it needlessly repeats the phrase "Jewish seminary," making it less concise than (D).

13) ➡ D

Concept(s) Tested: Precision/commonly confused words
Choice (D) is correct because "to accept" is to approve of or regard favorably, and it makes sense to say, "the city council *approved of* Mr.

ANSWER KEY – CHAPTER 2

Hornby's proposal."

14) ➡ A

Concept(s) Tested: Concision
Choice (A) is correct because it is the clearest and most concise choice. Choice (B) is incorrect because it is redundant: "about" and "approximately" are synonyms. Choices (C) and (D) are incorrect because it is already implied that a photon must travel to reach Earth, making any mention of "traveling" unnecessary.

15) ➡ B

Concept(s) Tested: Combining sentences
Choice (B) is correct because it effectively turns the first sentence into a subordinate clause describing the subject of the sentence, "Jefferson Davis." Other choices are unnecessarily wordy, or contain verb tense issues.

Grammar Skills Practice 31

☑
1.	ⓒ	4.	ⓓ	7.	ⓒ	10.	ⓐ	13.	ⓑ
2.	ⓓ	5.	ⓐ	8.	ⓓ	11.	ⓒ	14.	ⓓ
3.	ⓐ	6.	ⓑ	9.	ⓑ	12.	ⓒ	15.	ⓑ

1) ➡ C

Concept(s) Tested: Noun agreement
Choice (C) is correct because the underlined noun must agree with the plural subject "Edgar Allen Poe and Nathaniel Hawthorne," and the only plural option is (C), "authors."

2) ➡ D

Concept(s) Tested: Appositive phrases
Choice (D) is correct because the underlined information is separated from the rest of the sentence with a comma, and it consists of a phrase that describes the subject of the sentence, William Pène du Bois. Thus, the underlined phrase must be an appositive, which begins with an article ("a," "an," or "the") and contains a noun or noun phrase.

3) ➡ A

Concept(s) Tested: Providing evidence
Choice (A) is correct because it provides a statistic that keeps the focus on the surface gravity of Mercury (a person's weight on Earth vs. his or her weight on Mercury).

4) ➡ D

Concept(s) Tested: Within-sentence punctuation/concision
Choice (D) is correct because no punctuation is necessary between the noun "supercontinent" and its name ("Pangea") because they work together to form a single noun phrase.

5) ➡ A

Concept(s) Tested: Combining sentences
Choice (A) is correct because the underlined portion effectively turns much of the first sentence into a participial phrase that describes the subject of the sentence, "the Cambodian temple-complex of Angkor Wat."

6) ➡ B

Concept(s) Tested: Verb tense, mood, and voice
Choice (B) is correct; the sentence refers to events from the 19th century, so the underlined verb should be in the past tense, making (B), "was disproven," correct.

7) ➡ C

Concept(s) Tested: Parallel structure/items in a list
Choice (C) is correct because the list maintains parallel structure, is not redundant, and uses correct punctuation. Choices (A) and (B) are redundant because they include the term "(pop) artist," which had already been mentioned in the sentence. Choice (D) is incorrect because it fails to include "and" between the last two names in the list.

8) ➡ D

Concept(s) Tested: Subject-verb agreement
Choice (D) is correct because the underlined portion must agree with the singular subject of the sentence, "Tofu," and only "is" agrees with a third-person singular subject.

9) ➡ B

Concept(s) Tested: Providing evidence
Choice (B) is correct because it provides an explanation, telling readers *why* giraffe's have black tongues and answering the question's prompt clearly and concisely.

10) ➡ A

Concept(s) Tested: Parallel structure
Choice (A) is correct; the underlined portion must match the verb tense introduced by "was found." Because "found" is a past participle, the underlined portion must also be a past participle ("given" in this case).

11) ➡ C
Concept(s) Tested: Precision
Choice (C) is correct because "to allow" is to permit or let something happen, and it makes sense to say that a sport involves getting "a heavy rubber ball through a hoop without *letting* the ball touch the ground."

12) ➡ C
Concept(s) Tested: Within-sentence punctuation
Choice (C) is correct because the semicolon effectively separates two independent clauses containing related information from each other. Choices (A) and (B) result in run-on sentences, and the use of "while" in choice (D) confuses the intended relationship between the clauses.

13) ➡ B
Concept(s) Tested: Conventional expressions
Choice (B) is correct because "to brush up on" is an English idiom meaning "to add to one's knowledge about a particular subject or topic," which makes sense in the context of the sentence.

14) ➡ D
Concept(s) Tested: Parallel structure
Choice (D) is correct because the underlined portion must maintain the same "noun-past participle" word pattern as the preceding modifier, "pinecone-topped," making "ivy-covered" the only acceptable answer.

15) ➡ B
Concept(s) Tested: Countable and uncountable nouns
Choice (B) is correct; because "hippos" is a countable noun, the correct comparative adjective is "fewer," not a form of "less."

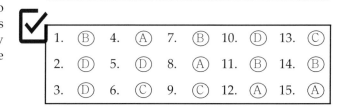
✓
1.	Ⓑ	4.	Ⓐ	7.	Ⓑ	10.	Ⓓ	13.	Ⓒ
2.	Ⓓ	5.	Ⓓ	8.	Ⓐ	11.	Ⓑ	14.	Ⓑ
3.	Ⓓ	6.	Ⓒ	9.	Ⓒ	12.	Ⓐ	15.	Ⓐ

1) ➡ B
Concept(s) Tested: Logical comparison
Choice (B) is correct; the sentence compares "the average height of a wealthy Englishman" to the average height of a poor Englishman. Because "average height" is singular, the singular pronoun "that" effectively replaces "average height" in the underlined portion.

2) ➡ D
Concept(s) Tested: Subordinate conjunction use
Choice (D) is correct because the sentence presents a contrast: "over 70 percent of the Earth's surface is covered in water"; "only about 1 percent" is drinkable. The choice that indicates contrast and fits with the syntax of the sentence is "Although." While "despite" also indicates contrast, the verb "is" would have to be "being" for "despite" to work in the sentence.

3) ➡ D
Concept(s) Tested: Appositive phrases
Choice (D) is correct; the appositive phrase "the inventor of the cyclotron" describes Ernest O. Lawrence, and an appositive must always appear immediately before or after the noun it describes. Only (D) correctly places the noun next to appositive that describes it.

4) ➡ A
Concept(s) Tested: Subject-verb agreement/ pronoun person and number
Choice (A) is correct; the underlined verb must agree with the gerund subject, "Treating." Gerunds are treated as third-person singular nouns, so "helps" agrees with "Treating." Moreover, the underlined pronoun must agree with the singular noun "wood," so the singular pronoun "it" is appropriate.

5) ➡ D
Concept(s) Tested: Concision
Choice (D) is correct; all the choices convey the same information (that New London used to be a large whaling port), yet (D) provides the clearest and most concise version of the sentence.

6) ➡ C

Concept(s) Tested: Pronoun clarity

Choice (C) is correct because the underlined portion must specify where researchers gather facts, and only (C), "the sleeping *nests*, makes sense in context.

7) ➡ B

Concept(s) Tested: Providing evidence

Choice (B) is correct because it gives an example of a science fiction novel (*The Forever War*) that is based on a real-world political situation (the Vietnam War), thus supporting the previous sentence's comment on works of science fiction reflecting real-world situations.

8) ➡ A

Concept(s) Tested: Within-sentence punctuation

Choice (A) is correct because the comma serves the same function here as a colon: it separates a piece of information from a definition of or elaboration on that information. In the sentence, the phrase "many of which...read today" is an elaboration on the "46 children's books" mentioned earlier in the sentence.

9) ➡ C

Concept(s) Tested: Parallel structure

Choice (C) is correct because the underlined portion must maintain the same word pattern as the other listed items in the sentence. The list is naming professional fields, so the underlined portion must also be a field, making "journalism" the correct choice.

10) ➡ D

Concept(s) Tested: Combining sentences

Choice (D) is correct because it clearly and concisely restructures the sentences by turning much of the first sentence into an appositive phrase. Other choices are unnecessarily convoluted or are incorrectly punctuated.

11) ➡ B

Concept(s) Tested: Modifier placement

Choice (B) is correct because it places the noun being modified, "the ancient city of Petra," directly after the phrase that modifies it, "Lying south of Amman, Jordan."

12) ➡ A

Concept(s) Tested: Within-sentence punctuation

Choice (A) is correct because no punctuation should separate a subject ("the *caste system*") from the verb that describes it ("is") if the verb comes immediately after the subject.

13) ➡ C

Concept(s) Tested: Combining sentences

Choice (C) is correct because the two sentences contain contrasting information: low-fat foods seem healthy; low-fat foods often replace fat with excessive amounts of sugar. The use of "but" in choice (C) effectively conveys this contrast.

14) ➡ B

Concept(s) Tested: Precision

Choice (B) is correct because "to secure" is to successfully gain or obtain something, and it makes sense to say that Tennessee Williams *obtained* his place as one of century's greatest playwrights.

15) ➡ A

Concept(s) Tested: Commonly confused words

Choice (A) is correct because "adverse" means "undesirable, or disadvantageous," which makes sense in the context of the sentence. Other choice may sound similar, but they have different meanings and do not fit the context of the sentence.

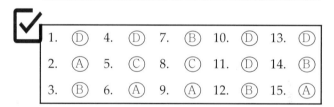

✓
1. Ⓓ	4. Ⓓ	7. Ⓑ	10. Ⓓ	13. Ⓓ
2. Ⓐ	5. Ⓒ	8. Ⓒ	11. Ⓓ	14. Ⓑ
3. Ⓑ	6. Ⓐ	9. Ⓐ	12. Ⓑ	15. Ⓐ

1) ➡ D

Concept(s) Tested: Participial phrases

Choice (D) is correct; the underlined portion cannot introduce another main verb, so it must introduce a participial phrase that modifies "The fangtooth fish," and the participial phrase must start with the present participle "having."

2) ➡ A

Concept(s) Tested: Combining sentences

Choice (A) is correct because the two sentences provide information about a new type of solar cell, but the relationship between the two clauses is self-evident and requires no transition words or conjunctions for clarification. Thus, a semicolon effectively joins the two sentences.

3) ➡ B

Concept(s) Tested: Within-sentence punctuation

Choice (B) is correct because a colon effectively separates a piece of information from a definition of or elaboration on that information. In the sentence, the phrase "their red blood…any blood type" is a definition of the term "universal donors" mentioned earlier in the sentence.

4) ➡ D
Concept(s) Tested: Providing evidence
Choice (D) is correct because it provides *an example* of agricultural artificial selection by explaining that humans developed modern-day from a type of grass millennia ago.

5) ➡ C
Concept(s) Tested: Parallel structure/subject-verb agreement
Choice (C) is correct because the three listed types of animals must all be plural to maintain parallel structure (note: "chimera" is the singular and plural form), and because the plural subject ("sharks, rays, and chimera") agrees with the third-person plural verb form "are."

6) ➡ A
Concept(s) Tested: Pronoun person and number
Choice (A) is correct because the underlined portion acts as the subject of the independent clause, so the subjective pronoun "he" correctly refers to "Pythagoras." Moreover, the phrase "his pupils" must come after "he" so that the reader knows to what noun "his" refers.

7) ➡ B
Concept(s) Tested: Precision
Choice (B) is correct because "to abdicate" is to renounce one's throne or retire from a position of power, and it makes sense to say that Cincinnatus *renounced his title* as dictator of Rome.

8) ➡ C
Concept(s) Tested: Logical comparison
Choice (C) is correct; the sentence compares Switzerland's chocolate consumption to every other nation's chocolate consumption, so "Switzerland consumes" provides the most logical comparison to "any other country." Moreover, it is important to note that the sentence does not literary mean that the region of Switzerland consumes chocolate; the sentence uses synecdoche by having "Switzerland" stand in for "the people of Switzerland."

9) ➡ A
Concept(s) Tested: Concision/conventional expressions
Choice (A) is correct because the phrase "generated through" is an English idiom meaning "produced by," which makes sense in the context of the sentence. Other choices either

convey a different and inaccurate meaning or are unnecessarily wordy.

10) ➡ D
Concept(s) Tested: Parallel structure
Choice (D) is correct because the underlined portion must follow the same "his + noun + modifiers" word pattern established by the other listed items, and only (D) maintains this structure.

11) ➡ D
Concept(s) Tested: Modifiers
Choice (D) is correct because the modifiers "critical" and "commercial" modify the noun "success," so they must be adjectives separated by the conjunction "and." Other choices are incorrect because they leave out "and," or they make either "critical" or "commercial" into adverbs.

12) ➡ B
Concept(s) Tested: Subject-verb agreement
Choice (B) is correct because the underlined verb must agree with the plural subject "some," and the only choice that agrees with a third-person plural subject is the verb phrase "have claimed."

13) ➡ D
Concept(s) Tested: Within-sentence punctuation
Choice (D) is correct because the short prepositional phrases "of the ancient Celtic people" and "in Northern Europe" are essential to the sentence; they define "priests." Essential information should not be separated by commas in most cases if it appears in the middle of a sentence. Only choice (D) avoids overusing commas.

14) ➡ B
Concept(s) Tested: Combining sentences
Choice (B) is correct; the first sentence references a fictional account of Mozart's death, while the second sentence provides the actual reason for his death. Thus, the sentences contain contrasting information, and the conjunction "but" as well as the phrase "in reality" convey this relationship accurately.

15) ➡ A
Concept(s) Tested: Pronoun person and number
Choice (A) is correct because the underlined pronoun refers to the singular noun "Pfizer," making the singular pronoun "it" correct.

1. Ⓓ	4. Ⓑ	7. Ⓐ	10. Ⓑ	13. Ⓒ
2. Ⓑ	5. Ⓒ	8. Ⓑ	11. Ⓑ	14. Ⓒ
3. Ⓐ	6. Ⓓ	9. Ⓓ	12. Ⓐ	15. Ⓓ

1) ➡ D

Concept(s) Tested: Parenthetical elements

Choice (D) is correct because parentheses are often used to separate grammatically non-essential information from the rest of a sentence. Other choices are incorrect because they either over-punctuate the sentence, or they place grammatically essential information in parentheses.

2) ➡ B

Concept(s) Tested: Combining sentences

Choice (A) is correct because the two sentences contain contrasting information: Alligators can move quickly; they "spend most of their time lying in wait." The use of "but" in choice (B) effectively conveys this contrast.

3) ➡ A

Concept(s) Tested: Relative clauses/verb tense, mood, and voice

Choice (A) is correct because the underlined portion refers to "the art movement known as Dadaism," making "which" the best choice because it is a relative pronoun (so it refers to the preceding information) that refers to non-human nouns/noun phrases. Moreover, "arose" is the correct verb form because the sentence refers to events that occurred in "the early 20th century."

4) ➡ B

Concept(s) Tested: Noun agreement

Choice (B) is correct because the underlined noun refers to the singular subject, "The monkey deity Hanuman," so the underlined noun must also be singular, making "a symbol" correct.

5) ➡ C

Concept(s) Tested: Precision

Choice (C) is correct because "to reject" is to abandon or refuse, and it makes sense to say that Imagism *abandoned* "the expansiveness of Romantic poetry in favor of conciseness." Although "shunned" is similar in meaning, it does not fit the context of the sentence because an inanimate object ("Imagism" in this case) cannot "shun," only sentient beings can "shun."

6) ➡ D

Concept(s) Tested: Providing evidence

Choice (D) is correct because it explains *why* people use alloys (their functions), claiming that "they are stronger or more resistant to corrosion than elemental metals."

7) ➡ A

Concept(s) Tested: Commonly confused words/subject-verb agreement

Choice (A) is correct because the adverb "there" is used to show that something exists, making it appropriate in the context of the sentence. Moreover, the underlined verb must agree with the plural phrase "a number of environmental conditions," making the third-person plural verb form "are" correct.

8) ➡ B

Concept(s) Tested: Correlative conjunction

Choice (B) is correct because a phrase beginning with "between" will always follow the pattern "between x and y." Moreover, choice (B) contains the only correctly paired conjunctions.

9) ➡ D

Concept(s) Tested: Pronoun number and person

Choice (D) is correct; the underlined pronoun refers to the singular subject, "The peregrine falcon." Because the writer is referring to both genders of the species, the gender-neutral, third-person singular pronoun "it" is the most appropriate choice.

10) ➡ B

Concept(s) Tested: Subordinate conjunction use

Choice (B) is correct because the sentence presents a contrast: baseball is "America's favorite pastime"; football is more popular and beloved. The choice that indicates contrast is "although."

11) ➡ B

Concept(s) Tested: Within-sentence punctuation/syntax

Choice (B) is correct; the underlined portion introduces a comparison between the Dead Sea and the Great Salt Lake, and (B) is the only choice that does so without introducing a verb ("is"), and thus creating a run-on sentence.

12) ➡ A

Concept(s) Tested: Combining sentences

Choice (A) is correct because the two sentences provide information about ocean acidification, but the relationship between the two clauses is self-evident and requires no transition words or conjunctions for clarification. Thus, a semicolon effectively joins the two sentences.

13) ➡ C

Concept(s) Tested: Modifier placement
Choice (C) is correct because it places the noun being modified, "Jackson Pollock," directly after the phrase that modifies it, "First receiving attention for his surrealistic portraits."

14) ➡ C

Concept(s) Tested: Participial phrases/concision
Choice (C) is correct because it succinctly yet fully conveys the writer's meaning. Choices (A) and (D) are unnecessarily wordy and awkward, while choice (B) changes the meaning.

15) ➡ D

Concept(s) Tested: Verb tense, mood, and voice
Choice (D) is correct because the sentence refers to past events, so the underlined verb should be in the simple past tense, making "developed" the correct choice.

Grammar Skills Practice 35

☑

1. Ⓒ	4. Ⓓ	7. Ⓓ	10. Ⓑ	13. Ⓐ
2. Ⓓ	5. Ⓑ	8. Ⓐ	11. Ⓓ	14. Ⓑ
3. Ⓐ	6. Ⓐ	9. Ⓒ	12. Ⓒ	15. Ⓑ

1) ➡ C

Concept(s) Tested: Indefinite pronouns/ Subject-verb agreement
Choice (C) is correct because the underlined portion must agree with the singular indefinite pronoun "everything." Furthermore, the action is occurring in a present tense, and only choice (C) is in a present tense and agrees with a singular noun: "everything… is sinking…"

2) ➡ D

Concept(s) Tested: Combining sentences
Choice (D) is correct because the two sentences provide information about harlequin-type ichthyosis. The relationship between the two clauses is self-evident and requires no transition words or conjunctions for clarification, so a semicolon effectively joins the two sentences.

3) ➡ A

Concept(s) Tested: Pronoun person and number
Choice (A) is correct; the underlined noun is later referred to using the singular pronouns "he or she." Thus, the underlined noun must also be singular, making "an individual" correct.

4) ➡ D

Concept(s) Tested: Verb tense, mood, and voice
Choice (D) is correct; the phrase "for about 13,000 years" indicates that something started in the past and continues today. In cases such as this, the perfect-progressive aspect ("has been doing/ has been done") is appropriate. Only choice (D) properly structures this aspect.

5) ➡ B

Concept(s) Tested: Gerunds/ Subject-verb agreement
Choice (B) is correct because the underlined portion must agree with the gerund "riding," which is the subject of the sentence. Since gerunds are always singular, it is correct to say that the "riding… was a hallmark…"

6) ➡ A

Concept(s) Tested: Syntax/run-on sentences
Choice (A) is correct because it clearly and concisely explains that the Dodge brothers worked on a farm, *then* they started their own company. Choices (B) and (D) are incorrect because they create run-on sentence, and (C) is incorrect because it contains a dangling modifier.

7) ➡ D

Concept(s) Tested: Countable/ uncountable nouns, Subject-verb agreement
Choice (D) is correct because the underlined portion must describe a quantity of "pronouncements," which are countable nouns. Thus, a smaller quantity must be described using "fewer."

8) ➡ A

Concept(s) Tested: Logical comparison
Choice (A) is correct because the sentence compares "the population of China" to the population of India. Because "population" is singular, the singular pronoun "that" effectively replaces "population" in the underlined portion.

9) ➡ C

Concept(s) Tested: Concision
Choice (C) is correct because it conveys all the information concisely and precisely. Choice (D) is vague, while choices (A) and (B) are wordy and convoluted. Furthermore, choice (C) effectively uses the active voice ("poachers kill") rather than the passive ("elephants are illegally killed").

10) ➡ B

Concept(s) Tested: Within-sentence punctuation

Choice (B) is correct because when contrasting information is introduced by the word "not," a comma must come before "not" to separate the contrast from the rest of the sentence.

11) ➡ D

Concept(s) Tested: Providing evidence

Choice (D) is correct because it clearly *refutes* the claim in the first sentence about "Neanderthals" being associated with stupidity by indicating that Neanderthals were likely intelligent and resourceful.

12) ➡ C

Concept(s) Tested: Restrictive clauses

Choice (C) is correct; "to maintain that" is a common English expression, so "maintain" must be followed by "that" for the sentence to make sense. Moreover, (C) more clearly illustrates the relationship between the Grand Canyon and its formation than does choice (D).

13) ➡ A

Concept(s) Tested: Relative clauses

Choice (A) is correct; the underlined pronoun introduces a relative clause that refers to "President Gerald Ford," and the relative pronoun "who" refers to the subjects of clauses.

14) ➡ B

Concept(s) Tested: Precision

Choice (B) is correct because "offensive" means "impolite or vulgar," and it makes sense to characterize a television show as "vulgar."

15) ➡ B

Concept(s) Tested: Concision

Choice (B) is correct because it clearly and concisely completes the sentence. Choice (A) and (D) are incorrect because they contain redundancies ("original" and "earliest," "destroyed" and "ruined"), and choice (C) is incorrect because it does not clarify *what* was destroyed.

Grammar Skills Practice 36

☑
1.	Ⓑ	4.	Ⓒ	7.	Ⓒ	10.	Ⓑ	13.	Ⓓ
2.	Ⓒ	5.	Ⓓ	8.	Ⓐ	11.	Ⓑ	14.	Ⓒ
3.	Ⓐ	6.	Ⓐ	9.	Ⓑ	12.	Ⓓ	15.	Ⓐ

1) ➡ B

Concept(s) Tested: Possessives/Parallel structure

Choice (B) is correct because it is accurately conveys the meaning of the sentence without redundancy. Choice (A) is redundant, choice (C) uses a plural pronoun ("those") to refer to a singular noun ("film industry"), and choice (D) changes the sentence's intended meaning.

2) ➡ C

Concept(s) Tested: Combining sentences

Choice (C) is correct because the two sentences contain contrasting information: films and television depict noisy space battles; no sound can travel in space. The use of "yet" in choice (C) effectively conveys this contrast.

3) ➡ A

Concept(s) Tested: Transition words

Choice (A) is correct; if something is "paradoxical," it is contradictory, and the underlined portion connects two contradicting ideas: Washington owned many slaves, but he opposed the institution of slavery. Thus, "paradoxically" is the best transition for the underlined portion.

4) ➡ C

Concept(s) Tested: Participial phrases

Choice (C) is correct; the underlined portion contains the subject of the sentence, "the Red Cross," and it introduces a participial phrase that describes the subject. Thus, the sentence has only one main verb, "set up."

5) ➡ D

Concept(s) Tested: Pronoun person and number

Choice (D) is correct; the underlined noun is later referred to using the singular pronouns "it." Thus, the underlined noun must also be singular, making "a bolt of lightning" correct.

6) ➡ A

Concept(s) Tested: Participial phrases

Choice (A) is correct because the underlined portion introduces a participial phrase that describes "Octopuses in captivity," so the present participle "sneaking" is correct. Choices (C) and (D) are incorrect because they create run-on sentences, and (B) is incorrect because a base verb form cannot introduce a participial phrase.

7) ➡ C

Concept(s) Tested: Subject-verb agreement

Choice (C) is correct; the underlined verb refers to the plural noun phrase "The film scores," making the third-person plural verb form "are" correct. Although choice (D) also contains "are," it is incorrect because the inclusion of "which" results in an incomplete sentence.

8) ➡️ A
Concept(s) Tested: Commonly confused words
Choice (A) is correct because "respectively" means "in the order already mentioned," and it makes sense to say that "France and Spain sided with the U.S...in 1778 and 1779" *in the order already mentioned.*

9) ➡️ B
Concept(s) Tested: Precision
Choice (B) is correct because, when referring to literature, and "account of" something is "a report or description" of it, and it makes sense to say that Schlesinger's book is *a description of* the Kennedy administration from 1960 to 1963.

10) ➡️ B
Concept(s) Tested: Logical comparison
Choice (B) is correct; the sentence compares the number of performances of *The Phantom of the Opera* to the number of performances of any other musical, which only (B) does clearly and concisely.

11) ➡️ B
Concept(s) Tested: Parallel structure
Choice (B) is correct because the underlined portion must maintain the same "past-tense verb + other information" word pattern as the other listed activities, and only (B) contains the aforementioned word pattern— "past-tense verb (traveled across) + other information (the United States)."

12) ➡️ D
Concept(s) Tested: Combining sentences
Choice (D) is correct because it organizes the events of the sentences in chronological order (from earliest to latest) and conveys information clearly and concisely. Other choices are incorrect either because they contain dangling modifiers, or because their phrasing is unnecessarily convoluted.

13) ➡️ D
Concept(s) Tested: Parenthetical elements
Choice (D) is correct because the phrase "seldom over a month" is not essential to the grammatical structure of the sentence, and parentheses are often used to separate grammatically non-essential information from the rest of a sentence.

14) ➡️ C
Concept(s) Tested: Providing evidence

Choice (C) is correct; in order to set up the information in the second sentence, the underlined portion should clarify the relationship between arm span and professional swimmers. Only choice (C) addresses both these points.

15) ➡️ A
Concept(s) Tested: Noun agreement/coordinate conjunction use
Choice (A) is correct because the terms "dolphins" and "whales" must agree in number, and because the conjunction "and" shows that *both* types of animal are examples of "aquatic mammals."

Grammar Skills Practice 37

1.	Ⓒ	4.	Ⓓ	7.	Ⓐ	10.	Ⓑ	13.	Ⓑ
2.	Ⓐ	5.	Ⓑ	8.	Ⓓ	11.	Ⓒ	14.	Ⓐ
3.	Ⓓ	6.	Ⓒ	9.	Ⓐ	12.	Ⓓ	15.	Ⓑ

1) ➡️ C
Concept(s) Tested: Appositive phrases
Choice (C) correctly provides an appositive that describes the subject, "Robert Clifton Weaver." Other choices contain convoluted wording or incorrect punctuation.

2) ➡️ A
Concept(s) Tested: Precision
Choice (A) is correct because "to incite" is to encourage or cause violent or destructive behavior, and it makes sense to say that a controversial ballet nearly *encouraged* or *caused* a riot.

3) ➡️ D
Concept(s) Tested: Subject-verb agreement/verb tense, mood, and voice
Choice (D) is correct; the underlined verb refers to the third-person singular subject, "the energy," and describes a general scientific fact, making the simple present tense appropriate. Thus, the third-person singular, simple present-tense verb form "converts" is correct.

4) ➡️ D
Concept(s) Tested: Combining sentences
Choice (D) is correct because it is the only choice that clarifies that *all* of *gimbap's* ingredients are "wrapped in dried seaweed and served in... slices."

5) ➡ B

Concept(s) Tested: Parallel structure

Choice (B) is correct because the underlined portion must maintain the same "number/statistic + plural noun" word pattern as the other listed statistics, and only (B) maintains this "number (over 2,000) + plural noun (casualties)" word pattern.

6) ➡ C

Concept(s) Tested: Concision

Choice (C) is correct because it is the clearest and most concise choice. Something that is "dubious" is unreliable information, which fits with the sentence's claim that "there is not reliable documentation that Ross was involved." Choices (A) and (D) are unnecessarily wordy, and choice (B) is incorrect because it is awkward and confusing to say that "Claims…are doubts."

7) ➡ A

Concept(s) Tested: Relative clauses

Choice (A) is correct; the pronoun "that" is generally used to introduce a relative clause that includes essential descriptive information, making (A) the most effective choice.

8) ➡ D

Concept(s) Tested: Providing evidence

Choice (D) is correct because it provides information proving that humans are not the most abundant animal species, claiming that there are millions of ants for each human.

9) ➡ A

Concept(s) Tested: Combining sentences

Choice (A) is correct because it is the only choice that contains a clear and logical flow of ideas. (A) immediately introduces the sentence's subject, "The language of the Frisians," and effectively places additional information about the Frisians in an appositive phrase.

10) ➡ B

Concept(s) Tested: Verb tense, mood, and voice

Choice (B) is correct because the simple present tense is appropriate for discussing general facts. The sentence is relaying a general fact about "Shakespeare's use of soliloquy," so the third-person singular, simple present-tense verb form "allows" is appropriate.

11) ➡ C

Concept(s) Tested: Concision

Choice (C) is correct because it clearly and concisely compares Charlemagne's height to that of an average man of his era. Choices (A) and (B) are unnecessarily wordy, and choice (D) does not provide a sufficient amount of information.

12) ➡ D

Concept(s) Tested: Parenthetical elements

Choice (D) is correct because the phrase that describes "room temperature," "approximately 72 degrees Fahrenheit," is not essential to the grammatical structure of the sentence, and parentheses can separate grammatically non-essential information from the rest of a sentence.

13) ➡ B

Concept(s) Tested: Commonly confused words

Choice (B) is correct because "except" means "not including," which makes sense in the context of the sentence. Other choices may sound similar to "except," but they have very different meanings that do not fit the sentence's context.

14) ➡ A

Concept(s) Tested: End-of-sentence punctuation

Choice (A) is correct because the two sentences are already quite long and convey complete thoughts, and should therefore be separated using a period. Other choices combine the sentences to create one long, unnecessarily confusing sentence.

15) ➡ B

Concept(s) Tested: Participial phrases

Choice (B) is correct because the underlined portion introduces a participial phrase that modifies the subject, "The presence of a tumor." Thus, the participial phrase should be separated from the rest of the sentence with a comma, and it should begin with the present participle "leading."

Grammar Skills Practice 38

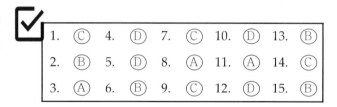

1.	Ⓒ	4.	Ⓓ	7.	Ⓒ	10.	Ⓓ	13.	Ⓑ
2.	Ⓑ	5.	Ⓓ	8.	Ⓐ	11.	Ⓐ	14.	Ⓒ
3.	Ⓐ	6.	Ⓑ	9.	Ⓒ	12.	Ⓓ	15.	Ⓑ

1) ➡ C

Concept(s) Tested: Precision

Choice (C) is correct because "influential" means "important and distinguished," and it makes sense to say that James Joyce, Gertrude Stein, and F. Scott Fitzgerald were *important and distinguished* artists.

2) ➡ B

Concept(s) Tested: Pronoun number and person/ conventional expressions

Choice (B) is correct; the pronoun in the

underlined portion refers to the singular noun "a wound," so the singular pronoun "it" is appropriate. Moreover, the phrase "protect from invasive organisms" makes more sense than does "protect with invasive organisms," as the latter phrase implies that the invasive organisms do the protecting, which is incorrect.

3) ➡ A
Concept(s) Tested: Subordinate conjunction use
Choice (A) is correct because the sentence discusses traditional practices within, or *among*, a certain Native American group, so the conjunction "among" effectively introduces the sentence.

4) ➡ D
Concept(s) Tested: Verb tense, mood, and voice
Choice (D) is correct because the sentence describes an event that occurred in the past, making the simple past tense verb form "exported" appropriate.

5) ➡ D
Concept(s) Tested: Possessives
Choice (D) is correct because it is the only choice that follows formal grammar rules and still indicates that the border in question lies between the two countries. Choices (A) and (B) could possibly refer to all of the two countries' borders. Choice (C) uses informal, conversational English. Only choice (D) uses a compound-subject possessive structure to accurately convey the information.

6) ➡ B
Concept(s) Tested: Combining sentences
Choice (B) is correct; the second sentence explains why Nebraska is Springsteen's darkest album, and when it is used as a conjunction, "as" can show that the second clause elaborates on the first, making it the correct choice. Other choices are incorrect because they contain either convoluted phrasing or incorrect verb usage.

7) ➡ C
Concept(s) Tested: Providing evidence
Choice (C) is correct because it clarifies that most Australians live near the coast because "the country's interior is…nearly uninhabitable." Thus, (C) effectively explains *why* Australians live in coastal regions.

8) ➡ A
Concept(s) Tested: Logical comparison
Choice (A) is correct because the sentence

compares "the solar power capacity of China" to the solar power capacity of Germany. Because "the solar power capacity" is singular, the singular pronoun "that" effectively replaces "the solar power capacity" in the underlined portion.

9) ➡ C
Concept(s) Tested: Within-sentence punctuation
Choice (C) is correct because all of the information in the underlined portion is essential to the meaning of the sentence, so it should not be separated from the rest of the sentence with any punctuation. Other choices are incorrect because they over-punctuate.

10) ➡ D
Concept(s) Tested: Verb tense, mood, and voice/ subject-verb agreement
Choice (D) is correct; the sentence discusses an author's work, and one should use the simple present tense when discussing the contents of a work of literature. (This is called the "literary present tense.") Moreover, the underlined verb refers to the plural noun "The writings," so the correct choice is the third-person plural, simple present-tense verb form "discuss."

11) ➡ A
Concept(s) Tested: Combining sentences
Choice (A) is correct because it clearly and concisely combines the sentences. Here the comma serves the same function here as a colon: it separates a piece of information from a definition of or elaboration on that information. In the sentence, the phrase "one of the longest… automotive history" is an elaboration on the manufacturing run that lasted from "1908 to 1927" mentioned earlier in the sentence.

12) ➡ D
Concept(s) Tested: Syntax
Choice (D) is correct because it effectively formats the sentence using the structure "So powerful is x that y occurs." The other choices do not properly arrange the subject and the verb to fit in with the rest of the sentence.

13) ➡ B
Concept(s) Tested: Modifier placement
Choice (B) is correct; the underlined portion introduces a participial phrase, so it must begin with a participle ("Written" in this case), and provide information that can clearly refer to the sentence's subject, the book *Main Street*. Other choices are incorrect because they refer to "Sinclair Lewis," who is NOT the subject of the sentence, resulting in dangling modifiers/

phrases.

14) ➡ C
Concept(s) Tested: Transition words
Choice (C) is correct because the second sentence qualifies information in the first sentence: all mammals have some body hair; some "lose this hair shortly after birth." The transition word "However" effectively conveys this exception.

15) ➡ B
Concept(s) Tested: Parallel structure
Choice (B) is correct because the underlined portion must maintain the same "past-tense verb + other information" word pattern as the other listed activities, and only (B) contains the aforementioned word pattern— "past-tense verb (patented) + other information (an improved method for producing light bulbs)."

Grammar Skills Practice 39

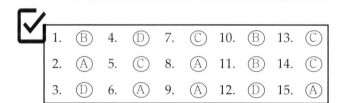

1.	Ⓑ	4.	Ⓓ	7.	Ⓒ	10.	Ⓑ	13.	Ⓒ
2.	Ⓐ	5.	Ⓒ	8.	Ⓐ	11.	Ⓑ	14.	Ⓒ
3.	Ⓓ	6.	Ⓐ	9.	Ⓐ	12.	Ⓓ	15.	Ⓐ

1) ➡ B
Concept(s) Tested: Relative clauses
Choice (B) is correct; the underlined portion introduces a relative clause that refers to a place, "gravel beds," and "where" effectively refers to "gravel beds" while introducing the relative clause, making (B) correct.

2) ➡ A
Concept(s) Tested: Precision
Choice (A) is correct because "to surpass" is to exceed or *outdo*, and it makes sense to say that English "is not expected to *outdo* Mandarin as the most spoken language."

3) ➡ D
Concept(s) Tested: Concision
Choice (D) is correct because it most clearly and concisely conveys information. All other choices contain redundancies or unnecessary wordiness, making them incorrect.

4) ➡ D
Concept(s) Tested: Dependent clauses
Choice (D) correctly punctuates the end of the dependent clause, "After the Associated Press... fishing companies," which must be separated by a comma from the main sentence ("it won the Pulitzer...") in order to avoid confusion. Choice (B) is incorrect because a semi-colon can only separate independent clauses (complete ideas.) Choice (C) creates a sentence fragment.

5) ➡ C
Concept(s) Tested: Verb tense, mood, and voice/ parallel structure
Choice (C) is correct because the underlined verb must maintain the same tense and aspect as the verb "kills" that appears earlier in the sentence, because both "kills" and "forces" describe a common subject, "the heat."

6) ➡ A
Concept(s) Tested: Relative clauses
Choice (A) is correct because the underlined portion introduces a relative clause that refers to "Charon" while showing possession over "responsibility," so the possessive relative pronoun "whose" is the most effective choice.

7) ➡ C
Concept(s) Tested: Combining sentences
Choice (C) is correct because the sentences are defining similar, but not identical terms ("domestication" versus "taming"), so the conjunction "whereas" serves to emphasize the differences between the two definitions.

8) ➡ A
Concept(s) Tested:
Choice (A) is correct because when contrasting information is introduced by the word "not," a comma must come before "not" to separate the contrast from the rest of the sentence.

9) ➡ A
Concept(s) Tested: Combining sentences
Choice (A) is correct because it clearly and concisely restructures the sentences by turning the first sentence into an appositive phrase. Other choices are incorrect because they contain convoluted phrasing.

10) ➡ B
Concept(s) Tested: Providing evidence
Choice (B) is correct because it provides an example of Caligula's cruelty and pettiness. Degrading politicians simply because one does not trust them is both cruel and petty.

11) ➡ B
Concept(s) Tested: Adverbs
Choice (B) is correct because it is the only choice that offers an adverb to modify the verb "tells." Choices (A), (C), and (D) offer adjectives, which cannot describe an action.

12) ➡ D
Concept(s) Tested: Commonly confused words
Choice (D) is correct because the word "averse" is an adjective that means "having a strong feeling of opposition." It would make sense to say that humans evolved the feeling of disgust so that we would have a strong feeling of opposition to substances that could spread disease.

13) ➡ C
Concept(s) Tested: Modifiers
Choice (C) is correct because it correctly uses an adverb to modify verb phrase "are becoming." Only (C) contains the an adverb ("increasingly") making it the correct choice.

14) ➡ C
Concept(s) Tested: Parallel structure
Choice (C) is correct because the underlined portion must maintain the "base verb + modifier + other information" word pattern established by the phrase "look ungainly on land," which only (C) does: "base verb (be) + modifier (unable) + other (to fly)."

15) ➡ A
Concept(s) Tested: Within-sentence punctuation
Choice (A) is correct because the modifiers in the underlined portion function as cumulative adjectives (adjectives not separated by commas that must be in a particular order to make sense), and because *Interchange* should not be separated by commas because it is essential to the sentence.

Grammar Skills Practice 40

☑
1.	Ⓑ	4.	Ⓑ	7.	Ⓓ	10.	Ⓑ	13.	Ⓒ
2.	Ⓓ	5.	Ⓐ	8.	Ⓒ	11.	Ⓓ	14.	Ⓑ
3.	Ⓐ	6.	Ⓒ	9.	Ⓐ	12.	Ⓐ	15.	Ⓑ

1) ➡ B
Concept(s) Tested: Subordinate conjunction use

Choice (B) is correct because the two sentences contain contrasting information: plastics have been used since ancient times; synthetic plastics are modern inventions. The use of "Though" in choice (B) effectively conveys this contrast.

2) ➡ D
Concept(s) Tested: Conventional expressions
Choice (D) is correct because "at the age of" is an English idiom used when describing a person's age when something occurred in their lives. Choice (B) is incorrect because it creates a run-on sentence, and choices (A) and (C) are incorrect because they contain awkward or unclear phrasing.

3) ➡ A
Concept(s) Tested: Commonly confused words
Choice (A) is correct because "errant" means "straying from the proper course." Although it often refers to a person's behavior, it also makes sense to describe a bad golf shot as "errant."

4) ➡ B
Concept(s) Tested: Participial phrases
Choice (B) is correct because the participial phrase, "portraying Kate…in *King Lear*" refers to "American actress Ruby Dee." When additional information about a subject comes at the end of a sentence, placing it in a participial phrase and separating the phrase from the rest of the sentence with a comma is generally appropriate.

5) ➡ A
Concept(s) Tested: Combining sentences
Choice (A) is correct it clearly and concisely restructures the sentences by turning the first sentence into an appositive phrase that describes the sentence's subject, "James Watt." Other choices are incorrect because they contain convoluted phrasing or unnecessary wordiness.

6) ➡ C
Concept(s) Tested: Commonly confused words
Choice (C) is correct because the underlined portion serves as the sentence's main verb, and only the phrase "may be" can serve as a main verb. Choice (A) is incorrect because "maybe" is an adverb, choice (B) is incorrect because a bare infinitive cannot act as a main verb, and choice (D) is incorrect because a participle ("being") cannot act as a main verb.

7) ➡ D
Concept(s) Tested: Logical comparison/parallel structure
Choice (D) is correct because the underlined portion must agree with the "The + comparative

adjective + noun phrase" word pattern established by "The more precise a doctor's instructions," and only (D) follows this pattern: "The + comparative adjective (easier) + noun phrase (they are...to follow").

8) ➡ C
Concept(s) Tested: Within-sentence punctuation
Choice (C) is correct because the sentence contains two independent clauses (ideas that could act as complete sentences) that present closely related information, and a semicolon effectively separates two such clauses containing related ideas.

9) ➡ A
Concept(s) Tested: Relative phrases
Choice (A) is correct because it effectively introduces a relative clause that refers to the "two volumes" mentioned previously in the sentence. Other choices do not effectively clarify the relationship between "two volumes" and the phrase at the end of the sentence.

10) ➡ B
Concept(s) Tested: Precision
Choice (B) is correct; a "nearly imperceptible fissure" is one that is difficult to see or detect, which makes sense in the sentence because the fissure is located in a "smooth rock face."

11) ➡ D
Concept(s) Tested: Parallel structure
Choice (D) is correct because the underlined portion must maintain the word pattern established by the previously listed professions. Thus, it maintains parallel structure to say that Baker was a "librarian, literary consultant, and author," and to place a description of what she wrote in a participial phrase at the end of the sentence.

12) ➡ A
Concept(s) Tested: Concision/tone
Choice (A) is correct because it is the clearest and most concise phrasing of the underlined portion. Choice (B) is incorrect because its informal tone (primarily in the use of the word "things") does not match the academic tone of the rest of the sentence. Choices (C) and (D) are incorrect because "external" and "environmental" are synonyms, so these choices contain redundancies.

13) ➡ C
Concept(s) Tested: Providing evidence
Choice (C) is correct because it provides statistical evidence confirming the claim in the first sentence. Other choices are incorrect because they stray from the topic established by the first sentence: the decline of the black rhino population.

14) ➡ B
Concept(s) Tested: Rhetorical style
Choice (B) is correct because it anthropomorphizes (attributes human qualities) to the tree by describing its branches as "grasping," which implies that the branches resemble hands.

15) ➡ B
Concept(s) Tested: Combining sentences
Choice (B) is correct because the underlined portion effectively turns the second sentence into a relative clause that refers to "a rock 'n roll soundtrack." Other choices contain improper punctuation or create run-on sentences.

Chapter 3 : Answers & Explanations

☑ 1. Ⓒ 2. Ⓑ 3. Ⓓ 4. Ⓒ 5. Ⓓ

1) ➡ C
Concept(s) Tested: Pronoun person and number/ commonly confused words
Choice (C) is correct; the underlined pronoun refers to the singular noun "a laundry soap called 'Rinso'" and shows possession over "slogans," making the third-person singular possessive pronoun "its" correct.

2) ➡ B
Concept(s) Tested: Logical comparison
Choice (B) is correct because the sentence containing the underlined portion compares the "fine particles" in Rinso to the particles "used in other soaps." Only (B) successfully compares the particles in Rinso to the particles in other soaps, making it the most appropriate choice.

3) ➡ D
Concept(s) Tested: Pronoun person and number
Choice (D) is correct because the underlined pronoun refers to the plural noun phrase "the sodium silicate particles," making the third-person plural pronoun "they" correct.

4) ➡ C
Concept(s) Tested: Logical sequence
Choice (C) is correct; much of paragraph 2 is spent explaining the reasoning behind Rinso's slogan. The added sentence sums and comments on this discussion, and should therefore come near the end of the explanation. It makes sense to place it before sentence 5, which elaborates on the marketers' strategy.

5) ➡ D
Concept(s) Tested: Providing evidence
Choice (D) is correct; the previous paragraph explains that many slogans (including Rinso's) are meant to connect a product to a desirable image or situation. Choice (D) provides information that best supports the claims made in the previous paragraph.

☑ 1. Ⓒ 2. Ⓓ 3. Ⓒ 4. Ⓒ 5. Ⓐ

1) ➡ C
Concept(s) Tested: Parallel structure/within-sentence punctuation
Choice (C) is correct because the first part of the underlined portion must maintain the same "singular noun + prepositional phrase" word pattern as the previously listed descriptions, which (C) does: "singular noun (the raven) + prepositional phrase (for its raspy caw)." Moreover, the underlined portion connects a dependent clause ("While the nightingale... raspy caws") to an independent clause ("the woodpecker's...pecking"), and a comma is the appropriate punctuation for connecting a dependent to an independent clause.

2) ➡ D
Concept(s) Tested: Parallel structure
Choice (D) is correct; the underlined portion must maintain the same word pattern as the previously listed nouns. (D) is correct because it maintains parallel structure and is the most concise choice.

3) ➡ C
Concept(s) Tested: Providing evidence
Choice (C) is correct because the conjunction "but" indicates contrast, and the underlined portion effectively contrasts the claim that "woodpeckers are noisy and destructive" by introducing ways that woodpeckers help the environment.

4) ➡ C
Concept(s) Tested: Improving focus
Choice (C) is correct; the first sentence of the paragraph establishes its topic: woodpecker's "protective physical features." Although the added sentence discusses woodpecker adaptations, it strays from the topic of "physical features" by discussing woodpecker behavior rather than anatomy.

5) ➡ A
Concept(s) Tested: Concision
Choice (A) is correct because it is the clearest and most concise version of the underlined portion.

Choices (B) and (C) are unnecessarily wordy, and choice (D) includes an incomplete and unclear comparison.

1) ➡ C
Concept(s) Tested: Transition words
Choice (C) is correct; the sentences that precede the underlined portion claim that most workers dream of vacations, while the sentence that contains the underlined portion points out that planning a vacation requires much work. Thus, the underlined portion must transition between the idea of a relaxing vacation and the reality that vacations require "work." The phrase "In reality" most effectively provides this transition.

2) ➡ B
Concept(s) Tested: Improving focus
Choice (B) is correct because the first and second sentences of paragraph 2 essentially say the same thing, making the second sentence redundant and therefore unnecessary.

3) ➡ C
Concept(s) Tested: Items in a list/parallel structure
Choice (C) is correct because the underlined portion is the last item in a list, so it must be separated from the other listed elements using a comma followed by the conjunction "and."

4) ➡ A
Concept(s) Tested: Providing evidence
Choice (A) is correct; the underlined portion is followed by a number of seemingly minor situations that can potentially ruin a vacation. Thus, it makes sense to introduce the list of situations by describing them as "minor oversights," making (A) the most effective choice. Although (B) conveys the same meaning as (A), it is incorrect because it does not match the structure of the sentence; one cannot say "It is little things...can make vacations difficult."

5) ➡ D
Concept(s) Tested: Within-sentence punctuation
Choice (D) is correct because a colon effectively separates a piece of information from a definition of or elaboration on that information. In the sentence, the phrase "at home" provides a definition of "where we are most comfortable."

1) ➡ A
Concept(s) Tested: Providing evidence
Choice (A) is correct; the sentence containing the underlined portion mentions Tubman's "greatest feat of liberation," and freeing "hundreds of slaves in a single night" is the most significant accomplishment mentioned in the answer choices, so (A) is the most logical choice.

2) ➡ D
Concept(s) Tested: Subordinate conjunction use
Choice (D) is correct because the use of the conjunction "although" shows that Tubman's unfamiliarity with the land was countered by the fact that "she was provided with excellent informants." Other choices fail to convey the relationship between the underlined portion and the information that follows it.

3) ➡ B
Concept(s) Tested: Modifiers
Choice (B) is correct; when two terms ("disease" and "ridden" in this case) work together to modify a single noun, they must be connected with a hyphen to show that they are acting as a single adjective. Thus, "disease-ridden" is correct because the two terms act as a single word that modifies "marshes."

4) ➡ D
Concept(s) Tested: Combining sentences
Choice (D) is correct because it effectively rephrases the first underlined sentence as a participial phrase that modifies "they" ("Union forces"). Other choices contain convoluted phrasing, which makes the connections between ideas unnecessarily confusing.

5) ➡ A
Concept(s) Tested: Improving focus
Choice (A) is correct because it effectively concludes the passage by briefly elaborating on one long-term benefit of the raid for the Union forces.

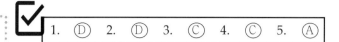

✓ 1. Ⓓ 2. Ⓒ 3. Ⓒ 4. Ⓑ 5. Ⓐ

1) ➡️ D

Concept(s) Tested: Combining sentences
Choice (D) is correct because it is the clearest and most concise version of the underlined portion. Unlike the other choices, (D) effectively conveys the relationship between the subject, verb, and direct object.

2) ➡️ D

Concept(s) Tested: Pronoun person and number
Choice (D) is correct because the underlined pronoun refers to the singular noun "an individual," making the third-person singular possessive pronouns "his or her" appropriate.

3) ➡️ C

Concept(s) Tested: Improving focus
Choice (C) is correct; the second paragraph discusses the relationship between humors and personality, so including information on Chinese astrology is unnecessary because it distracts from the paragraph's main topic.

4) ➡️ C

Concept(s) Tested: Verb tense, mood, and voice/parallel structure
Choice (C) is correct because the verbs in the underlined portion must maintain the tense established by other verbs in the paragraph. By looking at nearby verbs ("played," "had"), we can determine that the underlined verbs must be in the past tense. Moreover, we must ensure that the underlined verbs agree with the nouns to which they refer; the first verb in the underlined portion refers to the singular noun "blood," making the third-person singular verb form "was" appropriate, and the second underlined verb refers to "those," making the verb form "had" appropriate.

5) ➡️ A

Concept(s) Tested: Providing evidence
Choice (A) is correct because the paragraph claims that humor build-ups caused "physical and mental illnesses," and choice (A) elaborates on this idea by clarifying that ancient physicians had methods of curing these "imbalances"—that is, the illnesses mentioned previously.

1) ➡️ D

Concept(s) Tested: Providing evidence
Choice (D) is correct because the passage is about a travel guide publishing company, and only (D) establishes this in the passage's topic sentence.

2) ➡️ C

Concept(s) Tested: Sentence fragments
Choice (C) is correct because it forms a clear and complete sentence containing both a subject and a verb. All other choices form sentence fragments: choices (A) and (B) are incorrect because a complete clause must precede a colon, and (D) is incorrect because it lacks a verb.

3) ➡️ C

Concept(s) Tested: Within-sentence punctuation
Choice (C) is correct because all of the information in the underlined portion is essential to the meaning of the sentence, so it should not be separated from the rest of the sentence with any punctuation. Other choices are incorrect because they over-punctuate.

4) ➡️ B

Concept(s) Tested: Precision
Choice (B) is correct because "different" means "distinct, or separate," and it makes sense to say that Let's Go "was publishing a dozen or more distinct titles every year." Other choices are similar in meaning, but they do not fit the context of the sentence, as they cannot effectively be applied to the publication of books.

5) ➡️ A

Concept(s) Tested: Logical sequence
Choice (A) is correct because mention of Koppell graduating from Harvard should come before the claim that "students continued the legacy" established by Koppell, since a legacy must come after the departure of the person who established said legacy. Thus, sentence 2 must come before sentence 1.

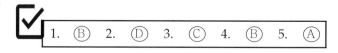

✓ 1. Ⓑ 2. Ⓓ 3. Ⓒ 4. Ⓑ 5. Ⓐ

ANSWER KEY – CHAPTER 3

1) ➡ B

Concept(s) Tested: Style and tone

Choice (B) is correct because the subject of the previous two sentences is the pronoun "they," and only (B) maintains this pattern by making the subject of the sentence containing the underlined portion "they" as well.

2) ➡ D

Concept(s) Tested: Improving focus

Choice (D) is correct; the main topic of paragraphs 2 and 3 is the reuse of unwanted items for art, so the sentence should be kept because it effectively provides a transition between paragraph 1 and the rest of the passage.

3) ➡ C

Concept(s) Tested: Within-sentence punctuation/ sentence boundaries

Choice (C) is correct; the two sentences contain a contrast: the suitcase pillars appear unstable (they "rest precariously") and they "appear to hold up the roof," implying that they provide structural stability. Only "yet" in choice (C) conveys this contrast, making it correct.

4) ➡ B

Concept(s) Tested: Commonly confused words

Choice (B) is correct; although all the choices are close to each other in terms of spelling, only the verb "to lose," meaning "to misplace," fits the context of the sentence.

5) ➡ A

Concept(s) Tested: Possessive nouns

Choice (A) is correct because the sentence refers to "items" in general, so the plural form of the noun is appropriate here. Moreover, the "items" do not show possession in this sentence, so no apostrophe is necessary.

Short Passage 8

✔ 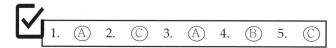 1. Ⓐ 2. Ⓒ 3. Ⓐ 4. Ⓑ 5. Ⓒ

1) ➡ A

Concept(s) Tested: Logical comparisons

Choice (A) is correct; the sentence containing the underlined portion compares the function of lysosomes to the function of a human's digestive organs ("the liver, kidneys, and intestines). Because "the function" is singular, it can effectively be replaced by the singular pronoun "that" in the underlined portion.

2) ➡ C

Concept(s) Tested: Concision

Choice (C) is correct because it is the clearest and most concise version of the underlined portion. Choices (A) and (B) are incorrect because they contain redundancies: "small" and "minute" are synonyms. Choice (D) is incorrect because it does not contain a verb, making the sentence that contains the underlined portion a sentence fragment.

3) ➡ A

Concept(s) Tested: Improving focus

Choice (A) is correct; the sentence prior to number 3 claims that a lysosome's crucial role is "waste removal," and the added sentence elaborates on this crucial role, making it an effective addition to the passage.

4) ➡ B

Concept(s) Tested: Noun agreement

Choice (B) is correct because the underlined portion refers to the plural noun phrase "obsolete parts of the cell," making the plural noun "the materials" appropriate. Choice (A), "they," is incorrect because it is ambiguous—it is unclear whether "they" refers to "obsolete parts" or "lysosomes."

5) ➡ C

Concept(s) Tested: Transition words

Choice (C) is correct because it effectively connects the circumstance of a cell becoming damaged (mentioned in the previous sentence) to the information in the sentence that contains the underlined portion.

Short Passage 9

✔ 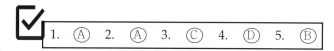 1. Ⓐ 2. Ⓐ 3. Ⓒ 4. Ⓓ 5. Ⓑ

1) ➡ A

Concept(s) Tested: Concision

Choice (A) is correct because it is the clearest and most concise version of the underlined portion. Choices (B) and (D) are incorrect because they contain redundancies: "independent thinking" and "autonomous thinking" are essentially the same. Choice (C) is incorrect because an adverb ("independently" in this case) cannot modify a noun (the gerund "thinking").

2) ➤ A

Concept(s) Tested: Improving focus

Choice (A) is correct; the first and second sentences contain contrasting information: Americans "pride themselves on their independent thinking," yet people "regularly conform to the opinions" of others. Only (A) acknowledges this contrast, making it the most appropriate choice.

3) ➤ C

Concept(s) Tested: Combining sentences

Choice (C) is correct because the two sentences provide information about Asch's experiment, but the relationship between the facts is self-evident and requires no transition words or conjunctions for clarification. Thus, a semicolon effectively joins the two sentences. Choice (A) is incorrect because it contains convoluted phrasing, (B) omits information, and (D) forms a run-on sentence.

4) ➤ D

Concept(s) Tested: Precision

Choice (D) is correct; the paragraph clarifies that only one study participant was not given instructions by Asch. Because the study participant did not have instructions, he or she can be described as unaware, or unwitting, making (D) correct. Although "clueless" has approximately the same meaning, it is often used as a pejorative term, so it does not fit the tone of the passage.

5) ➤ B

Concept(s) Tested: Providing evidence

Choice (B) is correct because it states that "scholars cast doubt" on Asch's experiments, and casting doubt is a form of criticism.

Short Passage 10

☑ 1. Ⓑ 2. Ⓓ 3. Ⓐ 4. Ⓓ 5. Ⓓ

1) ➤ B

Concept(s) Tested: Providing evidence

Choice (B) is correct because the sentence after the underlined portion describes velvet as "precious and costly," so it makes sense to introduce the passage by claiming that velvet is "associated with wealth and elegance." Because the passage

discusses both velvet's production and its history, choices (C) and (D) are each too narrowly focused to introduce the passage as a whole. Choice (A) does not as clearly link to the claim that velvet is "precious and costly," making (B) the best choice.

2) ➤ D

Concept(s) Tested: Within-sentence punctuation/ restrictive clauses

Choice (D) is correct because the phrase "such as polyester and nylon" is a restrictive clause—it limits the meaning of the noun phrase "synthetic materials" that precedes it—so no comma is necessary between "materials" and "such." In other words, "such as polyester and nylon" is necessary to the coherence of the sentence, so it should not be separated by a comma.

3) ➤ A

Concept(s) Tested: Syntax

Choice (A) is correct because it clearly names the sentence's subject, "The loops," and explains what is done to them (they "are sliced apart"). Other choices either include an ambiguous subject (as in (B) and (C)) or lack a main verb (as in (D)).

4) ➤ D

Concept(s) Tested: Dangling modifier

Choice (D) is correct; the phrase that precedes the underlined portion, "gradually making...Silk Road," must refer to "velvet." Only (D) places "velvet" next to the modifying phrase.

5) ➤ D

Concept(s) Tested: Transition words

Choice (D) is correct because the establishment of "several Italian cities" that specialize in producing velvet is a consequence of velvet being "embraced by the elite classes and church leaders" of Europe, so "Consequently" provides an effective transition.

Short Passage 11

☑ 1. Ⓒ 2. Ⓒ 3. Ⓑ 4. Ⓓ 5. Ⓓ

1) ➤ C

Concept(s) Tested: Participial phrases

Choice (C) is correct because it clearly and concisely introduces a participial phrase that modifies "vestibular system." Choice (A) is incorrect because it conveys the same meaning as (C), but is less concise. Choice (B) is incorrect because the prepositional phrase "within the inner ear" should not be separated from the rest of the sentence using commas. Choice (D) is incorrect because it is unnecessarily wordy.

2) ➡ C
Concept(s) Tested: Improving focus
Choice (C) is correct because it links the discussion of "chambers" in paragraph 1 to the main topic of paragraph 2—the structure of the vestibular system—so it provides the most effective transition.

3) ➡ B
Concept(s) Tested: Subject-verb agreement/conventional expressions
Choice (B) is correct; the underlined verb refers to and must agree with the singular subject, "Each of the three circular tubes," in person and number, so the third-person singular verb form "specializes" is correct. Moreover, if someone or something has a specific purpose, they are said to "specialize in" something, so (B) contains the correct verb form and forms an appropriate idiom.

4) ➡ D
Concept(s) Tested: Combining sentences
Choice (D) is correct because a colon effectively separates a piece of information from a definition of or elaboration on that information. In the sentence, the list "up-and-down, side-to-side, or tilted" is an elaboration on the "directional information" mentioned earlier in the sentence.

5) ➡ D
Concept(s) Tested: Subject-verb agreement/verb tense, mood, and voice
Choice (D) is correct because the underlined verb refers to and must agree with the plural noun phrase "muscle groups." Moreover, it must maintain the present tense established by previous verbs in the sentence ("interact" and "control"), so the third-person plural, present-tense verb form "allow" is correct.

Short Passage 12

✓ 1. Ⓑ 2. Ⓐ 3. Ⓑ 4. Ⓒ 5. Ⓑ

1) ➡ B
Concept(s) Tested: Noun agreement/parallel structure
Choice (B) is correct; in the underlined portion, "a wildlife biologist" must be singular in order to agree with the preceding pronouns that refers to it, "he or she." Moreover, the last word of the underlined portion must be "learning" in order to maintain parallel structure with "improving," making (B) the appropriate choice.

2) ➡ A
Concept(s) Tested: Improving focus
Choice (A) is correct because it provides a concise and accurate summary of the wildlife biologist job descriptions mentioned, so it appropriately concludes the paragraph.

3) ➡ B
Concept(s) Tested: Items in a list
Choice (B) is correct because the final element in a list must be separated from the other listed elements with a comma followed by the conjunction "and" or "or."

4) ➡ C
Concept(s) Tested: Conventional expressions
Choice (C) is correct because "to take inventory" of something is to record how many of something there are, which makes sense in the context of the sentence. Choices (B) and (C) convey approximately the same meaning, but (C) is incorrect because "to ascertain inventory" is not an accepted English idiom. Choice (D) is incorrect because the underlined portion must contain the main verb of the sentence, and (D) lacks a proper verb form— "taking" is a participle as it is used in (D).

5) ➡ B
Concept(s) Tested: Providing evidence
Choice (B) is correct; "hiking, boating, or even flying in helicopters" are all exciting and possibly dangerous activities, so a contrast to these would be safe or mundane activities, and "analyzing data and writing reports" is safe and (to most people) mundane.

Short Passage 13

✓ 1. Ⓒ 2. Ⓑ 3. Ⓓ 4. Ⓒ 5. Ⓑ

1) ➡ C
Concept(s) Tested: Precision
Choice (C) is correct because a "prerequisite" is a necessity or requirement, and it makes sense to say, "Factories required machinery (*a requirement for industrial productivity*)..."

2) ➡ B

Concept(s) Tested: Providing evidence
Choice (B) is correct because the added sentence clarifies that Darby "knew that malted grains were roasted using coke" because he worked as "an apprentice at a malt mill," so the added sentence provides relevant information.

3) ➡ D

Concept(s) Tested: Conventional expressions
Choice (D) is correct because the infinitive ("to + base form of verb") is appropriate when claiming that someone "was the first to do" something, so the infinitive "to produce" is correct.

4) ➡ C

Concept(s) Tested: Within-sentence punctuation
Choice (C) is correct because a short prepositional phase ("in 1779" in this case) does not generally need to be separated from the rest of a sentence using any form of punctuation. Other choices are incorrect because they over-punctuate the underlined portion.

5) ➡ B

Concept(s) Tested: Sentence boundaries
Choice (B) is correct because a period is the most straightforward way to separate the two clauses from each other. Choices (A) and (C) create run-on sentences, and (D) uses an inappropriate pronoun to refer to the location "England."

Short Passage 14

☑ 1. Ⓒ 2. Ⓑ 3. Ⓒ 4. Ⓓ 5. Ⓑ

1) ➡ C

Concept(s) Tested: Style and tone
Choice (C) is correct because the passage maintains a neutral, academic tone throughout, which (C) effectively maintains. Choice (A) is too casual and colloquial, choice (B) is too condescending, and choice (D) is too flowery for the passage's academic tone.

2) ➡ B

Concept(s) Tested: Within-sentence punctuation
Choice (B) is correct; the sentence containing the underlined portion consists of a dependent clause ("When waves...the shore") and an independent clause ("the energy...up"). When a dependent clause comes before an independent clause, a comma must separate the two clauses, making (B) correct.

3) ➡ C

Concept(s) Tested: Improving focus/ logical sequence
Choice (C) is correct because the added sentence concludes the cycle in which waves move up and down the shore. Because sentence 3 is the last sentence that discusses this cycle, the added sentence should come after sentence 3 to clearly conclude the explanation.

4) ➡ D

Concept(s) Tested: Verb tense, mood, and voice
Choice (D) is correct because the sentence containing the underlined portion describes a general process, and general processes are usually described using the simple present tense. Moreover, the previous sentence takes the simple present tense (as evidenced by the verb "are"), so the present-tense verb form "occur" is correct.

5) ➡ B

Choice (B) is correct because it relates to the previous sentence without introducing a new topic of discussion, thus providing a suitable conclusion to the passage. Choices (A) and (D) are incorrect because they introduce a new topic, and conclusions should wrap up previous discussions, not introduce new ones. Choice (C) is incorrect because it breaks from the academic tone of the passage to introduce a personal anecdote.

Short Passage 15

☑ 1. Ⓓ 2. Ⓓ 3. Ⓓ 4. Ⓐ 5. Ⓓ

1) ➡ D

Concept(s) Tested: Providing evidence
Choice (D) is correct because the underlined portion provides one of only two examples of Pig Latin in the passage, making it a constructive addition to the paragraph.

2) ➡ D

Concept(s) Tested: Improving focus
Choice (D) is correct because the main similarity between the preceding example and the following one is that they add sounds, making (D) the only possible transition.

3) ➡ D

Concept(s) Tested: Commonly confused words
Choice (D) is correct because "additions" are extras or add-ons, which makes sense in the context of the paragraph, as Kinabayo involves

adding sounds to Cebuano words.

4) 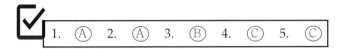 A
Concept(s) Tested: Improving focus
Choice (A) is correct; the coded languages described in paragraphs 1 and 2 were meant to be spoken playfully as language games, whereas the coded language described in paragraph 3 is designed for communication despite social barriers. Choice (A) effectively conveys this contrast.

5) 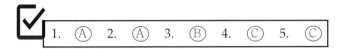 D
Concept(s) Tested: Parallel structure
Choice (D) is correct because the phrases "to be housebound" and "to have bound feet" must maintain the same "infinitive verb + noun" word pattern, which only (D) does.

Short Passage 16

✓ 1. Ⓐ 2. Ⓐ 3. Ⓑ 4. Ⓒ 5. Ⓒ

1) 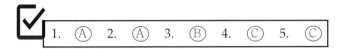 A
Concept(s) Tested: Providing evidence
Choice (A) is correct because data entry is generally a highly repetitive task, making it the most appropriate example.

2) 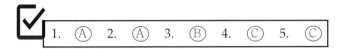 A
Concept(s) Tested: Logical comparison
Choice (A) is correct because it provides the clearest comparison between "people who listened to music" while working and "people who did not" listen to music while working.

3) 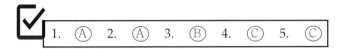 B
Concept(s) Tested:
Choice (B) is correct because it is the only choice that mentions what ("the music" in this case) "may not block every sound," making it the clearest and most comprehensive choice.

4) 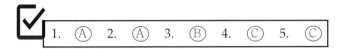 C
Concept(s) Tested: Precision/style and tone
Choice (C) is correct because it maintains the academic tone of the rest of the passage. Choices (A) and (D) do not fit the context of the sentence, as one cannot "get" or "fix" concentration. Choice (B) is incorrect because it is too colloquial, so it breaks the passage's tone to say that concentration is "bumped up."

5) 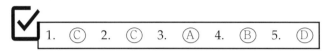 C
Concept(s) Tested: Logical sequence
Choice (C) is correct because paragraph 1 discusses the positive effects of listening to music during repetitive work, so it makes sense for the second paragraph to discuss the effects of listening to music during "cognitively taxing work." Thus, paragraph 4 includes an effective transition from paragraph 1, and should therefore be placed before paragraph 2.

Short Passage 17

✓ 1. Ⓒ 2. Ⓒ 3. Ⓐ 4. Ⓑ 5. Ⓓ

1) 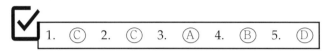 C
Concept(s) Tested: Providing evidence
Choice (C) is correct because it provides a clear and effective description of Neanderthals. Choices (A) and (D) are incorrect because they do not provide as much information as (C), and (B) is incorrect because it is unnecessarily wordy.

2) 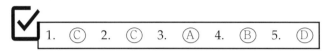 C
Concept(s) Tested: Providing evidence
Choice (C) is correct because it provides useful information: the valley is named after Neander even though he did not own it. Without the added portion, the reader would have difficulty discerning the exact nature of Neander's relationship to the valley he frequently visited.

3) 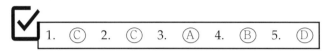 A
Concept(s) Tested: Precision
Choice (A) is correct because "to inspire" is to encourage or influence, especially artistically, and it makes sense to say, "the valley had influenced Neander to write dozens of" hymns.

4) 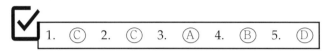 B
Concept(s) Tested: Providing evidence
Choice (B) is correct; the underlined portion must support the claim that Neander's "goal was to make church music accessible to common people." Creating songs "that people could easily memorize" is one way of making music accessible, so (B) is the most appropriate choice.

5) 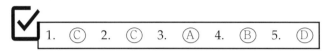 D
Concept(s) Tested: Possessive nouns/pronoun clarity
Choice (D) is correct because the sentence references both Neander and Bach, so the underlined portion must specify which of the two

men had one of his hymns adapted into a cantata. Since Bach wrote the cantata, we can infer that Neander wrote the hymn on which it was based, making "Neander's" the correct choice.

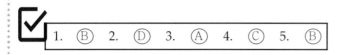

Short Passage 18

☑ 1. Ⓑ 2. Ⓓ 3. Ⓐ 4. Ⓒ 5. Ⓑ

1) ➡ B
Concept(s) Tested: Providing evidence
Choice (B) is correct because the underlined portion should provide an example of misbehavior in children's literature, which the example of stealing "a handful of helium balloons" provides.

2) ➡ D
Concept(s) Tested: Within-sentence punctuation
Choice (D) is correct because all of the information in the underlined portion is essential to the meaning of the sentence, so it should not be separated from the rest of the sentence with any punctuation. Other choices are incorrect because they over-punctuate.

3) ➡ A
Concept(s) Tested: Improving focus
Choice (A) is correct; the sentence that comes after number 3 rephrases and elaborates on the correct choice to number 3, as indicated by the phrase "Simply put." Because the sentence after number 3 discusses irony, it makes sense that it elaborates on the "dramatic irony" mentioned in choice (A).

4) ➡ C
Concept(s) Tested: Transition words
Choice (C) is correct because the information in the sentence that contains the underlined portion elaborates on the information in the previous sentence, and the transition word "moreover" effectively shows that one idea elaborates on another.

5) ➡ B
Concept(s) Tested: Modifiers/conciseness
Choice (B) is correct because it is the clearest and most concise version of the underlined portion. Choices (A) and (D) are unnecessarily wordy, and (C) is redundant ("persistent" and "relentless" mean essentially the same thing in the context of the sentence).

Short Passage 19

☑ 1. Ⓑ 2. Ⓒ 3. Ⓓ 4. Ⓐ 5. Ⓒ

1) ➡ B
Concept(s) Tested: Within-sentence punctuation
Choice (B) is correct because all of the information in the underlined portion is essential to the meaning of the sentence, so it should not be separated from the rest of the sentence with any punctuation. Choices (A) and (C) are incorrect because they over-punctuate, and (D) is incorrect because "and" changes the meaning of the sentence.

2) ➡ C
Concept(s) Tested: Precision/concision
Choice (C) is correct because "to advocate" is to publicly speak in support of a certain cause, which makes sense in the context of the sentence. Choice (D), "speak," is not correct because it does not provide as specific a description as does "advocate." Choices (A) and (B) are incorrect because they are unnecessarily wordy: "to advocate" is an action, so there's no need to say that someone "does" or "engages in" it.

3) ➡ D
Concept(s) Tested: Improving focus
Choice (D) is correct because it effectively summarizes the responsibilities of social workers that are outlined in paragraph 1, and it maintains a focus on the goals of social workers, which is elaborated on in paragraph 2.

4) ➡ A
Concept(s) Tested: Logical comparison
Choice (A) is correct because the sentence containing the underlined portion compares the counseling provided by LCSWs to the counseling "provided by psychological therapists." Because "counseling" is singular, it can effectively be replaced by the singular pronoun "that" in the underlined portion.

5) ➡ C
Concept(s) Tested: Relative and restrictive clauses
Choice (C) is correct because the underlined pronoun refers to "a teenager," and the relative pronoun "who" effectively refers to a person. Although "whom" and "whose" also refer to people, they are incorrect here because the teenager is the subject of the phrase "is failing classes"; thus, the subject pronoun "who" must be

ANSWER KEY – CHAPTER 3

used

Short Passage 20

1. Ⓒ 2. Ⓒ 3. Ⓓ 4. Ⓑ 5. Ⓑ

1) ➡ C
Concept(s) Tested: Correlative conjunctions
Choice (C) is correct because when two options come after the word "neither," the word "nor" must be placed between the two options.

2) ➡ C
Concept(s) Tested: Providing evidence
Choice (C) is correct; paragraph 2 discusses the process by which matter changes states from solid to liquid and from liquid to solid. Choice (C) effectively sets up this topic of discussion, whereas other choices either are too general or fail to focus on the right topic.

3) ➡ D
Concept(s) Tested: Verb tense, mood, and voice
Choice (D) is correct because the underlined verb must maintain the present tense established by the other verb in the sentence, "lose." Thus, the present tense verb phrase "become bonded" is the most appropriate choice.

4) ➡ B
Concept(s) Tested: Sentence clarity
Choice (B) is correct because it clarifies *what* ("atoms") is "vibrating." Choices (A) and (C) are incorrect because they fail to mention "atoms," making them ambiguous. Choice (D) is incorrect because it anthropomorphizes (gives human qualities to) atoms by saying they have "a sense of calm," which does not match the otherwise academic tone of the passage.

5) ➡ B
Concept(s) Tested: Parallel structure
Choice (B) is correct because the underlined portion must maintain the "like + prepositional phrase" word pattern established by the phrase "Like in a liquid," which (B) does: "like + prepositional phrase (in a solid)."

Short Passage 21

1. Ⓑ 2. Ⓐ 3. Ⓓ 4. Ⓐ 5. Ⓑ

1) ➡ B
Concept(s) Tested: Rhetorical styles
Choice (B) is correct because the metaphor in the previous sentence equates businesses in a recession to ships in a storm, and only (C) maintains this metaphor.

2) ➡ A
Concept(s) Tested: Providing evidence
Choice (A) is correct because the first example in the sentence containing the underlined portion mentions services that ordinary individuals need during a recession. Choice (A) also lists services that are necessary during a recession while maintaining the same word pattern as the first example.

3) ➡ D
Concept(s) Tested: Conventional expressions/ concision
Choice (D) is correct because the phrase "The reason is that" is used to introduce an explanation of a previous statement. All other choices are incorrect because they are unnecessarily wordy.

4) ➡ A
Concept(s) Tested: Within-sentence punctuation
Choice (A) is correct; when a quote is used within a sentence, it must be separated from the rest of the sentence with commas, and the first letter of the quote must be capitalized.

5) ➡ B
Concept(s) Tested: Improving focus
Choice (B) is correct; it provides a reason that "repair services thrive" during a recession. Because it provides background information for sentence 3, the best place for the added sentence is after sentence 2.

Short Passage 22

1. Ⓓ 2. Ⓑ 3. Ⓐ 4. Ⓓ 5. Ⓐ

1) ➡ D
Concept(s) Tested: Improving focus
Choice (D) is correct; paragraph 1 focuses on the plot and inspiration for the film *Embrace of the Serpent*. Although the plot involves collection of natural rubber, the process of rubber extraction is not relevant to the film's plot, so the added sentence is unnecessary.

2) ■■▶ B
Concept(s) Tested: Possessive pronouns
Choice (B) is correct because the underlined pronoun refers to "the diaries of two white scholars"; in other words, "the scholars' diaries." Thus, a plural possessive pronoun is appropriate at the underlined portion, making "theirs" the appropriate choice.

3) ■■▶ A
Concept(s) Tested: Subject-verb agreement/conventional expressions
Choice (A) is correct because the underlined verb refers to and must agree with the plural noun phrase "two scholars," so the third-person plural verb form "seek" is correct. Moreover, the phrase "seek the help" is always followed by the preposition "of," making (A) correct. Although (D) conveys the same meaning, the phrase "seek help" must be followed by "from," not "of" as is the case here.

4) ■■▶ D
Concept(s) Tested: Providing evidence
Choice (D) is correct because it provides more plot details than any other choice. Choice (A) is incorrect because it discusses the film's casting and production but not its plot, and choice (B) and (C) are incorrect because they are not as broad as choice (D).

5) ■■▶ A
Concept(s) Tested: Providing evidence
Choice (A) is correct because it clarifies that the "cultural details" suggested by indigenous people "influenced Guerra's creative decisions" by inspiring him to "transform the script" entirely. Although other choices mention minor changes made to the film on account of indigenous people's suggestions, they are not as dramatic as the creative decision mentioned in (A).

✓ 1. Ⓐ 2. Ⓒ 3. Ⓓ 4. Ⓓ 5. Ⓒ

1) ■■▶ A
Concept(s) Tested: Improving focus
Choice (A) is correct because the second sentence of the passage implies that the passage's focus is "chronically lonely people," so it makes sense that the first sentence mentions "training in social perceptiveness" for those "who suffer from loneliness."

2) ■■▶ C
Concept(s) Tested: Precision
Choice (C) is correct because it makes sense to describe the responses of someone who has trouble reading social cues as "unfriendly." Choice (A) is incorrect because it is too general, and it is unclear what a "wrong response" would be. Choice (B) is incorrect because describing the response of a socially awkward person as "menacing" is too strong, as "menacing" means "threatening or ominous." Choice (D) is incorrect because a response cannot accurately be described as "unapproachable."

3) ■■▶ D
Concept(s) Tested: Pronoun person and number/precision
Choice (D) is correct; the underlined pronoun refers to the plural noun phrase "all volunteers," so the plural pronoun "They" is appropriate. Moreover, it makes more sense to say that the volunteers were "asked to identify emotions," since "to impel" is to intensely persuade someone to do something, which does not make sense regarding volunteers.

4) ■■▶ D
Concept(s) Tested: Style and tone/parallel structure
Choice (D) is correct; the underlined sentence must maintain the same structure as the previous sentence, which explains what the introduction of the experiment said and how this introduction affected volunteers' scores. Only (D) maintains this structure.

5) ■■▶ C
Concept(s) Tested: Transition words
Choice (C) is correct because the last two sentences of the passage present a contrast: lonely people are capable of interpreting social cues; lonely

people lose this ability in social situations because of anxiety. Only "However" successfully conveys this contrast, making it the correct choice.

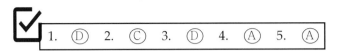

1. (D) 2. (C) 3. (D) 4. (A) 5. (A)

1) ➡ D
Concept(s) Tested: Noun agreement
Choice (D) is correct because the underlined noun, "hallways," is referred to earlier in the sentence by the plural pronoun "them," so "hallways" must also be plural.

2) ➡ C
Concept(s) Tested: Conjunction use/ parallel structure
Choice (C) is correct because the underlined portion must maintain the pattern set by "serving to...divide spaces," which is accomplished by (C), "and to link [them]."

3) ➡ D
Concept(s) Tested: Precision
Choice (D) is correct because "to develop" is to emerge, expand, and become more elaborate, and it makes sense to say, "Since their emergence and expansion, hallways have proven...influential." Although "to grow" has a similar meaning, it does not work in the context of the sentence because it is unclear whether it refers to growth in the size of hallways, or the gradual emergence and expansion of hallways.

4) ➡ A
Concept(s) Tested: Improving focus
Choice (A) is correct because the first half of paragraph 2 discusses the social impact of hallways, whereas the second half of the paragraph talks about their structural impact. Therefore, the added sentence should be kept because it introduces the topic of the second half of the paragraph: the structural functions of hallways.

5) ➡ A
Concept(s) Tested: Transition words
Choice (A) is correct because the fact that an interior hallway is often "the safest place...during extreme weather" is a consequence of their providing "interior support for the weight of a building." Thus, the transition word "Consequently" effectively describes the relationship between the two sentences.

1. (A) 2. (C) 3. (C) 4. (B) 5. (C)

1) ➡ A
Concept(s) Tested: Precision
Choice (A) is correct because an "outcropping" describes a rock formation, and it makes sense that the narrator would see a pine tree clinging to a rock formation during a backpacking trip.

2) ➡ C
Concept(s) Tested: Dangling modifiers
Choice (C) is correct because it places the noun being modified, "I," directly after the phrase that modifies it, "hesitating near the pine." Other choices contain unnecessarily convoluted and confusing phrasing.

3) ➡ C
Concept(s) Tested: Sentence clarity
Choice (C) is correct because it shows the spatial relationship between the crest, the rock plain, and the narrator. Thus, (C) is correct because it is the most concise and the most descriptive choice.

4) ➡ B
Concept(s) Tested: Improving focus
Choice (B) is correct; the narrator mentions "the others" in paragraph 1, and the added sentence contains the only mention of who "the others" are, so it provides new and relevant information.

5) ➡ C
Concept(s) Tested: Syntax/sentence clarity
Choice (C) is correct because it clearly explains the relationship between "the vast mountain canyons" and the narrator's current location. Other choices are unnecessarily wordy, and/or they use prepositions that confuse the spatial relationship described in the sentence.

SAT Writing & Language Test 1 : Answers & Explanations

1. Ⓒ	5. Ⓒ	9. Ⓒ	13. Ⓑ	17. Ⓓ	21. Ⓒ	25. Ⓓ	29. Ⓓ	33. Ⓓ	37. Ⓒ	41. Ⓑ
2. Ⓓ	6. Ⓐ	10. Ⓓ	14. Ⓒ	18. Ⓒ	22. Ⓑ	26. Ⓒ	30. Ⓑ	34. Ⓒ	38. Ⓓ	42. Ⓐ
3. Ⓓ	7. Ⓑ	11. Ⓒ	15. Ⓐ	19. Ⓐ	23. Ⓑ	27. Ⓓ	31. Ⓐ	35. Ⓑ	39. Ⓓ	43. Ⓒ
4. Ⓓ	8. Ⓐ	12. Ⓒ	16. Ⓒ	20. Ⓐ	24. Ⓓ	28. Ⓐ	32. Ⓒ	36. Ⓐ	40. Ⓐ	44. Ⓑ

1) ➡ C

Concept(s) Tested: Concision/modifiers
Choice (C) is correct because it is the clearest and most concise version of the underlined portion. All other choices convey the same idea as (C), but they are unnecessarily wordy and/or contain misplaced modifiers.

2) ➡ D

Concept(s) Tested: Transition words
Choice (D) is correct; the *reason* that a robot "appears to be making decisions" is that it can "'plan' an adaptive behavior" using algorithms. Thus, the phrase "For this reason" logically transitions from an explanation of a robot's "adaptive behavior" to its apparent decision-making abilities.

3) ➡ D

Concept(s) Tested: Improving focus
Choice (D) is correct; the sentence that precedes the underlined portion provides two "typical" branches of robotics: software and mechanical. Because the sentence containing the underlined portion discusses an atypical type of robotics— one "inspired by biological organisms"—it makes sense to use the adverb "even," which emphasizes that this type of robotics is unusual or surprising.

4) ➡ D

Concept(s) Tested: Within-sentence punctuation

Choice (D) is correct because "for example" is non-essential information, so it should be set apart by commas. Only choice (D) sets the phrase apart using commas.

5) ➡ C

Concept(s) Tested: Verb tense, mood, and voice

Choice (C) is correct because the paragraph containing the underlined portion provides hypothetical examples of tasks that *could be* completed by cockroach-like robots (they "may be able to get through rubble," and they "could also be used to diagnose..."). The future conditional verb phrase "could someday serve" maintains the hypothetical mood of the paragraph.

6) ➡ A

Concept(s) Tested: Improving focus

Choice (A) is correct because it emphasizes that "soft robotics" is still an emerging field with many practical applications. In other words, it broadens the scope of the paragraph.

7) ➡ B

Concept(s) Tested: Sentence boundaries

Choice (B) is correct because the underlined portion must contain the sentence's subject, and only (B) provides a subject ("That speed"), making it the only grammatically acceptable choice.

8) ➡ A

Concept(s) Tested: Improving focus/transition words

Choice (A) is correct because it effectively introduces the studies regarding cockroach agility discussed in the paragraph while smoothly transitioning away from the previous paragraph that discussed cockroach robots' speed.

9) ➡ C

Concept(s) Tested: Concision

Choice (C) is correct because it is the clearest and most concise version of the underlined portion. Choices (A) and (B) are incorrect because they do not provide enough information for the reader to imagine the set-up of the experiment. Choice (D) is incorrect because it is unclear what it means for a ceiling to be "accommodating."

10) ➡ D

Concept(s) Tested: Pronoun clarity

Choice (D) is correct; the sentence before the underlined portion mentions both researchers and cockroaches, so using the pronoun "they" could be confusing. We can infer that the noun in the underlined portion should be "cockroaches" because they are able to "splay their legs out to the side and scoot on their bellies."

11) ➡ C

Concept(s) Tested: Correlative conjunctions

Choice (C) is correct because any time the phrase "not only" appears in a sentence, it must be followed by "but also," and only (C) effectively incorporates "but also" into the sentence.

12) ➡ C

Concept(s) Tested: Sentence clarity/independent clauses

Choice (C) is correct; the underlined portion must include the sentence's subject. Since the sentence containing the underlined portion continues to discuss the student's announcement, it makes sense that the subject should be "the student," making (C) correct.

13) ➡ B

Concept(s) Tested: Verb tense, mood, and voice

Choice (B) is correct because it clearly situates "the school board" as the subject, which creates a concise, active-voice clause. Other choices are awkwardly worded, passive-voice clauses.

14) ➡ C

Concept(s) Tested: Interpreting graphs, charts, and diagrams

Choice (C) is correct because the chart reveals that black students still tend to be segregated at "black" high schools, and Latinos at "Latino" high schools, which supports the claim made in (C). Choice (A) and (D) represent misreadings of the chart. Choice (B) does not necessarily support the previous sentence, due to the majority of the U.S. population being white.

15) ➡ A

Concept(s) Tested: Precision

Choice (A) is correct because "to be inspired by" something is to be motivated or encouraged by it, and it makes sense to say, "The Kingston protest *was motivated/encouraged* by" an earlier black high-school protest.

16) ➡ C

Concept(s) Tested: Providing evidence

Choice (C) is correct because it provides a specific example of how "severely overcrowded" the Farmville school was. Choices (A) and (D) are incorrect because they repeat information from the paragraph rather than provide elaboration or description. Choice (B) is incorrect because it does not support the claim that the school was "severely overcrowded," so it is off-topic.

17) ➡ D

Concept(s) Tested: Sentence clarity/sentence boundaries

Choice (D) is correct; the underlined portion must provide the sentence's main verb. The main verb should come immediately after the subject of the sentence, "A quiet, studious 11th-grader," making "was" the best choice. All other choices are incorrect because they create sentence fragments.

18) ➡ C

Concept(s) Tested: Commonly confused words

Choice (C) is correct because "discreet" means "careful, or cautious," and it makes sense to describe Johns's "recruitment of friends" as *cautious*. Although "discrete" sounds the same, it means "separately," so it does not fit the context of the sentence, making (A) incorrect. Choice (B) and (D) are incorrect because they do not make sense in the context of the sentence.

19) ➡ A

Concept(s) Tested: Combining sentences/precision

Choice (A) is correct because the two sentences list the consecutive events that unfolded during the Farmville walk-out. The relationship between the facts is self-evident and requires no transition words or conjunctions for clarification. Thus, a semicolon effectively joins the two sentences, along with the precise word "interval."

20) ➡ A

Concept(s) Tested: Within-sentence punctuation

Choice (A) is correct; when a quote is used within a sentence, it must be separated from the rest of the sentence with a comma, and the first letter of the quote must be capitalized.

21) ➡ C

Concept(s) Tested: Logical sequence

Choice (C) is correct; in sentence 4, the phrase "Understanding the gravity of the situation" refers to Johns recognizing that protesting "carried real risks." Because sentence 4 refers to the added sentence, it should come right after it.

22) ➡ B

Concept(s) Tested: Relative clauses

Choice (B) is correct because the underlined pronoun introduces a relative clause that refers to "their cause," and the relative pronoun "which" effectively begins a relative clause that refers to a non-human noun ("their cause" in this case).

23) ➡ B

Concept(s) Tested: Noun agreement

Choice (B) is correct because the underlined portion provides an example of "daily life," and the only choice that can be described as a part of daily life is "experiences in the workplace." Other choices give examples of objects ("desks" and "cubicles") or locations ("the workplace"), which cannot be categorized as situations or experiences in "daily life."

24) ➡ D

Concept(s) Tested: Noun agreement/modifiers

Choice (D) is correct because the generalized plural word "managers" is best paired with the plural "employees." Moreover, if the participle "including" is preceded by a comma, it is more clearly referring to "methods" than to "employees."

25) ➡ D

Concept(s) Tested: Improving focus

Choice (D) is correct because it adds a relevant counter-argument to the discussion. Often, an argument can be strengthened if a counter-argument is introduced and then minimalized.

26) ➡ C

Concept(s) Tested: Providing evidence

Choice (C) is correct; the topic sentence of the paragraph says that monitoring employees "has the potential to benefit everyone," so the example

in the underlined portion should support this topic statement. Choice (C) provides the most effective support by claiming that data "can improve working conditions."

27) ➡ D

Concept(s) Tested: Possessive nouns

Choice (D) is correct because the underlined noun refers to "companies" in general, and should therefore be plural. Moreover, "companies" shows possession over "purposes," so the plural possessive noun "companies' " is correct.

28) ➡ A

Concept(s) Tested: Providing evidence

Choice (A) is correct because it gives an example of improved working conditions (more effective keyboards) as a result of the data gathered from employee monitoring. The other choices do not relate as closely to improved working conditions or to employee monitoring.

29) ➡ D

Concept(s) Tested: Concision

Choice (D) is correct because it is the clearest and most concise version of the underlined portion. All other choices are unnecessarily wordy and/or contain redundancies.

30) ➡ B

Concept(s) Tested: Style and tone

Choice (B) is correct because it maintains the academic tone of the rest of the passage. All other choices are too conversational and casual in tone, as they unnecessarily use adverbs ("really" and "even") or colloquialisms ("deal with").

31) ➡ A

Concept(s) Tested: Within-sentence punctuation

Choice (A) is correct because all of the information in the underlined portion is essential to the meaning of the sentence, so it should not be separated from the rest of the sentence with any punctuation. Other choices are incorrect because they over-punctuate.

32) ➡ C

Concept(s) Tested: Pronoun person and number/ commonly confused words

Choice (C) is correct because the underlined

pronoun refers to the singular noun "Google," and it shows possession over "innovations," so the third-person singular possessive pronoun "its" is correct.

33) ➡ D
Concept(s) Tested: Logical sequence
Choice (D) is correct because paragraph 5 elaborates on paragraph 3. Thus, paragraph 4 should come after paragraph 5 in order to make the relationship between paragraphs 3 and 5 clear.

34) ➡ C
Concept(s) Tested: Pronoun person and number
Choice (C) is correct; the pronoun in the underlined portion refers to the singular noun phrase "a slip of paper," so the singular pronoun "it" effectively replaces "a slip of paper" in the underlined portion.

35) ➡ B
Concept(s) Tested: Within-sentence punctuation
Chioce (B) is correct because a pair of commas is needed to separate the non-essential phrase "to his astonishment" from the rest of the sentence.

36) ➡ A
Concept(s) Tested: Providing evidence
Choice (A) is correct because paragraph 2 focuses on Nash's success as an author. Explaining that his work was popular with both critics and "the public alike" best indicates Nash's success.

37) ➡ C
Concept(s) Tested: Improving focus
Choice (C) is correct because sentence 3 mentions critics' reactions to Nash, so it makes sense that an example of a critic's reaction comes immediately after sentence 3.

38) ➡ D
Concept(s) Tested: Sentence boundaries/within-sentence punctuation
Choice (D) is correct because the relative pronoun "when" effectively refers to "the 1930s" while introducing a relative clause that describes the era. Moreover, relative clauses are generally separated from the noun(s) they describe using commas.

39) ➡ D
Concept(s) Tested: Conventional expressions
Choice (D) is correct because "to shy away" from something is to avoid it, and it makes sense to say that Nash "did not *avoid* pointed social commentary," seeing as he wrote a poem that criticizes the greed of bankers during a time when "many Americans lost

their savings."

40) ➡ A
Concept(s) Tested: Improving focus
Choice (A) is correct; the underlined portion transitions from discussing Nash's political commentaries to his observations about ordinary life. Thus, it makes sense to begin the paragraph with the contrasting conjunction "But" to show that the paragraph that follows will discuss a different aspect of Nash's writing than the previous paragraph did.

41) ➡ B
Concept(s) Tested: Relative clauses
Choice (B) is correct because the underlined pronoun refers to "wife and two daughters," and the relative pronoun "who" effectively refers to people. Although "(to) whom" also refers to people, "whom" is used for a clause's object; in this clause, the wife and daughters are the subject.

42) ➡ A
Concept(s) Tested: Providing evidence
Choice (A) is correct because the added sentence provides a relevant example of Nash's focus on ordinary life in his poems, thus supporting the paragraph's topic sentence.

43) ➡ C
Concept(s) Tested: Sentence clarity/verb tense, mood, and voice
Choice (C) is correct because "boast and swagger" contrasts with "run from real danger," and the conjunction "yet" effectively conveys this contrast. All other choices are incorrect because they fail to convey contrast. Choice (C) also correctly uses the literary present tense.

44) ➡ B
Concept(s) Tested: Providing evidence
Choice (B) is correct because it is the only choice that mentions the duration ("emphasizes the longevity") of Nash's literary career.

SAT Writing & Language Test 2 : Answers & Explanations

1. Ⓑ	5. Ⓐ	9. Ⓐ	13. Ⓓ	17. Ⓓ	21. Ⓓ	25. Ⓓ	29. Ⓓ	33. Ⓒ	37. Ⓑ	41. Ⓓ
2. Ⓒ	6. Ⓑ	10. Ⓑ	14. Ⓑ	18. Ⓐ	22. Ⓐ	26. Ⓑ	30. Ⓑ	34. Ⓒ	38. Ⓒ	42. Ⓐ
3. Ⓓ	7. Ⓒ	11. Ⓒ	15. Ⓐ	19. Ⓒ	23. Ⓐ	27. Ⓓ	31. Ⓒ	35. Ⓐ	39. Ⓐ	43. Ⓑ
4. Ⓐ	8. Ⓒ	12. Ⓒ	16. Ⓑ	20. Ⓑ	24. Ⓒ	28. Ⓒ	32. Ⓐ	36. Ⓓ	40. Ⓒ	44. Ⓑ

1) ➡ B

Concept(s) Tested: Precision

Choice (B) is correct because "to excel at" something is to be exceptionally good at it, which makes sense in the context of the sentence. Although the other choices have similar meanings, they are incorrect because they do not fit the context of the sentence. Also, it is not logical to say that a successful athlete "wins" a sport.

2) ➡ C

Concept(s) Tested: Improving focus/transition words

Choice (C) is correct; the paragraph that contains the underlined portion discusses ways in which a person's genes make a difference in a particular sport. Therefore, (C) most logically follows the passage's main proposition; it quickly clarifies that no one, including the writer, denies the obvious counter-claim.

3) ➡ D

Concept(s) Tested: Logical comparison

Choice (D) is correct; the sentence compares the stride length and weight carried by a runner with long legs to the stride length and weight carried by other runners. Without the word "do," however, it is possible to read the sentence as having something to do with a runner carrying other runners.

4) ➡ A

Concept(s) Tested: Providing evidence

Choice (A) is correct because it provides a concise example of how genetics can give some athletes an advantage, and it matches the style and tone of the paragraph's previous examples. Other choices are

incorrect because they fail to mention the role of inheritable traits in athletics.

5) ➡ A

Concept(s) Tested: Verb tense, mood, and aspect

Choice (A) is correct because the author's claim that "Kenyans and Ethiopians have some special gene" is a conjecture that is undermined by the rest of the paragraph, and the verb "would" is used to show that something is a conjecture or opinion.

6) ➡ B

Concept(s) Tested: Providing evidence

Choice (B) is correct; the added sentence should provide an example of how lifestyle influences athletic ability. Since traveling "a number of miles on foot" each day is a lifestyle that would affect someone's long-distance running abilities, (B) provides the most effective example.

7) ➡ C

Concept(s) Tested: Syntax/commonly confused words

Choice (C) is correct because the determiner "which" serves to limit the noun "players." The conjunction "whether" is incorrect because it must always be followed by two options, which is not the case here.

8) ➡ C

Concept(s) Tested: Possessive nouns and pronouns

Choice (C) is correct because the underlined pronoun shows possession over "players," making the possessive pronoun "its" appropriate. Moreover, "players" shows possession over "risk of injury," so the plural noun "players'" must also be possessive.

9) ➡ A

Concept(s) Tested: Providing evidence

Choice (A) is correct; the underlined portion should explain *why* identifying "genes that control production of collagen" is important, which (A) does by explaining that collagen forms a body's connective tissues. Thus, (A) effectively connects the body's production of collagen to predicting the risk of sports injury.

10) ➡ B

Concept(s) Tested: Combining sentences

Choice (B) is correct because the two sentences contain contrasting information: Geneticists have found a connection between genetics and proneness to tendon and ligament injury; geneticists claim that the science of predicting injuries is not fully developed. The use of "but" in choice (B) effectively conveys this contrast.

11) ➡ C

Concept(s) Tested: Improving focus

Choice (C) is correct because it effectively restates the passage's central claim that genetics alone cannot accurately predict athletic talent. Choice (A) is incorrect because it is not as substantial as (C): the phrase "as we have thought" is unclear and does not strengthen the author's previous claims. Choice (B) is incorrect because it undermines the author's main claim, and (D) is incorrect because it addresses only a small part of the passage while ignoring the passage's main claim.

12) ➡ C

Concept(s) Tested: Concision

Choice (C) is correct because it is the clearest and most concise version of the underlined portion. All other choices are incorrect because they are unnecessarily wordy and/or contain redundancies.

13) ➡ D

Concept(s) Tested: Within-sentence punctuation

Choice (D) is correct because a colon effectively separates a piece of information from a definition of or elaboration on that information. In the sentence, the list "a tight corset...to the hair" provides an elaboration of "their own clothes."

14) ➡ B

Concept(s) Tested: Improving focus

Choice (B) is correct; the question asks wich choice "sets up a contrast" in the sentence. The most effective contrast to "celebrity" is "pariah," meaning a social outcast.

15) ➡ A

Concept(s) Tested: Transition words

Choice (A) is correct because "therefore" indicates consequence. In this case, women riding bikes was considered scandalous; *consequently*, Annie Londonderry's announcement was surprising.

16) ➡ B

Concept(s) Tested: Verb tense, mood, and voice

Choice (B) is correct; the underlined verb phrase indicates a plan for the future that was announced in the past. Thus, "was going to ride" is the correct choice. Although (D) is also in a past tense, it is incorrect because it creates ambiguity about her announcement and whether she still planned to ride.

17) ➡ D

Concept(s) Tested: Providing evidence

Choice (D) is correct because changing one's name to match that of a commercial sponser is an extreme way of *promoting* the sponsor. Other choices are incorrect because they are unsupported by the passage; the passage states that Londonderry promoted the company for money, but it never states that she wanted to please, own, or show gratitude towards the company.

18) ➡ A

Concept(s) Tested: Providing evidence

Choice (A) is correct because it provides relevant, non-redundant information regarding *how* Londonderry made the journey.

19) ➡ C

Concept(s) Tested: Pronoun clarity

Choice (C) is correct; presumably, the writer does not mean that *corsets* could dress comfortably and still be respectable. Thus, the underlined term must describe a group who could "still be respectable" without wearing corsets. Since a corset is an article of women's clothing, the writer must intend to refer to "women."

receive free tickets..."

20) ➡ B

Concept(s) Tested: Logical sequence

Choice (B) is correct; sentence 3 summarizes the trip, and the added sentence describes the last portion of it. The conclusion of the trip should be mentioned before a summary of the entire trip, so the added sentence should go after sentence 2.

21) ➡ D

Concept(s) Tested: Precision

Choice (D) is correct because "to hinder" is to prevent by creating difficulties, and it makes sense to say that women's heavy swimwear *prevented* them from doing any actual swimming.

22) ➡ A

Concept(s) Tested: Improving focus

Choice (A) is correct because the last paragraph focuses mainly on Kellermann's controversial swimsuit, so the underlined portion should maintain this focus, which only (A) does. All other choices are incorrect because they focus on other aspects of Kellermann's career.

23) ➡ A

Concept(s) Tested: Modifier placement

Choice (A) is correct because it clearly places "passengers" after their modifier, "when feeling restless." The other choices imply that the pilots or the blame are restless.

24) ➡ C

Concept(s) Tested: Improving focus

Choice (C) is correct because the paragraph that contains the underlined portion mentions three possible benefits of becoming an airline pilot, and the introduction, "People become airline pilots for several reasons" effectively introduces these three benefits.

25) ➡ D

Concept(s) Tested: Pronoun person and number

Choice (D) is correct because the first underlined pronoun refers to the plural noun "pilots," so the plural noun "they" is appropriate. Moreover, the plural possessive pronoun "their" is necessary to indicate that "families" belong to "pilots." Choice (B) is incorrect because it uses the object pronoun "them"; it would be incorrect to say that "*them* often

26) ➡ B

Concept(s) Tested: Verb tense, mood, and voice

Choice (B) is correct because the underlined verb phrase should maintain the same word pattern established in the previous sentence, "Pilots *may have*." The phrase "pilots' schedules *may offer*" maintains this pattern. Moreover, using the word "may" conveys that the statements are generalities and do not apply to every situation.

27) ➡ D

Concept(s) Tested: Subject-verb agreement/noun agreement

Choice (D) is correct because the preposition "between" must always be followed by two choices. Thus, "flights" must be plural to indicate that we are talking about *two* flights and to agree with "between." Moreover, the underlined verb refers to and must agree with "a layover," making the third-person singular verb form "is" correct.

28) ➡ C

Concept(s) Tested: Combining sentences

Choice (C) is correct because the pronoun in the underlined portion must be "they" to effectively refer to "pilots." Moreover, (C) effectively connects the participial phrase that modifies "they" ("Provided that they are patient") to an independent clause using a comma, making it the only grammatically correct choice.

29) ➡ D

Concept(s) Tested: Providing evidence

Choice (D) is correct because it provides relevant, non-redundant information regarding *why* pilots have a disincentive to switch employers.

30) ➡ B

Concept(s) Tested: Interpreting graphs, charts, and diagrams

Choice (B) is correct because the points on the graph from the mid-1990s onwards stray dramatically from the line of best fit, indicating that compared to the past, sometimes airlines profit greatly and sometimes they lose large amounts of money. Thus, airlines nowadays have "increasingly volatile profit margins."

31) ➤ C

Concept(s) Tested: Correlative conjunctions

Choice (C) is correct because the term "not only" must always be followed by the term "but also," making (C) the only acceptable answer.

32) ➤ A

Concept(s) Tested: Providing evidence

Choice (A) is correct because it is the only choice that adds to the discussion of airline pilot job growth by providing statistics to support the sentence's claim. Other choices deviate from the topic established in the sentence, blurring the focus of the paragraph.

33) ➤ C

Concept(s) Tested: Style and tone/parallel structure

Choice (C) is correct because it maintains the word pattern established in the previous sentence by the phrase "One route is to..."

34) ➤ C

Concept(s) Tested: Parallel structure/verb tense, mood, and voice

Choice (C) is correct because the underlined verb phrase must maintain the same tense and aspect as the other verb phrase of the sentence, "was composing," which "was creating" does effectively.

35) ➤ A

Concept(s) Tested: Combining sentences

Choice (A) is correct because it effectively combines the sentences into a single list of nouns ("battles, adventures, romances, and the triumph...") that maintains parallel structure.

36) ➤ D

Concept(s) Tested: Providing evidence

Choice (D) is correct because it provides the most detailed explanation of why *Ramcharitmanas* is difficult to translate, and examples of the information in (D) are discussed throughout the paragraph.

37) ➤ B

Concept(s) Tested: Improving focus

Choice (B) is correct because it elaborates on relevant, non-redundant information about the importance of *Ramcharitmanas* in Hindu culture.

38) ➤ C

Concept(s) Tested: Precisiont

Choice (C) is correct because the paragraph discusses what Tulsidas did to make classic Hindu stories easier for common people to understand and remember. In other words, Tulsidas attempted to make "the Hindu religon *more accessible* to common people."

39) ➤ A

Concept(s) Tested: Pronoun clarity

Choice (A) is correct because, as it is used in the sentence, the pronoun "what" effectively means "the things that," so (A) shows the relationship between "Hindu sacred texts" and "contained."

40) ➤ C

Concept(s) Tested: Modifiers/syntax

Choice (C) is correct because the adverb phrase "mainly as a script to be acted out" explains *how* Tulsidas "thought of the *Ramcharitmanas*." To maintain sentence clarity, the adverb "mainly" should introduce the rest of the adverb phrase, making (C) the ony acceptable choice.

41) ➤ D

Concept(s) Tested: Conventional expressions

Choice (D) is correct because "to know something by heart" is to have it memorized. The sentence that follows the underlined portion implies that the audience has the *Ramcharitmanas* memorized since they know when and how to react to various parts of the poem.

42) ➤ A

Concept(s) Tested: Style and tone

Choice (A) is correct because the phrase "Vividly colored" clearly conveys a positive yet fact-based description of sets and costumes. Other choices are incorrect because they are more opinionated than fashionable.

43) ➤ B

Concept(s) Tested: Relative clauses

Chioce (B) is correct because a non-essential relative clause ("in which a giant effigy of a demon is burned" in this case) must be separated from the rest of the sentence using commas.

44) ➤ B

Concept(s) Tested: Logical sequence

Choice (B) is correct because the phrase "the whole town" in sentence 3 refers to "the town of Ramnagar" mentioned in sentence 1. Thus, sentence 3 should come immediately after sentence 1.

SAT Writing & Language Test 3 : Answers & Explanations

1. Ⓑ	5. Ⓒ	9. Ⓓ	13. Ⓓ	17. Ⓐ	21. Ⓒ	25. Ⓐ	29. Ⓐ	33. Ⓑ	37. Ⓐ	41. Ⓑ
2. Ⓓ	6. Ⓐ	10. Ⓐ	14. Ⓑ	18. Ⓐ	22. Ⓒ	26. Ⓑ	30. Ⓓ	34. Ⓑ	38. Ⓑ	42. Ⓒ
3. Ⓐ	7. Ⓓ	11. Ⓒ	15. Ⓒ	19. Ⓑ	23. Ⓐ	27. Ⓑ	31. Ⓒ	35. Ⓓ	39. Ⓒ	43. Ⓑ
4. Ⓑ	8. Ⓑ	12. Ⓐ	16. Ⓓ	20. Ⓓ	24. Ⓒ	28. Ⓒ	32. Ⓓ	36. Ⓐ	40. Ⓒ	44. Ⓓ

1) ➡ B

Concept(s) Tested: Improving focus

Choice (B) is correct because the passage as a whole discusses family leave policies in the U.S., so it makes sense for the introduction to intorduce this focus by mentioning "family-leave policies."

2) ➡ D

Concept(s) Tested: Possessive nouns

Choice (D) is correct because the underlined portion discusses "mothers and babies" in general, so the plural forms of both nouns are appropriate. Moreover, both "mothers' " and "babies' " show possession over "health," so the underlined nouns must be possessive.

3) ➡ A

Concept(s) Tested: Pronoun person and number

Choice (A) is correct because the underlined pronoun refers to the singular noun "the leave" in the previous sentence, and the third-person singular pronoun "it" effectively refers to "the leave."

4) ➡ B

Concept(s) Tested: Verb tense, mood, and voice

Choice (B) is correct; to determine what tense the underlined verb should take, look to other nearby verbs in the paragraph. In the sentence that follows the underlined portion, the verbs are in the present-perfect tense ("have tried" and "has required"). Since the paragraph does not indicate a shift in tense between the two sentences, the underlined verb should also be in the present-perfect, making "have created" the correct choice.

5) ➡ C

Concept(s) Tested: Providing evidence

Choice (C) is correct; the paragraph discusses the need for more extensive and universal family leave policies, and because the added sentence does not clarify how the aging Baby Boomer generation fits into this need, it should not be included in the paragraph.

6) ➡ A

Concept(s) Tested: Improving focus

Choice (A) is correct because the third paragraph provides statistics revealing that millions of Americans must care for elderly or disabled family members. If the law mentioned in paragraph 2 only helps a small portion of the population, the information in paragraph 3 proves that "the law does little to help millions of people," making (A) the best choice.

7) ➡ D

Concept(s) Tested: Commonly confused words

Choice (D) is correct because the underlined pronoun refers to the plural noun phrase "People in 'Generation X'" and shows possession over "aging parents," so the third-person plural possessive pronoun "their" is appropriate.

8) ➡ B

Concept(s) Tested: Precision

Choice (B) is correct because "universal" means "affecting everyone," and based on the information in the passage, it makes sense to say that the need for family leave *affects everyone.*

9) ➡ D

Concept(s) Tested: Logical sequence

Choice (D) is correct; sentence 4 claims that everyone needs more extensive family leave policies ("the need is universal"), and the added sentence provides examples of multiple age groups that would benefit from better policies. Because sentence 1 provides examples that support the general statement made in sentence 4, sentence 1 should come after sentence 4.

10) ➡ A

Concept(s) Tested: Within-sentence punctuation

Choice (A) is correct because the sentence containing the underlined portion presents a conditional "If... then" statement, and a comma must always separate the "If..." part of a conditional statement from its consequence.

11) ➡ C

Concept(s) Tested: Providing evidence

Choice (C) is correct because it provides a broad "social impact" of inadequate family leave policies. All other choices are incorrect because they describe personal impacts of inadequate family leave policies.

12) ➡ A

Concept(s) Tested: Providing evidence

Choice (A) is correct because it explains why the narrator is "a little dubious" about the exhibit he or she is visiting. After all, a ramp made entirely of tape would not appear stable and therefore would not inspire confidence.

13) ➡ D

Concept(s) Tested: Commonly confused words/verb tense, mood, and voice

Choice (D) is correct because the underlined verb must maintain the tense established by other verbs in the paragraph/passage. The sentences prior to the underlined verb contain the simple past-tense verbs "contemplated" and "appeared," so it makes sense that the underlined verb should also be in the simple past tense, making "led" the correct choice.

14) ➡ B

Concept(s) Tested: Style and tone

Choice (B) is correct; the two sentences before the underlined portion have "they" (referring to "Engineers and artists") as their subjects, and (B)

maintains this sentence pattern, making it the correct choice.

15) ➡ C

Concept(s) Tested: Providing evidence

Chioce (C) is correct because it provides the most detailed account of the appearance of the exhibit, thus helping "the reader visualize the exhibit." Although (D) mentions the texture of the exhibit's ramp, this does not greatly help the reader imagine what the exhibit as a whole looks like.

16) ➡ D

Concept(s) Tested: Pronoun person and number

Choice (D) is correct because "my friend and I" acts as the subject of the sentence, so all the pronouns should be subject pronouns. It would be incorrect, after all, to say "could *me* really enter?" Moreover, "my friend" must come before "I" because it is conventional English to put other nouns and pronouns before "I" when "I" is part of a subject.

17) ➡ A

Concept(s) Tested: Within-sentence punctuation

Choice (A) is correct because all of the information in the underlined portion is essential to the meaning of the sentence, so it should not be separated from the rest of the sentence with any punctuation. Other choices are incorrect because they over-punctuate.

18) ➡ A

Concept(s) Tested: Precision/transition words

Choice (A) is correct because the adverb "apparently" means "insofar as can be seen, or evidently," which makes sense in the context of the passage. The narrator has just described seeing "no indications of a weight limit" and seeing people "running and jumping inside." Thus, the narrator is clearly speaking about what is evident, making (A) the best choice.

19) ➡ B

Concept(s) Tested: Combining sentences/concision

Choice (B) is correct because the sentences convey contrast: the boat is tied to the dock; the wind pushes the boat away from the dock. The conjunction "but" effectively shows this contrast. Moreover, (B) is the clearest choice because it forms an active-voice sentence.

20) ➡ D

Concept(s) Tested: Verb tense, mood, and voice

Choice (D) is correct because the underlined verb is part of a conditional, hypothetical statement, so the verb must take the subjunctive mood. In other words, when expressing a hypothetical situation, use the past-tense, third-person plural verb form, in this case "were."

21) ➡ C

Concept(s) Tested: Interpreting graphs, charts, and diagrams/parallel structure

Choice (C) is correct because the chart shows that as the diameter of a rope (its thickness) increases, so too does the rope's tensile strength. Moreover, (C) maintains the sentence structure: "the thicker the rope...the more force...the higher..."

22) ➡ C

Concept(s) Tested: Improving focus

Choice (C) is correct because connects to the beginning of the passage by recalling that the "plastic tape looked thin and weak," yet it maintains the focus of the passage by referencing the exhibit's tensile strength.

23) ➡ A

Concept(s) Tested: Providing evidence

Choice (A) is correct because the previous examples list ways that a language can express love or affection, and the phrase "flowery terms of endearment" fits with this pattern.

24) ➡ C

Concept(s) Tested: Improving focus

Choice (C) is correct; paragraph 2 discusses the origins of Romance languages and lists the languages that comprise "the Romance family," so it makes sense that the underlined portion would introduce this topic by briefly describing "a language family."

25) ➡ A

Concept(s) Tested: Providing evidence

Choice (A) is correct; the sentence that contains the underlined portion discusses the size of the Romance language family, so the underlined portion should add information regarding the number of Romance-language speakers, which (A) does effectively.

26) ➡ B

Concept(s) Tested: Parallel structure

Choice (B) is correct because the underlined portion must maintain the same word pattern as the previously listed countries, which choice (A) does. All other choices are incorrect because they begin with a preposition, which does not maintain the parallel strucutre of the list.

27) ➡ B

Concept(s) Tested: Concision

Choice (B) is correct because it is the clearest and most concise version of the underlined portion. All other choices are unnecessarily wordy.

28) ➡ C

Concept(s) Tested: Improving focus
Choice (C) is correct; the underlined sentence acts as the conclusion of the paragraph, which discusses the reasons for Vulgar Latin's evolution over time. Because the underlined sentence does not wrap up the discussion or elaborate on a previous point, it should be deleted. Concluding sentences should not introduce new topics that go unexplained.

29) ➡ A

Concept(s) Tested: Commonly confused words

Choice (A) is correct because "to affect" is to influence, and it makes sense to say that a "Roman presence in a region *influenced* the development of Romance languages." Choice (B) is incorrect because "effect" is more often used as a noun, and its meaning when used as a verb does not fit the context of the sentence. Choices (C) and (D) are incorrect because making the verb passive reverses the intended meaning of the sentence.

30) ➡ D

Concept(s) Tested: Combining sentences

Choice (D) is correct because the two sentences provide information about the development of Romance languages, but the relationship between the facts is self-evident and requires no transition words or conjunctions for clarification. Thus, a semicolon effectively joins the two sentences.

31) ➡ C

Concept(s) Tested: Subordinate conjunction use

Choice (C) is correct because the sentence containing the underlined portion conveys contrast: In Roman-dominated areas, Vulgar Latin became the main language; in other areas, local languages remained more intact. The conjunction "whereas" effectively conveys this contrast.

32) ➡ D

Concept(s) Tested: Style and tone

Choice (D) is correct because it effectively maintains the academic tone of the rest of the passage. Choices (A) and (B) are incorrect because they are too informal, and choice (C) is incorrect because it does not provide clear information.

33) ➡ B

Concept(s) Tested: Logical sequence

Choice (B) is correct because the phrase "Many of these groups" must refer to the "populations" mentioned in sentence 1, so the added sentence should go between sentences 1 and 2.

34) ➡ B

Concept(s) Tested: Improving focus

Choice (B) is correct because the added sentence provides more information than the underlined portion; the added sentence narrows the focus to urban parks in the United States, which accurately summarizes the focus of paragraph 1.

35) ➡ D

Concept(s) Tested: Interpreting charts, graphs, and diagrams

Choice (D) is correct because the chart assumes that the "average value of a nearby park" is "5 percent," which means that city planners generally believe that the presence of a park raises nearby property values by about 5 percent.

36) ➡ A

Concept(s) Tested: Interpreting charts, graphs, and diagrams

Choice (A) is correct because it provides an accurate assessment of the last row of the chart. This states that higher property values due to parks yield $6,953,377 in tax revenue, thus increasing the city's income "by about $7 million annually."

37) ➡ A

Concept(s) Tested: Improving focus

Choice (A) is correct because it sets up the example that follows: even an extreme commercial center such as the Las Vegas Strip now concedes the crucial budgetary benefits of adding a park.

38) ➡ B

Concept(s) Tested: Style and tone

Choice (B) is correct because the use of the term "benefits" conveys positivity, and the wording of (B) maintains the academic tone of the passage as a whole. Choice (A) and (C) are incorrect because they are too informal, using colloquialisms such as "all kinds" and "really great." Choice (D) is incorrect because it does not necessarily convey a positive attitude, as "indescribable returns" is vague.

39) ➡ C

Concept(s) Tested: Prepositional phrases/syntax

Choice (C) is correct because it properly arranges the two prepositional phrases in the underlined portion; it first states who doctors talk to ("their patients") and what they talk about ("nearby parks"). All other choices are incorrect because they rearrange the prepositional phrases, which changes the intended meaning of the sentence.

40) ➡ C

Concept(s) Tested: Sentence clarity

Choice (C) is correct because it states *what* "may prevent floods." All other choices are incorrect because they fail to clarify that "parks" are what help prevent flooding, and that it is parks that absorb water.

41) ➡ B

Concept(s) Tested: Logical sequence

Choice (B) is correct; sentence 4 provides an example of the building projects described in sentence 2, so sentence 4 should come between sentences 2 and 3 because examples generally follow the processes they describe.

42) ➡ C

Concept(s) Tested: Verb tense, mood, and voice

Choice (C) is correct because the underlined portion

must serve as the main verb of the sentence, and only (C) provides a main verb in the present-perfect tense. All other choices are incorrect because they are participles, which look like verb forms but act as modifiers, and so cannot be a sentence's main verb.

43) ➡ B

Concept(s) Tested: Comparisons

Choice (B) is correct; the sentence needs a superlative form of the adjective, as in "least," because it compares a specific set of places to all other palces. Thus, (B) correctly refers to "*The* places *that seem least likely...*" out of all other places.

44) ➡ D

Concept(s) Tested: Within-sentence punctuation

Choice (D) is correct because the "bird-viewing preserve" is a regular noun phrase, so there is no need to capitalize it or to put it in quotes or parentheses.

Made in the USA
San Bernardino, CA
06 November 2017